STEWARD OF HEADWATERS

U.S. ARMY CORPS OF ENGINEERS
ST. PAUL DISTRICT 1975 – 2000

Theodore **Catton**
Matthew **Godfrey**

authors
Theodore Catton & Matthew Godfrey

layout and cover designer
Emily Chavolla

editor
Shannon Bauer

additional contributors
Kevin Bokay, Rick Magee, Matt Pearcy, Brad Perkl, Kenton Spading

Steward of Headwaters, U.S. Army Corps of Engineers 1975 - 2000
printed by the U.S. Army Corps of Engineers, St. Paul District, 2012

The St. Paul District

CANADA

DETROIT
DISTRICT

NORTH
DAKOTA

MICHIGAN

Minnesota

OMAHA
DISTRICT

St. Paul

Wisconsin

SOUTH
DAKOTA

N

IOWA

St. Paul District boundaries

St. Paul District office

Table of Contents

Lock and Dam 3, Mississippi River: the river is seen here in high water, October 1995. (Photo courtesy of St. Paul District, Corps of Engineers)

1 Introduction

The U.S. Army Corps of Engineers, St. Paul District, is one of forty-one districts in the Corps' organization. As the northernmost district in the Mississippi Valley Division, it centers on the headwaters of the Mississippi River and the uppermost section of the river's nine-foot navigation channel. The St. Paul District oversees civil works projects and conducts disaster relief within the geographic boundaries of the district, implements the Corps' regulatory program in the states of Minnesota and Wisconsin and assists with other Corps' missions wherever needed. The following history updates the book *Creativity, Conflict & Controversy: A History of the St. Paul District, U.S. Army Corps of Engineers*, published in 1979.[1] This book describes how the St. Paul District responded to enormous changes in the Corps' missions and organization in the last quarter of the twentieth century.

The St. Paul District in the Environmental Era

The U.S. Army Corps of Engineers has been the federal government's leading civil works agency for more than two centuries. It built its reputation largely on river and harbor improvements, such as the nine-foot navigation channel in the Mississippi River and dikes and dams for flood control and hydroelectric power. In the 1960s and 1970s, the environmental movement fundamentally altered the public outlook on the Corps' works. Many people recognized rivers and lakes and wetlands to be some of the most vulnerable elements of the natural environment. Dams, some argued, were perhaps the most egregious example of heavy-handed transformations of the landscape. Engineering projects that were unquestioningly termed "improvements" in the past were condemned by environmentalists as misguided and destructive. Moreover, the public developed a more skeptical attitude toward government and technocracy and demanded greater participation in public land management decisions. In response, the

Corps reinvented its public image, evolving from the nation's leading dam builder to its principal steward of water resources. Seeking to win public confidence, it navigated through a changed political landscape of environmental impact studies and public review. More than a few social scientists and environmentalists marveled at the Corps' success, though many still contended that the Corps wrought environmental damage wherever it worked.

The St. Paul District has played a significant role in the "greening" of the Corps. It embraced the Corps' new mission of environmental management on the Upper Mississippi River – a project that Congress has continually funded since 1986. When the Corps performed maintenance on the nine-foot channel, it placed dredged material so as to create islands and back channels that would provide new wildlife habitat. The Corps came to occupy a key role in interagency administration of the river, mediating between environmentalists and recreational-use interests on the one hand and flood-prone communities and commercial-navigation interests on the other.

The St. Paul District similarly embraced the Corps' expanded mission in regulatory matters, particularly its role in protecting wetlands. The district took initiative in redrawing regulatory boundaries to conform to state lines so that it could work more effectively with state regulatory programs in Minnesota and Wisconsin. Since these states had two of the most aggressive wetlands protection programs in the nation, the St. Paul District forged ahead of many other districts in proving the Corps' commitment to the protection of this resource.

The St. Paul District demonstrated environmental sensitivity in other areas, from new project designs such as the $115-million Rochester, Minnesota, Flood Control Project to restoration efforts such as the Weaver Bottoms Rehabilitation, both of which were recognized with the Chief of Engineers Award of Excellence – the most prestigious award given to civil works projects. Since 1975, the St. Paul District has received four Awards of Excellence, an outstanding record. The professionalism the district has cultivated in the course of improving its environmental standing extends to other programs, including innovations in the development of recreational facilities and the making of one of the Corps' strongest district history programs.

Unlike most districts, the St. Paul District does not participate in military programs, but rather focuses exclusively on civil works. This is one factor that encourages the district to excel in its areas of specialization. Moreover, it is said that the individuals who comprise the St. Paul District tend to be less mobile within the organization, less inclined to seek or accept a reassignment, more loyal to their sense of place than is characteristic of most district staff. Longevity has both advantages and disadvantages for the organization, but one of its advantages is producing people with a greater commitment to quality of living. Many people in the St. Paul District are reluctant to transfer elsewhere because they like St. Paul and the region – they have a personal stake in the environment. Yet, the human resource may be less significant than the geographic and political setting in explaining the St. Paul District's orientation.

Most of this region is flat. The major exception is the "Driftless Area" of southwest Wisconsin, so-named because it escaped glaciation during the Ice Ages and is lacking glacial "drift" or deposit, therefore exhibiting a much older geologic imprint of uplift and dissection by water erosion. Other hills include the Mesabi Range and the Vermillion Range in northeast Minnesota, which form the divide with the Great Lakes Basin. Generally, the topography of the St. Paul District shows the marks of past continental glaciers, which left behind thousands of natural lakes and prairie potholes, as well as low, rounded hills, kettle moraines, ancient flood plains, and dry river channels.[3] The Red River Valley, the flattest area in a region known for its flatness, is the bed of the gigantic glacial Lake Agassiz. Its rich, black soil is extraordinarily fertile.

Indeed, most of the area within the St. Paul District features soil that is highly productive for agriculture – another consequence of past glaciation. The continental glaciers not only covered the original land surface with a deep, flat layer of glacial till, they also imported and deposited limestone and other minerals that made good soil-building material. Deposits of loess in some areas and lacustrine materials of old lakebeds in others formed additional mantles of good soil. Most of the St. Paul District, from North Dakota's Red River Valley in the west to Wisconsin's central counties in the east, has yielded rich farm crops for more than a century.[4]

The climate of this region is continental, marked by temperature extremes from winter to summer, as well as by dramatic temperature shifts within each season. For its mid-continent location it is also relatively humid, with 30 to 40 inches of annual precipitation. Rainfall is generally highest in the summer, with much of it occurring in torrential thunderstorms. These climatic conditions, added to the flat topography and the abundance of water, make large areas of the St. Paul District particularly flood prone.

Because the region is mid-continent and devoid of mountain barriers, the rivers and lakes have provided pathways of commerce for centuries. Since the nineteenth century, the Mississippi River has served as the main artery of commerce with the outside world. The Twin Cities of Minneapolis and St. Paul, formed at the river's farthest point of navigation at St. Anthony Falls, became the region's largest metropolitan area very early. The U.S. Army Corps of Engineers opened an office in St. Paul in 1866 for the purpose of surveying the Upper Mississippi and its tributaries – a permanent presence that eventually became the St. Paul District.

Upper and Lower Locks at St. Anthony Falls, Minneapolis: The falls were the highest point of navigation on the Mississippi River when the Corps of Engineers opened an office in St. Paul in 1866. (Photo courtesy of St. Paul District, Corps of Engineers)

Throughout its history, the St. Paul District has made the Mississippi River its central focus. In the 1930s, it oversaw dredging of a nine-foot channel for navigation as far upriver as St. Anthony Falls. This project assisted farmers and industry by facilitating the transportation of grain downstream and coal upstream. The project had unintended environmental consequences, however, as the dumping of dredge material in backwaters along the edges of the river harmed vegetation and wildlife habitat in these sensitive wetland areas.

By the 1960s and 1970s, public concern for the ecological and recreational values of the Mississippi River vied with more traditional considerations of its navigability and susceptibility to flooding. In the last quarter of the century, the Corps devoted increasing attention to reclamation and preservation of the river's natural features.[5]

In addition to lakes and rivers, the region contains a vast amount of wetlands. Outside of Alaska, the St. Paul District encompasses more wetlands than any other Corps' district in the nation – much of it in the form of prairie potholes and inland fresh marshes that interface with agricultural lands. Long maligned by the general public as worthless, these areas were once converted to farmland as fast as they could be ditched and drained. In the last quarter century, however, the public value of wetlands has changed radically. The Corps of Engineers now plays an important role in preserving the nation's wetlands, and the St. Paul District occupies a strategic place in this effort.

ST. PAUL DISTRICT BOUNDARY

St. Paul District boundary: The current boundaries, after the realignment in 1979, of the St. Paul District include portions of five states. (Map courtesy of St. Paul District, Corps of Engineers)

Political Setting of the St. Paul District

The St. Paul District overlaps portions of five farm states. Agriculture built these state economies and continues to have a strong influence on state politics. In North Dakota, South Dakota and Iowa, farmers and farming-based communities are a dominating factor in most local governments. In Minnesota and Wisconsin, agricultural interests similarly control most county governments. However, in Minnesota and Wisconsin, there are large cities, as well as numerous small cities, and the state economies are more diversified, meaning that urban and nonagricultural interests have a greater influence at the state level.

Wisconsin in the last quarter of the twentieth century has remained less urban than the nation as a whole. Though highly industrialized, comparatively few of its people live in large cities. The majority of Wisconsin residents live in cities of less than 50 thousand, or towns, or in the country; about twenty percent live on farms. Minnesota, with slightly fewer people than Wisconsin, has the larger metropolitan area of the two states: the Twin Cities. Minnesota's next largest cities, Duluth and Rochester, each have fewer than 100 thousand inhabitants. Yet even Duluth and Rochester are larger than North Dakota's largest city of Fargo, which contains a population of 75 thousand.

Wisconsin, Minnesota and North Dakota received large numbers of German and Scandinavian immigrants in the nineteenth century. All three states developed political traditions of agrarian dissent and populism. In Wisconsin, the Republican Party embraced a persistent progressive wing. In Minnesota, the state Democratic Party fused with the leftist Farmer-Laborites in 1944 to form the Democratic-Farmer-Labor party, which occupies the left of the political spectrum to this day. In North Dakota, leftist farmers formed the Nonpartisan League, which gained control of the state government for a few years in the early twentieth century. The Nonpartisan League eventually vanished into the Democratic Party, and the Republican Party prevails in the state today. In each of these states, liberal and conservative divisions do not run along predictable fault lines, and the Corps encounters politically active citizens both in rural and urban contexts.

This district history is organized into ten chapters (including an introduction and a conclusion). Six central chapters focus on a Corps' mission or program: navigation, flood control, wetlands protection, recreation, cultural resources management and disaster relief. The two remaining chapters address organizational change: the first concentrating on internal reform and the second discussing external relationships. Since the main theme of this history is how the St. Paul District participated in the Corps' efforts to reinvent itself in the environmental era, we begin with the chapter on internal reform of the organization.

Chapter 1 Endnotes

1 Raymond H. Merritt, *The Corps, the Environment, and the Upper Mississippi River Basin* (Washington, D.C.: Historical Division, Office of Administrative Services, Office of the Chief of Engineers, 1984).

2 William E. Lass, *Minnesota: A Bicentennial History* (New York: W.W. Norton & Company, Inc., 1977), 3.

3 Richard Nelson, *Current, Wisconsin: A Bicentennial History* (New York: W.W. Norton & Co., Inc., 1977), 12-13.

4 John H. Garland, ed., *The North American Midwest: A Regional Geography* (New York: John Wiley & Sons, Inc., 1955), 6.

5 Lass, *Minnesota*, 4-5.

Site survey: Mike Dahlquist (left) and Jim Sentz look at survey information for the St. Cloud, Minnesota, erosion control project. (Photo by Shannon Bauer, courtesy of St. Paul District, Corps of Engineers)

2 Reinventing the St. Paul District

During the past thirty years, the Army Corps of Engineers has proven adept at embracing new missions to meet the changing needs of the nation. In particular, the Corps has responded to environmentalism. As early as the 1970s, the Corps' adaptability became the subject of an in-depth study by the Brookings Institution, *Can Organizations Change? Environmental Protection, Citizen Participation, and the Corps of Engineers*. The authors of the study were cautiously optimistic that the Corps could assimilate new environmental values into its varied missions and that its environmental mission could be translated into new programs.[1] In the following decades, the Corps moved toward more environmentally-sensitive approaches in its traditional workload involving river and harbor dredging and flood control projects; and, at the same time, the Corps came to occupy a central role in the growing federal commitment to protection of wetlands.

These impressive changes notwithstanding, the Corps faced additional challenges in demonstrating it could improve its efficiency. Efforts to downsize the federal bureaucracy and to trim the Department of Defense after the end of the Cold War fell heavily on the Army Corps of Engineers, especially in the 1990s. The Corps responded with successive plans and initiatives to streamline its decentralized administrative organization of divisions and districts, to revamp the way it conducted business and to stretch federal dollars by means of cost-sharing agreements with local sponsors.

The St. Paul District faced in microcosm the challenges that beset the whole Corps. Most of the pressure for organizational change came from Congress and from within the executive branch of the federal government; therefore, most of the direction to change sprang from the Corps' Headquarters Division, or HQUSACE, and emanated outward through the field divisions to the districts in the Corps' organization. However, the districts continued to serve as primary points of contact for members of Congress, so political pressures at the district level shaped the process of organizational change as well. In general, the St. Paul District underwent a transformation during the past thirty years in step with other Corps' districts and in response to national trends and developments.

Organizational change in the St. Paul District may be divided into two principal areas: realignment of the district's geographical boundaries (and, later, its transfer from one division to another) and modifications in the district's internal organization. This chapter examines organizational change in these two contexts. A third area of organizational change, which involves how the district and the Corps interact with other agencies, governments and nongovernment organizations, is addressed in Chapter Nine.

Realignment: The St. Paul District and the Corps

The Corps is a decentralized organization with offices and key personnel distributed widely throughout the United States so as to be near the resource and available to local and state officials and members of Congress in their respective districts. In the nineteenth century, officers were stationed in various cities, and the projects in their charge defined the geographic range of their respective offices. The Corps began to refer to projects as "districts" in the 1890s and gave names to the districts in 1908. It described the geographic boundaries of each district for the first time in 1913. The districts took shape within a divisional organizational structure, each district officer reporting to a division commander. There were five divisions in 1889, nine in 1908 and eleven by the end of World War II, while the number of districts fluctuated. After World War II, Congress reduced the number of districts.[2]

The St. Paul District dates to 1866, when Major Gouverneur Kemble Warren opened an engineer's office in St. Paul and initiated a survey of the Upper Mississippi River and its tributaries. The earliest description of the St. Paul District's boundaries included the Mississippi River drainage from the river's headwaters to the lower end of Lock 1 between St. Paul and Minneapolis, together with the Red River of the North drainage as far as the international boundary with Canada, and the Rainy River drainage in northern Minnesota, which encompasses the boundary waters area. The district was enlarged in 1919 by the addition of the Mississippi River from Lock 1 downstream to the mouth of the Wisconsin River. It was enlarged again in 1930 by the addition of the whole Wisconsin River drainage. The boundaries were extended further in 1940 to include more of the Mississippi River down to Lock and Dam 10 at Guttenberg, Iowa. A portion of the Upper Peninsula of Michigan draining into Lake Superior and Isle Royale were added to the district in 1941. The St. Paul District was originally part of the Northwest Division. It was transferred to the Upper Mississippi Valley Division and then to the North Central Division – where it remained when discussion about another reorganization of the Corps ensued in 1978.[3]

Realignment of District Boundaries

When the Corps examined alternatives for a realignment of districts and divisions in 1978, it was the largest such reorganization effort since World War II. The underlying reason for reorganization was recognition of the fact that the Corps had a declining workload. The era of large-scale water resource development projects had passed. Changing environmental considerations, coupled with rising construction costs, led to a steady winnowing and down-scaling of project proposals. Soon after taking office in 1977, President Jimmy Carter identified water resource development projects as some of the most egregious examples of the pork-barrel politics that he had promised to fight in his presidential campaign. Carter prevailed on Congress – particularly on the Democratic leadership – to cut many projects from the annual appropriation bill in 1977, and he vetoed the bill altogether in 1978. This political fight "left deep scars" and was one of the primary sources of Carter's troubled relations with Congress, according to Carter's memoir.[4] But it established a precedent that subsequent presidents would follow – of challenging the close relationship that Congress had long enjoyed with the Army Corps of Engineers.[5] Thus, the Corps had to adjust to an uncertain future in which new projects would be smaller and more varied and appropriation bills would be sorely contested by Congress and the Administration.

Another reason for reorganization was to bring the districts into better alignment with major river basins. Increasingly, river basins drew attention as rational geographic units for interagency planning, and river basin commissions were formed to guide such efforts. The Upper Mississippi River Basin Commission, established in 1972 by President Richard Nixon at the request of seven state governors, was one such body. The commission sought to improve public decision-making by bringing together ten different federal agencies that oversaw land and water resource programs in the river basin and by encouraging maximum participation by the public.[6] The growing emphasis on interagency regional planning caused the Corps to reexamine its district boundaries with the intent of making the Corps a more effective team player.

Baldhill Dam, Sheyenne River, N.D.: The district operates and maintains approximately sixteen multi-purpose reservoirs, mainly for flood control, and another thirteen locks and dams for navigation. (Photo by Ken Horner, courtesy of St. Paul District, Corps of Engineers)

These two factors – declining workload and watershed management – led the Corps to study various alternatives for a nationwide reorganization of divisions and districts. Looking at the Upper Midwest, the Corps considered eliminating both the Rock Island and Chicago districts by dividing the Rock Island District between the St. Paul and St. Louis districts, and splitting the Chicago District between the St. Paul and Detroit districts. Either scenario would have added responsibilities and personnel to the St. Paul District and enlarged its profile on the Upper Mississippi River. Both scenarios encountered resistance by Illinois' congressmen, who did not want a closure of either Illinois office.[7]

Instead, a plan emerged in which the St. Paul District would be divided. On May 25, 1979, Major General Richard Harris, North Central Division commander, announced the reorganization plan for the Upper Midwest. He recommended transferring the area of the St. Paul District that drained into Lake Superior – parts of Minnesota, Wisconsin and the Upper Peninsula of Michigan, as well as Isle Royale – to the Detroit District. In addition, he proposed eliminating Chicago District, transferring the area that borders Lake Michigan to the Detroit District and transferring the area comprising the Illinois River drainage to the Rock Island District. In concept, this proposal sought to allow the St. Paul District to focus on the Upper Mississippi River and to allow the Detroit District to focus on the Great Lakes. Rounding out this conceptual plan, Major General Harris proposed the transfer of the St. Louis District from the Lower Mississippi Valley Division to the North Central Division. The whole North Central Division was to benefit from this conceptual framework, in which three western districts (St. Paul, Rock Island and St. Louis) would share responsibility for the Upper Mississippi River all the way down to its confluence with the Ohio River, and two eastern districts (Detroit and Buffalo) would share responsibility for the Great Lakes.[8]

Although the plan had merit conceptually, it had little to recommend it politically. The Illinois politicians quickly blocked the move to close the Chicago office, and local interests in St. Louis successfully resisted the transfer of that district to the North Central Division, leaving just one part of Harris's proposal alive: the realignment of the St. Paul and Detroit districts. At issue was the Corps' presence in Duluth. Predictably, Congressman James Oberstar, whose congressional district included Duluth, opposed the transfer. Oberstar was close to the Corps. Before his election to Congress in 1974, he had served as administrative assistant to his predecessor, Congressman John Blatnik, and had been an administrator for the House Committee on Public Works from 1971 to 1974. He preferred to deal with an office in St. Paul rather than Detroit, and he pointed out that the St. Paul District in its present configuration served almost the whole state of Minnesota. However, Oberstar, a Democrat, received no support from Minnesota's other members of Congress. In the previous election year, the Republicans had campaigned on a platform of reduced government, and Minnesotans had elected two new Republican senators and a Republican governor, none of whom opposed the plan.[9] Moreover, the Carter Administration favored the realignment and Vice President Walter Mondale, Minnesota's most influential Democrat, was loyal to the administration initiative. Oberstar finally withdrew his opposition to the realignment after conferring by telephone with Mondale's office. The transfer was formally announced a few days later in mid-November 1979.[10]

What did the St. Paul District and the Corps gain or lose by this realignment? The harbor at the extreme western end of Lake Superior serves the cities of Duluth, Minnesota, and Superior, Wisconsin. Harbor improvements by the Corps date from 1867 in Superior and 1871 in Duluth. The ports were combined in 1896, and the facilities were subsequently expanded and modified by ten separate River and Harbor Acts, the latest (in 1960) authorizing the Corps to increase the depth of several channels and slips to accommodate deep-draft Great Lakes vessels. The Corps had completed most of the harbor-deepening project by 1968 at a cost of $14.5 million. All previous harbor improvements had amounted to $1.5 million, while the cost of maintenance from the first year they were authorized until 1979 was $18 million.[11] The harbor area is about 19 square miles and contains 17 miles of dredged channels. Most of the cargo shipped in and out of the harbor consists of iron ore, grain, coal and limestone. The extensive facilities and the amount of commerce make this harbor one of the most important on the Great Lakes and in the nation.[12]

In 1979, the Duluth field office had an annual budget of $3.5 million and employed about a hundred people at peak season. Dredging and other activities contributed another $1.2 million to the area economy. Despite initial concern that the realignment would cost Duluth money and jobs, the personnel and dredging equipment in Duluth were not relocated. The Corps' personnel in the Duluth office accepted the change with equanimity; some happily anticipated a greater degree of autonomy in working under the supervision of the more distant Detroit office.[13] Duluth's port director, Davis Helberg, noted that dealing with Detroit would pose some logistical challenges but this could be offset by the Detroit District's greater involvement in Great Lakes operations.[14]

Duluth jetties, Minnesota: Transfer of the Duluth harbor from St. Paul District to Detroit District took place in 1979. (Photo by Casondra Brewster, courtesy of Detroit District, Corps of Engineers)

The realignment mainly impacted the St. Paul District office, where twenty-eight employees were slated for transfer to Detroit to supervise Duluth-area operations.[15] It resulted in the loss of several construction projects at a time when the St. Paul District already faced a declining workload. It also eliminated the district's most visible point of contact with the general public – the Marine

Museum in Duluth, which attracted hundreds of thousands of visitors annually.[16] On the other hand, it allowed the St. Paul District to focus on rivers, as the reorganization plan had originally conceived, and officials presumed that the Detroit District benefited by the infusion of expertise from St. Paul for managing projects on the Great Lakes.[17]

The challenge of leading the St. Paul District personnel through the process of realignment fell largely on the shoulders of the new district engineer, Colonel William W. Badger, who took command of the district in June 1979. The reduction in size of the district from four major watersheds to three, and its loss of the harbors on Lake Superior – which cut the district's dredging work by half – left Colonel Badger with limited options. He assumed charge of an office that was already top heavy with senior staff and imposed a virtual hiring freeze for two years. In the political climate surrounding the realignment, he found it difficult to be innovative. In an effort to justify more senior-level positions, he proposed to his division commander, Major General Harris, that his people could take responsibility for river dredging, geophysical investigations and hydropower studies for all districts in the North Central Division. The St. Paul District, Badger suggested, could even handle all small flood control projects throughout the division. Harris cautiously agreed that the St. Paul District would become one of the lead districts for low-head hydropower studies, but he could not make the St. Paul District a regional resource center for the other items on Badger's agenda. It was not possible, Harris explained, "in light of the reorganization decision."[18]

The search for projects required much of the district engineer's energy. Prior to his assignment to the St. Paul District, Colonel Badger had served the Chief of Engineers as special assistant for international programs. It was a new position, in which Colonel Badger had helped to develop a growing overseas program for the Corps largely funded by foreign governments. After his arrival in St. Paul, Badger tried to involve the St. Paul District in water conservation projects in Gabon, Nigeria, China and elsewhere overseas.

This search for additional work outside the district brought little reward. By the end of his three-year tenure, Colonel Badger was focusing on planning, concerned about further reductions in the workload in the future. He had become worried that he would "not have the projects in the pipeline that will keep the district healthy in the future," he told an interviewer. "This may sound like survivalism, and in a way it is. I look at the district as a national asset, especially during a time of mobilization."[19]

Although the St. Paul District lost Duluth in the realignment of 1979, it survived; and in the 1980s, efforts to change the organizational structure of the Corps focused primarily on staff development, staff organization and project management – internal developments that will be discussed later in this chapter. These innovations could only go so far, however, in addressing the organizational problems that were evident in 1979: declining workload, rising overhead costs and, as a further consequence of the Corps' diminishing horizons, an aging professional workforce. Moreover, as military construction declined toward the end of the Cold War, the Army Corps of Engineers found another one of its primary missions fading. As a result, Corps' leadership called for renewed discussion of a major reorganization of the Corps' field structure. This time, the St. Paul District was on the list for elimination.

In 1988, the new Chief of Engineers, Lieutenant General Henry Hatch, initiated a comprehensive review of the Army Corps of Engineers' missions, goals and structure. He identified reorganization of the Corps' divisions and districts as a vital component of reinventing the Corps. The effort gained momentum with passage of the Energy and Water Development Appropriations Act of 1990, which directed the Corps to "initiate a broadbased conceptual study of potential field organizational structures." Congressional reports accompanying the appropriations bill for fiscal year 1991 reinforced this directive.[20]

In June 1990, Chief of Engineers Hatch formed a study team under Fred H. Bayley III, chief of engineering in the Vicksburg District, Lower Mississippi Valley Division, to develop alternative approaches to reorganization. The study team's report, called the Bayley Report, proposed five alternative conceptual approaches for reorganization: realignment, regionalization, decentralization, elimination of division offices and a "combination option." Pursuant to Congressional directive, the report was merely conceptual; it did not recommend specific changes that would impact one district or another. The Bayley Report was submitted to Congress on January 4, 1991.[21]

In the meantime, other developments were afoot that would have a crucial effect on the reorganization process and its outcome. With the end of the Cold War, the Department of Defense began to examine the need for reorganization of the entire U.S. military, with an emphasis on military installations that might be closed or consolidated. This wider effort commenced in mid-1988 after Secretary of Defense Dick Cheney established the Commission on Base Realignment and Closure, or BRAC Commission. Recognizing that base closures would affect local economies, that the economic consequences would fall unevenly across the nation and that the process would therefore become highly politicized, Congress attempted to cope with this problem in the Defense Authorization Amendments and Base Realignment and Closure Act of October 24, 1988, which provided that the Secretary of Defense and Congress must accept all or none of the recommendations by the BRAC Commission. However, this only raised the political stakes. Reluctant to accept the BRAC Commission's early recommendations, Congress passed the Defense Base Realignment and Closure Act of 1990, which established another commission to review the recommendations made by the Department of Defense. The latter commission's recommendations would also require approval or rejection in their entirety. As these developments were brewing in 1990, Corps' leadership began to consider whether the Corps' plan for reorganization should be incorporated into the BRAC plan. Given the way Congress had picked apart the Corps' previous reorganization effort in the late 1970s, it appeared that the BRAC process might offer the Corps the best chance for pushing its own reorganization plan through Congress. As a result, when Acting Assistant Secretary of the Army (Civil Works) Dr. G. Edward Dickey submitted the Bayley Report to Congress on January 4, 1991, he averred that the next phase of the Corps' reorganization effort would be aimed at inclusion in the BRAC process.[22]

By this time, Chief of Engineers Hatch had formed a second reorganization study team for the specific purpose of hitching the Corps' effort to the BRAC Commission's wagon. Lieutenant General Arthur E. Williams headed the new team. While the team included many members of the Bayley team, it worked on an independent report using various methodological tools provided by the BRAC Commission, most notably a "D-PAD Model." In essence, the D-PAD computer analysis involved scoring each district and division on numerous capabilities and weighting the relative importance of those capabilities in order to determine the most efficient scenario for realignment. After the D-PAD analysis was completed, the team sought intuitive input from twenty senior leaders in the organization "to supplement the purely analytical results" from D-PAD.[23] District leaders, however, were not invited to participate in the process.[24]

The Williams team worked from November 1990 to February 1991 and produced its own report, "The U.S. Army Corps of Engineers Reorganization Study." It made specific recommendations to realign the existing ten divisions and thirty-five districts in the contiguous United States into six divisions and twenty-two districts. The plan called for a parallel realignment of divisions for the Corps' civil works and military support missions, but division and district boundaries would conform to watershed boundaries for the civil works mission, whereas division boundaries would conform to state borders for the military support mission. Just one district in each division would be responsible for military construction throughout the division's jurisdiction (compared to fifteen districts with a military construction mission under the existing structure). The plan would eliminate 2,600 jobs and transfer 6,600 others. The authors estimated a cost for implementation of $266 million and annual savings of $112 million.[25]

The plan called for the closing of the St. Paul District together with twelve other districts. The St. Paul District would be combined with the Rock Island and St. Louis districts to form a single district for all of the Upper Mississippi River with its central office in St. Louis. The plan contemplated expansion of the North Central Division and relocation of its headquarters to Louisville, Kentucky.

The Williams team released the scores used in its D-PAD analysis together with its recommendations. These scores revealed that the St. Paul District ranked high in the two broad categories of "flexibility and expendability" and "quality of life/ competence," – it had a skilled professional staff and it was admirably situated in St. Paul to take advantage of educational opportunities and other services. It was average in "operational efficiencies" – a general measure of the cost of doing work. Its score suffered, however, in the two broad categories of "mission essentiality" and "mission suitability." These categories reflected the basic problem of a declining workload, and the D-PAD analysis indicated that the St. Paul District was feeling that pinch more than other districts. Indeed, the D-PAD analysis ranked the St. Paul District in twenty-first place among thirty-six civil works districts. (Districts with military construction were ranked separately.)[26]

As soon as the Corps' reorganization plan was completed, members of Congress whose districts would suffer the loss of a division or district office – including Congressman Bruce Vento (DFL-Minnesota), whose congressional district included St. Paul – began to pressure the Administration to scuttle the plan. They threatened to oppose the military base closures initiative if it included Corps' offices. Members of Congress argued that the Corps could not be included under BRAC because congressional oversight of the Corps fell to the Senate and House committees on public works, not the committees on armed services. Anxious to protect the BRAC process, Secretary of Defense Cheney announced in April that he would not propose the Corps reorganization plan. Although he supported it in principle, the Administration would not try to include the Corps' reorganization with the Administration's current push to close thirty-one military installations around the nation. Not content with Cheney's announcement, Congressman Vento went to Corps' headquarters in Washington, D.C., to confirm the plan was tabled. "There is no proposal or decision as of today to close the St. Paul District office," he told reporters afterwards.[27]

A month later, on May 24, 1991, Cheney announced the reorganization plan for the Corps. Although it was now separate from the base-closing plan submitted in April, there was no change in the Corps' approach.[28] Immediately the Corps' concept for reorganization fell under attack. Governor of Minnesota Arne H. Carlson and Governor of Wisconsin Tommy Thompson argued that the reorganization plan was poorly conceived; the Corps would be unable to provide the same quality of service from a remote location in Buffalo, New York, or St. Louis, Missouri.[29] Other critics charged that the reorganization plan was based on politics. For example, it seemed the St. Paul District and Rock Island District offices were to be consolidated with the St. Louis District office, the smallest of the three, because the latter happened to be located in the district of House Majority Leader Dick Gephardt. Congressmans Vento and Oberstar responded to Cheney's announcement by going to the chairman of the House appropriations subcommittee on energy and water development, Congressman Tom Bevill (D-Alabama), and obtaining a formal commitment that none of the Corps' appropriations for the next fiscal year could be used to close or relocate the St. Paul District office.[30]

At this point, the BRAC Commission entered the debate over the Corps' reorganization plan. In a clear signal to Congress that it wanted to include the Corps within its purview, it invited various witnesses to testify at a June 5 hearing on the Corps' reorganization. On July 1, it made its recommendations on base closures. The recommendations included a provision that would allow Congress an opportunity to develop its own plan for reorganizing the Corps but at the expiration of one year (July 1, 1992) the Administration's reorganization plan for the Corps would go into effect under BRAC's authority. On July 10, President George H. W. Bush presented the BRAC Commission recommendations to Congress without comment on this provision.[31]

In the fall of 1991, Congress passed a series of acts that firmly detached the Corps from the BRAC process and crushed the Corps' reorganization plan. First, it explicitly rejected the one-year deadline for developing a plan of reorganization for the Corps when it approved the BRAC recommendations on base closures. Second, it prohibited the expenditure of funds for closing Corps' division or district offices in both the public works and armed services appropriations bills. Finally, for good measure, it included a provision in the appropriations bill for 1992 that defined what could be considered a

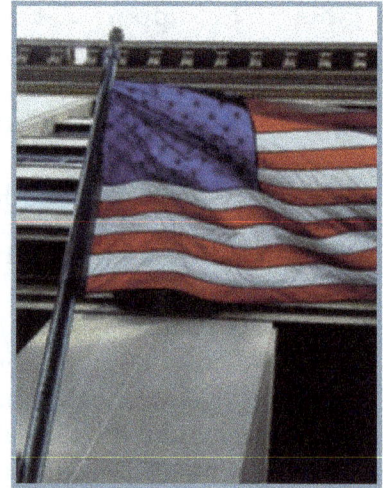

The Corps of Engineers Centre: A Brief History

The building that housed the Army Corps of Engineers, St. Paul District, from 1993 to 2010, enjoys a rich history, with ties to the flourishing fur trade industry of the nineteenth century; nationally renowned Minnesota architect Clarence Johnston; and Minnesota's favorite son, Charles Lindbergh.

The building at 333 Sibley in St. Paul was first constructed as an industrial structure to house the manufacturing and sales activities of the Gordon & Ferguson Company, a fur corporation first founded by Richards Gordon in 1854. In 1912, the company, under the leadership of Charles Gordon, Richards' son, began planning construction of the building at Sibley and 4th Street. Gordon hired the famed Minnesota architect, Clarence Johnston, for the project. At a cost of $250,000, the structure, named the Gordon & Ferguson Building, covered nearly half of a city block to the height of nine stories, with eight above ground and one below. The main entrance was originally located on Sibley Street. While housed in this structure, the Gordon & Ferguson Company prospered, even manufacturing the flight suit worn by Charles Lindbergh on his precedent-setting, non-stop flight from the United States to Paris in "The Spirit of St. Louis." By 1944, the Gordon & Ferguson Company had outgrown its residence, and it abandoned the building, leaving it vacant for nearly fifteen years.

In 1958, John J. Kaplan, president and treasurer of the Globe Paper Box Manufacturing Company of St. Paul, purchased and refurbished the structure, renaming it the Nalpak Building (Kaplan spelled backwards). Under their ownership, the structure housed mostly state offices, including the Minnesota Department of Administration, Records Management Division; the Minnesota Council on Developmental Disabilities; and the Minnesota Department of Human Rights. The Army Corps of Engineers, St. Paul District, began leasing portions of the building in 1988 for eighty employees of the district's Construction-Operations Division. In 1993, after more than 53 years in the old Post Office, the St. Paul District adopted the building as its headquarters. The structure was completely renovated for the district and renamed the Corps of Engineers Centre.

-Matt Pearcy, St. Paul District Historian (from 2001-2006)

military installation under BRAC. A military installation did not include "any facility used primarily for civil jurisdiction or control of the Department of Defense."[32]

In the spring of 1992, the Administration went back to the drawing board. Officials who had worked for months to develop a plan of reorganization under the BRAC process felt disappointed and chastened by Congress's action. Newly appointed Assistant Secretary of the Army (Civil Works) Nancy Dorn told a House committee in March 1992: "The message that Congress sent was clear. While there may be a need to reorganize the Corps to meet the challenges of the 21st century, the proposed plan was unacceptable and there should be an opportunity for Congressional involvement in any future plan." Congressman Vento, who impugned the previous year's effort as a "sort of top-down type of slam dunk effort to reorganize the Corps," welcomed Dorn's "fresh perspective."[33]

The Corps formed a field advisory committee to develop a new reorganization plan. In contrast to the Williams' team, the field advisory committee included representatives from every district and division. Louis E. Kowalski, Planning Division chief, served as the St. Paul District representative. After several months of data gathering, a smaller task force, under the leadership of Brigadier General Albert J. Genetti, Jr., produced a report in July 1992. That same summer saw a change of Corps' leadership, according to the usual four year rotation of the chief of engineers, Lieutenant General Arthur E. Williams, who had been closely involved with reorganization over the previous year-and-a-half, replaced Hatch. During September and October, he reviewed the new reorganization plan with the Assistant Secretary of the Army (Civil Works) and other Administration officials and released it on November 19, 1992, shortly after the election.

The new proposal reflected the influence of Congress. Districts would be given a robust standing in the new field organization while divisions would be consolidated and downsized. The number of divisions in the contiguous United States would be reduced from eleven to six, and the number of districts would be increased by one to thirty-six. However, some district capabilities would be consolidated: planning and engineering functions would be transferred from twenty-one districts to the remaining fifteen, which would be called technical centers.[34]

The St. Paul District was identified as one of the technical centers. Staff writers for the *News-Tribune* were quick to note the turnaround. "The St. Paul District office of the Army Corps of Engineers that was to all but close under a plan last year, instead will almost double in size to more than 800 workers under a major restructuring," they wrote. District Engineer Richard W. Craig explained that the St. Paul office had been selected to be a technical center because it had a nearby airport and a significant technical staff already in place and it could obtain room to expand. (He was prepared to relocate the office from the old post office building to the Sibley Building at 5th and Sibley streets one block away.)[35]

Ironically, in developing a plan more to Congress's liking, the Corps cut itself off from the new Administration. Chief of Engineers Williams was premature in unveiling the plan two weeks after the election, without even a pause for consultation with President-elect Bill Clinton's nominees for Secretary of Defense or Secretary of the Army. One day after President Clinton took office, Secretary of Defense Les Aspin announced that the plan was withdrawn.[36]

Restructuring under the Clinton Administration

Chief of Engineers Williams gradually lowered the drumbeat for reorganization, despite the investment that he and so many other Corps' officials had put into it.[37] He was in an awkward position with the new Administration and needed to build credibility with Secretary of Defense Aspin and other incoming civilian political appointees in the Department of Defense. Moreover, he understood that the rank and file in the organization were tired of all the uncertainty and stress that had accompanied the reorganization effort and they needed a reprieve. Many people who worked under Williams were relieved when the new Chief told Congress he would prefer not to restudy the issue. The St. Paul District Commander, Colonel Craig, applauded Williams' position. The St. Paul office had been on a roller coaster ride – facing closure, then expansion and then uncertainty again – and Craig wanted to restore his staff's confidence. "We've been down at the lowest levels, and we've been at the highest levels," Craig told an interviewer. "We're on a norm now, and we recognize the turf that we're on, and, hopefully, we won't go up or down."[38]

The Clinton Administration made its effort to introduce organizational change in the Corps part of a much larger strategy of "reinventing government." In his election campaign, Clinton promised to make government work better while costing less money to the taxpayers. On March 3, 1993, Clinton requested Vice President Albert Gore head a taskforce of some two hundred people to conduct an intensive review of how the federal government performed. The effort, called the National Performance Review, had six months to make its report. After the taskforce completed its work in October, the Clinton Administration drafted legislation to implement various changes in government processes. The legislation addressed numerous agencies in all the departments of the executive branch. Clinton's plan for the Corps appeared in Section 3201 of the bill:

The Secretary of the Army shall reorganize the U.S. Army Corps of Engineers by reorganizing the Headquarters offices, reducing the number of Division offices, and restructuring the District functions so as to increase the efficiency of the U.S. Army Corps of Engineers and reduce staff and costs, with the goal of achieving approximately $50 million in net annual savings by fiscal year 1998.[39] The legislation was eventually enacted as the Federal Workforce Restructuring Act of 1994.

The Clinton Administration's strategy for "restructuring" the Corps – a term it preferred to "reorganization" – followed from the National Performance Review. It focused on the headquarters and divisions and eliminated various functions that were redundant with functions carried out at the district level. For example, it divested the divisions of responsibility for technical review. It also worked on consolidating (regionalizing) human resources offices and finance offices in the Corps. These initiatives resulted in significant reductions of "full time equivalent" positions, or FTEs, in the headquarters and division offices. While some of these changes were anticipated, a decisive innovation in the Clinton plan was that it accomplished these changes using the "General Expenses" account in the Corps' budget, thereby obviating the need for Congress to approve a line item for the cost of "reorganization."[40] Moreover, by leaving all districts intact, it recovered control of the reorganization process from Congress. However, the problem of realigning the divisions and districts remained.

The Clinton Administration commenced its own study of reorganization of the Corps' field structure in June 1994, when Acting Assistant Secretary of the Army (Civil Works) John Zirschky called a conference of about two hundred people comprising division and district Corps' personnel and representatives of non-federal Corps' partners to examine relationships between headquarters, divisions and districts. For obvious reasons, this effort was accompanied by little fanfare. Eventually, the Clinton Administration arrived at a plan that did not differ too much from the plan the Corps unveiled in November 1992. Instead of reducing the number of divisions from eleven to six, they were reduced to eight. There were two significant innovations. Divisional offices in Portland and Omaha became regional offices, and all of the districts on the Mississippi River were combined under one command, the Mississippi Valley Division. As with the Clinton Administration's other restructuring efforts, this approach allowed the plan to be implemented using General Expense accounts of the headquarters and divisions. Rather than closing any division offices, they were converted (and downsized) to regional centers. The new divisional structure went into effect on April 1, 1997, with full implementation – expressed most simply in terms of reduced FTEs – to be accomplished by April 1, 2002.[41]

The divisional restructuring placed the St. Paul District in a new division. It was transferred from the North Central Division to the Mississippi Valley Division with headquarters in Vicksburg, Mississippi. The change was not entirely comfortable. Colonel J. M. Wonsik, district engineer, characterized the St. Paul District and the North Central Division as "introspective" in the way they conducted business, while the Mississippi Valley Division was "aggressive" in its practices. Concerned that his district risked losing its edge, he encouraged his staff to communicate more with their counterparts in the other districts within the Mississippi Valley Division and to learn from the district's "new neighbors." Wonsik advised his staff to examine what the districts on the lower Mississippi River were doing and "steal shamelessly what other people are doing very, very well." He also wanted his people to take every opportunity to help those districts' staffs learn from them. In his view, realignment of the Mississippi Valley Division presented an opportunity for "crossfertilization" between districts.[42]

Reorganization had a significant impact on employee morale and productivity. People feared for their jobs and all the discussion about redundancy and streamlining lowered people's sense of commitment. The concern about job loss was most critical in 1991, when Corps' leadership proposed to deactivate the St. Paul District. But the duration of the process upset people as well. In the mid-1990s, the office was under constant pressure to reduce FTEs, and people grew impatient with the continuing uncertainty as reorganization was simply held in abeyance. Finally, the divisional restructuring that took effect in 1997 provided a measure of relief by simply bringing an end to the process, but it too left a mark on the St. Paul District staff. It accentuated the St.

Paul District's vulnerability even as districts strengthened their position within the organization. Change was unsettling. Although the realignment brought opportunity, it also caused insecurity. Wonsik told an interviewer in January 1998, with apparent misgivings, "It felt like we were traded from the [Minnesota] Vikings to the [Green Bay] Packers."[43] All factors combined, morale in the district probably reached a low point during Wonsik's tour from 1995 to 1998.

Changes in Internal Organization

Engineering a Victory for Our Environment

A CITIZEN'S GUIDE TO THE U.S. ARMY CORPS OF ENGINEERS

YOU AND WHOSE ARMY?

A Sierra Club Special Publication

This cartoon from a Sierra Club publication, published in the early 1970s, presents the Corps of Engineers as a large, powerful force that bullied small, weak environementalists.

Much of the restructuring that occurred under the Clinton Administration involved changing how staffs were organized within each office or how the Corps got its work done. Some of these initiatives flowed from the National Performance Review; other initiatives began much earlier. Like the reorganization effort, these internal organizational changes were made in response to two broad imperatives. First, the Corps sought to reinvent itself in light of its increasing role in environmental protection. Second, the Corps sought to change the way it managed civil works projects in order to perform more efficiently at less cost.

Addressing Environmentalism

The environmental movement of the 1960s and 1970s reflected profound shifts in public attitudes about the environment and resulted in numerous laws aimed at reforming society's relationship to the natural world. The American people's new environmental awareness extended into many areas, including wilderness preservation, endangered species protection, reduction of air and water pollution and hazardous waste cleanup. The broad ranging issues that underpinned the environmental movement were as interwoven as they were varied. They stemmed from such broad societal trends as the nation's rising affluence in the post-World War II era, the increasing scientific understanding of ecology and the environment and the threats posed to humanity's very existence by the development of nuclear weapons, the pressures of population growth and the depletion of nonrenewable resources.[44] Practically all facets of

24

environmentalism impinged on the Army Corps of Engineers' missions. Moreover, the Corps acquired new missions specifically aimed at protecting the environment.

Environmentalism was an outgrowth of conservation, but it also differed from conservation in fundamental ways. Traditional conservation, which blossomed in the early twentieth century, posited that the federal government had a responsibility to protect and manage natural resources for efficient and sustainable use for the good of the nation. The conservation movement resulted in legislation directed at ensuring an efficient and democratic approach to resource development. In contrast to the great giveaway of public domain that characterized public land policy in the late nineteenth century, conservation laws in the early twentieth century emphasized the commons: water resources, forest lands, fish and wildlife, scenic wonders. One of the first great legislative acts of the conservation movement was the Reclamation Act of 1902, which sought to develop rivers for purposes of irrigating arid Western lands. A central tenet of the conservation movement was the role of the scientific expert in resource management. Fledgling federal agencies like the Reclamation Service and the Forest Service assembled staffs of experts in their respective scientific disciplines and emphasized centralized planning in resource development. The Corps of Engineers, long recognized for its expertise in river and harbor improvement, fit easily into the traditional conservation milieu.

In contrast to the earlier conservation movement, the environmental movement of the 1960s and 1970s displayed a mistrust of federal resource management and a refusal to defer to scientific experts. More broadly, the new environmentalism emphasized the interconnectedness of the natural world. It doubted the ability of federal agencies concerned primarily with developing a single resource such as timber or water to consider the ramifications of their actions on the total environment. Indeed, environmentalists found that federal agencies such as the Forest Service, Atomic Energy Commission and Corps of Engineers were among the worst offenders against the environment.[45] Supreme Court Justice William O. Douglas did not mince words when he called the Corps of Engineers "public enemy number one."[46]

To address these concerns, Congress enacted the National Environmental Policy Act, or NEPA, of 1969. This law, the most important environmental legislation of the era, mandated federal agencies to coordinate their efforts in managing the nation's resources and to integrate public review and comment into all of their resource planning efforts. These guiding principles of national environmental policy recognized the need for a more holistic approach to the environment as well as the need to make decision-making more public and democratic.[47] NEPA provided a clarion call for agencies such as the Army Corps of Engineers to reform their planning processes.

Various studies of the Corps have stated that the agency responded admirably to the new requirements mandated by NEPA. One study characterized the Corps' response as "sincere, swift, and impressive."[48] Another study praised the Corps for the amount of autonomy it gave to environmental analysts in conducting environmental reviews. An internal study by the Corps' Historical Division stated that the agency "developed new procedures to insure that environmental issues were properly addressed. Consequently the Corps became the first federal water resources agency to institutionalize environmental views."[49]

The critical provision of NEPA was the requirement that federal agencies produce an Environmental Impact Statement, or EIS, for each proposed action significantly affecting the environment. The EIS evaluated environmental impacts from the standpoint of various scientific and social-scientific disciplines to arrive at a well-rounded understanding of the consequences of an action. Rather than complain that the EIS requirement was onerous, the Corps built the EIS into its project authorization process and publicly stated that the EIS was helpful in allowing it to do a better job. The procedure for completing an EIS included an opportunity for public comment, so it deflected criticism that the Corps ignored public opinion.[50]

Corps' leadership at Headquarters initiated organizational changes to increase public participation and environmental sensitivity in Corps' decision-making, and the divisions and districts soon emulated their example. Agency policy required that the district engineer hold public meetings when proposing a project. The object was to give local interests the "full opportunity to express their views on the character and extent of the improvement desired, on the need and advisability of its execution, and on their general willingness and ability to cooperate with the Federal Government."[51]

In the early to mid-1970s, a number of districts experimented with citizen advisory boards.[52] A flood control project in Minneapolis exemplified the new emphasis on public participation. To help plan the project on Bassett Creek, which runs through the city, the St. Paul District assisted in forming a nine-member commission composed of interested citizens rather than experts. The Corps developed a flood control plan incrementally with frequent input by the commission and its consulting engineer, and the Corps prepared an EIS in tandem with this process. A member of the commission, Edward Silberman, lauded the result. "In the Bassett Creek flood-control problem, incremental plan development has been so effective that the Commission did not have to take a formal vote to adopt its final plan," he wrote. "This was not an accident but rather the result of a carefully conducted melding of bureaucratic and public input by the Bassett Creek Flood Control Commission with important assistance from its consulting engineers."[53]

NEPA's EIS requirement also led the Corps to hire new staff with expertise in fisheries biology, wildlife biology, archeology, history, economics and sociology. As a result of this infusion of new staff skills into the organization, the Corps acquired greater sensitivity to environmental concerns. The interdisciplinary team that prepared an EIS for a project was usually situated in an environmental branch attached to the Planning Division. Indeed, the basic function of the environmental branch was to produce EISs. One of the challenges in changing the internal organization of the Corps was to integrate these units effectively into corporate decision-making. Engineers referred to the new staff positions as the "exotic disciplines," and they tended to accord these specialists less respect than they did their fellow engineers. It took time to develop an interdisciplinary ethos in the agency.[54]

In the St. Paul District, the Environmental Branch was originally housed within the Engineering Division. The relationship was not a smooth one. The district's first chief ecologist, Dr. Barbara Gudmandson, was fired in December 1971. She appealed her dismissal and was reinstated in April 1972, but was replaced one month later by chief ecologist Keith B. Larson. A year-and-a-half after taking the job, Larson resigned in protest, claiming that the district engineer, Colonel Rodney Cox, had significantly altered a draft EIS, which in its original form found a proposed $18-million coal terminal at Pig's Eye Lake in St. Paul to be environmentally unsound. At a press conference, Larson also disclosed that someone in the Corps had altered the conclusions of several contracted environmental reports prepared by forty-five scientists from colleges and universities in Minnesota, Wisconsin and North Dakota. Environmental groups expressed concern. A Sierra Club spokesman charged the Corps with removing environmental staff whenever they became effective and called for an independent citizens' review of operations in the St. Paul District office. A representative of the Minnesota Environmental Control Citizens Association asserted that the district's Environmental Branch was "window dressing that has turned out to be pie in the face of the Corps."[55] These public controversies notwithstanding, the district stayed the course in its effort to integrate environmental review into its planning process.[56]

President Jimmy Carter and First Lady Rosslyn Carter on board the Delta Queen at Lock and Dam 6, on August 18, 1979. (Photo by Lyle Nicklay, courtesy of St. Paul District, Corps of Engineers)

By 1980, the so-called exotic disciplines had made further inroads into the engineer-dominated agency. Some of the environmental staff was located in the Environmental Resources Branch under the direction of Robert Post, while some of it was in the Planning Branch headed by J. Robert Calton. Both of these staff groups remained in the Engineering Division under Roger Fast. Colonel Badger, district engineer, wanted to combine the two branches and elevate the latter to division status – separating the two staff groups from the Engineering Division. However, Calton and Fast, both veterans of more than thirty years in the district, opposed the change. Colonel Badger waited for the two men's retirements in 1980 and 1981, respectively, and then appointed Louis Kowalski as chief of the Planning Branch and moved him into an office next to his own. His new chief of the Engineering Division, Peter Fischer, occupied an office on the other side. The position of these offices on either side of the district engineer's office, Colonel Badger found, prepared the district staff for the change that followed one year later. With the approval of the Chief of Engineers, Colonel Badger created the Planning Division on April 4, 1982. He appointed Robert Post assistant chief of the Planning Division as well as chief of the environmental resources staff.[57]

The Planning Division took the lead in encouraging the Corps to embrace more environmentally sensitive approaches in its project designs. Certainly the clearest manifestation of the Corps' increasing sensitivity to the environment was its advocacy of nonstructural measures for flood control. Traditionally, the Corps supported structural improvements – primarily dams and levees – to reduce flood hazards. As Corps' planners increasingly took an interdisciplinary view of river systems and their floodplains, they favored alternatives to dams and levees. These included buyouts of private property in the floodplain (and relocation of existing buildings away from the floodplain) and other means of social engineering to change land uses in flood-prone areas.[58] In 1979, the St. Paul District produced a report on The Development of Nonstructural Alternatives.[59] The change from structural to nonstructural flood controls is discussed in more detail in subsequent chapters.

If diversification of staff specializations within the Corps was an important factor encouraging greater consideration of nonstructural projects, President Jimmy Carter's controversial reform effort was another factor. Carter saw a need to revise how the Corps justified civil works projects to Congress in order to make the Corps move away from its long-standing commitment to construction of dams and levees. The Corps' traditional emphasis on hard structures, Carter found, was embedded in the Flood Control Act of 1936 as amended in 1938. The law provided for full funding of flood control structures. Local communities were far more supportive of structural than nonstructural flood controls because hard structures, such as dams and levees, were

Colonel William Badger, district engineer, and First Lady Rosslyn Carter. (Photo by Lyle Nicklay, courtesy of St. Paul District, Corps of Engineers)

federally funded while nonstructural remedies entailed costs that had to be born by local governments. In 1977, Carter issued executive orders and proposed legislation that aimed to end this bias by introducing cost-sharing requirements for local governments on all flood controls – regardless of whether they were structural or nonstructural. The Administration termed this initiative a "redirected public works program." Although Carter implemented the costsharing plan administratively, the plan did not receive congressional sanction until nine years later.[60]

As the Corps began to propose nonstructural solutions for flood control, environmental organizations took note. In 1975, *Audubon* ran an article praising the Corps' "new look" in flood control. It cited the example of Prairie du Chien, Wisconsin, where the Corps recommended evacuation of the floodplain as the only economically justifiable solution to flood hazards. "No dams. No levees," *Audubon* commented. "Instead, the Corps recommended that one hundred and fifty-seven buildings be relocated out of the flood-prone area, that another forty-eight buildings be purchased and demolished by the federal government, that thirty-three homes be raised above flood levels, and that seven other buildings be flood-proofed. The Corps also recommended that the cleared floodplain become a greenbelt, protected by state and local regulation."[61]

Environmentalists were not the only group to note the change in the Army Corps of Engineers. Respected journals such as *The Nation* and *Business Week* commented on the Corps' new approach to flood control. The agency was adapting, these journals pointed out, because growing concern about the environment had exposed serious limitations in the Corps' traditional benefit-cost analysis of proposed projects. One writer characterized the organizational change in the Corps as an "internal struggle" between engineers trained to "optimize economic aspects" of a project and others who wanted to modify projects "to enhance or preserve the environment."[62]

The popular magazine *Ms.* examined organizational change in the Corps from a feminist perspective, noting not only the infusion of non-engineer specialists into the ranks of this peculiarly civilian unit of the Army but the Corps' push to recruit more women as well. Speaking of the latter initiative, one official was quoted, "We have a real shortage. We could use a lot more."[63] The increasing numbers of women in the Corps changed the face of the organization. The Corps was not alone in taking affirmative action to hire more women in the 1970s; other federal agencies with traditionally male-dominated staffs, such as the U.S. Department of Agriculture Forest Service, underwent a similar transition during the decade.

In the 1970s, the Corps of Engineers acquired a new mandate relating to environmental protection. It became the administrator of regulatory programs aimed at protecting the nation's wetlands. In 1972, Congress passed the Federal Water Pollution Control Act (later known as the Clean Water Act). Section 404 of the law prohibited the discharge of dredged or fill material into the "waters of the United States" without a permit from the Army Corps of Engineers. During the next few years, environmentalists sought to affirm that the law applied to wetlands as well as navigable waterways. Environmentalists pushed the Corps to assert its regulatory responsibility under the law as widely as possible. Although the Corps initially resisted taking an aggressive stand on wetlands protection, judicial decisions in the mid-1970s forced the Corps to take a wider view of its "Section 404" responsibilities. According to historian Jeffrey K. Stine, the regulatory responsibilities of the Corps fundamentally altered its relationship with the environmental community. Some of the Corps' staunchest critics in the environmental community suddenly began courting the Corps because of its key role under Section 404 of the Clean Water Act.[64]

The evolution of the Corps' regulatory program for the protection of wetlands and the regulatory activities of the St. Paul District in Minnesota and Wisconsin will be discussed in detail in another chapter. Suffice it to say here that Section 404 of the Clean Water Act had a profound effect on the Corps' organization. To staff the program, the Corps recruited ecologists who specialized in ecological processes and values associated with wetlands, and it hired biologists who specialized in aquatic flora and fauna. Like the interdisciplinary teams that prepared EISs, the ecologists and biologists who evaluated Section 404 permit applications brought new perspectives to the organization. By 1991, the Section 404 permitting program funded thirty-one positions, including field office positions located at Bemidji and Duluth, Minnesota, and Waukesha, Fox River, Green Bay and La Crosse, Wisconsin. Ben A. Wopat was chief of the Regulatory Branch, which was attached to the Construction-Operations Division.[65] By 2001, the Regulatory Branch had grown to thirty-nine positions with field offices in Two Harbors and Brainerd, Minnesota, and Waukesha, Green Bay, Stevens Point and La Crosse, Wisconsin. Robert J. Whiting was chief of the Regulatory Branch, while Wopat was assistant chief of the Construction-Operations Division.[66]

The St. Paul District's Section 404 responsibilities involved the organization directly with state officials in Minnesota and Wisconsin. For purposes of wetlands regulation, the St. Paul District's jurisdiction covered all of these two states. The district boundaries followed state lines rather than watersheds. The staff was organized into sections, one for each state. From 1977 to about 1987, there was a Surveillance and Enforcement Section. In the 1990s, a Metro Permit Section was created. The locations of some of the field offices changed frequently. Organizational changes in the Corps provided tangible evidence that it was adapting to new public concern for the environment. Changes in staff organization and personnel enabled the Corps to address new legal requirements, such as the EIS, effectively.

Organizational changes facilitated the Corps' move toward nonstructural approaches to flood control and its increasing role in environmental protection – particularly wetlands protection. How these changes became manifested in particular projects and programs will be explored in subsequent chapters.

Prairie du Chien, Wisconsin, nonstructural flood control project: In 1978, the city of Prairie du Chien relocated numerous residents whose homes stood in a floodplain. This house was the first to be moved under guidlines jointly developed by the St. Paul District and the city. Shown here is the homeowner, a man in his eighties who had built the house himself more than fifty years earlier. (Photo courtesy of St. Paul District, Corps of Engineers)

Improvements in Business Operations

The civil works program was once the lifeblood of the Corps of Engineers, and new civil works projects were what sustained the program. [67] As the average size of new civil works projects decreased in the 1960s and 1970s, the administrative cost of moving any given project through consecutive phases of planning, design and construction rose proportionally. Moreover, small projects sometimes brought the Corps into direct competition with private- sector engineering firms, further highlighting the cost of its project-related work. By the mid-1970s, the Corps faced significant pressure to reduce costs. During the next two decades, the Corps introduced various new approaches in how it funded and managed civil works projects. Two initiatives were of particular importance: cost-sharing and project management.

While these initiatives developed out of specific changes in the Corps' civil works program – namely the smaller size of projects and the Corps' greater sensitivity to the environment – they also mirrored much broader public concerns about the federal bureaucracy. Public confidence in government fell sharply in the 1960s and early 1970s in response to the U.S. embroilment in Vietnam, the civil unrest in American cities, the degradation of the environment and, finally, the Watergate scandal. In the last quarter of the twentieth century, U.S. presidents made various attempts to reform the federal bureaucracy and to overcome the deep public cynicism toward government. President Jimmy Carter saw the public's cynicism as rooted in mistrust of public officials and sought to restore government's credibility. President Ronald Reagan responded to the public's disillusionment by promising to cut taxes and to get government off people's backs. President Bill Clinton believed the way to restore public confidence in government was to make bureaucracy function more efficiently, in large part by making it emulate certain aspects of the private sector. Organizational changes in the Corps mirrored these presidential initiatives, each of which cut across the whole federal bureaucracy: a heightened commitment to openness and accountability in the Carter years, an emphasis on downsizing and cost reduction in the Reagan-Bush years and a commitment to innovation and efficiency in the Clinton years. Not since the Progressive Era and the New Deal had the United States experienced such a sustained effort to reform how its government worked.

Some of the initiatives designed to make the Corps more open to public scrutiny and public input have been discussed above. The St. Paul District supported efforts in the 1970s to involve the public in decision-making through citizen advisory boards and hearings on EISs. In May 1979, President Carter introduced legislation aimed at stimulating greater involvement by state and local governments in the Corps' civil works projects through mandatory cost-sharing. He proposed a requirement that state and local governments contribute 5 to 10 percent of the cost of each new river or harbor improvement project. In addition, state governments would contribute 5 percent and local governments would contribute 20 percent of the cost of each new flood control project. The state or local government would be responsible for its share of the cost from the project's inception – beginning in the planning phase. Carter contended that the requirement for local participation would increase the quality of consideration of potential projects, "thereby improving the public's ability to judge the comparative merits of many water project opportunities." By the same token, it would give state and local governments a firmer role in rejecting unwanted federal projects.[68] Congress did not pass this legislation, though it would adopt the cost-sharing model seven years later in the Water Resources Development Act of 1986. In the meantime, the Corps moved to implement cost-sharing agreements administratively wherever state and local governments were willing to cooperate.

For many flood-prone communities in the St. Paul District, the cost-sharing initiative was unwelcome. The editors of Fargo's *The Forum* objected that the partnership would be unequal. "Hardly any state has the experience in construction of water projects that has been amassed by the Army Corps of Engineers and the U.S. Bureau of Reclamation," they noted. Most of the obvious water projects were already built, so it was unfair to require state and local governments to share costs of determining whether water projects were economically feasible.[69] The St. Paul *Pioneer Press* was more receptive to the Carter proposal but agreed with *The Forum* that the legislation would not pass Congress. Environmental groups, meanwhile, wanted the states to contribute up to a fourth of the cost of water projects.[70]

The Reagan Administration intensified the push to implement cost-sharing agreements between the Corps and state and local governments. After Reagan took office, Colonel William W. Badger, district engineer, was surprised by the strength and swiftness of the message that the new Administration delivered through Headquarters to the district engineers. "The essence of the new policy arrived very quickly and the comments about what we could say and could not say about cost-sharing were very exact," Badger said in a March 1982 interview. The intent of the policy was to shift some of the burden and responsibility for civil works from the federal to the state level. Ironically, Badger noted, in its haste to federalize or decentralize the Corps' operation, the Administration was moving the Corps "toward a more centralized operation." Like a good soldier, Badger delivered the new Administration's message that new projects would require significantly greater state and local participation.[71]

Colonel Ed Rapp, who replaced Colonel Badger as district engineer in 1982, continued to take the Reagan Administration's message to state and local governments within the St. Paul District. He held cost-share discussions with Wisconsin state officials over a highway project at La Crosse. In Minneapolis, city officials "signed up for cost-sharing" on the Bassett Creek flood control project. In North Dakota, Rapp held "preliminary" but "significant" discussions concerning cost-sharing at Lake Darling. When the City of Rochester in Minnesota refused to share costs with the Corps for flood control on the South Zumbro River, Rapp was philosophical: "They could afford cost-sharing," he told an interviewer. "They just chose to see if they could get a better deal somewhere else." Much of the colonel's discussion with local sponsors remained theoretical, while Congress deliberated over the cost-share proposal, laying the groundwork for future projects. "The Administration is getting in their licks," he commented, "and I was glad we were able to support the Administration's firm position."[72]

In addition to wanting more cost-share agreements, the Reagan Administration sought to accelerate and streamline the Corps' planning process. It wanted faster decisions, more results, less study. "Signals very quickly came down through the system," Badger recalled. "People were stating over and over again that government should get off the people's backs."[73] In particular, the Corps' Section 404 program for the protection of wetlands came under attack. The Reagan Administration criticized the Corps' permitting as excessively ponderous and obstructionist, and it wanted the Corps to streamline its process for reviewing and issuing permits.[74] While this position found congressional support in some parts of the country, it was not popular in Minnesota and Wisconsin. The people of Minnesota and Wisconsin were generally sensitive to loss or degradation of wetlands, since the region contained such an abundance of wetlands, lakes, rivers and potholes, and they did not want to roll back the Corps' involvement in wetlands protection. As the Reagan Administration moved to weaken the Corps' Section 404 program nationwide, the St. Paul District worked hard to preserve its cooperative relations with the state governments. The greatest challenge to the Section 404 program in the St. Paul District, in Colonel Badger's view, was that the Corps was regulating with uniform regulations nationwide when the regions were "drastically different." The states of Minnesota and Wisconsin wanted more stringent standards than the Corps could support in other regions.[75]

Construction on the South Fork Zumbro River Flood Control Project, 1993: Although the city of Rochester initially balked at cost-sharing measures, the project later became one of the St. Paul District's showcases for how to involve communities in flood control. (Photo courtesy of Russel Snyder, St. Paul District, Corps of Engineers)

Congress passed the Water Resources Development Act of 1986, or WRDA-86, ending a decade-long stalemate over the Army Corps' civil works program. This landmark act not only included new project authorizations – the first in twelve years – but also added force to the Corps' efforts to develop more responsive and cost-efficient ways of conducting business. WRDA-86 required the Corps to obtain cost-share agreements with local sponsors for virtually all new flood control projects. In general, the non-federal share was between twenty-five and fifty percent of the cost of the project, with at least five percent cash. Since the federal government would no longer bear the entire cost of acquiring land and relocating buildings out of the way of reservoirs, the law made future reservoir projects much less likely. WRDA-86 also required local sponsors contribute fifty percent of the cost for feasibility studies. This provision had two major consequences. First, it significantly reduced the number of feasibility studies undertaken, since local sponsors were reluctant to fund a feasibility study when the project authorization was in doubt. Second, it encouraged the local sponsor to take a much larger role in the project through its design and construction phases. WRDA-

86 placed an even heavier burden on the local sponsor for coastal harbor projects (a provision that did not adversely affect the St. Paul District). It did not require cost-sharing for inland waterways; however, Section 1404 imposed a fuel tax on commercial users. Revenue collected from the fuel tax would eventually contribute fifty percent toward new inland waterway projects through the Inland Waterways Trust Fund.[76]

WRDA-86 energized the Corps. As so many years had elapsed without the passage of a water resources bill, people began to wonder what would happen to the Corps' civil works mission. Was the Corps simply going to do maintenance on existing projects and use the continuing authorities program to complete those projects that had been in progress for the past twelve years? WRDA-86 gave the Corps a more promising future, and it ratified the move toward cost-sharing that the Corps had been slowly implementing without congressional sanction since the Carter years. Colonel Joseph Briggs, St. Paul District commander when WRDA-86 was passed, described the effect as dramatic. "This [was] brand new in terms of how we were going to cost share and all of the new requirements placed upon different customers, whether the customers were within the Corps or outside of the Corps," Briggs commented in 1988.[77]

As new cost-share projects came on line, the Corps gained experience in its new relationship with local sponsors or "partners." Much effort went to cost-accounting so that sponsors would be cooperative and responsible in making regular payments to keep the project running. Colonel Roger L. Baldwin, St. Paul District commander from 1988 to 1991, commented that this first stage in the new relationship was developing smoothly. "We go out monthly and tell sponsors that they've got to have a check for so much in to the Treasurer or in to the Finance and Accounting Officer by such a date so that we can maintain the financial progress of the project, and we've had, happily, no problems here," he told an interviewer in 1991. "That system is established and working well." Baldwin anticipated that project closeouts, when both parties conduct final audits and reconcile their respective allowable costs, might raise disputes. Although the St. Paul District was keeping financial records for each project, it had not yet closed out any projects nor had it developed procedures for working with sponsors in that area.[78]

Partnering with local sponsors occasionally led to disputes and the threat of litigation, as when the City of Minneapolis disputed real estate credits in cost-accounting for the Bassett Creek Project. To keep such disputes out of the courts, the Corps developed a process called Alternative Dispute Resolution in 1988. As Chief of Engineers Arthur E. Williams explained the program, Alternative Dispute Resolution "helps to create an atmosphere in which the clash of alternative viewpoints can be synergized into creative solutions. A neutral, third party mediator helps find a middle ground to facilitate decisions which are acceptable to all parties."[79] The St. Paul District was the first in the nation to use Alternative Dispute Resolution to resolve a real estate credit dispute.[80]

Another aspect of cost-sharing was the need to demand decisions by the sponsor to keep a project moving. Delays drove up costs. In one case, the St. Paul District redesigned a project five times before the local sponsor approved it. Colonel Richard W. Craig, St. Paul District commander from 1991 to 1993, suggested that the Corps, and the St. Paul District in particular, had to get "a little tougher" with local sponsors who hesitated to make decisions. "We have small communities out there that have a tough time coming up with the money," he stated. The St. Paul District had exceptionally good relations with partnering communities, Craig noted, but project costs were higher as a result.[81] By the mid-1990s, the St. Paul District's costs for engineering design were running ten to twelve percent higher than most other districts. Since the entire Corps performed engineering design at about ten percent higher cost than private engineering firms, the St. Paul District ran the risk of losing customers to the private sector.[82]

As more cost-sharing projects developed, it became clear the Corps must adopt a new process for moving projects through their planning, design and construction phases more efficiently. The Corps' traditional method of managing feasibility studies and projects was termed "functional management." A project was passed from planning to engineering to construction, or from one functional unit to the next, and each functional unit assigned a different manager to the project. Project review occurred vertically in the organization. Planners at the district level, for example, submitted their work to planners at the division and headquarters levels. The problem with this process was that projects frequently bounced back and forth from one functional unit to another, with no single person responsible for keeping the project on schedule and on budget. Working within what were referred to as "stovepipes," staff members became invested in their functional unit rather than in each project.[83]

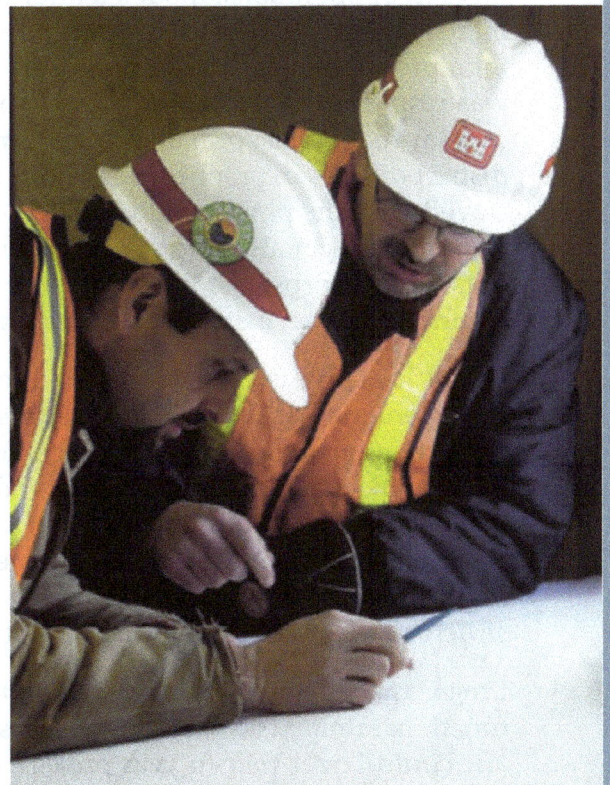

The St. Paul District began experimenting with project management before other districts. Colonel Badger detailed what he termed "management by objective" in a memorandum dated April 30, 1981.[84] Project managers had oversight of projects, but functional managers supervised the technical people who performed the engineering or environmental work on projects. It was a "matrix system" in which project managers and functional managers shared dual supervision over the staff. In an effort to promote teamwork – one of the essential goals of project management – Badger contracted with a consultant to conduct team-building courses for the Engineering Division and the project managers. He also emphasized cross-training in order to improve communication between functional units.[85]

Site survey: Mike Dahlquist (left) and Jim Sentz look at survey information for the St. Cloud, Minnesota, erosion control project. (Photo by Shannon Bauer, courtesy of St. Paul District, Corps of Engineers)

Without firm direction from Headquarters, however, the stovepipes continued to operate in spite of the district commander's best efforts to move projects along. After three years as district engineer, Badger expressed great frustration with the technical staff members who held projects back. Increasingly, he went to congressmen and senators to apply outside pressure on the Corps in order to work projects through the system. "I have come to the conclusion … I can't just wait until all the minutia is done before sending a project forward and the technocrats or termites, the minutia people at that level, ask a lot of questions and send it back," he told an interviewer in 1981. "I can't live with a system that runs back and forth between termites. What I have to do is wrap up my projects, kick them up to the higher Headquarters." To his chagrin, Badger found himself in favor of "going outside the system, getting the language written into law so that the Corps system is short-circuited."[86]

Discussion of the need for changing the "Corps system" intensified after Congress passed WRDA-86. Cost-sharing highlighted how often the Corps understated project costs and fell behind with project schedules. In response, the Corps adopted a new method of operations, modeled after the private sector, which it called "project management." Initiative 88, distributed to all district engineers in July 1988, called for a project manager to be assigned to each civil works project. The project manager was responsible for keeping projects on schedule and on budget. The project manager oversaw a team of specialists drawn from the different functional units within the district office.[87] In practice the team remained fluid, but the project manager generally stayed with the project and provided continuity through the life of the project.[88] The project manager also served as a consistent contact for the local sponsor and others outside the Corps who had an interest in the project – an important public relations feature of project management known as "one door to the Corps."[89]

Under Initiative 88, Headquarters directed each district office to implement project management. All district commanders were directed to appoint a civilian as a deputy district engineer for project management, or DDE (PM). (Later the acronym changed to DPM, which was an abbreviation for deputy district engineer for program and project management.) Although the DPM reported to the district engineer, headquarters created an Office of Project Management that fostered and protected the development of project management. Under the Chief Engineer's directive, the new organizational structure was to be established without adding new staff positions.[90]

Project management introduced a matrix system – it did not do away with the functional units. The project managers had two significant limitations: they did not have any control over year-to-year project funding, which remained in the hands of Congress and the president, and they did not control the resources, which were still organized by function. Nonetheless, the project managers were supported as leaders in the new system. Chief of Engineers Lieutenant General Henry Hatch affirmed that the deputy district engineer for project management had equal rank with the chiefs of engineering and construction in each district. Hatch established a Project Management Division at the Headquarters level and directed district engineers to create similar divisions. By 1991, the St. Paul District had a Programs and Project Management Division. In effect, the project management initiative resulted in its own stovepipe.[91]

The St. Paul District made a relatively smooth transition to project management. It had been a leader in developing interdisciplinary teams during the 1970s and 1980s and anticipated the push from Headquarters.[92] It easily implemented procedures that were developed for the whole Corps, notably Life Cycle Project Management. District commanders provided project team meetings. They fostered better communication between functional division chiefs and project managers. Problems with the matrix organization persisted a decade after Initiative 88, however, particularly among some of the senior civilians. As District Engineer Colonel Kenneth Kasprisin remarked, "Anytime you change people, process, organization, or culture, it creates other issues … People get into a very comfortable routine, and anything that takes them out of that routine, out of that comfort zone, brings consternation."[93]

Cost-sharing and project management were the big drivers of internal organizational change in the 1980s and 1990s, but the Corps pursued other innovations as well. Following the National Performance Review by the Clinton Administration in 1993 and passage of the Government Performance and Results Act later that year, the Corps furthered its efforts to streamline procedures. In 1996, for example, the Corps revised its document review process to eliminate redundancies at the headquarters, division and district levels. To Headquarters fell the task of "policy review" – ensuring the Corps complied with law and administration policy. Divisions limited their review to "quality assurance review" – ensuring quality of planning and engineering in accordance with approved quality assurance plans implemented for each district. Districts were responsible for "technical review" – controlling the technical adequacy of the planning and engineering documents. Previously, the review process wended through the district, division and Headquarters of the Army Corps and could include the former Washington Level Review Center, the Assistant Secretary of the Army (Civil Works) and the Office of Management and Budget as well. The revised review process compressed review time and reduced costs.[94]

While the National Performance Review and the Government Performance and Results Act provided a certain amount of philosophical guidance to the Corps' reorganization efforts, much change resulted simply from the brute requirement of having to reduce full-time equivalent employees to mandated levels. Critics referred to this hatchet method of change as "salami slicing." Across the nation, efforts to "downsize" the Corps resulted in a reduction of 1,770 FTEs, or about six percent of the workforce, between 1990 and 1995.[95]

Conclusion

In the last quarter of the twentieth century, the Corps faced two imperatives for organizational change. First, environmentalism created a host of new public values and legislative mandates to which the Corps responded. Second, government reform initiatives led the Corps to introduce fundamental changes in how it conducted business. These new imperatives forced change in the St. Paul District in two ways. Sometimes the district responded to decisions that occurred at a higher level in the Corps, the Administration or Congress, as with realignment of district boundaries and staff reductions. In other instances, the district took initiative in developing new approaches to its work, as when it teamed with local citizens on the Bassett Creek Flood

Control Commission. Environmental Impact Studies, public review, cost-sharing, project management – these were the mechanics of internal organizational change in the Corps in the 1970s, 1980s and 1990s. In the following chapters, we will see how the St. Paul District put these new mechanisms to work in executing the Corps' various missions.

Chapter 2 Endnotes

1 Daniel A. Mazmanian and Jeanne Nienaber, *Can Organizations Change? Environmental Protection, Citizen Participation, and the Corps of Engineers* (Washington, D.C.: The Brookings Institution, 1979), p. 187.

2 Raymond H. Merritt, *Creativity, Conflict & Controversy: A History of the St. Paul District, U.S. Army Corps of Engineers*, (Washington, D.C.: Government Printing Office, 1979), pp. 56-57.

3 Merritt, *Creativity, Conflict & Controversy*, pp. 60-61. See also Paul K. Walker, "Corps Historian Explains Past Reorganization Experience," in The Reorganization Wrap-Up 1, no. 1 (19 November 1992): p. 14. The North Central Division was established in 1954.

4 Jimmy Carter, *Keeping Faith: Memoirs of a President*, (New York: Bantam Books, 1982): pp. 78-79. Also see Martin A. Reuss, *Reshaping National Water Politics: The Emergence of the Water Resources Development Act of 1986*, (U.S. Army Corps of Engineers, Institute of Water Resources, 1991), pp. 49-52.

5 President George Bush and President Bill Clinton both asserted stronger executive control over the U.S. Army Corps of Engineers through their political appointees in the position of Assistant Secretary of the Army (Civil Works).

6 George W. Griebenow, "A Team Called Great," *Water Spectrum* 9, No. 1 (Winter 1976- 77): pp. 18-19.

7 Raymond Merritt, "New Directions: Transitions in the St. Paul District, Corps of Engineers, 1976-1982," unpublished manuscript, n.d., St. Paul District, pp. 92-93.

8 Duluth *News-Tribune*, 26 May 1979.

9 Merritt, "New Directions," pp. 94-95. On Oberstar's background see <http://bioguide.congress.gov> (September 2002).

10 Duluth *News-Tribune*, 11 November 1979.

11 U.S. Army Corps of Engineers, North Central Division, *Water Resources Development by the U.S. Army Corps of Engineers in Wisconsin*, (Chicago: North Central Division, 1979), p. 124.

12 U.S. Army Corps of Engineers, Water Resources Support Center, "The Ports of Duluth, MN and Superior, WI; Taconite Harbor, Silver Bay, and Two Harbors, MN; and

Ashland, WI," *Port Series* No. 49 (Washington, D.C.: Government Printing Office, 2000), p. 1.

13 Merritt, "New Directions," p. 94.

14 *Duluth Herald*, 12 November 1979.

15 *Duluth Herald*, 12 November 1979.

16 Merritt, "New Directions," p. 94; Merritt, *Creativity, Conflict & Controversy*, p. 406.

17 U.S. Army Corps of Engineers, Office of the Chief of Engineers, Engineer Profiles: The District Engineer, Interviews with Colonel William W. Badger, by Frank N. Schubert (Washington, D.C.: U.S. Army Corps of Engineers, 1983) [hereafter cited as Badger Interviews], p. 24.

18 Merritt, "New Directions," p. 126.

19 Badger Interviews, pp. 81-82.

20 Donita M. Moorhus and Gregory Graves, "The Limits of Vision: A History of the U.S. Army Corps of Engineers 1988-1992," unpublished ms, January 1999, Office of the Chief Engineers, Office of History, pp. 29-30.

21 The Reorganization Wrap-Up 1., no. 1 (19 November 1992), p. 7.

22 Moorhus and Graves, "The Limits of Vision," pp. 31-32. See also "Background Paper on Corps of Engineers Reorganization" in Senate Committee on Environmental and Public Works, Reorganization of the Corps of Engineers, Hearing before the Committee on Environment and Public Works, 102d Cong., 2d sess., December 30, 1992, p. 12.

23 Don Cluff, Memorandum for all USACE Division and District Commanders, no date, File "Reorganization," Box 6250, St. Paul District administrative records, St. Paul [hereafter cited as SPDAR].

24 Colonel Richard W. Craig interview by John O. Anfinson, 20 July 1993.

25 Moorhus and Graves, "The Limits of Vision," p. 33; Don Cluff, Memorandum for all USACE Division and District Commanders, no date, File "Reorganization," Box 6250, SPDAR.

26 Don Cluff, Memorandum for all USACE Division and District Commanders, no date, File "Reorganization," Box 6250, SPDAR.

27 Minneapolis *Star-Tribune*, 13 April 1991.

28 Office of Assistant Secretary of Defense, News Release, 24 May 1991, File "Reorganization," Box 6250, SPDAR.

29 Arne H. Carlson to Michael P. W. Stone, 26 April 1991, and Tommy Thompson to Richard Cheney, 7 June 1991, File 1105 Upper Mississippi River Basin Association Meetings (91), Box 4465, SPDAR.

30 Unidentified news clipping, File "Reorganization," Box 6250, SPDAR.

31 Moorhus and Graves, "The Limits of Vision," p. 36.

32 Moorhus and Graves, "The Limits of Vision," pp. 36-37.

33 House Subcommittee on Water Resources of the Committee on Public Works and Transportation, Water Resources Development Act of 1992 and the Reorganization of the U.S. Army Corps of Engineers, 102d Cong., 2d sess., 4, 11, 19, 25 March 1992, p. 618.

34 The Reorganization Wrap-up 1, no. 1 (19 November 1992).

35 Minneapolis Star-Tribune, 20 November 1992.

36 Moorhus and Graves, "The Limits of Vision," p. 39.

37 Senate Committee on Appropriations, Energy and Water Development Appropriations Fiscal Year 1994, 103rd Cong., 1st sess., S. Hrg. 103-299 Part 1, May 1993, pp. 163-165; House Subcommittee on Investigation and Oversight of the Committee on Public Works and Transportation, U.S. Army Corps of Engineers Proposed Reorganization Plan, 103rd Cong., 1st sess., Serial 103-23, May 1993, pp. 449-454.

38 Craig Interview.

39 U.S. Congress, House, Proposed Legislation: "Government Reform and Savings Act of 1993," Message from the President of the United States, 103d Cong., 1st sess., House Doc. 103-155, 1993, p. 14.

40 Prepared statement of Lt. General Joe N. Ballard, Chief of Engineers, U.S. Army Corps of Engineers, before the Senate Appropriations Committee Subcommittee on Energy and Water Development, 24 April 1997, <http://web.lexis-nexis.com> (September 2002).

41 Prepared statement of Lt. General Joe N. Ballard, Chief of Engineers, U.S. Army Corps of Engineers, before the Senate Appropriations Committee Subcommittee on Energy and Water Development, 24 April 1997, <http://web.lexis-nexis.com> (September 2002); House Subcommittee on Energy and Water Development of the Committee on Appropriations, Energy and Water Development Appropriations for 2000, Part 1, 106th Cong., 1st sess., 1999, pp. 128-129.

42 Colonel J. M. Wonsik, interview by John O. Anfinson, 20 January 1998, pp. 4-5.

43 Wonsik Interview, p. 5.

44 The best comprehensive source on the historical development of modern environmentalism is Samuel P. Hays, Beauty, Health and Permanence: Environmental Politics in the United States, 1955-85 (New York: Cambridge University Press, 1987).

45 Mazmanian and Nienaber, *Can Organizations Change?*, p. 1.

46 William O. Douglas, "The Public be Dammed," *Playboy*, 16 (July 1969), p. 186.

47 Lynton Keith Caldwell, *The National Environmental Policy Act: An Agenda for the Future* (Bloomington: Indiana University Press, 1998), p. xiv.

48 Jeanne Nienaber Clarke and Daniel McCool, *Staking out the Terrain: Power Differentials Among Natural Resource Management Agencies* (Albany: State University of New York Press, 1985), p. 18.

49 Martin Reuss, *Shaping Environmental Awareness: The United States Army Corps of Engineers Environmental Advisory Board 1970-1980* (Washington, D.C.: Historical Division, Office of Administrative Services, Office of the Chief of Engineers, 1983), p. 1.

50 Nienaber and McCool, *Staking out the Terrain*, p. 16.

51 Clement and Lopez, *Engineering a Victory for our Environment*, pp. 2-11.

52 Mazmanian and Nienaber, *Can Organizations Change?*, p. 38.

53 Edward Silberman, "Public Participation in Water Resource Development," *Journal of the Water Resources Planning and Management Division* (May 1977), p. 122.

54 Mazmanian and Nienaber, *Can Organizations Change?*, pp. 39-47. See also Taylor, Making Bureaucracies Think, pp. 93-95.

55 St. Paul *Dispatch*, 19 October 1973.

56 According to Taylor, the St. Paul District was not the only district to experience tension between its environmental staff and project engineers. "In the Corps, although cantankerous environmental units were sometimes threatened with dispersal, the threat never materialized." Writing in the early 1980s, Taylor praised the Corps for protecting the relative autonomy of the environmental units. "Because they are in a separate group, headed by someone in their own specialty, environmental analysts can more easily support one another. A group spirit can develop and be maintained against a hostile or indifferent internal environment." Taylor, *Making Bureaucracies Think*, p. 108.

57 Merritt, "New Directions," pp. 127-130.

58 Interagency Floodplain Management Review Committee, *Sharing the Challenge: Floodplain Management into the 21st Century*, (Washington, D.C.: Government Printing Office, 1994), pp. 118-119.

59 Cited in Merritt, "New Directions."

60 Clarke and McCool, *Staking out the Terrain*, pp. 24-25.

61 "Corps' new look in flood control: no dams, levees," *Audubon 77* (July 1975): pp. 103- 104.

62 Steve Slade, "Army Corps of Engineers: Caught in Midstream," *The Nation* 221 (6 September 1975): pp. 179-181; "Cost-benefit trips up the corps," *Business Week* (19 February 1979): pp. 96-97.

63 "The Civilian Side of the U.S. Army: The Corps of Engineers," Ms. 11 (September 1982): p. 77.

64 Jeffrey K. Stine, "Regulating Wetlands in the 1970s: U.S. Army Corps of Engineers and the Environmental Organizations," *Journal of Forest History* (April 1983): p. 61.

65 U.S. Army Corps of Engineers, St. Paul District, "Organization – Position Charts, February 1991," p. 6.

66 U.S. Army Corps of Engineers, St. Paul District, "Organization Directory and Position Chart, August 2001," p. 7.

67 Nationwide, military construction gradually overtook civil works as the most significant portion of the agency's budget. In addition, maintenance and operation of existing works overtook construction of new works as a major share of the overall civil works budget.

68 *The Forum* (Fargo-Moorhead), 25 May 1979.

69 *The Forum* (Fargo-Moorhead), 25 May 1979.

70 The St. Paul *Pioneer Press*, 17 May 1979.

71 Badger interview, 30 March 1982, pp. 83-85.

72 Colonel Ed Rapp, interview by Mickey Schubert, 7 July 1983, pp. 6-7.

73 Badger Interviews, pp. 40-43.

74 Reagan appointed William R. Gianelli, a former head of the California State Water Resources Division, to the position of Assistant Secretary of the Army (Civil Works). Gianelli stated that one of his primary objectives was to streamline the Corps' Section 404 permitting process. See William R. Gianelli, interview by Martin A. Reuss, August 1, 1985.

75 Badger Interviews, p. 43.

76 Bory Steinberg, "The Federal Perspective," in *Water Resources Administration in the United States: Policy, Practice, and Emerging Issues,* edited by Martin Reuss (East Lansing: Michigan State University Press, 1993), pp. 264-267.

77 Colonel Joseph Briggs, interview by Mickey Schubert, May 24, 1988, p. 9.

78 Colonel Roger L. Baldwin, interview by John O. Anfinson, 1 July 1991, pp. 12-13.

79 Arthur E. Williams, "The Role of Technology in Sustainable Development," in *Water Resources Administration in the United States,* p. 128.

80 Baldwin Interview, p. 13.

81 Craig Interview, p. 17.

82 Colonel Kenneth Kasprisin, interview by Virginia Gnabasik, 13 July 2001, p. 3.

83 Lisa Mighetto and William F. Willingham, *Service – Tradition – Change: A History of the Fort Worth District, U.S. Army Corps of Engineers, 1975-1999* (Fort Worth, TX: U.S. Army Corps of Engineers, 2000), p. 98.

84 William W. Badger, Memorandum, 30 April 1981, File Oral History DES, Box 7842, SPDAR.

85 Badger Interviews, p. 7.

86 Badger Interviews, pp. 58-59.

87 Steinberg, "The Federal Perspective," p. 271.

88 Charles P. Spitzak, interview by Ted Catton, 9 May 2002, p. 1.

89 Kasprisin Interview, p. 2.

90 Mighetto and Willingham, *Service – Tradition – Change*, p. 99.

91 U.S. Army Corps of Engineers, St. Paul District, "Organization – Position Charts, February 1991," p. 1; Mighetto and Willingham, *Service – Tradition – Change*, p. 98.

92 Spitzak Interview, p. 1.

93 Kasprisin Interview, p. 2.

94 "Prepared Statement of Lt. General Joe N. Ballard, Chief of Engineers, U.S. Army Corps of Engineers, Department of the Army, before the Senate Appropriations Committee Subcommittee on Energy and Water Development," 24 April 1997, <http://web.lexis-nexis.com> (September 2002).

95 Mighetto and Willingham, *Service – Tradition – Change*, p. 102.

Navigation: Several barges being locked through Lock and Dam 10 in Guttenberg, Iowa. (Photo by Shannon, Bauer, courtesy of St. Paul District, Corps of Engineers)

3 Civil Works Program I: The Upper Mississippi

Meandering over 2,000 miles from Minnesota's Lake Itasca to the Gulf of Mexico, the Mississippi River was once described by Mark Twain as the "crookedest river in the world, ... not a commonplace river, but on the contrary ... in all ways remarkable."[1] The upper portion of the waterway, stretching from the river's headwaters to Guttenberg, Iowa, has been managed by the Corps of Engineers since the early nineteenth century. Throughout these years, the Upper Mississippi has been a vital lifeline of commerce and recreation for the Midwest. It has also functioned as a center of biodiversity and cultural heritage. To facilitate the different functions of the river and to preserve environmental quality, the St. Paul District has the task of dredging, straightening and widening the river; of ensuring that residents in the Upper Mississippi River Basin have adequate flood protection; and of mitigating the environmental effects caused by these activities.

The district's navigation and flood control mission on the Upper Mississippi both fall under the umbrella of its civil works program. At the dawn of the twenty-first century, the civil works program was drastically different than in 1975. Laws such as the National Historic Preservation Act of 1966 and the National Environmental Policy Act of 1969, or NEPA, forced the Corps to become more environmentally conscious. Whereas large structures such as dams and reservoirs characterized the Corps' flood control efforts for much of the twentieth century, non-structural solutions were increasingly prevalent by 2000. Throughout the 1900s, the Corps dredged the Upper Mississippi River and other waterways with little consideration of the environmental effects on wildlife habitat and fish populations; but by 2000, the St. Paul District dredged far less than before, used the dredged material for constructive purposes and carried out an Environmental Management Program that restored habitat on the Upper Mississippi. In addition, although the federal government largely paid for most civil works projects, cost-sharing measures implemented in the 1980s shifted some of the expenses to local sponsors, allowing local participation and involvement and establishing high levels of trust and cooperation. But some critics charged that the Corps still had a long way to go in accepting environmental responsibility and pointed to the controversial Upper Mississippi River/Illinois Waterway Navigation Study, which supposedly used skewed benefit-cost analyses to justify extensive navigational developments on the Mississippi, as proof. Although there was some merit to the critics' contentions, it was clear that the Corps of Engineers generally and the St. Paul District specifically had made great changes in the last quarter of the twentieth century. As John Anfinson, former district historian, related, there was now "a much more open mind in St. Paul District as an organization to doing better by the environment and [still] meeting the needs of people who want flood protection and navigation."[2]

Dredging the river: A Corps' dredge in operation on the Upper Mississippi River. (Photo courtesy of St. Paul District, Corps of Engineers)

The Upper Mississippi River Basin Commission and GREAT I

After the passage of NEPA in 1969, the Corps faced numerous attacks from environmental organizations, such as the Sierra Club, for its alleged support of navigation interests on the Upper Mississippi and on the detrimental effects of its dredging program on fish and wildlife. Through leadership and cooperation on a number of studies and commissions about the Upper Mississippi, including the Great River Environmental Action Team, or GREAT, and the Upper Mississippi River Basin Commission, the St. Paul District gradually embraced its role as protector of the river. Although criticism came from all sides, the St. Paul District continued to try to balance the different uses of the river.

Dredging the Mississippi River: The Dredge Hauser, a small dredge operated by the St. Paul District. (Photo courtesy of St. Paul District, Corps of Engineers)

Even before NEPA passed, Congress decided the time had come to coordinate navigation interests with wildlife and fish habitat protection and appointed the Corps of Engineers as the leader in this management. In 1962, a resolution adopted by the Senate Committee on Public Works called for the development of "a comprehensive plan of improvement for the Upper Mississippi River Basin." In response, the Corps initiated the Upper Mississippi River Comprehensive Basin Study, an examination of the river by an interagency committee chaired by the division engineer of the North Central Division. By the 1970s, this committee had morphed into the Upper Mississippi River Basin Coordinating Committee, containing representatives from the Departments of Agriculture; Commerce; Health; Education and Welfare; Housing and Urban Development; Interior; and Transportation, as well as individuals from the Environmental Protection Agency and the Federal Power Commission. After consulting with seventy federal and state agencies about how to solve the water and land resource problems on the Upper Mississippi, the committee published its report in 1972, calling for "an orderly development of water and related land resources" through cooperation between federal, state and local agencies, including the Corps.[3]

Complementing the recommendations of the study was a request from several Upper Mississippi Basin governors for the completion of a river management plan. By executive order, President Richard Nixon established the Upper Mississippi River Basin Commission in 1972 to satisfy this demand. The commission immediately focused on the Corps' nine-foot navigation channel. In the Rivers and Harbors Act of 1930, Congress authorized the Corps to dredge the Upper Mississippi to a depth of nine feet so that larger barges could traverse the river. During the years, the Corps often dredged three or four feet below the nine feet requirement in the interest of reducing the frequency of dredging operations. Along with the deeper dredging, the Corps constructed a series of twenty-nine locks and dams big enough for larger vessels.[4] The pools created by the locks and the disposal of dredged material in side channels leading to open backwater areas accelerated sedimentation in backwaters. These backwaters served as important fish and wildlife habitat, so the loss of approximately twenty-five percent of these areas to marshlands heavily impacted fish and wildlife populations.[5]

According to Upper Mississippi River Basin Commission chairman George W. Griebenow, for years "commercial fishermen, biologists, and sportsmen ... expressed deep concern" over Corps maintenance of the nine-foot channel. Their main complaint was that commercial navigation dominated the Upper Mississippi to the detriment of recreation and fish and wildlife management, even though Congress had established the Upper Mississippi River Wildlife and Fish Refuge in 1924 to preserve lands and waters for waterfowl.[6] The situation intensified in the late 1960s and early 1970s, when the Upper Mississippi River Comprehensive Basin Study called for a twelve-foot channel and the Corps examined this possibility. Environmentalists worried that such deep dredging would cause the Mississippi to overflow into wetlands, that the increase in dredged disposal material would further damage already impaired wildlife habitats and that a deeper channel was not economically justified.[7] The Corps did not disagree; in the early 1970s an EIS prepared by the Corps on the nine-foot channel revealed, in the words of two St. Paul District employees, that dredging and channel maintenance caused "significant damage to the fragile backwaters, marshes, and sloughs" of the Upper Mississippi. However, the Corps at that time seemed unable or unwilling to mitigate these effects, in part because of questions over whether it was authorized to alleviate the damage.[8]

Based on information gained from the EIS, Representatives Albert Quie (R-Minnesota) and Vernon Thomson (R-Wisconsin), together with the Minnesota/Wisconsin Boundary

Area Commission, recommended the Upper Mississippi River Basin Commission delineate a river system management plan that would coordinate navigation, fish and wildlife interests, recreation, watershed management and water quality. At the same time, a lawsuit brought by the state of Wisconsin in the 1970s against the Corps temporarily halted dredging activities on the Upper Mississippi, convincing Congress that an investigation of dredging was needed. Congress appropriated $375,000 for a study in 1974 and provided $9.1 million more when it officially authorized the examination in the Water Resources Development Act of 1976. Upon the suggestion of the North Central Division of the Corps and the U.S. Fish and Wildlife Service, the Upper Mississippi River Basin Commission transformed its Dredged Spoil Disposal Practices Committee into the Great River Environmental Action Team, a collection of appointees from Iowa, Wisconsin and Minnesota, including representatives from the Corps, the U.S. Geological Survey, the Environmental Protection Agency, the Soil Conservation Service, the Bureau of Outdoor Recreation and the Department of Transportation, with members from other interested organizations serving as ex-officio members. William R. Pearson, the chief of special studies for the St. Paul District, cochaired the study, which was divided into three parts: GREAT I examined the Upper Mississippi from the Twin Cities in Minnesota to Guttenberg, Iowa; GREAT II investigated the river from Guttenberg to the mouth of the Missouri River at Saverton, Missouri; and GREAT III studied the river from Saverton to its confluence with the Ohio River at Cairo, Illinois.[9]

From 1975 to 1980, GREAT I explored the question of how the St. Paul District's navigation and dredging could be coordinated with other river uses. As two members of the study related, because the team consisted of individuals from a variety of backgrounds, it was able to provide "a meaningful interdisciplinary approach through education and understanding of the many resources and physical factors involved with a river system so diverse as the Upper Mississippi." In order to give different aspects of the river equal emphasis,

Cooperation: The GREAT I studay area. (Map courtesy of St. Paul District, Corps of Engineers)

the team divided into twelve work groups, each led by a different agency: dredging requirements, side channel openings, material and equipment needs, sediment and erosion control, fish and wildlife management, plan formulation, dredged material uses, recreation, water quality, commercial transportation, floodplain management and public participation and information. The Corps led the dredging requirements and material and equipment needs work groups. Dennis Cin, St. Paul District chief of the Mississippi River Maintenance Section, chaired the dredging requirements group, and Wayne Knott, an engineer for the district, led the material and equipment needs team.[10]

The Dredge William A. Thompson: The Thompson was the largest dredge in the St. Paul District's Fleet. After 67 years of service, the William A. Thompson was replaced by a new dredge in 2005. (Photo courtesy of Marc Krumholz, St. Paul District, Corps of Engineers)

As it studied the river, GREAT I developed three different levels of goals: short-range or day-to-day decisions about the Mississippi; midterm, defined as those programs that could be completed within the study's time frame; and long-range, referring to the master plan of overall river management.[11] By 1978, GREAT I was reporting several accomplishments within its short- and mid-term goals. For one, it had helped convince the district to implement a reduced-depth dredging program in 1976 that ended the practice of dredging three or four feet below the required nine-foot depth. This change reduced the amount of material dredged from the Upper Mississippi from 1.6 million cubic yards to 650,000 cubic yards. For another, GREAT I recommended the Corps use advance site preparation to ensure that dredged material did not enter wetlands. Instead of depositing dredged spoils in backwaters, the Corps began placing them in seven pre-selected disposal sites on land, thus decelerating sedimentation in backwaters and creating recreational beaches at some areas. Finally, and perhaps most importantly, GREAT I facilitated communication among management agencies, the Corps and the general public, in large part through its Public Participation and Information Program, which held eleven public town meetings, nineteen special hearings and forty-one citizen executive board meetings about the Upper Mississippi.[12]

Between 1979 and 1980, the study's different work groups submitted their individual reports. In September 1980, GREAT I published its general report, using information compiled by the different work groups and containing eighty recommendations on how the St. Paul District could better manage the Upper Mississippi. Among its suggestions was that Congress provide the Corps with additional authority and funding to implement wildlife enhancement projects, that the Corps place dredged material at pre-selected sites and that the Corps alter side channels and make structural flow modifications to alleviate sedimentation in backwaters.[13] When district officials saw the report, they did not entirely agree with its conclusions but decided to support them anyway. As Colonel Badger, district engineer from 1979 to 1982, related, "We can never fully agree with a multi-agency report. But I think the effort that went into it was good, the ideas were good, and they [were] trying to do the right thing."[14] Other districts within the Corps, however, criticized St. Paul for allowing state and local entities to dictate how the Corps should conduct its affairs, and some officials even referred to St. Paul District employees as "ecofreaks" because of their environmental concerns.[15]

To ensure that GREAT I's proposals were realized, Badger produced an implementation report, detailing what recommendations the St. Paul District considered to be of highest priority, how the district would execute these recommendations and what legislation and funding were needed. In this report, Badger discussed three possible future programs: the Basic Program, which would continue nine-foot channel dredging with only incidental considerations of fish and wildlife and recreation interests; the First Priority Program, which would consider fish and wildlife, recreation and water quality issues in nine-foot channel dredging; and the GREAT I Program, which would fully execute GREAT I's suggestions by significantly enhancing recreation and fish and wildlife opportunities. Taking the costs and benefits into consideration, Badger concluded the First Priority Program was the best plan to follow.[16]

Dredging the Mississippi River: J. Skrede, a member of the crew on the Dredge Dubuque, positions pipe that will carry dredge material. (Photo courtesy of, St. Paul District, Corps of Engineers)

To implement this program, Badger recommended that the St. Paul District receive $3 million a year from Congress in order to protect the fish and wildlife habitat on the Mississippi from Minneapolis to Guttenberg. This money would go toward purchasing land rights from owners in order to build new dredge disposal sites and would also be used to slow down the sedimentation occurring in the Upper Mississippi's backwaters.[17] As Badger stated, the plan enabled the district to "swim in the middle of the river" by balancing navigational interests and environmental concerns.[18] This middle-ground approach, however, infuriated proponents of navigation. The Upper Mississippi River Waterway Association

denounced it because it "literally puts confiscation of private lands within the grasp of environmentalists," while the U.S. Coast Guard believed it would eventually cause safety problems for river vessels. On the other hand, many environmental organizations, such as the Fish and Wildlife Service and the Minnesota Pollution Control Agency, generally supported the program as a step in the right direction, although they also claimed the Corps was not going far enough in environmental protection.[19]

By 1992, the St. Paul District had worked hard to execute the First Priority Program. The district had developed a forty-year dredged material placement plan for fifteen active dredging sites, taking into consideration economic, environmental, cultural and social impacts on each location. In addition, the district developed a comprehensive Channel Maintenance Management Plan which governed the placement of dredged material. It successfully reduced the average annual dredging volume from 1.6 million cubic yards to only 650 thousand cubic yards. In the opinion of one project manager in the St. Paul District, the reduced dredging was one of the major environmental changes the district made in the last quarter of the twentieth century.[20] At the same time, the district implemented the Weaver Bottoms Rehabilitation Project in 1987 to decrease sedimentation and restore habitat in that backwater lake, which was situated between Winona, Minnesota, and Wabasha, Minnesota. Although the Corps had deferred some of GREAT I's recommendations, it had taken significant steps toward alleviating the problems it considered most pressing, and it continued to develop plans for future mitigation efforts.[21]

Complementing the GREAT I study was another analysis of the Upper Mississippi coordinated by the Upper Mississippi River Basin Commission. On October 21, 1978, President Jimmy Carter signed the Inland Waterway Authorization Act, which directed the commission to compile a Comprehensive Master Plan for the Management of the Upper Mississippi River System. This authorization resulted from a controversial

Environmental Restoration

Environmental Restoration: The first Upper Mississippi River Environmental Management Program project completed by the St. Paul District included the backwater restoration in 1987 of Island 42. The Corps excavated the channel in the center of the left photo. Pictured on the right is Island 42, a fill site. (Photo courtesy of Dan Wilcox, St. Paul District, Corps of Engineers)

Corps' proposal to replace Lock and Dam 26 at Alton, Illinois, with two new locks that could accommodate larger barges, thereby improving navigational use of the Upper Mississippi. Railroad interests feared the new locks would be a boon to barge companies. Environmentalists worried about the ecological effects of increased navigation. Both tried to prevent the construction of the locks through unsuccessful appeals to Congress and the courts. Although opponents could not halt construction of one of the locks, they were able to convince Congress to forestall building the second lock until a master study had been conducted.[22]

According to the 1979 Annual Report of the Upper Mississippi River Basin Commission, the Comprehensive Master Plan intended to "seek a balance of present and future commercial navigation activities with the economic, recreational, and environmental objectives" of the river by specifically examining how an enlargement of navigational capacity would affect the Mississippi. After seeking public input, the commission adopted a Plan of Study on August 15, 1979, divided into four work teams – Resources and Transportation, Dredged Material Disposal Demonstration, Computerized Analytical Inventory and Analysis and Public Participation and Information – and commenced the study, hoping to complete it in four years.[23] On September 11, 1979, the Upper Mississippi River Basin Commission entered into a Memorandum of Agreement with the Corps, stating that the Corps would take an active role in developing the master plan.[24] The St. Paul District had the responsibility of determining the navigational carrying capacity of the Upper Mississippi, as well as evaluating the cost and benefits of depositing dredge spoil material in additional contained areas out of the floodplain.[25]

The commission worked on the master plan for two years before issuing the report to Congress in late 1981. Upon its appearance, environmentalists were disappointed, believing that the plan sacrificed environmental interests for the sake of navigation. In the report, the Upper Mississippi River Basin Commission, with input from the Corps, concluded the second lock at Lock and Dam 26 was justified, but that Congress should also provide more than $20 million for the next two years to control erosion along tributary streams and to protect backwater lakes and sloughs. The plan also called for the establishment of a ten year environmental management program. The Sierra Club, however, saw these proposals as mere smoke and mirrors. "The commission's tangible recommendations are for improving navigation on the river," Jonathan Ela, Midwest representative of the Sierra Club, stated. "The environmental stuff they recommend is puff." Rod Searle, chairman of the UMRBC, disagreed. The barge industry, he declared, was "not as happy as Mr. Ela would want us to believe. Since we don't have everybody happy (with the plan), that leads me to believe that we've certainly accomplished something."[26] For the St. Paul District, the plan merely reinforced many of the recommendations offered by GREAT I, especially backwater rehabilitation and erosion mitigation, and showed the value of interagency planning on the Upper Mississippi. Although President Ronald Reagan abolished the Upper Mississippi River Basin Commission due to budget constraints soon after it issued its master plan, the commission, together with GREAT I, had developed recommendations that pushed the district toward formulating an environmental management program on the river.

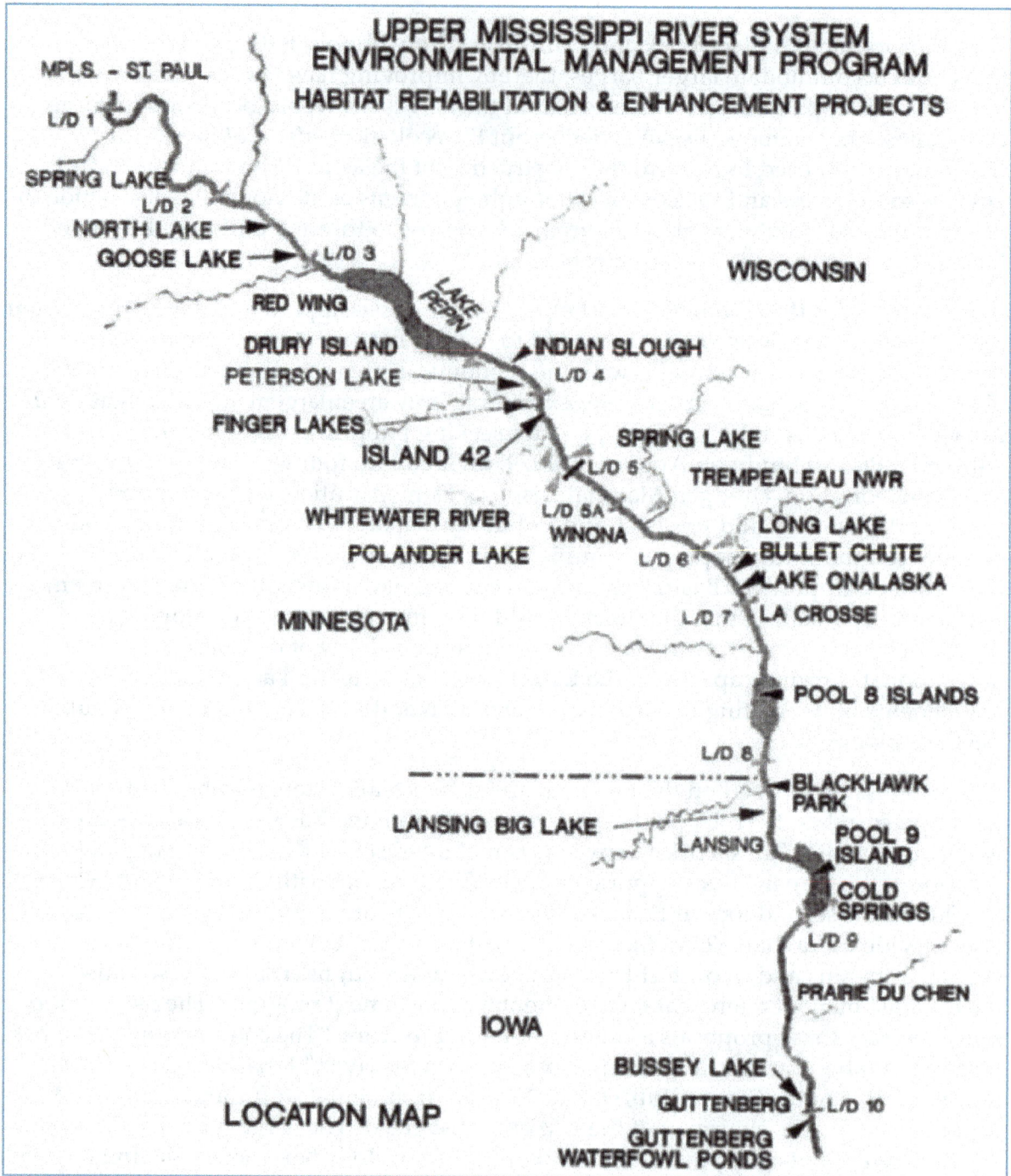

UPPER MISSISSIPPI RIVER SYSTEM
ENVIRONMENTAL MANAGEMENT PROGRAM
HABITAT REHABILITATION & ENHANCEMENT PROJECTS

Upper Mississippi River: Locations of habitat rehabilitation and enhancement projects conducted by the St. Paul District for the Upper Mississippi River System Environmental Managment Program. (Map courtesy of St. Paul District, Corps of Engineers)

Upper Mississippi River System Environmental Management Program

Indeed, largely because of the Upper Mississippi River Basin Commission's report suggesting the establishment of a ten-year environmental management plan, Congress authorized the Upper Mississippi River System Environmental Management Program, or EMP, in the Water Resources Development Act of 1986. According to a report on the program, it was "designed to protect and balance the resources of the Upper Mississippi River Basin and guide future river management." In order to accomplish this, five elements received emphasis: habitat rehabilitation and enhancement, long-term resource monitoring, recreation projects, the economic impacts of recreation, and navigation traffic monitoring. In terms of resources, the habitat rehabilitation and enhancement and long-term resource monitoring were the largest components, while the recreation facets received no funding "due to a low federal priority." Habitat rehabilitation and enhancement projects consisted of restoring river and floodplain habitats degraded by dredging or other activities, while the resource monitoring program called for biological and ecological research to determine what actions would best preserve the river's ecosystem. Federal management of the program lay with the Corps, which coordinated with the U.S. Fish and Wildlife Service, the U.S. Geological Survey, the Upper Mississippi River Basin Association (an organization formed by Illinois, Iowa, Minnesota, Missouri and Wisconsin after the UMRBC's demise) and representatives from five Upper Mississippi states. Although the North Central Division of the Corps chaired the project as a whole, the St. Paul District supervised habitat rehabilitation and enhancement in Minnesota and Wisconsin.[27]

In order to implement the EMP, the St. Paul District consulted with river management agencies, the Fish and Wildlife Service and the River Resources Forum. The forum, first created in 1981 as the Channel Maintenance Forum (renamed the River Resources Forum in 1990), was an interagency team chaired by the Corps and the Fish and Wildlife Service to continue the coordination of channel maintenance and other river-related projects instigated by GREAT. Together, these groups evaluated different pools and areas along the Upper Mississippi and made a priority list of areas needing restoration. The first project completed by the St. Paul District included backwater restoration in 1987 at Island 42, located in Pool 5 of the Upper Mississippi between Locks and Dams 4 and 5 in Minnesota. Because backwater sloughs were not receiving enough water flow to maintain dissolved oxygen levels for fish, the district excavated a channel, built a structure to bring fresh water into the sloughs and dredged the area to create a deep-water fish habitat.[28]

Another important undertaking included the Pool 8 Islands Habitat Project, involving a section of the river near Stoddard, Wisconsin. When the Corps completed construction of Lock and Dam 8 in 1937, it submerged the floodplain of Pool 8, initially enhancing the fish and wildlife habitat. But by the late 1980s, nearly 80 percent of the islands in Pool 8 had eroded, leading to increased wind fetch and turbidity. These conditions destroyed aquatic plants used by migrating canvasback ducks for food. In 1989, the St. Paul District, under the leadership of project manager Gary Palesh, began restoration on seven islands in Pool 8, reconstructing them from dredged material and protecting them with riprap and vegetation. The district also constructed six rockfill "seed" islands to try to stimulate growth and recommended periodic water drawdowns. The first two phases of construction were completed in 1999, and the project received the Minnesota Society of Professional Engineers' Seven Wonders of Engineering award in 2002. According to St. Paul District hydraulics engineer Jon Hendrickson, "River currents and sediment deposits were returned to a more natural condition, wind-driven wave action was reduced and floodplain habitat was restored," leading to a large increase in the number of canvasback ducks in the area.[29]

By 2003, the district had finished twenty habitat restoration projects, many led by Palesh and Don Powell, with two more under construction and seven in the planning and design stage.[30] Although Congress originally authorized the EMP for only fifteen years, its life-span was extended indefinitely in the 1999 Water Resources Development Act, providing the district reported on its EMP activities every six years.[31] In 1999, Powell and Palesh estimated the program had "brought environmental benefits to more than 10,000 acres of habitat on the Upper Mississippi River."[32] Indeed, the EMP had two major impacts on the St. Paul District: first, it provided steady work, and, second, it showed the district not only cared about the environment but could successfully implement projects to alleviate environmental damage. As District Engineer Colonel Richard W. Craig related in 1993, "We do [EMP] business very well ... We're always going to do those types of environment-related activities very well because we have people here that are more interested in those types of projects than people in other regions of the country."[33] Colonel Roger L. Baldwin, district engineer from 1988 to 1991, concurred, recognizing that both environmental and navigation interests had praised EMP projects. The EMP, he continued, "has demonstrated that we are capable of pulling off a major program that consists of many separable elements and have done so with a variety of constituencies and stakeholders in these individual projects."[34]

Locks and Dams 1-10 Rehabilitation

Facelift: Lock and Dam 5A after its rehabilitation. (Photo courtesy of Carl Gray, St. Paul District, Corps of Engineers)

Despite the success of the EMP, some organizations still believed the Corps promoted navigation on the Upper Mississippi above environmental concerns. Whether or not this was an accurate criticism, the Corps continued to maintain the nine-foot channel and its locks and dams. Indeed, beginning in the late 1970s, the St. Paul District undertook a major rehabilitation effort at Locks and Dams 1-10 on the Upper Mississippi. Because the Corps had first built these structures, which had fifty-year design lives, in the 1930s, they were all nearly fifty years old and in need of extensive maintenance in order to operate effectively for another fifty years. The first efforts began on Lock and Dam 1 in 1979 with five major objectives: improving hydraulic operation, improving structure stability, extending the lock's service life, providing more protection to the lock's foundation and improving recreational and aesthetic aspects.[35] One of the main problems, however, included completing the rehabilitation without disrupting barge traffic on the river. In order to fulfill this goal, the Corps mainly worked on the locks and dams in the winter, usually reopening the structures in May. According to Craig Hinton of the district's Dredging and Structures Section, this meant that the rehabilitation was "intensive work in a short time, under the worst conditions."[36]

In 1983, the district completed the renovations on Lock and Dam 1, rededicating the structure in June. That same year, it began rehabilitating the other locks and dams as part of a $225 million effort. Throughout the 1990s, work was completed on various locks and dams; but by 2003, some were still undergoing maintenance to be completed by the end of 2004. According to John Bailen, chief of the Engineering Division, the rehabilitation would allow Locks and Dams 1-10 to continue to operate efficiently for another fifty years.[37]

The Midwest Flood of 1993

But not all were convinced that locks, dams and levees were appropriate for the Mississippi River. The Corps faced serious debates about its entire flood control function when a flood of historic proportions hit regions around the Upper Mississippi in the summer of 1993. Problems began when a low-pressure system stalled over the Midwest for two months, dumping large amounts of rain on the area. This started a chain reaction of flooding on the Upper Mississippi. In portions of the river stretching from the Quad Cities of Illinois to St. Louis, Missouri, water levels were at times more than three feet higher than previous records. On this stretch, the river broke through numerous levees constructed by agriculturists to protect rich farmland near the Mississippi, and water poured into surrounding areas, causing significant damage. Several roads, including major arteries such as Interstate 29 and U.S. 40 near St. Louis, closed due to flooding, while water inundated a treatment plant in Des Moines, Iowa, contaminating the drinking supply of 250 thousand people. The floods also submerged locks on the Upper Mississippi, forcing the Corps to close the waterway to barge traffic and causing an estimated $300 million in losses to the shipping industry. When the waters finally receded, at least fifty-two people were dead, 2,300 were injured, 56 thousand were homeless and property damage totaled more than $10 billion.[38]

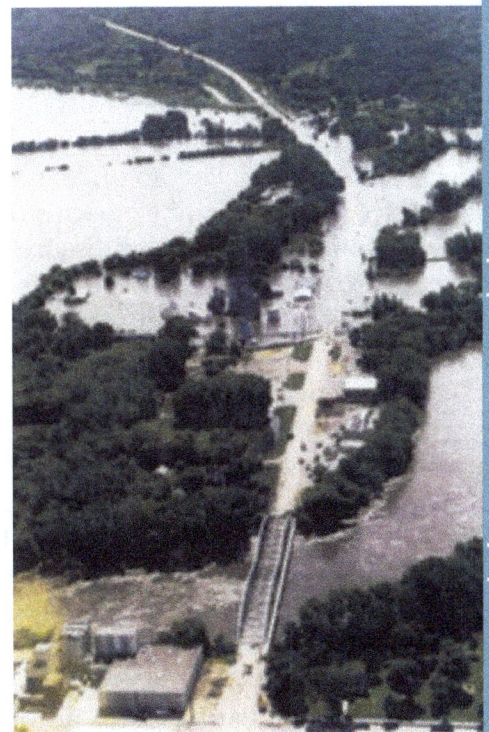

Flooding: St. Peter, Minnesota, 1993.
(Photo courtesy of St. Paul District, Corps of Engineers)

Using complicated and technical comparisons of peak flood stage/discharge data and stage/discharge damage curves, the Corps claimed that its flood control projects and response efforts actually prevented more than $8 billion in damages, but others believed the levees worsened the flood. According to an article in the *Engineering News Record*, several environmental groups argued that the construction of levees along the Mississippi River aggravated conditions "by restricting flow and raising water levels to unnatural heights." They also created a false sense of security that encouraged communities to build in the floodplain.[39] The devastation wreaked by the river was proof, many said, that levees could not work alone. Therefore, politicians and environmental organizations called for a reexamination of flood control on the Mississippi. "If we continue down the old path, we do so at our own peril," said Jim Tripp of the Environmental Defense Fund.

Representative Jim Lightfoot (R-Iowa) echoed these sentiments. "The Corps is very good at what they do," he admitted. "But quite frankly, I think their book needs to be rewritten."[40] Bill Bertrand, chairman of the Upper Mississippi River Conservation Committee, believed the Corps needed to implement "ecosystem planning," whereby wetlands would be restored, levees would be removed and the river would be returned "to a more natural condition."[41]

The Corps defended levees against these attacks, believing its flood control system on the Mississippi River truly did protect communities. In this system, reservoirs restrained tributary flows, while smaller levees protected agricultural land and urban levees and floodwalls shielded city centers. Reservoirs were designed with enough storage capacity to offset some of the flood stage increases caused by the channelization of the river, while agricultural levees were constructed to overtop during heavy flooding to relieve pressure on urban levees.[42] According to the Corps, then, the real problem in 1993 was not its flood control system but a phenomenal natural event. "The paramount purpose of the levee system is to prevent loss of life," Gene Gamble, a Corps' spokesman, related. "That's what they did well."[43] Gary L. Dyhouse, a St. Louis District hydrologist, agreed. "There are many reasons for changes in a flood elevation besides levees," he claimed. "Contrary to the beliefs of some, the Great Flood of 1993 … was not caused by levees." Instead, Dyhouse continued, unprecedented rainfall triggered flooding and made water levels rise to extraordinary heights. "The Great Flood of 1993 was probably the largest flood seen at St. Louis since the first European settlers entered the area in the 1700s," he concluded.[44] Yet the Corps also realized that levees alone could not adequately protect river communities and lands. Besides, they were not always aesthetically pleasing. "A wall all along the Mississippi River is not something a lot of people would support," Colonel Richard Craig, district engineer of the St. Paul District, admitted.[45] Therefore, the Corps reiterated that nonstructural solutions such as relocation, floodplain zoning and land-use planning were, in the words of Dyhouse, "good companion measures that should be included with traditional structural flood reduction measures like levees and reservoirs."[46] The Corps also declared it would not finance the repair of any levees destroyed by the flood that local sponsors had not properly maintained.[47]

Because of extensive flood damages, criticisms arose about federal financial assistance to natural disaster victims. When the federal government intervened in emergencies, taxpayers ended up paying for cleanup and repairs to private residences, in part because the federally funded National Flood Insurance Program, first established in 1968, covered areas at risk. This irritated Americans such as Richard Reeves, a syndicated columnist who wondered why citizens had to pay "higher taxes and insurance premiums to protect property that is uninsurable under any rational system."[48] Such complaints dovetailed with cries for better floodplain management and for a revised flood insurance program. In part because of these criticisms, Congress ordered the North Central Division to conduct a study on flood control on the Upper Mississippi. David Loss, a project manager in the St. Paul District, chaired this examination, and the resulting report reiterated that the federal government needed to use other flood prevention methods besides levees, including purchasing land in the floodplain and improving flood insurance.[49]

Navigation: Several barges being locked through Lock and Dam 10 in Guttenberg, Iowa. (Photo by Shannon Bauer, courtesy of St. Paul District, Corps of Engineers)

Additional studies reached the same conclusions. A post-flood examination conducted by the North Central Division explained that although floods could not be "100 percent controlled," they could be "greatly reduced and better managed with structural and nonstructural improvements."[50] Likewise, the Interagency Floodplain Management Review Committee appointed in 1994 to investigate existing floodplain and watershed management programs on the Upper Mississippi, recommended the implementation of policies that focused first on "inappropriate use of the floodplain;" second, on "minimizing vulnerability to damage through both structural and nonstructural means;" and, third, on "mitigating flood damages when they do occur." It also recommended that the National Flood Insurance Program mandate floodplain management before allowing communities to participate in the program. In addition, the Interagency Floodplain Management Review Committee proposed that federal agencies, including the Corps, increase floodplain management education and outreach, but hardly any of the committee's recommendations were ever legislatively enacted.[51]

Upper Mississippi River-Illinois Waterway System Navigation Study

No matter what solutions the Corps proposed, many environmentalists remained convinced the organization would continue to restrict rivers to the detriment of the environment. Accusations surrounding a Corps' navigation study in the late 1990s only reinforced this perception. As part of its navigation planning function, the Corps began two separate reconnaissance studies in 1990 on the Illinois Waterway and the Upper Mississippi River in order to identify sites and structures needing navigation improvements. In 1993, the Corps combined these two reconnaissance studies into a system feasibility study, which examined what the Corps could do on the Upper Mississippi and the Illinois to relieve traffic congestion and delays.[52]

Repairs: Richard Princko and Joe Kupietz, tender boat operators at the maintenance and repair unit in Fountain City, Wisconsin, remove a clamp bar and bottom seal during dewatering of the lock at lower St. Anthony Falls, Minneapolis in 2003. (Photo by Shannon Bauer, courtesy of St. Paul District, Corps of Engineers)

Congestion on the Upper Mississippi had been a worrisome problem for years. As increasing numbers of barges traversed the river, delays became commonplace at many locks and dams. Part of the problem was that most of the locks on the Upper Mississippi were only 600 feet long, while most towboats pushed lines of fifteen barges approximately 1,200 feet long. This meant that when a tow approached the lock, it would have to be dismantled into two separate tows in order to pass through, causing a delay of roughly an hour. Of special concern to the Corps were Locks 11 through 25. Because of regular delays on these sixteen locks, the navigation study specifically examined whether or not it was feasible to increase their length to 1,200 feet. The Corps also explored whether or not to expand seven locks close to St. Louis.[53]

The feasibility study, entitled the Upper Mississippi River-Illinois Waterway System Navigation Study, lasted into the twenty-first century, costing about $50 million. The St. Paul District participated in the study, along with the Rock Island and St. Louis districts, under the supervision of first the North Central Division and then the Mississippi Valley Division. By 1998, the economics work group, chaired by Donald Sweeney of St. Louis District, determined that the costs of lock expansion, which approached $1 billion, far outweighed the benefits. The group, therefore, recommended that enlargements not occur. Sweeney claimed that after his team issued this finding, he was relieved from his duties and replaced by another economist. Eventually, he argued, the Corps developed a draft report showing that large-scale expansion of the seven locks was economically viable. Sweeney charged senior Corps' officials, including Major General Russell L. Fuhrman, deputy chief of engineers and deputy commanding general of the Corps; Major General Phillip R. Anderson, Commanding General of the Mississippi Valley Division; and Colonel James V. Mudd, district engineer of the Rock Island District, with deliberately altering data in order to produce this favorable benefit-cost analysis. Sweeney officially filed an affidavit with the U.S. Office of Special Counsel detailing these charges, and the Office of Special Counsel instructed the Department of Defense to investigate. In November 2000, the Inspector General of the Army issued a report that substantiated some of Sweeney's charges, specifically that Mudd improperly told Corps' employees to use a lower N-value (a variable measuring how much consumers would be willing to pay for better barge transportation) than was warranted, and that Fuhrman and Anderson told subordinates that the Corps should act as an advocate for navigational interests. The report also found that an attitude of "Grow the Corps" existed, whereby divisions and districts were pressured to deliver projects.[54]

After the Inspector General released his findings, environmental groups expressed anger, but not amazement, with the Corps' conduct. Even before Sweeney delineated his suspicions, an article in *Forbes* magazine argued that "it is foreordained that the Corps will ask for new locks, and will say that without them the competitiveness of U.S. grain exports is at risk."[55] An editorial in the Minneapolis *Star Tribune* agreed. "The remarkable thing" about the Inspector General's findings, it concluded, "was how plainly the Corps' conduct on the Mississippi and Illinois rivers locks project illustrates what so many have suspected but been unable to prove."[56] Likewise, Ted Williams, in an essay in *Audubon*, saw the controversy as just another chapter in an ongoing history: "The Corps' military pooh-bahs have traditionally used trick arithmetic to justify environmentally hurtful, make-work projects."[57] Williams' perception was that the Corps routinely manipulated its benefit-cost analyses to validate projects it wanted.

This opinion was nothing new. Since the 1970s critics had disparaged the Corps' benefit-cost system, which used various figures to produce a ratio comparing the benefits accruing from a project with the amount of money expended. According to the national economic development criterion employed by the Corps, if a project had a ratio of 1.0 or greater (meaning that for every dollar spent, benefits greater than a dollar resulted), it was economically justified. But in the 1970s, economist Robert H. Haveman of the University of Wisconsin argued that two-thirds of the Corps' projects could not "pass a rigorous and correct cost-benefit test."[58] Others believed the benefit-cost process was inherently flawed because of the discount rates used in the calculations. Since water projects usually stretched over long periods of time, the Corps, like other government agencies, used discount rates, usually a figure lower than the current market interest rate, to equalize future dollar values with present rates. As Stephen A. Thompson of Millersville University in Pennsylvania explained, "Public spending uses a discount rate lower than that used by private markets. Low discount rates favor capital-intensive projects that produce benefits many years into the future; this is precisely the character of most water projects."[59] Thus, according to journalist Steve Slade, "The Corps's outdated benefit-cost type of analysis is consistently biased toward endorsing proposed construction projects."[60] Attorney Michael S. Baram extended this argument, stating that "by manipulating the discount rate, assigning arbitrary values to identified costs and benefits, excluding costs that would tilt the outcome against the preferred option, and using self-serving assumptions about distributional fairness," the Corps could easily justify any desired project.[61]

Another problem with benefit-cost analysis was the difficulty of making an economic estimate on environmental effects. As Ted Williams questioned about the Upper Mississippi River-Illinois Waterway System Navigation Study, "What, I wondered, is the dollar value of the two dozen bald eagles ... [or] the pileated woodpecker" that would be displaced by the lock expansion? Williams, quoting a study performed for the Fish and Wildlife Service in 1999, placed "the economic contribution of fishing, hunting, wildlife viewing, and sightseeing along the Upper Mississippi at $6.6 billion per year," but such figures were difficult to verify.[62]

In some ways, then, the controversy over the Upper Mississippi River-Illinois Waterway System Navigation Study was part of an ongoing disagreement over the benefit-cost system itself. Even though the Inspector General's report castigated the Corps, it recognized the subjectivity of the benefit-cost process and supported some of the changes the Corps had made in its economic analysis of lock construction because of this.[63] But the damage had been done, and the Upper Mississippi River-Illinois Waterway System Navigation Study came to a halt in 2000 while the National Academy of Sciences' National Research Council conducted an independent review. On February 28, 2001, the National Research Council issued its findings and recommended the study broaden its scope to focus on both environmental and economic factors. Acting on these recommendations, the study acquired a new name, the Restructured Upper Mississippi River-Illinois Waterway Navigation Study, and began again in the summer of 2001, with a projected completion date in 2004.[64]

Even though no one from the St. Paul District was implicated in the scandal, the district, as well as the Corps as a whole, still learned some lessons from the process. Although the benefit-cost manipulations were disturbing, the charges that the Corps was primarily interested in navigation and as an organization concentrated on getting work for itself regardless of the cost to taxpayers was perhaps more damaging. Some Corps' personnel clearly needed to change their perspective, but in the St. Paul District, which had traditionally been more environmentally conscious than other Corps' units, the issue, according to Colonel Kenneth Kasprisin, district engineer from 1998 to 2001, was more about projecting an accurate image than about revising its benefit-cost analyses. "I think that the Corps has a very high integrity," Kasprisin asserted. "I think that we take a lot of pride in what we do." The problem, he continued, was conveying that impression to the public, and he called on the Corps in general to improve its efforts "to tell our story of what it is that we do to help the communities."[65]

While the Corps continued to address criticism of its handling of the Upper Mississippi River, the 2002 publication of an interim report by the Restructured Upper Mississippi

River-Illinois Waterway Navigation Study began to rectify the challenging issues in the original study. "A collaborative process has been applied in restarting the restructured navigation study," the report stated, and this process consisted of consulting with "other Federal agencies, state agencies, the public, and economic and environmental non-governmental organizations" about how "to give equal consideration of fish and wildlife resources and navigation improvement."[66] For the duration of the study, this collaboration was to continue. The question remained as to how the Corps would deal with the problems associated with benefit-cost analyses, but, as the successes of GREAT I and the UMRBC master plan showed, consistent coordination with other agencies would help.

Endangered Species – Lampsilis higginsii

As the Corps dealt with the problems arising from the Upper Mississippi River-Illinois Waterway Navigation Study, the St. Paul District faced difficulties from another source: mussels on the Upper Mississippi. The district became concerned with mussels because some varieties were endangered species and because an exotic species, the zebra mussel, threatened to destroy the native population. In 1973, Congress passed the Endangered Species Act, which required federal agencies to ensure their actions did not harm any endangered species or its habitat. This complicated matters for the St. Paul District because of the presence of *Lampsilis higginsii*, or the Higgins' eye pearly mussel, in several waterways under its jurisdiction, including the Upper Mississippi and St. Croix rivers. Because of a decrease in abundance and range of the Higgins' eye, the Fish and Wildlife Service listed it as an endangered species in 1976.[67]

That same year, various individuals and agencies expressed concern for the Higgins' eye mussel. When the St. Paul District held public hearings on its nine-foot channel maintenance dredging, for example, the Fish and Wildlife Service conveyed its trepidation about the effects of this action on the Higgins' eye, especially in the eastern channel at Prairie du Chien, Wisconsin. In response, the district held a meeting with commercial clammers, Prairie du Chien's city council and representatives from the State of Wisconsin, as well as the Wisconsin Department of Natural Resources and GREAT, to determine exactly where in the east channel the mussel resided. The group discovered that, although mussel beds existed in the southern part of the channel, they were not known in the northern part. Based on this information, the district decided to dredge the east channel from the north, rather than the south. Marian Havlik, a Wisconsin resident who had educated herself about the Higgins' eye, objected to this effort, believing it would still disrupt the mussel's habitat. The Corps, however, believed that because of a slow river current, the dredged material could settle before reaching the mussel beds. Besides, the mussels had already survived heavy periods of natural siltation due to flooding, and the short duration of the dredging would not harm them. All interested agencies and commercial clammers accepted the district's revised plan.[68]

But after the dredging, Havlik went through the spoil and found, in her own words, "hundreds of Higgins' Eye shells."[69] Angry that the St. Paul District had not listened to her, Havlik wrote President Jimmy Carter and United States representatives and senators from Wisconsin and Minnesota, protesting that the Corps had knowingly violated the Endangered Species Act by not conducting a thorough survey of Higgins' eye mussels before dredging.[70] Perhaps exasperated at the outcry Havlik made, some Corps' personnel began referring to her as "that clam lady," but her actions helped the St. Paul District become more aware and knowledgeable about the Higgins' eye mussel. Before this incident, Havlik related, "There was no one in the Corps who could identify a mussel species." After her protests, she said, "The Army Corps realized that never again could it dredge a channel without first doing a survey of mussel species in the path of the dredge boat."[71]

Endangered Species

(Left) Male and female Higgins eye mussels. (Photo by Mike Davis, courtesy of Minnesota Department of Natural Resources)
(Right) Nonnative species zebra mussels without infestation next to native infested zebra mussels. (Photo courtesy of St. Paul District, Corps of Engineers)

As the district continued to discover Higgins' eye mussels in its dredging areas, it developed a greater concern for them. In 1977, for example, the district discovered the half-shell of a dead clam in dredged spoils from the Minnesota River. Although the clam could not positively be identified as a Higgins' eye, the district stopped work for two days while a malacologist investigated. Such inconveniences led James Braatz, a St. Paul District spokesman, to declare in 1980, "The problem with the Higgins' Eye is that it keeps cropping up where we want to work." To solve the Higgins' eye issue, the district advocated the establishment of specified areas outside of dredging sites where the species could be placed and protected. The Fish and Wildlife Service investigated this possibility, but took no action in the 1980s.[72]

In the 1990s, anxiety about the mussel increased after the St. Paul District learned that an exotic mussel species, *Dreissena polymorpha*, or the zebra mussel, had invaded the Upper Mississippi River. The zebra mussel, usually around one inch long, is native to central Asia but migrated to Europe in years past. In 1985 or 1986, commercial barges with the mussel attached entered the Great Lakes, unintentionally leaving the creature behind. Thereafter, the mussel was carried to the Mississippi River by recreational and commercial crafts. Once in the Mississippi, the mussel created three problems: first, it used strong threads to attach itself to any hard substrate, including water intakes,

Mussels: Corps' bilogists relocate immature Higgins eye mussels pursuant to the Biological Opinion. Left to right: Randy Urich, Dan Kelner and Dennis Anderson. (Photo by Shannon Bauer, courtesy of St. Paul District, Corps of Engineers)

pipes, valves, buoys, screens and other underwater structures, causing clogging and sinkage; second, its large numbers could ruin fish spawning habitat; and third, it could potentially eliminate the Higgins' eye and other native mussels by competing for food and attaching to their shells, thereby preventing them from migrating or burrowing.[73] The St. Paul District initiated a monitoring process of the zebra mussel at its locks and dams in 1992; but by the end of the decade, the population of the organism had exploded on the Upper Mississippi.[74]

In 2000, the Fish and Wildlife Service issued a Final Biological Opinion for the operation and maintenance of the nine-foot channel navigation project which concluded that because of barge movement, the project would continue to facilitate the growth of zebra mussel populations, thereby diminishing the survival chances of the Higgins' eye. The Service recommended the Corps conduct a study as to the feasibility of relocating populations of the Higgins' eye mussels to stimulate their population growth, and a reconnaissance/feasibility study commenced. In April 2002, the St. Paul District released a draft relocation plan under the direction of biologist Dennis Anderson. This report proposed establishing ten sites throughout Minnesota, Illinois, Iowa and Wisconsin, where the Corps could place Higgins' eye mussels in order to ensure that at least five new populations survived. The ten-year plan, estimated to cost $2.66 million, also called for raising juvenile mussels on certain fish species at hatcheries and then transplanting these mussels to the relocation sites.[75] The next decade would show whether or not this plan enhanced Higgins' eye populations, but the Corps was optimistic. Meanwhile, the St. Paul District worked on a zebra mussel reconnaissance study, but what solutions this proposed remained to be seen. For the foreseeable future, the zebra mussel, in the words of one district official, would continue to be a "multi-million-dollar pest" to the Corps.[76]

Conclusion

By 2003, civil works projects on the Upper Mississippi River had produced numerous opportunities for the St. Paul District to show its concern for the environment and to demonstrate its cooperation with federal, state and local entities. Although the Upper Mississippi River Navigation Study and the Midwest Flood of 1993 produced new concerns about the Corps' commitment to environmental values, the St. Paul District's work on commissions, such as GREAT and the Upper Mississippi River Basin Commission, together with its implementation of the EMP and its efforts to preserve the Higgins' eye mussel, evinced the district's environmental awareness. Events on the Upper Mississippi showed that balancing the interests of different parties was difficult and controversial, and that most of the time the Corps could not satisfy all viewpoints. The key, according to District Engineer Colonel William Badger, was to "swim in the middle of the river" and hope that a moderate approach appeased some of the concerns.[77]

Chapter 3: Endnotes

1 Mark Twain, *Life on the Mississippi* (Boston: James R. Osgood and Company, 1883), p. 21.

2 John O. Anfinson interview by Matthew Godfrey, St. Paul, MN, 25 October 2002, p. 21.

3 Upper Mississippi River Basin Coordinating Committee, *Upper Mississippi River Comprehensive Basin Study Main Report* (Chicago: Upper Mississippi River Basin Coordinating Committee, 1972), pp. 1-3, 129-133.

4 Raymond H. Merritt, *The Corps, the Environment, and the Upper Mississippi River Basin* (Washington, D.C.: Historical Division, Office of Administrative Services, Office of the Chief of Engineers, 1984), pp. 53-58, 93.

5 "Study Calls for Swift Costly Safeguards for River Wildlife," *Crosscurrents* 4 (March 1981): p. 3. *Crosscurrents* is the St. Paul District's newsletter.

6 George W. Griebenow, "A Team Called GREAT," Water Spectrum 9 (Winter 1976- 77): pp. 21-23. See also U.S. Army Corps of Engineers, St. Paul District, *A Public Trust: An Executive Summary of GREAT I* (St. Paul, MN: U.S. Army Corps of Engineers, St. Paul District, n.d.), p. 3, copy in File 870 Great River Environmental Action, Box 3851, St. Paul District administrative records, St. Paul, Minnesota [SPDAR]. For an example of environmental complaints, see "The Mississippi River: The 20th Century's Grand Canal?" *Outdoor America* 37 (September 1972): pp. 1, 3 and "Walton League Opposes Dredge and Fill Projects on Upper Mississippi River," *Outdoor America* 37 (January 1972): p. 9.

7 Merritt, *The Corps, the Environment, and the Upper Mississippi River Basin*, pp. 65-72.

8 William R. Pearson and Dennis E. Cin, "The GREAT River Study – A New Perspective in River Management," p. 2, File 870 Great River Environmental Action, Box 3851, SPDAR.

9 GREAT I Plan of Study, Upper Mississippi River (Head of Navigation to Guttenburg, Iowa) (n.p., n.d.), pp. 1-3; U.S., Congress, House, Committee on Public Works and Transportation, Water Resources Subcommittee, Water Resources Development – 1976: Hearings Before the Subcommittee on Water Resources of the Committee on Public Works and Transportation, House of Representatives, 94th Cong., 2d sess., 1976, p. 644; Griebenow, "A Team Called GREAT," pp. 19-20; Pearson and Cin, "The GREAT River Study," p. 3.

10 Pearson and Cin, "The GREAT River Study," pp. 3-5; Raymond Merritt, "New Directions: Transitions in the St. Paul District, Corps of Engineers, 1976-1982," unpublished manuscript, St. Paul District, pp. 13-14.

11 Pearson and Cin, "The GREAT River Study," pp. 4-5.

12 "The GREAT River Study – GREAT I," pp. 4-7, manuscript in File 870 Great River Environmental Action, Box 3851, SPDAR; A Public Trust, p. 7; see also "Dredged Material Developed into Beaches," Crosscurrents 4 (July 1981): p. 1.

13 A Public Trust, pp. 11, 14; unidentified newspaper clipping, File 870 General History – Environment (73-79), Box 3848, SPDAR.

14 U.S. Army Corps of Engineers, Office of the Chief of Engineers, Engineer Profiles: The District Engineer, Interviews with Colonel William W. Badger, by Frank N. Schubert (Washington, D.C.: U.S. Army Corps of Engineers, 1983), p. 25 [hereafter cited as Badger Interviews].

15 Quotation in Ben A. Wopat interview by Matthew Pearcy, St. Paul, MN, 25 April 2002, p. 19, Oral History File, St. Paul District, St. Paul, Minnesota; see also Merritt, "New Directions," p. 14.

16 U.S. Army Corps of Engineers, St. Paul District, Implementation for GREAT I Study (St. Paul, MN: St. Paul District, U.S. Army Corps of Engineers, 1981), pp. 26-31. This report was actually written by Dennis Cin and William Spychalla. Merritt, "New Directions," p. 129.

17 "Corps Seeks $3 Million to Guard River Habitat," Quad-City Times, 1 September 1981; "Corps to Spend $3 Million on Mississippi Cleanup," Post-Bulletin (Rochester, MN), 18 April 1983.

18 Badger Interviews, p. 48.

19 Unidentified newspaper clipping, File 870 General Historical Activities Correspondence, Mississippi River, 1981, Box 3854, SPDAR.

20 Russel K. Snyder interview by Matthew Godfrey, St. Paul, MN, 23 October 2002.

21 U.S. Army Corps of Engineers, St. Paul District, Great I Implementation Status Report and Future Program (St. Paul, MN: U.S. Army Corps of Engineers, St. Paul District, 1992), pp. 7-11, 28-31.

22 Upper Mississippi River Basin Commission Annual Report/Fiscal Year 1979 (n.p., n.d.), p. 8, copy in Box 1674, SPDAR; "Mississippi Basin Commission's New Master Plan Draws Fire," Minneapolis *Tribune*, 6 January 1982.

23 Upper Mississippi River Basin Commission Annual Report/Fiscal Year 1979, pp. 8- 9.

24 "Memorandum of Agreement Between U.S. Army Corps of Engineers and the Upper Mississippi River Basin Commission," File 1517-08, Box 1637, SPDAR.

25 Jerry E. Smith, Colonel, Corps of Engineers, Deputy Division Engineer, Memorandum, 24 January 1979, File 1517-08 Survey Report – Miss. Rv. Basin (79), Box 1637, SPDAR.

26 Quotations and information in "Mississippi Basin Commission's New Master Plan Draws Fire," *Star Tribune*, 6 January 1982.

27 U.S. Army Corps of Engineers, North Central Division, *Upper Mississippi River System Environmental Management Program*, Sixth Annual Addendum (Chicago: U.S. Army Corps of Engineers, North Central Division, 1991), pp. 2-4; U.S., Congress, House, Committee on Transportation and Infrastructure, Water Resources and Environment Subcommittee, Proposals for a Water Resources Development Act of 1998: Hearings Before the Subcommittee on Water Resources and Environment of the Committee on Transportation and Infrastructure, House of Representatives, 105th Cong., 2d sess., 1998, pp. 255-256.

28 U.S. Army Corps of Engineers, St. Paul District, *Great I Implementation Status Report and Future Program*, p. 50; U.S. Army Corps of Engineers, North Central Division, Water Resources Development in Minnesota 1995 (Chicago: North Central Division, 1995), p. 18.

29 Quotation in "Corps of Engineers Mississippi River Pool 8 Environmental Project Wins State Award," St. Paul District News Release, 29 January 2002; see also U.S. Army Corps of Engineers, St. Paul District, "Pool 8 Islands Phase II Habitat Project, Stoddard, Wisc.," <http://www.mvp.usace.army.mil/environment/default.asp?pageid=136> (6 June 2003).

30 U.S. Army Corps of Engineers, St. Paul District, "Mississippi River Environmental Management Program, Minn/Wis/Iowa," <http://www.mvp.usace.army.mil/environment/default.asp?pageid=74> (6 June 2003).

31 U.S. Army Corps of Engineers, St. Paul District, "Mississippi River Environmental Management Program, Minn/Wis/Iowa," <http://www.mvp.usace.army.mil/environment/default.asp?pageid=74> (6 June 2003).

32 Don Powell and Gary Palesh, "EMP Benefits More Than 10,000 Acres of Habitat," *Crosscurrents* 22 (February 1999): p. 4.

33 Colonel Richard W. Craig interview by John O. Anfinson, St. Paul, MN, 20 July 1993, p. 14, Oral History File, St. Paul District, St. Paul, Minnesota.

34 Colonel Roger L. Baldwin interview by John O. Anfinson, St. Paul, MN, 1 July 1991, p. 8, Oral History File, St. Paul District, St. Paul, Minnesota.

35 "The Rebirth of Lock and Dam 1," *Crosscurrents* 4 (May 1981): pp. 1-2.

36 Quotation in "Major Rehab Begins at Lock 3, Continues at Lock 2," *Crosscurrents* 11 (January 1988): p. 11; see also Badger Interviews, pp. 71-72.

37 "Lock and Dam No. 2 Rehab," *Crosscurrents* 10 (February 1987): p. 4; see also Colonel Ed Rapp interview by Mickey Schubert, 7 July 1983, p. 1, Oral History File, St. Paul District, Minnesota; "Lock & Dam No. 3 Rehabilitation Project Dedicated," *Crosscurrents* 14 (December 1991): p. 3. For the status of the lock and dam rehabilitation, see the various listings for each lock under U.S. Army Corps of Engineers, St. Paul District, "Mississippi Locks and Dams," <http://www.mvp.usace.army.mil/navigation/default.asp?pageid=145> (6 June 2003).

38 Michael C. Robinson, "Nightmare in the Heartland: The Great Midwest Flood of 1993," APWA (American Public Works Association) *Reporter* 60 (September 1993): pp. 6-7; "1993 Reviewed," *Crosscurrents* 17 (January 1994): p. 4; Lt. Col. Gary M. Koenig, "The Great Flood of 1993," File 1993 Flood, Cultural Resource Management Files, St. Paul District, St. Paul, Minnesota; David Tenenbaum, "Rethinking the River," *Nature Conservancy* 44 (July/August 1994): p. 11.

39 "Corps Finds Itself in Middle of a Heated Policy Debate," *Engineering News Record* 225 (26 July 1993): p. 14.

40 Quotations in "Flood Control System Under a Microscope," *USA Today*, 9 August 1993.

41 Quotations in Tenenbaum, "Rethinking the River," p. 14.

42 Charles Camillo, MVD Historian, Memorandum for Matt Pearcy, MVP Historian, 28 July 2004, copy provided by Matthew Pearcy. Camillo is the Mississippi Valley Division historian.

43 Quoted in "Flood Control System Under a Microscope," *USA Today*, 9 August 1993.

44 Gary R. Dyhouse, "Myths and Misconceptions of the 1993 Flood," <http://www.mvs.usace.army.mil/dinfo/pa/fl93info.htm> (6 June 2003).

45 Craig Interview, p. 17.

46 Dyhouse, "Myths and Misconceptions of the 1993 Flood."

47 "Information Paper, Subject: Floodplain Management," 22 October 1993, File Briefing Book: Hearing Before the House Committee on Public Work and Transportation Subcommittee on Water Resources and Environment on Federal Flood Control and Floodplain Policy and Midwest Floods, Room 7112 Civil Works/Policy Division/Legislative Initiatives Branch, Headquarters, U.S. Army Corps of Engineers, Washington, D.C.; "A Tougher Army Corps," Kansas City *Star*, 17 October 1993.

48 Richard Reeves, "Hurricane$, Earthquake$, and Flood$: If People Want to Build Their Houses in Dangerous Places, Why Should the Rest of Us Pay When Disaster Strikes?" *Washington Monthly* 26 (April 1994): p. 12.

49 "Costly Flood Control," *Washington Post*, 10 July 1995; "Agencies Told to Explore Alternatives to Levees," *Star Tribune*, 26 August 1993; "In the Flood's Wake," *Star Tribune*, 29 August 1993.

50 U.S. Army Corps of Engineers, Rock Island District, "The Great Flood of 1993 Post-Flood Report," <http://www.mvr.usace.army.mil/PublicAffairsOffice/HistoricArchives/Floodof1993/pafr.htm> (6 June 2003).

51 Interagency Floodplain Management Review Committee, *Sharing the Challenge: Floodplain Management into the 21st Century* (Washington, D.C.: Government Printing Office, 1994), pp. v, 98.

52 U.S. Army Corps of Engineers, Rock Island District, St. Louis District, St. Paul District, Upper Mississippi River-Illinois Waterway System Navigation Study: Responses to Issues Raised at the Public and NEPA Scoping Meetings of November 1994, Interim Product (Washington, D.C.: U.S. Army Corps of Engineers, 1995), pp. 1-2.

53 U.S. Army Corps of Engineers, Upper Mississippi River-Illinois Waterway System Navigation Study, pp. 3, 8.

54 Elaine Kaplan, U.S. Office of Special Counsel, to The President, 6 December 2000, <http://www.osc.gov/reading.htm> (1 November 2002); U.S. Army Inspector General Agency Report of Investigation (Case 00-019), ibid.; see also "Corps Adjusted Data to Justify Project, Probe Finds," *Star Tribune*, 7 December 2000

55 Bruce Upbin, "A River of Subsidies," *Forbes* 161 (23 March 1998): p. 86.

56 "Corps of Engineers," *Star Tribune*, 15 December 2000.

57 Ted Williams, "Trouble on the Mississippi," *Audubon* 102 (July/August 2000): p. 45.

58 "Cost-Benefit Trips Up the Corps," *Business Week* (19 February 1979): p. 96.

59 Stephen A. Thompson, *Water Use, Management, and Planning in the United States* (San Diego, CA: Academic Press, 1999), p. 164.

60 Steve Slade, "Caught in Mid-Stream," *The Nation* 221 (6 September 1975): p. 179.

61 Michael S. Baram, "Cost-Benefit Analysis: An Inadequate Basis for Health, Safety, and Environmental Regulatory Rulemaking," *Ecology Law Quarterly* 8 (No. 3, 1980): p. 489.

62 Williams, "Trouble on the Mississippi," pp. 40-41.

63 U.S. Army Inspector General Agency Report of Investigation (Case 00-019), pp. 3- 4, <http://www.osc.gov/reading.htm> (1 November 2002).

64 U.S. Army Corps of Engineers, Rock Island District, "Frequently Asked Questions," Restructured Upper Mississippi River-Illinois Waterway Navigation Study, <http://www2.mvr.usace.army.mil/umr-iwwsns/index.cfm?fuseaction=home.faq> (6 June 2003).

65 Colonel Kenneth Kasprisin interview by Virginia Gnabasik, St. Paul, MN, 13 July 2001, p. 12.

66 Restructured Upper Mississippi River-Illinois Waterway Navigation Study, "Interim Report – Executive Summary," p. 1, <http://www2.mvr.usace.army.mil/umr-iwwsns/documents/IR072502ES.pdf> (6 June 2003).

67 U.S. Army Corps of Engineers, St. Paul District, "Draft April 2002, Definite Project Report and Environmental Assessment for Relocation Plan for the Endangered Higgins' Eye Pearlymussel (Lampsilis higginsii)," copy provided by Dennis Anderson, biologist, St. Paul District.

68 Norman C. Hintz, Acting District Engineer, to Honorable Hubert H. Humphrey, 27 October 1976, File 1520-01 Mississippi River – Dredging (1976), Box 1660, SPDAR.

69 Quoted in Pat Middleton, "The Clam Lady of America's Rivers: Marian Havlik," <http://www.greatriver.com/clam.htm> (6 June 2003).

70 Marian E. Havlik to Brigadier General Robert L. Moore, 15 August 1976, (copies to Thomas Kleppe, Patrick Lucey, Wendell Anderson, Robert Ray, Gaylord Nelson, William Proxmire, Hubert Humphrey, Walter Mondale, and Richard Clark), File 1520-01 Mississippi River – Dredging (1976), Box 1660, SPDAR; Middleton, "The Clam Lady of America's Rivers."

71 Quoted in Middleton, "The Clam Lady of America's Rivers."

72 Quoted in "Small Creature Might Mussel in on River Dredging Work Again," *Tribune*, 31 December 1980; see also Bruce Bigelow, "Clams in Need Has Biologist Friends Indeed," *Crosscurrents* 4 (February 1981): p. 4.

73 Robert Whiting Memorandum, 15 November 1990, File 1105 Environmental Resource Branch General Correspondence (1990), Box 1560, SPDAR; "Draft April 2002, Definite Project Report and Environmental Assessment for Relocation Plan for the Endangered Higgins' Eye Pearlymussel (*Lampsilis higginsii*)."

74 Robert J. Whiting Memorandum, 23 November 1992, File 10-1-7a Exotic SpeciesStudy (1992), Box 4338, SPDAR; Dennis Anderson, personal communication with the authors, 11 July 2002.

75 "Draft April 2002, Definite Project Report and Environmental Assessment for Relocation Plan for the Endangered Higgins' Eye Pearlymussel (*Lampsilis higginsii*)"; U.S. Army Corps of Engineers, St. Paul District, "Corps Reveals Draft Plan to Revive Endangered Mussel Species," Press Release, 18 April 2002, <http://www.mvp.usace.army.mil/news_media/news/PA-2002-0046.htm> (1 November 2002).

76 Robert J. Whiting Memorandum, 28 November 1994, File 1105 Mussel Activity (1994), Box 5601, SPDAR.

77 Badger Interviews, p. 48.

Zumbra River: Channel modifications on the South Fork Zumbra River in Rochester, Minnesota, showing the pedestrian bridge and riprap implemented by the St. Paul District, 1995. (Photo courtesy of St. Paul District, Corps of Engineers)

4 Civil Works Program II: Flood Control Projects

Throughout the last quarter of the twentieth century, much of the St. Paul District's civil works efforts focused on the Mississippi River. However, that waterway was not the district's only responsibility; it also performed flood control projects on rivers and lakes throughout North Dakota, Minnesota and Wisconsin. Just as district undertakings on the Mississippi showed the impact of environmentalism on the Corps' civil works mission, so too did these other flood control projects demonstrate the evolution of the St. Paul District's environmental awareness. In these other regions, the Corps faced different problems than in the Mississippi River Basin. For one thing, agriculture dominated the Northern Great Plains, where many of these projects were built, leading to conflicts between urban environmentalists intent on halting undertakings and rural agriculturists who, in their estimation, needed the projects to survive. For another, the flat topography and cold climate of the Northern Great Plains ensured that Corps' activities would consist primarily of flood control, with few navigational concerns. Indeed, the La Farge project in Wisconsin, the Devils Lake undertaking in North Dakota, the Grand Forks/East Grand Forks project in North Dakota and Minnesota and the South Fork Zumbro River undertaking in Minnesota, raised several interesting quandaries for the district and are especially good examples of the controversial issues and innovative solutions that developed between 1975 and 2003.

La Farge, Wisconsin

The La Farge Project in southwestern Wisconsin was an attempt to tame the Kickapoo River, a waterway that flows 95 miles through nine communities ranging in population from a hundred to more than seven hundred. The river mainly traverses hilly farmland before emptying into the Wisconsin River only 16 miles from the Wisconsin's juncture with the Mississippi. Other than the development of the Corps' Upper Mississippi River policies, perhaps no other project better highlights the impact of the National Environmental Policy Act, or NEPA, and the environmental movement on the Corps' civil works program. The beginnings of the project stretched back to the 1930s, when Kickapoo Valley residents, tired of floods that had inundated the region in 1907, 1912, 1917 and 1935, asked the Corps for assistance. In 1938, the Corps performed a preliminary examination of the river but the outbreak of the Second World War stalled any decisive action. In January 1962, the St. Paul District issued a report recommending that a dam and reservoir be constructed at La Farge for flood control, fish and wildlife enhancement and recreation purposes, and Congress authorized the project that same year. In order to build the dam and reservoir, the district acquired 348 tracts of land, totaling 8,569 acres, from private residents in the Kickapoo Valley in 1969.[1]

La Farge: An artist concept drawing of La Farge Lake and Dam produced in 1972. (Photo courtesy of St. Paul District, Corps of Engineers)

LA FARGE LAKE AND DAM

When the Corps began constructing the dam, Congress had just passed NEPA, thereby requiring federal agencies to take into account environmental effects of their actions. Bolstered by this statute, environmentalists quickly objected to the La Farge Dam, believing that the resulting 1,800-acre lake would inundate a scenic portion of the Kickapoo River, would be environmentally unsound and would damage endangered plant species such as arctic primrose and northern monkshood. The Corps' own Environmental Advisory Board, created on April 2, 1970, to provide recommendations and aid to Corps' leadership on environmental issues, requested the La Farge project be used as a test case to implement Environmental Advisory Board suggestions as to how the Corps should interface with the public on controversial issues. However, in 1971, Environmental Advisory Board chairman Charles H. Stoddard charged both the St. Paul District and the North Central Division with, in the words of historian Martin Reuss, "undermining the Board's efforts in the case of the La Farge Dam." Stoddard

La Farge Project Map

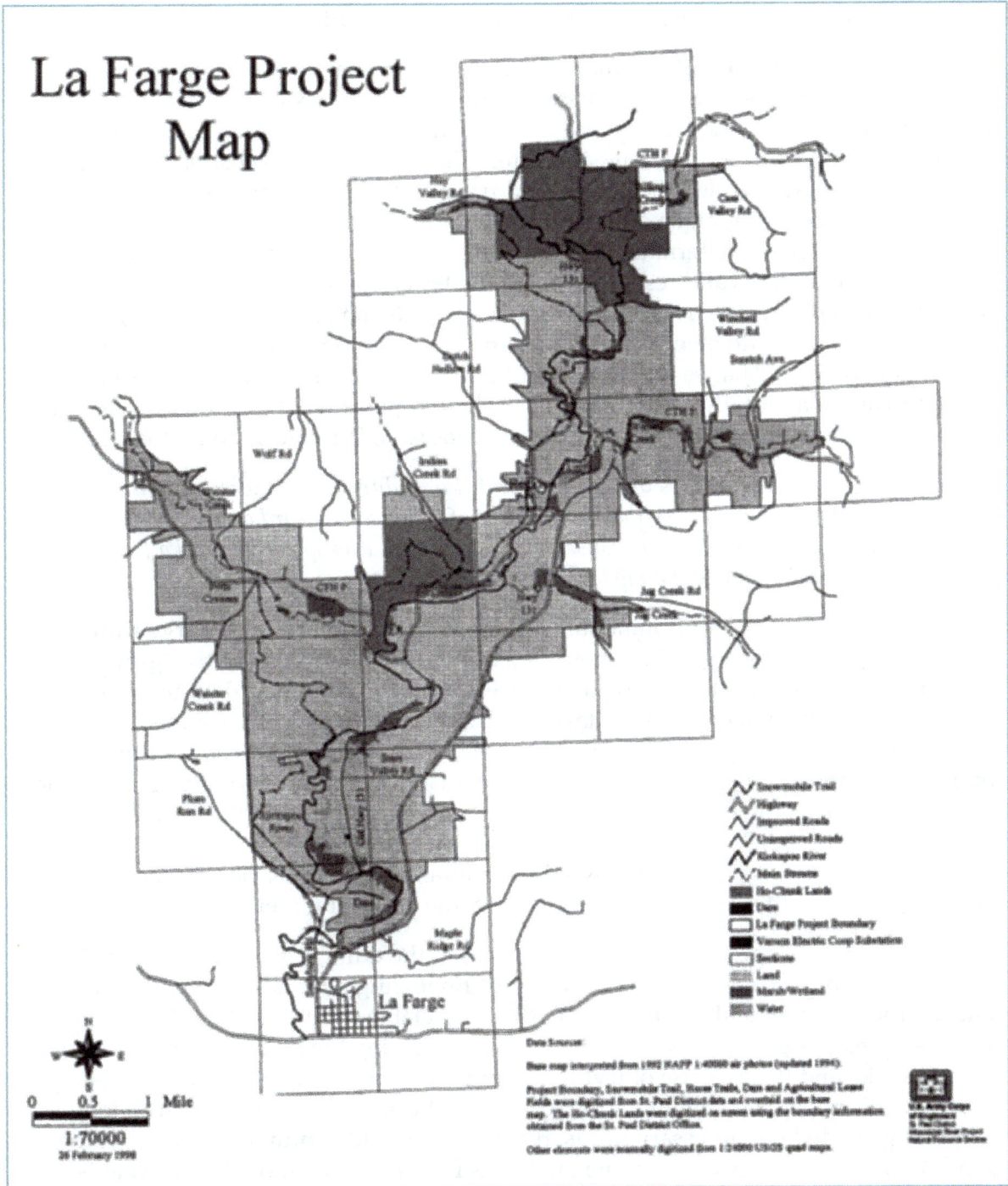

La Farge: Project map, 1998. (Mapo courtesy of St. Paul District, Corps of Engineers)

believed that district and division representatives had pressured state officials to review recommendations for flood control rather than forming an independent panel for that purpose, meaning that no significant dialogue had been conducted about flood control alternatives. Instead, construction of the dam merely continued.[2]

In the early 1970s, the Sierra Club filed two lawsuits against the Corps to stop Corps' work at La Farge but both were dismissed. Late in 1974, the issues reached a head. Wisconsin Governor Patrick Lucey and U.S. Senator Gaylord Nelson (D-Wisconsin), both former proponents of the dam, called for a halt to construction after a University of Wisconsin report revealed the lake would probably be rich in nutrients and susceptible to weeds and algae due to farmland runoff. Lucey and Nelson asked the St. Paul District to consider alternatives to the dam and reservoir. Schooled in traditional Corps' beliefs that dams and reservoirs were the best flood control devices regardless of environmental effects, District Engineer Col. Max Noah reluctantly agreed, but observed, "I think we do owe it to the [Kickapoo Valley] community as a whole to continue the project."[3] James Braatz, St. Paul District spokesman, also expressed skepticism about alternatives, stating the original proposal was "the only way to go."[4] Such comments prompted the *Capital Times* in Madison, Wisconsin, to editorialize,

> *Nothing better exemplifies the ossified, stratified, obdurate bureaucratic mind at work than the attitude of the Army Corps of Engineers toward any suggestion that, maybe, the dam they are constructing across the Kickapoo River at La Farge might be an environmental mistake.*[5]

The differences between environmentalists and the Corps over the La Farge Dam reflected the general tensions that abounded in the 1970s between the two groups. Whereas environmentalists perceived engineers as narrow-minded dam builders who were insensitive to environmental concerns, engineers saw environmentalists as unrealistic "tree-huggers."[6] Part of the problem was different perceptions of flood control. Environmental groups such as the Sierra Club endorsed nonstructural solutions to flooding, such as removing development from the floodplain and other management techniques, while the Corps still focused mainly on structural answers, such as dams and reservoirs. Although the Corps would eventually begin to implement nonstructural solutions, the La Farge Project saw it clinging to the structural method.

The St. Paul District agreed to study alternatives to the dam. It formed a partnership team for that purpose and even issued a report reviewing alternatives, but it still believed that the dam and reservoir were the only viable solutions. After the partnership team issued a report in March 1975, affirming the eutrophic nature of the proposed lake and the expense of trying to improve its water quality, Noah defiantly declared, "It's never been my intention to review alternatives," adding that as long as Congress provided the necessary funds, the district would continue to construct the dam.[7] A Kickapoo Valley organization, Citizens for Kickapoo, agreed with Noah's stance, presenting Governor Lucey with a 7,000-name petition in support of the dam. Faced with the obstinacy of Noah and Kickapoo Valley residents, Nelson, who wanted to relocate individuals from the floodplain and create a riverway park system, and

U.S. Senator William Proxmire (D-Wisconsin), who was concerned about the escalating costs of the dam, took the matter to the Senate Subcommittee on Public Works and eliminated construction funding in November 1975. In response, La Farge residents burned Proxmire in effigy and buried him in a mock funeral, angered that he had helped place the project in a state of "bureaucratic limbo."[8]

Proxmire's vilification highlighted another significant theme – the battles between urban and rural residents over flood control. Most of the opposition to La Farge came from residents of Madison and Milwaukee; most of the proponents were centered in the Kickapoo Valley. "Kickapoogians" believed the recreation potentials of the dam and reservoir were needed in order to stimulate the area's economy and claimed the reservoir was necessary to prevent farmland flooding. They resented the intrusion of "outsiders," people who they believed had no economic interest in the project. Jane Johnson, a resident of La Farge, expressed her discontent with Nelson and others who were "playing on our emotions," while Bernice Schroeder, also a La Farge citizen, stated that opposition to the dam "shows the insensitivity of the urban people to the needs and wants of the people here."[9] Ward Rose's despair went even deeper, as he believed it did not matter what La Farge residents actually wanted because, "We are going to end up with what some rotten politicians want us to have."[10] Environmentalists disagreed, arguing that "the fate of the Kickapoo Valley is of great concern to all Wisconsin residents, as the Kickapoo River is an important natural treasure enjoyed by residents from all areas of Wisconsin."[11] The St. Paul District was caught in the middle, wanting to build the dam and reservoir but facing intense opposition from the other side.

By the time Nelson and Proxmire successfully persuaded Congress to cut the dam's funding, the Corps had spent approximately $18 million and completed nearly forty percent of the project. The dam itself lay across the valley, stopping just at the river. A concrete intake tower was finished, as was a conduit tunnel and a maintenance building.[12] Because no taxes were levied on the lands the Corps had purchased from valley residents, the community suffered a decrease in tax revenue. Those who sold the property criticized the Corps for removing them from their homes for no purpose. With such problems, it became imperative either to de-authorize the project or to find another solution. Several proposals were introduced, including Nelson's idea to build a riverway park for the National Park Service to administer. But early in 1976, the Interior Department declared that the stretch of the Kickapoo River, including La Farge, did not meet the criteria for national park or scenic waterway status.[13] In 1977, President Jimmy Carter recommended the abandonment of the La Farge Project as part of his fight against unnecessary flood control projects, advocating instead the need to focus on nonstructural alternatives in the Kickapoo Valley.[14]

The need to resolve the flooding became more urgent in 1978 when the region experienced severe summer inundations that caused an estimated $10 million in damages.[15] After water at a depth of six feet flowed down its main street, Soldiers Grove, a community of five hundred on the Kickapoo, worked with the Department of Housing and Urban Development to relocate its homes and businesses a half-mile away, placing them out of the floodplain.[16] Other towns, including La Farge, were not

La Farge Project: The La Farge Project soon after work was suspended, 1979. The concrete intake tower is in the foreground. (Photo courtesy of St. Paul District, Corps of Engineers)

so willing to uproot. Thus, when Steven Gunderson (R-Wisconsin) began serving in the House of Representatives in 1981, he decided to try to find a less radical solution to the Kickapoo Valley's problems. Gunderson asked the St. Paul District to consider completing the dam as a dry dam, with no resulting reservoir. District Engineer Colonel William Badger agreed to study the proposal, but admitted that ultimately, Congress had the responsibility of telling the district what to do with the project. "I'd be willing to do whatever Congress, in its wisdom, decides," Badger stated.[17] But Congress took no steps toward deauthorization, leaving Badger somewhat frustrated: "It really creates problems for me because it is not being funded and yet I have to maintain it. I have to keep it clean and keep security on it."[18]

Despite Badger's concerns, the dam remained in limbo. In 1983, Congress appropriated funds for the dry dam study, which was completed in 1984. This report concluded that neither a dry dam nor a wet dam was feasible for several reasons, including poor benefit-cost ratios and inadequate flood protection.[19] With no relief forthcoming, some Kickapoo Valley residents decided to take matters into their own hands and instituted lawsuits against the Corps to force the completion of the dam. In October 1985, Martha Rose Driscoll, who had sold 200 acres to the Corps in 1970; Ronald Driscoll; and Pat Driscoll filed a suit seeking $110,000 in damages and requiring the St. Paul District to finish the dam. Two months later, Leita Slayton, Darold and Loretta Hanson and Schwert Farms filed a similar suit, claiming that stoppage of the project had led to "loss of jobs, tax revenues, and profits," and that the lack of flood protection "hurt property values and left crops unprotected."[20] U.S. District Judge Barbara Crabb dismissed the suits in December 1988, but stated that if residents "were to show that the Corps acted improperly, they might be entitled to have the Corps redetermine whether the project should be completed." Pat Driscoll thus redirected his efforts and filed another suit in December 1989, asking the Corps sell acquired land back to the landholders if it could not finish the dam.[21] In September 1990, U.S. District Judge John C. Shabaz dismissed the suit, stating that because Congress had not provided funds to the Corps for the dam, the Corps could not be obligated to complete it.[22]

With no solution forthcoming, La Farge residents and the St. Paul District continued to wait. Some of the land itself, however, was still in use. The St. Paul District leased the maintenance building to the town of Stark, Wisconsin, and more than a thousand acres of land to nearby farmers. In addition, the Corps allowed some events to occur in the vicinity, including annual dog training clinics by the Blackhawk Retrievers Club and a couple of gatherings by the Rainbow Family, a group promoting alternative lifestyles.[23] A final resolution of the project was still necessary.

In 1991, Governor Tommy G. Thompson of Wisconsin asked the people in the Kickapoo River Valley to study the problem and devise a solution. Assisted by Alan Anderson, an economic development specialist with the University of Wisconsin-Extension, the residents developed a proposal for the government to transfer the disputed 8,500 acres of land to the state which would then have a local board administer it as public land. In addition, the locals asked the St. Paul District to complete improvements to State Highway 131, a road the Corps was supposed to have relocated after the dam was constructed. Thompson, stating that the plan went "far towards putting this twenty-five year source of pain and conflict behind us all," asked Gunderson to usher it through Congress.[24]

In June 1994, Gunderson and U.S. Representative Thomas Petri (R-Wisconsin), together with U.S. Senators Russell D. Feingold (D-Wisconsin) and Herbert H. Kohl (D-Wisconsin) introduced legislation implementing the proposal. It stated the land would be transferred to the state of Wisconsin and designated as the Kickapoo Valley State Reserve. It also set up a local citizen's board to manage the land and provided $17 million to complete the road construction and to develop recreational features. The law also provided for a part of the 8,500 acres to be given to the Ho-Chunk Indian Nation, which resided in the area. Since the early 1970s, numerous surveys in the Kickapoo River Valley had uncovered hundreds of archeological sites in the area. When Alan Anderson discovered this in the process of developing the transfer proposal, he contacted the Ho-Chunk to determine the tribe's view of these historic and cultural resources. Two Ho-Chunk leaders, Joann Jones and Chloris Lowe, subsequently asked the federal government give all 8,500 acres to the Ho-Chunk. The Water Resources Development Act of 1996 stipulated that no more than 1,200 acres be given to the tribe and stated that negotiations over the final amount had to be concluded with the Ho-Chunk before the State of Wisconsin could receive its land.[25]

For several months, the Corps and state representatives negotiated with the tribe. In October 1997, the two sides agreed the tribe would take 1,200 acres – 840 acres south of Wildcat Mountain State Park and 360 acres near Black Hawk Rock in the southern section of the reserve.[26] After this land reverted to the Ho-Chunk, the remaining acreage would go to the State of Wisconsin to be governed by the Kickapoo Reserve Management Board. The board promised not only to preserve the unique environmental characteristics of the valley but also to promote its use "in a manner that encourages an appreciation and advocacy of a natural area." Kickapoogians hoped that increased tourism would arise from this settlement and that the natural reserve would mitigate future flooding.[27]

Meanwhile, the St. Paul District used the $17 million provided in the law to improve State Highway 131 and to clean up some environmental hazards. The district filled in the concrete intake tower, capped numerous wells, extricated contaminated soil from old dumping sites and conducted real estate surveys. When these necessary functions were completed, the district transferred the deeds to the land to the state and the Department of the Interior. Except for the ongoing construction on State Highway 131, the Corps no longer had a presence at La Farge.[28]

The unfinished dam remained at the site, a symbol, according to former district historian John Anfinson, of the impact of NEPA. Anfinson and others did not see the incomplete dam as a Corps' failure; instead, it merely represented how NEPA had affected the Corps' civil works program. Had the project been constructed before the passage of the act, nothing could have been done to stop the destruction of endangered plants, scenic beauty and archeological remains. After NEPA became law, it was no longer appropriate for the Corps to build without any regard for environmental effects and the project was stopped. As Anfinson related, "The Corps did an excellent job of building that project and working on that project and doing what it was supposed to do. It couldn't do anything about NEPA being passed and implemented," except adapt itself to the new regulations.[29] Because of controversies like La Farge, it became increasingly clear to the Corps that such adaptation was both necessary and desirable.

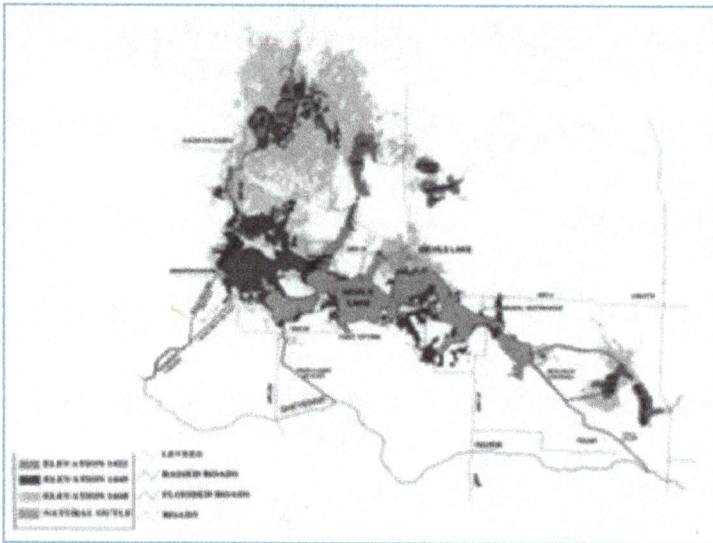

Devils Lake: Map of Devils Lake, North Dakota, and the vicinity. (Map courtesy of St. Paul District, Corps of Engineers)

Devils Lake, North Dakota

Although the La Farge project ultimately reached a reasonable and acceptable solution for all sides, such an answer remained elusive for the St. Paul District and the residents of Devils Lake, North Dakota. Perhaps no other project illustrated the difficulties that could result when congressional delegations from different states pursued opposing solutions to the same problem, and perhaps no other project presented as many interested parties – federal, state, local and international – all clamoring for what they thought was best for Devils Lake. Whereas most flood control situations occurred on rivers, Devils Lake was a closed-basin lake with unpredictable water levels. As the lake continued to rise and inundate property in the 1990s, Devils Lake residents pushed for the St. Paul District to build an outlet into the Red River of the North. This proposal met neither legal nor Corps' standards and caused an outcry from various other "publics," including the Canadian government whose officials claimed that it would dump damaging levels of saline into the Red River, which ultimately flowed into Canada; the Spirit Lake Tribe, which believed that the water was sacred and should not be manipulated; and environmentalists, who believed that the adverse environmental effects of an outlet exceeded its benefits. Caught in the middle of these various perceptions, the Corps struggled to find a solution that would meet the different concerns and still be within its own rigid justification guidelines.

Devils Lake: A flood control diversion channel constructed by the North Dakota State Water Commission in the northeastern part of the Devils Lake watershed. (Photo by Lyle Nickly, courtesy of St. Paul District, Corps of Engineers)

Devils Lake, described by North Dakota journalist Peter Salter as "a wooded jewel in [the] middle of the prairie,"[30] lies at the extremity of a closed subbasin of the Red River of the North Basin in north central North Dakota. Unlike most lakes, the waterway has no natural outlet unless its water level reaches approximately 1,457 feet above mean sea level, whereupon it spills into the Sheyenne River.[31] Surrounded by the communities of Devils Lake, Minnewaukan, Fort Totten and the Spirit Lake Indian Reservation, the lake has been an important economic resource in the area for many years, bringing in approximately $50 million annually from recreation.[32] Because of climatic swings, water levels have traditionally fluctuated between rising and falling cycles. Around 1860, the lake entered a falling phase that dropped the water level from 1,438 feet to 1,402 feet.[33] The lake then shifted into a rising cycle that eventually resulted in flooding. In 1979, lake levels reached 1,426 feet, wiping out railroad bridges and culverts.[34] The lake continued to rise, leading Congress to authorize the Corps in 1983 to conduct studies to determine the best way to protect communities from the rising water. Many residents believed the only solution was to provide a man-made outlet for the water. "It is impossible to manage the water level in the lake without an outlet," an editorial in a local newspaper suggested.[35] Jack Zaleski, managing editor of the Devils Lake *Journal*, agreed. "The cost of no outlet. . .will, in the long run, be very expensive," he stated.[36]

St. Paul District leaders did not necessarily oppose construction of an outlet but explained it would not be feasible until the lake rose an additional seven feet.[37] Colonel Edward Rapp, district engineer from 1982 to 1985, cautioned community members to consider rising lake levels in their long-term context: "In a very real sense, mother nature owns all that property below the natural outlet at 1,457 feet." Rapp declared that floodplain management was necessary no matter what other flood control solutions were implemented and committed the district to a thorough investigation of the problem, no matter how long it took. "You should not be panicked into a quick fix which could be bad in the future," he counseled the community.[38] In the meantime, the Corps installed levees to protect the City of Devils Lake to a level of 1,440 feet, a project that was completed in 1987.[39]

Part of the reason for the district's reluctance to place an outlet in the lake was the complicated nature of a conduit. William Spychalla, Devils Lake project manager, explained there were several obstacles the district needed to overcome before an outlet could be constructed. For one thing, the outlet was embroiled in a larger debate over the Garrison Diversion reclamation project.[40] Authorized in legislation passed by Congress on August 5, 1965, the Garrison Diversion Unit would have provided water to eastern North Dakota from the eastern end of Lake Sakakawea, a reservoir first formed by the construction of Garrison Dam in the late 1940s. The original authorization of the unit called for the diversion of Missouri River water to Devils Lake to reduce its high salinity, while also recommending the discharge of Devils Lake water into the Sheyenne River, which drains into the Red River, thereby tying an inlet and an outlet together. In 1974, the Bureau of Reclamation abandoned this plan because of adverse effects it would have on the water quality of the Sheyenne and Red rivers, but the idea continued to be debated. Some entities, including Canada and the state of Minnesota, objected to the strategy because diversions would allegedly transfer water and biota from the Missouri River Basin to the Red River, which ran into Canada, in violation of the 1909 Boundary Waters Treaty between Canada and the United States.[41]

Because of public clamor for an outlet, the St. Paul District studied the possibilities and concluded in a 1988 draft feasibility report that an outlet could be constructed at the western end of Devils Lake. The report also proposed studies on regulating upper basin drainage areas, evacuating low-lying structures and regulating lakeshore development. That summer, however, North Dakota and other Midwestern states entered a period of severe drought which dropped the lake from its 1987 high of 1,428 feet to 1,422 feet by 1993, prompting fears of fish kills and other recreational and environmental harm from the high salinity of the remaining water. The Corps thus examined how to solve both high- and low-water problems in the lake. In 1990, Congress appropriated funds for a reconnaissance study for a complete lake management plan conducted by the Corps and the Bureau of Reclamation, and, in February 1992, a draft report tentatively found that both an outlet and an inlet were economically feasible.[42] Some officials within the St. Paul District were not comfortable with this recommendation. Colonel Richard W. Craig, district engineer from 1991 to 1993, believed the district acted too quickly in recommending feasibility. "I'm not sure it's in the best interests of the Corps for there to be a Devils Lake project," he stated in 1993. The ultimate solutions, he believed, were more policy-oriented than technology-oriented.[43]

Conditions again changed in the summer of 1993, when wet conditions drastically elevated water levels. Between June and November, the lake rose five feet to 1,427 feet, and its expansion continued. In 1991, the edge of the lake was approximately six miles away from the City of Minnewaukan; but by 1995, water was lapping at the community's sewage lagoon. Hence, the Corps implemented emergency flood

Devils Lake

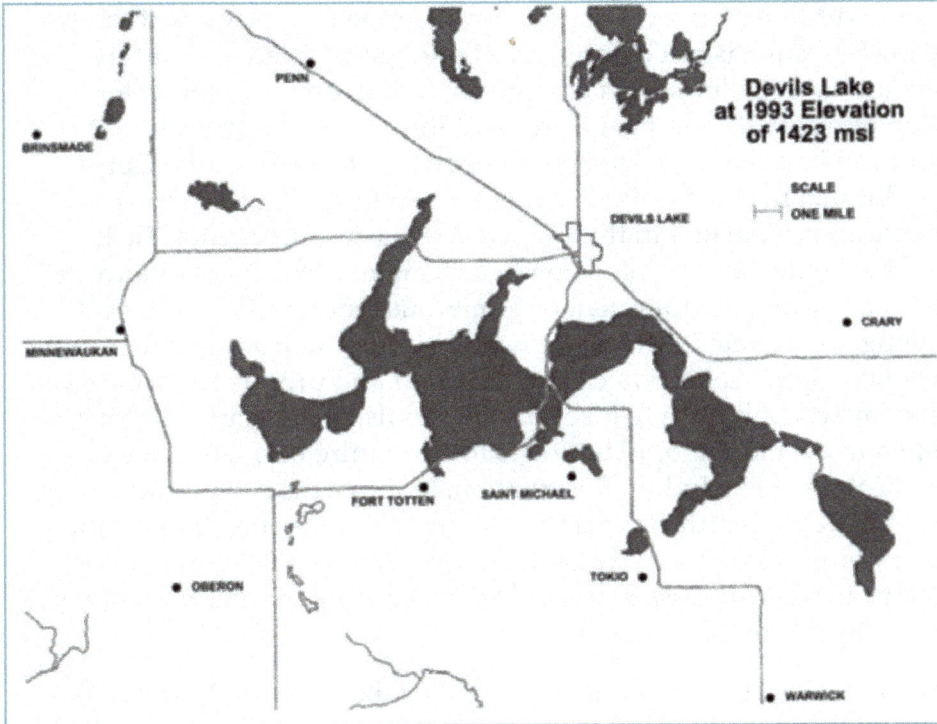

Devils Lake
at 1993 Elevation
of 1423 msl

SCALE
ONE MILE

PENN

BRINSMADE

DEVILS LAKE

CRARY

MINNEWAUKAN

FORT TOTTEN   SAINT MICHAEL

OBERON

TOKIO

WARWICK

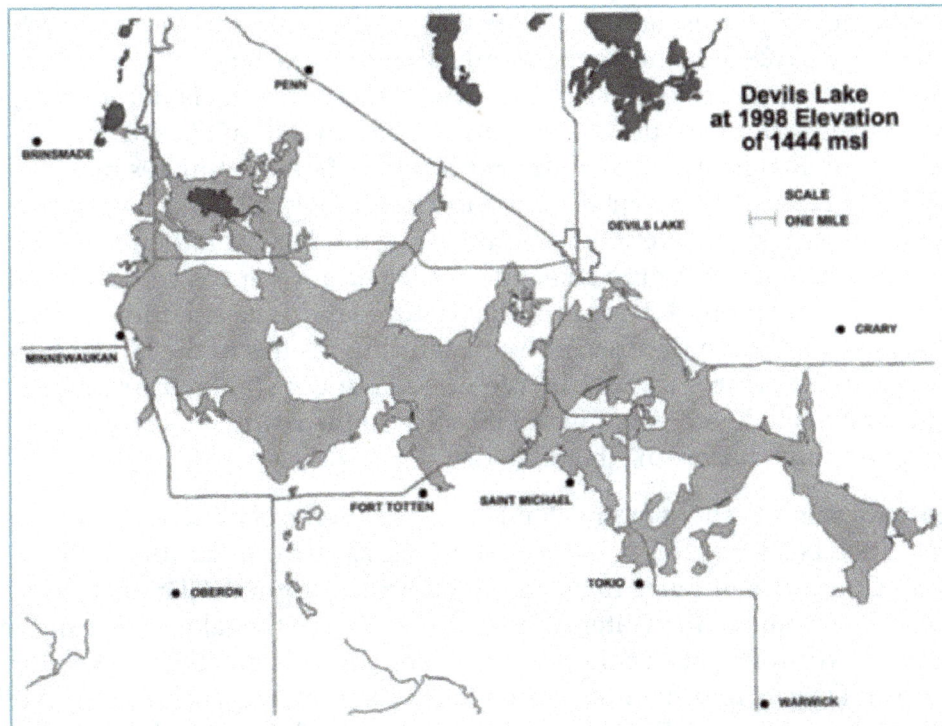

Devils Lake
at 1998 Elevation
of 1444 msl

SCALE
ONE MILE

PENN

BRINSMADE

DEVILS LAKE

CRARY

MINNEWAUKAN

FORT TOTTEN   SAINT MICHAEL

OBERON

TOKIO

WARWICK

Two maps of Devils Lake, North Dakota, show the dramatic expansion of the water in the 1990s. (Maps courtesy of North Dakota Department of Natural Resources)

measures in coordination with other federal, state and local agencies to protect lakeside communities from the water's rapid expansion, including the construction of a protective berm around Minnewaukan's lagoon.[44] When the lake continued to rise in 1994 and 1995, the St. Paul District completed a contingency plan that outlined measures the district could take, including an emergency outlet, upper basin water management, relocation of residents and businesses and infrastructure protection.[45] In June 1996, the City of Devils Lake requested emergency assistance from the Corps to raise its levees an additional five feet (later extended to ten feet), and the Corps complied.[46] The district also participated in the Devils Lake Basin Interagency Task Force formed in 1995. This organization, according to chairman Michael J. Armstrong, used "the coordinated activity and commitment of numerous federal, state and local government entities along with elected officials, private citizens, environmental groups and representation from the Spirit Lake Sioux Tribe" to "find and propose intermediate solutions to reduce the impacts of high lake levels in the Devils Lake Basin." By 1997, the task force had helped to develop floodplain maps for the entire basin, to relocate twenty-one homes on the Spirit Lake Indian Reservation, to move the sewage lagoon in Minnewaukan, to create with the North Dakota State Water Commission 30 thousand acre-feet of upper basin storage under the Available Storage Acreage Program and to implement agricultural programs to assist farmers who had lost money from flooding or from the Available Storage Acreage Program.[47]

Despite the best efforts of the district and the task force, the lake continued to rise, causing alarm for those living around it. In 1996, the lake sat at 1,438 feet and engulfed approximately 77 thousand acres. This was a significant increase from 1993, when the lake rested at 1,428 feet and covered only 45 thousand acres. As the water continued to spread, seventy-eight homes in the area qualified for the Federal Emergency Management Administration's flood insurance buyout, while the Spirit Lake Nation moved more than fifty homes on the reservation. Some estimates placed flood damages at $70 million.[48] Just as important were the psychological effects. Bobby Michels, a lifetime Devils Lake resident, farmed the same land as his father. In 1993, his property was a good distance from the lake; but in 1996, the water rested only a mile from his house after swallowing 150 acres of his pasture land. The situation convinced him to sell his farm and leave the area, notwithstanding his ties to the land. "I don't have any qualms about leaving," he stated. "We've been under so much stress here." John Grann, a farmer who had lost 7,000 of his 8,000 acres to the rising water, agreed. "It's pretty hard to have any optimism," he related.[49]

Faced with this situation, many Devils Lake residents clamored again for a man-made outlet, believing this solution would alleviate the situation. As Tim Heisler, Ramsey County emergency management director, argued, "There's only one solution, getting rid of some of the water. We need to stabilize the lake."[50] Acting on this public sentiment, North Dakota's congressional delegation, consisting of Senators Kent Conrad and Byron Dorgan and Representative Earl Pomeroy, requested in May 1996 that the St. Paul District prepare an Emergency Outlet Plan, and the district complied, issuing the report in August 1996. This plan, prepared under the direction of Thomas Raster, a civil engineer for the district, delineated the best place for an outlet as the West Bay of Devils Lake, where water would be pumped through Twin Lakes and the Fort Totten Indian

Reservation until it reached a natural divide and flowed downhill to the Sheyenne River. The report also indicated that had an outlet been in place since 1985, it would have only lowered the lake's level by one foot because of pumping capacities, high salinity concerns and Sheyenne River water levels. In addition, the same outlet concerns raised in the 1980s still existed: Canada, Minnesota, environmental organizations and citizens living along the Sheyenne River did not want Devils Lake water in their river, whether because of water transfer issues or because of fears that an outlet would exacerbate Sheyenne River flooding. Likewise, the Corps needed permission from the Spirit Lake Nation before outlet construction could begin since the unit would run across its reservation.[51]

Aware of these concerns, the federal government still decided to take action. In March 1997, President Bill Clinton sent a supplemental disaster aid bill to Congress that included $32.5 million to complete the design of an emergency outlet.[52] Canada immediately registered its objections. Lloyd Axworthy, Canadian minister of foreign affairs, told the Winnipeg *Free Press* that Canada continued to oppose "any interbasin transfers of water as these may cause serious biota problems and degrade water quality in other basins." Manitoba Premier Gary Filmon explained that Canada could not "support actions that will have adverse and possibly disastrous consequences for Manitoba and Canada." Filmon urged Axworthy "to push every diplomatic button necessary to block the U.S. congressional proposal for the emergency outlet."[53]

Devils Lake: A house surrounded by the rising water shows the predicament faced by many Devils Lake, North Dakota, residents. (Photo courtesy of the North Dakota State Water Commission)

This was not the first time the Corps clashed with Canada over a flood control project. In the 1970s and 1980s, the Corps examined ways to protect the city of Minot, North Dakota, from Souris River floods. The Souris River begins in Saskatchewan, flowing south for 217 miles before entering the United States and North Dakota. The river continues in a southeasterly direction through Minot to Velva, North Dakota, where it turns to flow north back into Canada, eventually joining the Assiniboine River in Manitoba, draining a 24,800-square-mile basin. Severe flooding in 1969 and 1970 pushed the Corps to develop a flood control plan for Minot; and in 1970, Congress authorized a two-pronged approach: modifying and straightening the channel and constructing a dam and reservoir at Burlington. Environmental groups and the U.S. Fish and Wildlife Service protested these proposals, especially since the resulting reservoir would periodically inundate the Upper Souris National Wildlife Refuge. Regardless, the channel modification plan proceeded on schedule and was completed in 1979. But the furor over the dam caused its deferment in 1982 in favor of a four-foot raise of Lake Darling Dam, a unit constructed in northern North Dakota by the Fish and Wildlife Service in the 1930s for migratory waterfowl management.[54]

Some groups protested the Lake Darling decision, leading local interests to begin discussions with Canada about other solutions. At the time, Canadians were developing plans for two dams in Saskatchewan to provide increased power development in the area. In the late 1980s, the Corps and Canadian officials reached an agreement whereby the United States would purchase 400,000 acre-feet of flood storage in the Canadian reservoirs, thereby providing Minot and other North Dakota communities with protection against a hundred- year flood event. Under the leadership of Louis E. Kowalski, chief of the St. Paul District's Planning Division from 1979 to 1996, the Corps successfully coordinated the agreement with Canada. Both dams, known as Rafferty and Alameda, were completed by the mid-1990s, giving North Dakota some measure of flood protection from the Souris River.[55] In this case, interaction with the Canadians resulted in a favorable outcome.

But cooperation between Canada and the United States on the Devils Lake issue was not as forthcoming. In June 1997, Congress, ignoring Canadian opposition to a Devils Lake outlet, passed a bill authorizing the expenditure of $5 million by the Corps for preconstruction engineering and design on an emergency outlet, as well as the preparation of an Environmental Impact Statement, or EIS.[56] The driving forces behind the bill included Senators Conrad and Dorgan, both of whom believed the outlet was the best alternative. Because of their efforts, Congress also appropriated $5 million in October for the initial building stages, requiring, however, that before any construction began, the Corps show that an emergency truly existed, that the outlet was technically sound, that it had a favorable benefit-cost ratio, that it would comply with NEPA and that it would not violate the Boundary Waters Treaty Act of 1909. Conrad and Dorgan also had to agree to shelve any plans for an inlet into Devils Lake, mainly because of the opposition of Senator Christopher Bond (R-Missouri), who publicly objected to the mixing of water between watersheds but privately worried that an inlet supplied with Missouri River water would reduce reservoir releases for commercial barge traffic on the river, thereby adversely affecting an economic segment of the State of Missouri.[57] Even with this funding, the Corps estimated it would take at least thirty months to construct the outlet, now designed to be a 14-mile-long pipeline running from the west end of Devils Lake along Peterson Coulee to the Sheyenne River.[58]

Devils Lake: Levee construction in 1998 on a southern section of the project adjacent to North Dakota Highway 57. (Photo courtesy of St. Paul District, Corps of Engineers)

As the Corps began the studies mandated by Congress, it also continued to investigate other ways of controlling the flooding, especially since the lake had risen in July 1997 to 1,443 feet. Not only were buildings threatened but essential roads and state parks faced damage as well. In the spring of 1997, Highways 20 and 57, which provide access to the south side of Devils Lake and the Spirit Lake Reservation, were flooded, necessitating road elevation measures, while four state parks, including Narrows and Grahams Island state parks, experienced flooding as well. Faced with these problems, the Corps worked with other agencies, including the North Dakota

State Water Commission and the Fish and Wildlife Service, to implement two other solutions to the problem: basin-wide water management and infrastructure protection. Together with the emergency outlet proposal, these constituted a "three-legged stool" approach to the problem, with each "leg" dependent to some degree on the others. The water management strategy built on the Available Storage Acreage Program started by the North Dakota State Water Commission and the Devils Lake Basin Interagency Task Force in 1995, expanding the number of acres used for upper-basin storage to 75,000 acres. Meanwhile, the Fish and Wildlife Service identified thirty-six projects in the Devils Lake area that had the potential to store 12,774 acre-feet of water permanently and completed eight of them in 1996. It also called for wetland restoration in the area. As part of the infrastructure protection "leg," the Corps and the state elevated seventeen roadbeds around Devils Lake in 1997 and relocated some pipes and pumps in the Ramsey County sewer system. The St. Paul District's Devils Lake levee raise project fit into the infrastructure protection category as well.[59] As Colonel John M. Wonsik, district engineer from 1995 to 1998, related in January 1998, balancing environmental concerns with the protection of the surrounding communities had made Devils Lake "a major challenge for the district."[60]

The district received help from other Corps' entities as mitigation measures continued. The Institute for Water Resources prepared a report to Congress explaining whether or not an emergency outlet met the required criteria, while staff at the Corps' headquarters assisted the district on two other issues: exploring the possibility of waiving the normal NEPA process in order to expedite the outlet's construction and consulting with Canada through the International Joint Commission, or IJC, established by the Boundary Waters Treaty of 1909 to deal with water quality matters affecting both the United States and Canada.[61] A decision on whether or not to expedite the NEPA process became more critical in October 1997 after a hearing before the Senate Committee on Environment and Public Works. In that hearing, Senators Conrad and Dorgan, Representative Pomeroy and North Dakota Governor Ed Schafer all pleaded for an accelerated process; while Gary Pearson, vice president of the Dakota Prairie Audubon Society, strongly counseled against such a waiver.[62] On December 19, the St. Paul District met with John H. Zirschky, Acting Assistant Secretary of the Army of Civil Works; to discuss an expedited schedule, but after consultation with the Council on Environmental Quality, the overseer of NEPA compliance, Zirschky decided the district should "comply fully with the NEPA by completing the Environmental Impact Statement and Record of Decision using a normal NEPA process." Zirschky counseled the district to try to complete the work by December 1999 to ensure a construction starting date in spring 2000.[63]

At the same time, consultations occurred among Corps' headquarters, the IJC and the Department of State over Canada's concerns with the emergency outlet. In October 1997, Raymond Chrétien, Canadian ambassador to the United States, reiterated his country's concern that "interbasin transfers have the potential to seriously damage Canadian waters and Manitoba's multimillion dollar fishery."[64] In March 1998, Zirschky asked the State Department to consult with the IJC about Devils Lake. Although initial reports indicated the outlet would have only a minimal effect on water quality once it reached the Canadian border, the Corps still committed itself to additional hydrologic, hydraulic and water quality modeling of the border water.[65]

But as the studies and consultations extended into 1999, problems developed with the Peterson Coulee outlet route. For one thing, the Spirit Lake Nation withdrew its support of the course, stating that "the proposed Western Emergency Outlet would violate a majority of the sacred sites of the Spirit Lake Nation without regard to tribal and Federal laws to protect these culturally sensitive areas."[66] For another, EIS study numbers indicated that the Peterson Coulee route did not have a favorable benefit-cost ratio. Finally, it seemed that Peterson Coulee could not meet water quality standards on both the Sheyenne and Red rivers unless fresher water could be brought into the outlet from the north. Although it was feasible to divert water from northwestern bodies such as Pelican Lake to Peterson Coulee, it would escalate project costs to between $75 and $110 million, making it even more difficult to justify the project economically. Because of these concerns, the St. Paul District examined other options, including diverting water from the eastern end of Devils Lake into the Stump Lakes. Since the Stump Lakes were within the Devils Lake basin, there would be no transfer of water and biota from one watershed to another. However, dumping water in the lakes would adversely affect a fish and wildlife refuge in the area. The need to examine these other alternatives delayed completion of the EIS.[67]

The lake rose to 1,447 feet in 1999. After discussions with Major General Russell L. Fuhrman, director of civil works for the Corps; Joseph Westphal, Assistant Secretary of the Army for Civil Works; and Conrad, Dorgan and Pomeroy, Major General Phillip R. Anderson, the Mississippi Valley Division commander appointed a team in May 1999 composed of division and district employees to decide what conditions would warrant the construction of the emergency outlet.[68] When the team issued its report in June, it concluded that none of the outlet plans had a favorable benefit-cost ratio. However, it also determined that if an outlet operated when the lake reached 1,454 feet, it "would have substantially lower adverse effects than a natural overflow" and could "protect the population around the basin at a certain elevation." It, therefore, recommended that construction of an outlet commence if the lake reached 1,453 feet, or six feet more than its current level.[69] Based on this report, Anderson informed Conrad, Dorgan, Pomeroy and Governor Schafer that "while I understand your concern and frustration in finding a timely remedy for the rising lake, I have not reached a conclusion that an outlet is a necessary or appropriate solution to the recent rise of water in Devils Lake."[70]

Upon hearing the report's recommendations and Anderson's conclusions, proponents of the outlet were infuriated. "My skin prickled when I read the report," Schafer related before suggesting that state workers might start an outlet "and see if anybody stops us." Schafer could not understand the Corps' benefit-cost analysis. "To me, this is like fourthgrade math," he declared. "It costs $100 million to build an outlet. It costs us $25 million in damages every time the lake rises a foot. So if they let it go up another six feet, that's $150 million in damages."[71] Conrad agreed. "The cost/benefit ratio is totally flawed," he stated. "The economic analysis of the Corps is completely detached from reality."[72] Residents living within striking distance of the lake's lapping waters were even more livid. "I wish powerful lobbyists could experience the anguish we in Devils

Lake feel whenever heavy rains or another winter storm further raises the level," one Devils Laker wrote. "Delaying actions of environmental organizations, downstream interests, and ... [the] Mississippi Valley Division have caused clinical depression among many of our citizens."[73] Others were not so refined in their expressions; some citizens began wearing T-shirts emblazoned with the phrase "Six More Feet My Ass."[74]

One cause of the outcry was that critics either did not understand or did not agree with the method the Corps used to calculate the benefit-cost ratio. When deciding on a flood control project on a river, the Corps looked at the probabilities of occurrence of a hundred- or five hundred-year flood event and then calculated the benefits and costs based on those risks. Applying this method to Devils Lake caused problems because Corps' data indicated that the lake had not flooded – or exceeded 1,457 feet msl – for hundreds of years. Since the probability of the lake reaching this elevation was unlikely, the project had a low benefit-cost ratio. A scenario-based approach recognizing that problems were occurring even though the lake was below 1,457 feet would produce a high benefit-cost ratio, but the rigidity of Corps' guidelines for flood control projects did not allow the application of such a scenario in its analyses.[75] Understandably, Devils Lakers could not comprehend why the Corps refused to abandon its guidelines, especially since the waterbody was a lake and not a river. But the Corps believed it had to maintain its standards, especially since Congress had stipulated when making its Devils Lake appropriation that the Corps use its normal economic evaluation principles and guidelines when analyzing benefits and costs. In the words of Colonel James T. Scott, district engineer from 1993 to 1995, "When you analyze [the lake] with those river methods, you find that there's no project authorized ... , but we can't cut through the politics, the red tape associated with our standard system."[76]

The district, then, faced a major dilemma. As Colonel William J. Breyfogle, who served as district engineer in St. Paul for six months in 1998, explained, on the one hand, studies showed the inadequacy of an outlet and its lack of economic viability because of the difficulty of predicting whether or not the lake would continue to rise. On the other hand, North Dakota's congressional delegation and residents in the area kept pushing for an outlet, believing it was the region's only hope. "I think that's why you didn't really see us doing anything besides just sitting back and studying it," Breyfogle commented, "because the powers in USACE knew that it was a losing battle."[77]

No matter what justification the Corps used for shelving the outlet, Conrad, Dorgan and others continued to fight for it. The situation reached a head in July 1999, when Conrad, frustrated by Anderson's outlet position, told the division leader that he was "done meeting with [the Corps] because they're not serious about this and the people of Devils Lake deserve better." After this stormy meeting, Conrad requested that all Senate business affecting the Corps, including promotions, be halted, and also, in the company of Dorgan and Pomeroy, met several times with White House Chief of Staff John Podesta, Joseph Westphal and other Clinton Administration officials to underscore the importance of an outlet. The pressure tactics worked, as Corps' headquarters assumed responsibility for Devils Lake flood control in July 1999, and in October, overruled Anderson's earlier decision by announcing the Corps would resume design and engineering work on the outlet.[78] When environmental groups heard about the

resumption, it was their turn to criticize the Corps. "The politicians have the Corps buffaloed on this one," remarked Gary Pearson of the Audubon Society. "At this point, the science has all been thrown out the window."[79] Many environmentalists believed the ultimate solution to the problem was better management of the floodplain, evacuation of those residing in the lake's bed and a restoration of wetlands in the area. In fact, using North Dakota State Water Commission documents from the 1950s and 1960s, environmentalists claimed that wetland drainage was the chief culprit of the rising lake. When they remarked that people should have known better than to settle in the lake bed, however, they were accused of being unsympathetic to the plight of Devils Lakers.[80]

Tensions between the different groups mounted as the lake steadily rose. Reaching an all-time high of 1,448 feet in August 2001, the lake persisted in creating problems. The St. Paul District, meanwhile, maintained its commitment to examining upper basin water storage and infrastructure protection. The district completed the levee raises around Devils Lake in 2001, receiving a 2001 Chief of Engineers Design and Environmental Merit Award for the project.[81] The district also continued with the EIS and outlet studies, but, because of the environmental and economic difficulties with the Peterson Coulee and Stump Lakes outlets, it began focusing on a Pelican Lake outlet, whereby fresh water coming into Devils Lake from the west would be diverted south into the Sheyenne (see map of Devils Lake and the vicinity). A draft EIS came out in February 2002; and, in February 2003, Chief of Engineers Lieutenant General Robert B. Flowers decided the outlet to Pelican Lake was the best course to pursue.[82]

Flooding at Devils Lake was one of the most complex and controversial problems the St. Paul District attempted to solve in the last quarter of the twentieth century. Along with the environmental issues that it raised about interbasin transfers, it also saw the Corps working and negotiating with several different entities, all of which had their own beliefs about what was best for Devils Lake. In addition, the Devils Lake project raised several questions about the process of deciding how and when flood projects are justified. Should a different economic standard exist for closed-basin lakes than for rivers? Is the benefit-cost ratio the best way to determine a project's economic viability? Should projects be allowed to continue because of political pressure when they do not meet environmental and economic standards? Who would stop them if the political pressure became too strong? The Corps would continue to wrestle with these questions. As David Loss, who assumed management of the project in 2000, related, Devils Lake showed the Corps that "we need to remain objective, look at the big picture, and understand that we are doing what is best for the federal interest" no matter what criticisms or pressures are levied.[83] Even then, the chances of pleasing all sides are slim.

Grand Forks, North Dakota/East Grand Forks, Minnesota

At the same time, the St. Paul District dealt with Devils Lake, it was also deepening its involvement in a flood control project on the Red River at Grand Forks, North Dakota, and East Grand Forks, Minnesota. As with Devils Lake, this project contained elements of controversy, especially since the Corps had initial difficulties in obtaining public support and cooperation. Unlike Devils Lake, however, a major catastrophe, the 1997 flood, helped to convince residents of both Grand Forks and East Grand Forks that the Corps' flood control plan was necessary. An examination of the project also shows some of the problems that arose from new cost-sharing measures that were delineated in the Water Resources Development Act of 1986.

The cities of Grand Forks and East Grand Forks rest in the heart of the Red River Valley, a predominantly agricultural region located approximately 70 miles south of the Canadian border. Characterized by its severe winters, the basin, situated in a flat glacial plain that allows water to spread in every direction, continually experienced spring flooding from the Red River, which forms near the cities of Wahpeton, North Dakota, and Breckenridge, Minnesota, and runs north for 400 miles before draining into Lake Winnipeg in Canada. Throughout the 1800s and 1900s, the Red flooded periodically, but severe floods became more frequent in the 1960s and 1970s. Flooding was exacerbated by the fact that spring snowmelt poured into the southern portions of the waterway and flowed north into still-frozen reaches of the river, creating ice jams that pushed the river from its banks and into the surrounding communities and farmland.[84]

Ice Jam on the Root River, 1982: Ice jams are one cause of frequent floods in the shallow river valleys of northwest Minnesota and northeast North Dakota. (Photo by Lyle Nicklay, courtesy of St. Paul District, Corps of Engineers)

In the spring of 1978, the river crested only a foot-and-a-half below the top of emergency levees in Grand Forks, intensifying an existing debate over the effects of agricultural diking on flooding. Beginning in 1975, farmers south of Oslo, Minnesota, had constructed dikes to protect

91

their crops from flooding. After the dikes successfully stopped the water, farmers constructed 38 more miles on the Minnesota side and 10 miles on the North Dakota side, providing them with protection against ten and fifteen-year flood levels. Following the 1978 flood, however, residents of Grand Forks charged that the more numerous Minnesota dikes had pushed water to the North Dakota side and called for their removal. The St. Paul District investigated the situation, and, according to Peter Fischer, a district hydrologist, concluded there was a "potential [for] adverse impacts if [farm] levee construction were to continue uncontrolled." The Corps instructed farmers to remove some of their dikes, but agriculturists refused to comply, stating the structures would remain until the state or the federal government provided sufficient flood protection. In reply, the Corps threatened legal action.[85]

Before anything could happen, the worst flooding since 1897 hit Grand Forks and East Grand Forks in the spring of 1979 and easily overtopped the farm dikes. The Red River crested at nearly 49 feet, more than 20 feet above flood stage, sending 82,000 cubic feet per second of water through its channel at Grand Forks. Almost before the water receded, politicians and citizens called for solutions to the flooding problems and looked to the Corps for answers.[86] U.S. Representative Arlan Stangeland (R-Minnesota) convinced the House Committee on Public Works and Transportation to hold a hearing in East Grand Forks on the 1979 floods and told his constituents that he could "no longer tolerate the lackadaisical attitude of the bureaucrats in Washington" about Grand Forks/East Grand Forks flooding.[87]

Because of Stangeland's influence, the St. Paul District examined more closely flood control in East Grand Forks. Actually, the district's authorization to perform studies on the Red River at East Grand Forks issued from the Flood Control Acts of 1948 and 1950. Following the passage of these laws, the district had prepared flood control plans but could not get the community to agree to local cooperation until 1975. After several years of analysis under the leadership of Martin McCleery, project manager, the district rejected any channel modification and dam and reservoir solutions in the early 1980s and tentatively proposed building earthen levees and concrete floodwalls in East Grand Forks at a cost of between $10.7 and $21.6 million to the federal government and between $9.8 and $11.6 million to the city. In part because of the cost and in part because the main plan the Corps favored would mean the relocation of numerous homes and businesses, the reaction of East Grand Forks residents to the proposal was, in the words of one newspaper account, "colder than dike patrol duty at 2 a.m. on a late March morning." In order to give itself time to explore its options, the city declared it would take a few years to make a final decision as to whether or not to implement the Corps' plan. In December 1986, the Corps completed a general design memorandum, which proposed placing a flood barrier around part of the city, constructing levees, floodwalls, closure structures and interior drainage facilities within the city, and evacuating residences and businesses that remained unprotected. But in July 1988, the city decided to withdraw its support for the project because of high economic and social costs. One month later, the project was classified as inactive.[88]

East Grand Forks' rejection of the flood control project highlighted some of the effects of new cost-sharing requirements implemented by the federal government in the Water Resources Development Act of 1986. These provisions stipulated that non-federal interests would have to pay from twenty-five to fifty percent of a flood control project's cost and fifty percent of any feasibility study undertaken by the Corps. In addition, local sponsors were responsible for real estate acquisition and relocation of businesses and residences.[89]

Since many buildings in East Grand Forks required moving, this cost, coupled with the other required funds, made the project too expensive for East Grand Forks. Although other factors were involved, cost-sharing measures ultimately convinced the city that federal flood control was too expensive and not worth the trouble. According to Colonel Kenneth Kasprisin, East Grand Forks was not alone. The problem with cost-sharing, he explained was "that there are a lot of communities that cannot pay; they don't have the money to pay." More and more, Kasprisin argued, the Corps would have to deal with its responsibilities to those communities that did not have the necessary funds.[90]

Meanwhile, the City of Grand Forks faced problems because the Corps could not find a project that met its economic feasibility guidelines. In the 1950s, the Corps had constructed a permanent levee project, but now no other projects had favorable benefit-cost ratios. "That doesn't mean the city can't protect itself physically," Tom Raster, an engineer for the St. Paul District, explained, "but we had to get a dollar or more back with every dollar we spent there. On Corps' standards, we couldn't do it." Because the district's hands were tied, the city dealt with the problem itself, improving emergency levees along the river and working on an upward channel diversion of the English Coulee. According to Raster, such improvements would protect the city against fifty-year flood levels. "The city, I think, is doing just a fantastic job of self-help, in light of federal limitations," he concluded.[91]

Red River Flooding: North Main Stem, 1997, at U.S. Highway 2 (Kennedy) Bridge. (Photo courtesy of St. Paul District, Corps of Engineers)

In 1985, however, city engineers and leaders in Grand Forks requested assistance from the St. Paul District to develop a more extensive flood control system. In response, the district completed a draft reconnaissance report in April 1991 that concluded a couple of different plans might exist with favorable benefit-cost ratios. Based on this determination, the Corps began feasibility studies of the different proposals in January 1994. But despite city officials' requests for help, the district had to try to heighten public support for flood control in Grand Forks. According to Edward McNally, who served as study manager for the feasibility report, city engineers realized Grand Forks did not have adequate flood protection, but the citizens themselves believed no problem existed. "They had flood fights that they had successfully been able to weather," McNally related, "and they had a spirit that said, 'We can do it again, and we don't need anybody's help.'" In addition, the flood of 1979 was a distant memory. Although flooding occurred in 1989, it did not approach the levels experienced in 1979. The challenge for the district, McNally explained, "was convincing them that the water could get" as high or higher than 1979, "and, in fact, at some point would get that high." Moreover, he continued, " it was in their interest to be proactive," especially if economically viable solutions were available.

As the feasibility study neared completion early in 1997, the public began to accept the Corps' position.[92] But before the study could be issued, nature proved the need for additional flood protection. During the winter of 1996-1997, a record amount of snow fell in the Red River Valley, including Grand Forks, which had an accumulation of 97.7 inches. In February and March, the National Weather Service predicted severe flooding in the Red River Valley. When a blizzard hit the region on April 6, it only added to the problems. Then, warmer temperatures arrived, causing a rapid snowmelt. With meltwater pouring in, the Red River rose to 53 feet at Grand Forks, far above flood level stage and four feet above the 1979 crest. Despite the best efforts of the Corps and the citizens of Grand Forks and East Grand Forks to prepare for the flooding, the water breached dikes and levees, sending torrents of water through the two cities, knocking out power and contaminating water supplies. Nearly everyone in East Grand Forks was forced to evacuate and ninety percent of Grand Forks' 52 thousand citizens had to leave as well, especially after fires broke out in the downtown area, burning eleven buildings. By the time the river crested at 54.3 feet, more than 26 feet above flood stage, water and fire had nearly wiped out both communities.[93]

In the wake of the devastation, citizens in Grand Forks and East Grand Forks clamored for the Corps to provide flood protection. As McNally related, "The issue at that point of [citizens] trying to say that there was not a potential for flooding and that they weren't really at risk ... was pretty much gone."[94] Before the flood hit, the Corps' feasibility study was calling for hundred-year flood protection plan consisting of construction of a ring levee around Grand Forks at a cost of $39 million, with local costs slightly less than $10 million.[95] In order to expedite the construction process, however, the Grand Forks feasibility study was never finalized; instead, planning, engineering and design authority for the East Grand Forks project was reactivated in May 1997, and the authority was expanded to include Grand Forks. As part of the planning, engineering and design process, the St. Paul District prepared a General Reevaluation Report to ascertain the best plans for flood protection in the two communities.[96]

In preparing the draft General Reevaluation Report, completed in August 1998, the Corps examined and rejected several primary strategies for flood protection, including upstream reservoir storage (because of the flat drainage area upstream) and evacuation (because of its social unacceptability). The district also determined that the alternative preferred by the two cities, a split-flow diversion channel, was not cost effective, having a benefit-cost ratio of 0.4. Instead, the Corps decided that a large setback levee and floodwall system along both sides of the river was the most feasible plan, whereby the Corps would build three "rings" of levees around the cities. But because the communities had already seen levees fail in the 1997 flood, they were reluctant to accept the Corps' analysis, and some even believed the district was intentionally skewing the figures against a diversion. To forestall such criticisms, consultants were hired to study the diversion channel, and they reached the same conclusion as the Corps – a diversion could not meet the economic standards and would be twice as expensive as the levees-only plan. The communities accepted these conclusions and, on February 26, 1998, voted to approve the levees-only project, which was estimated to cost $342.7 million, $170.8 million of which was required as the non-federal cost.[97]

Throughout 1998, the Corps worked to finalize its General Reevaluation Report and the EIS under the leadership of Lisa Hedin, project manager, and Edward McNally, technical manager. In doing so, it encountered some opposition from residents of both communities over the placement of the levees. In order to provide the best flood protection, the levees would have to be set back on the riverbank, requiring the removal of residences and other structures. Just as in the 1980s in East Grand Forks, landowners were not pleased with this requirement, but district officials, through a series of public meetings and studies conducted by outside consultants, finally convinced citizens that most of the structures could not be protected and would have to be removed. At the same time, the public's objections forced the Corps to examine other options, and in some cases, the district was able to use innovative alternatives, such as a mechanically stabilized earthwall and an invisible floodwall, to preserve some of the structures.[98]

With the levee placement resolved, the district completed its Final General Reevaluation Report and Environmental Impact Statement in 1999, issuing it less than eighteen months from its conception rather than the normal thirty-two to forty-eight months, in large part because of the diligent work of the project's planning team. This effort was recognized in September 1999, when the district received an Outstanding Planning Achievement Award for Civil Works for the Grand Forks/East Grand Forks General Reevaluation Report and EIS from the deputy commander. The expedited schedule also allowed Congress to authorize the project in an omnibus spending bill in 1999, meaning that plans for construction could proceed.[99]

Only two years after the devastating flood, then, the Corps had the authorization and money for the Grand Forks/East Grand Forks project. This was not only important for the two communities but also for the St. Paul District, which was experiencing a decline in large flood control projects. In 1995, for example, Colonel James T. Scott, outgoing district engineer, noted that "St. Paul's workload is falling off." He lamented this drop, especially since the district "has had a great history of flood control and navigation within its area of responsibility."[100] The Grand Forks/East Grand Forks project reversed that decline and proved itself a boon to the district, both in terms of workload and employment. In the words of McNally, it was a "big step" for the district to receive authorization for the project.[101] Colonel William Breyfogle echoed those sentiments, stating that Grand Forks was "something that we could do that would really make a difference."[102]

With congressional funding, Phase I construction on the levees themselves began in the summer of 2001, with the completion date of the entire project estimated to be 2004. Upon its completion, Grand Forks and East Grand Forks would have protection against a 210-year flood equivalent to the 1997 disaster.[103] The St. Paul District involved both communities in meetings, making their leaders feel like part of a team.[104] Grand Forks and East Grand Forks residents questioned the project before the 1997 flood, but they later cooperated with the district, providing suggestions and accepting Corps' decisions, albeit with some grumbling. The productive collaboration stemmed in part from the good relationships that district employees established with residents during the flood fight in 1997, in part from the communities' desire to protect themselves against future floods and in part from the Corps' willingness to use outside consultants to validate its conclusions.

South Fork Zumbro River at Rochester, Minnesota

Probably the best example of citizen cooperation on a civil works project was the South Fork Zumbro River Flood Control project at Rochester, Minnesota, completed in the 1990s. As Colonel James T. Scott said in 1995, this undertaking was "one of those classic projects that I would recommend to other district engineers to look at and to study if they want to know how to run a project."[105] Few other developments enjoyed the amount of local financial support as Rochester and few won as many awards. Although there were some environmental controversies, the project was one of the major civil works successes for the St. Paul District in the last quarter of the twentieth century.

The city of Rochester, located in southeastern Minnesota about 80 miles south of St. Paul, is located on the floor of the South Fork Zumbro River Valley. At Rochester, three other streams join the Zumbro, a 50-mile tributary of the Mississippi, including Cascade Creek from the west, Silver Creek from the east and Bear Creek from the south. Some describe Rochester as sitting in a bowl, as the southern and western parts of the city consist of high undulating land while the eastern and northern ends have high bluffs and steep ridges. Because of the topography of the area and the confluence of the four waterways, Rochester, with approximately a third of the city located in the floodplain, is susceptible to flooding, especially after heavy rainstorms.[106]

Flash flooding had periodically inundated the city since its founding in 1854. In order to solve this problem, Congress authorized the Corps to complete a study on the Rochester area in 1936, but little action occurred until a major flood in 1962 caused more than $1.6 million in damages. By 1972, the St. Paul District completed preliminary examinations of channel improvements, floodwalls and levees for Zumbro River, Bear Creek and Cascade Creek; and by the mid-1970s, the U.S. Department of Agriculture's Soil Conservation Service (now known as the Natural Resources Conservation Service) had initiated plans to construct seven headwater reservoirs in the area. Congress endorsed these proposals in 1974; and for the next four years, the Corps worked with the Soil Conservation Service, the Minnesota Department of Natural Resources and local interests to develop the plans, completing a Phase I General Design study in 1977.[107]

Before the Corps could complete any further reports, however, a torrential rainstorm devastated Rochester. On the evening of July 5, 1978, approximately six inches of rain fell on the city, swelling Cascade Creek, Bear Creek and the Zumbro itself. By the next morning all three waterways had overflowed, pouring water into downtown Rochester. When the Zumbro finally crested at 23 feet, it was 19 feet higher than it had been twenty-four hours earlier. The deluge of water killed five people, forced five thousand more from their homes and caused $60 million worth of damage.[108] In response to the

Zumbra River Flooding: Rochester, Minnesota, 1978. (Photo by Russ Snyder, courtesy of St. Paul District, Corps of Engineers)

flood, Representative Albert H. Quie (R-Minnesota) asked Congress to authorize the construction of the planned flood control project, stating that had it been in place in time for the rainstorm, "damage to personal property and public buildings would have been minimal."[109]

Unfortunately, declarations of the necessity of the Rochester project occurred when congressional and executive support for federal water projects was ebbing. Because of environmental concerns, budget deficits and the policies of both Jimmy Carter and Ronald Reagan, no omnibus water resource authorization bills passed between 1976 and 1986, and the Rochester project itself received no funding. Although the undertaking seemed worthwhile, construction funds were unavailable until 1986.[110]

In the mid-1980s, Congress and the Reagan Administration agreed that local and state governments should make significant contributions towards flood control projects. Based on that idea, Congress passed the Water Resources Development Act of 1986 which implemented new cost-sharing requirements and authorized a hundred and fifteen flood control projects for construction or study, including the project at Rochester.[111] Under the new stipulations, Rochester had to contribute more than $17 million to the estimated $68 million necessary for the project, rather than the $7 million under the old plan, but the city was prepared. Although the project had hung in limbo for several years, city leaders believed it would eventually gain approval. In 1982, Rochester had added a one percent increase to the state sales tax and devoted the proceeds to flood control, collecting $10 million by 1987. These accumulated funds, together with the money that continued to accrue, largely handled the city's cost-

The South Fork Zumbro River, before and after: The first photograph (top) shows the construction of walls along the river near the Civic Center. Note the house in the background that the project would protect. The second (below) shows the completed project, with the area of the first image in the lower right quadrant. (Photos by Russ Snyder, courtesy of St. Paul District, Corps of Engineers)

Hsharing requirements. As Jim Gagnon, a St. Paul District project manager, explained, the city "had great foresight in setting up the sales tax."[112]

By assuming a portion of the project's costs, Rochester not only fulfilled its legal requirements, but also made itself a partner with the Corps, enabling city leaders to offer suggestions and work with the district to ensure its desires were met.[113] St. Paul District employees, who were not used to such involvement, soon realized local sponsors could provide meaningful dialogue and useful ideas in a project's construction. Although conflicts inevitably developed, both the district and the city learned to work well together, providing the Corps with an example of what could happen with good partnerships.[114]

With cost-sharing funds and congressional authorization in place by 1987, the city signed a Local Cooperation Agreement and construction began. Following its 1970s proposal, the district, under the leadership of project manager Deborah Foley, began deepening and widening the channels of Zumbro River and Cascade and Bear creeks. Most of the undertakings occurred in downtown commercial areas, residential neighborhoods, parks and a municipal golf course. In order to provide slope protection, the district lined banks of the waterways with riprap, concrete and steel-sheet piling. Coupled with the storage reservoirs built by the Soil Conservation Service in the 1980s and 1990s, these changes provided Rochester with protection from a two hundred-year flood event.[115]

Despite the district's best efforts, controversies arose. By 1990, the estimated cost of the project had escalated from $86 million to $120 million, and the district had to spend much time justifying these increases to the city. Because of the higher costs, Congress also had to reauthorize the project. Reflecting these delays, the Corps calculated the project could not be completed in 1994, as it had originally estimated, but would now stretch into 1997. The city objected to this revised timeline, forcing the district to reconsider its reckonings. Upon a reexamination, the district determined that if all went well, it could complete the project in late 1995. "There will be no slack in the schedule," Foley admitted, "but it's a doable schedule."[116]

At the same time, environmental criticisms began to emerge. Although the Corps tried to mitigate the riprapping effects, many residents complained about the aesthetic degradation of the river, as well

Zumbro River: Channel modifications on the South Fork Zumbro River in Rochester, Minnesota, showing the pedestrian bridge and riprap implemented by the St. Paul District, 1995. (Photo courtesy of St. Paul District, Corps of Engineers)

99

as the destruction of numerous trees lining the Zumbro's banks. One letter to the Rochester *Post-Bulletin* objected to the Corps' "rape of nature," stating the project destroyed "dozens of beautiful oak trees and a pristine area of wildflowers, flowering shrubs and trees, a sanctuary for birds, squirrels and other wildlife."[117] Others called the project "outdated, expensive, impractical, and destructive," believing it would only create "riprapped mud flats" at the expense of numerous trees.[118] As one critic bluntly declared, "If this is [the Corps'] idea of 'aesthetic design,' please refrain from showing me any more of it."[119] In response to the complaints, the district intensified its efforts to provide aesthetically pleasing features, laying topsoil and sod over riprap, commissioning artist Anne Plummer to create a mural for a downtown section of floodwall, placing decorative handrails throughout the project, using native plants for landscaping and emphasizing sustainable development wherever possible.[120]

Other problems arose from the destruction of wildlife habitat, especially fisheries, because of channel deepening. The Minnesota Department of Natural Resources requested the Corps purchase lands adjacent to the Keller Wildlife Management Area to mitigate these impacts. Although it initially rejected that proposal, the Corps eventually acquired 140 acres near the Keller area and deeded them to the State of Minnesota. The Corps also placed rock structures in the river to serve as current deflectors and fish cover, concentrated water depths in low-flow channels during dry seasons and used rock clusters, groins and weirs to create fish-spawning pools. In addition, the city's Park and Recreation Department stocked the Willow Creek Golf Course and Chester Woods reservoirs with fish.[121] These measures helped to dissipate some of the criticism, as did a prevailing belief that the project was necessary despite the environmental costs. "Any destruction of trees and natural habitat is a cause for regret," an editorial in the *Post-Bulletin* explained. "We would prefer a natural, meandering stream, but not at the cost of a never-ending risk of a disastrous flood."[122]

As construction continued in the early 1990s, the Corps and the city were happily surprised when costs began dropping. In October 1991, construction bids for one portion of the project came in at less than sixty percent of the original estimate, providing a considerable savings.[123] Innovations led to lower costs as well. For example, moving residences rather than building a half mile of proposed levee at the upstream end of Cascade Creek saved $800,000 and decreasing the scope of channel modifications on that creek from 9,000 to 4,000 feet recovered an additional $5 million, while also preserving existing parks and neighborhoods. According to Foley, value engineering accounted for a discount of $4 million. These reductions meant that instead of the $123 million projected in the early 1990s, the total cost of the Corps' portion of the project decreased to $97 million.[124]

When the Corps finished its construction in August 1995, one month ahead of schedule, all parties seemed pleased. Rochester Mayor Chuck Canfield declared it "the best project in the country" and many citizens agreed.[125] Even before final completion, people were using the 6.5 miles of recreational trails developed along the river, as well as the pedestrian plazas and picnic shelters. Frank Star, a planner for the district who helped design the recreational aspects, said he "felt good" when he saw how much people enjoyed the trails.[126] Others in the district also recognized the "enthusiastic local response" to the project, proudly claiming that "rather than mere satisfaction, the project has elicited delight from ... the citizens of Rochester, for its flood protection and social and economic benefits."[127]

People outside of the St. Paul District also acknowledged the superiority of the project. In 1996, when the Minnesota Society of Professional Engineers proclaimed it one of the "Seven Wonders of Engineering" for that year, the judges emphasized the effective coordination between the Corps and the city.[128] That same year, the project won the prestigious Award of Excellence from the Chief of Engineers Design and Environmental Awards Program. Although a Corps' award, a non-Corps' jury, which had to be unanimous, selected the winner. By 2004, the St. Paul District received four other Awards of Excellence – for the Lock and Dam 1 rehabilitation in 1983; for the Weaver Bottoms Rehabilitation Project in 1989; for the St. Paul, Minnesota, Flood Control Project in 1998; and for the Pool 8 Islands Project in 2004. In addition, Foley received the Corps' Project Manager of the Year Award in 1996, and George V. Fortune, a design engineer on the Rochester project, received the 1996 Corps' Design Engineer of the Year Award.[129]

For those associated with the project, it was not difficult to understand why it received so many accolades. Foley attributed it to numerous factors, including her capable district staff, the coordination between the district and the city and the recreational and aesthetic elements.[130] Russel K. Snyder, a project manager and landscape architect in the district, believed the Rochester project was an ideal example of how cost-sharing created a working partnership between the Corps and a local sponsor.[131] A Corps' summary of the project explained that its success stemmed from cooperation between federal, state and local government agencies which generated "innovative solutions to benefit the public." No better example existed, the summary continued, "of recreational planning, attractive design, and environmental sensitivity integrated with high quality, cost effective urban flood control." In fact, it concluded, the major reason for the project's success "was the spirit of partnering and teamwork that prevailed throughout its design and construction," whereby the local sponsors "became active members of the project team."[132]

This project, then, was a showcase for the St. Paul District's competence in civil works. Although environmental concerns were raised about the project, the Corps' own mitigating efforts, coupled with aid from the city, mollified these criticisms to a large degree. Perhaps no other project developed better cooperation between the district and the local sponsor, and this cooperation, as with the Grand Forks/East Grand Forks project, ensured the success of the undertaking. Relationships were not always perfect between district representatives and city leaders, but the creation of a team mentality facilitated good relations and enabled the Corps to implement efficiently a project that provided security, recreation and economic benefits. As Colonel James Scott declared, "It was just a win/win situation."[133]

Conclusion

The civil works projects discussed above were by no means the only important undertakings for the St. Paul District between 1975 and 2000. As with Rochester, other projects received prestigious awards, such as the St. Paul Flood Control Project. Undertakings other than Devils Lake also had international implications. As with Grand Forks/East Grand Forks, other Corps' work received more attention after disastrous floods, such as the Red River Project at Wahpeton, North Dakota, and Breckenridge, Minnesota. Finally, other undertakings besides the La Farge Project, including the Prairie du Chien Project of the 1970s and 1980s, were drastically affected by environmental concerns. But the La Farge, Devils Lake, Grand Forks/East Grand Forks and South Fork Zumbro undertakings clearly highlighted the major themes that the St. Paul District faced in the last quarter of the twentieth century. Environmentalism, cost-sharing, benefit-cost analyses and cooperation with international, federal, state and local agencies all influenced the district and the Corps throughout this period. Because of these issues and because of important legislation such as NEPA and the Water Resources Development Act of 1986, the Corps' civil works program changed dramatically. The successes of the St. Paul District resulted in large part from its willingness to accept that change – difficulties with environmentalists, local communities and politicians arose, at least to some degree, from inflexible attitudes. As Colonel Kenneth Kasprisin explained, if district employees "see [the] opportunities with ... change then we'll continue to do extremely well. If they hide from it ... then there will be problems."[134] Nowhere was this more apparent than in the St. Paul District's civil works program.

Chapter 4: Endnotes

1 "La Farge Lake and Channel Improvement, Kickapoo River, Wisconsin," Water Resources Fact Sheet, 3 September 1975, pp. 1-2, Box 6407, SPDAR; Merritt, *Creativity, Conflict and Controversy*, pp. 413-414.

2 Martin Reuss, *Shaping Environmental Awareness: The United States Army Corps of Engineers Environmental Advisory Board*, 1970-1980 (Washington, D.C.: Historical Division, Office of Administrative Services, Office of the Chief of Engineers, 1983), 1, 14, 20.

3 Quotation in "Corps to Look at Alternatives to La Farge Dam Construction," *Winona Daily News*, 12 January 1975. See also Merritt, *Creativity, Conflict and Controversy*, p. 415.

4 Quoted in "Corps Coached Pro-Dam Group on Pressure Tactics," *Capital Times* (Madison, WI), 10 January 1975.

5 "Kickapoo Alternatives," *Capital Times*, 9 January 1975.

6 Quotation in John Anfinson interview by Matthew Godfrey, St. Paul, MN, 25 October 2002, p. 21; see also Jamie W. Moore and Dorothy P. Moore, *The Army Corps of Engineers and the Evolution of Federal Flood Plain Management Policy* (Boulder: Institute of Behavioral Science, University of Colorado, 1989), p. 91.

7 Quotation in "Corps Builds, No Matter What," *Capital Times*, 18 March 1975; see also "National Register of Historic Places Registration Form, La Farge Reservoir and Lake Dam," Section 8, p. 33, File La Farge Management, Box 6410, SPDAR.

8 Quotation in "Congressmen Still Fret Over La Farge Dam," *La Crosse Tribune*, 25 January 1976; see also Merritt, *Creativity, Conflict and Controversy*, p. 416; "National Register of Historic Places Registration Form," Section 8, pp. 34-37.

9 "Army Halts LaFarge Dam Work," *Wisconsin State Journal*, 10 April 1975.

10 "Study Proposals Inundate La Farge," *La Crosse Tribune*, 27 April 1976.

11 "June 19 LaFarge Dam Hearing Hit by Audubon Society," *Courier Press* (Prairie du Chien, WI) 22 June 1981.

12 Richard J. Otto interview by Matthew Godfrey, St. Paul, MN, 23 October 2002, p. 3. Otto, a recreation and natural resources planner in the La Crescent, Minnesota, field office of the St. Paul District, had charge over the La Farge project for many years after its deauthorization.

13 "National Register of Historic Places Registration Form," Section 8, p. 37; "Kickapoo Denied Designation as Park, Waterway," *La Crosse Tribune*, 27 June 1976.

14 Merritt, *The Corps, the Environment, and the Upper Mississippi River Basin*, 78.

15 "Draft, Position Paper, La Farge Lake and Channel Improvement, Wisconsin," 3 December 1981, p. 2, File 1501-07 Reference Paper Files – La Farge, Wisconsin, Box 7932, SPDAR.

16 Merritt, *The Corps, the Environment, and the Upper Mississippi River Basin*, 79.

17 Unidentified newspaper clipping, 20 February 1981, File 870 La Farge, Wisconsin (1980-1981), Box 3864, SPDAR.

18 Badger Interviews, p. 22.

19 U.S. Army Corps of Engineers, St. Paul District, *Special Report: Reevaluation of La Farge Dam, Kickapoo River Valley, Wisconsin, Dry Dam and Wet Dam Alternatives* (St. Paul, MN: U.S. Army Corps of Engineers, St. Paul District, 1984), p. 43.

20 Quotes in "Lawsuits Push Dam Project," *La Crosse Tribune*, 19 December 1985; see also "LaFarge Dam Project Subject of Suit Filed Against Fed. Govt," Courier Press, 30 October 1985.

21 "La Farge Dam Fight Not Over Yet," *La Crosse Tribune*, 7 January 1990.

22 "Dam Project Dead in Water," *La Crosse Tribune*, 6 September 1990.

23 "LaFarge Project Waits for Deauthorization," *Crosscurrents* 10 (May 1987): pp. 8-9; "St. Paul District Successfully Manages Rainbow Event," *Crosscurrents* 15 (July 1992): pp. 1- 4; Otto Interview, pp. 3-4.

24 Tommy G. Thompson, Governor, to The Honorable Steven Gunderson, 14 April 1994, File La Farge Correspondence, Box 6407, SPDAR.

25 "Master Plan for the Kickapoo Valley Reserve," p. 2-3, File 1110-2-1150a La Farge Flood Control Record of Decision, Box 6417, SPDAR; Marcy West to Dawn Make

Strong Move, 13 February 1997, File LaFarge Ho Chunk, Box 6410, SPDAR; Ron Wilber to Larry Garvin, HoChunk Researcher, 10 February 1997, File LaFarge Ho Chunk, Box 6410, SPDAR; U.S., Congress, House, Committee on Public Works and Transportation, Water Resources and Environment Subcommittee, The Water Resources Development Act of 1994 and Issues Related to Reauthorization of the Civil Works Program of the U.S. Army Corps of Engineers: Hearings Before the Subcommittee on Water Resources and Environment of the Committee on Public Works and Transportation, House of Representatives, 103d Cong., 2d sess., 1994, p. 113; U.S. Army Corps of Engineers, St. Paul District, "Information Paper, Subject: Proposed De-authorization of the La Farge Dam Project," 24 July 1995, copy provided by Richard J. Otto, St. Paul District; "Focus: Kickapoo Valley – Ho-Chunk Add to Trust Holdings," *Wisconsin State Journal*, 29 October 1997; John Anfinson Interview, pp. 12-14.

26 "Focus: Kickapoo Valley – Ho-Chunk Add to Trust Holdings," *Wisconsin State Journal*, 29 October 1997; John Anfinson Interview, p. 13.

27 "Master Plan for the Kickapoo Valley Reserve," pp. 1-2.

28 Otto Interview, pp. 6-8.

29 John Anfinson Interview, p. 15. Anfinson tried to get the incomplete dam listed on the National Register of Historic Places in 2000, even though it was not yet eligible under the fifty-year requirement. Although he insisted that the dam deserved listing because of its significance as a symbol of the effects of NEPA, the Wisconsin State Historic Preservation Office did not agree with his arguments and rejected the nomination.

30 "City, State Under Dangerous Siege," The Bismarck *Sunday Tribune*, 15 September 1996.

31 The North Dakota State Water Commission estimated the natural outlet at 1,459 feet. See Notes from Thomas Raster, Civil Engineer, St. Paul District, 19 November 2003, copy in possession of the author.

32 "History and Effects of Devils Lake Flooding," Devils Lake Outlet EIS Newsletter 1 (March 1998): p. 2.

33 "Devils Lake Flood Fact Sheet, February 1998," File Devils Lake Miscellaneous, Box 6447, SPDAR.

34 "Devils Lake Floodwaters Flow," *Grand Forks Herald*, 17 May 1979.

35 Unidentified newspaper clipping, File 228-10 IHP Devils ('83), Box 3846, SPDAR. 36 "Corps Dike is Needed, But is Step Backwards in Managing Lake Level," *Devils Lake Journal*, 29 August 1984.

37 "Lake Outlet Apparently is On Hold," *Devils Lake Journal*, 16 August 1984.

38 Unidentified newspaper clipping, File 229-10 IHP Devils ('83), Box 3846, SPDAR.

39 U.S. Army Corps of Engineers, St. Paul District, *Operation and Maintenance Manual: Section 205 Flood Control Project, Devils Lake, North Dakota* (St. Paul, MN: U.S. Army Corps of Engineers, St. Paul District, 1992), pp. 1-2.

40 "Lake Outlet Apparently is On Hold," *Devils Lake Journal*, 16 August 1984.

41 Garrison Diversion Conservancy District, "Abbreviated History, 1944-2001," <http://www.garrisondiv.org/pages/publicinfo/history/index.epl> (5 February 2004); "Garrison Diversion and the Devils Lake Outlet: The Canadian Position," <http://www.canadianembassy.org/ environment/garrison-e.asp> (6 June 2003); "Statement of Gary L. Pearson on Behalf of the Dakota Prairie Audubon Society Submitted at the Hearing of the Committee on Environment and Public Works, United States Senate, Regarding the Proposal to Construct An Emergency Outlet from Devils Lake to the Sheyenne River in North Dakota," 23 October 1997, <http://80-web.lexisnexis. com.weblib.lib.umt.edu:2048/congcomp/document?_m=7701530145029adf8c74d315 780642db&_docnum=7&wchp=dGLbVtb-lSlAA&_md5=259852c2189ade895507a0b950f5775d> (6 June 2003).

42 U.S. Army Corps of Engineers, St. Paul District, *Devils Lake Feasibility Study: Concept-Level Plan of Study* (St. Paul, MN: U.S. Army Corps of Engineers, St. Paul District, 1995), pp. 2-3; North Dakota State Water Commission [NDSWC], "Assessment of Potential Devils Lake Flood Damages, October 1994," p. 2, copy in File Devils Lake – Roads, Box 6452, SPDAR.

43 Colonel Richard W. Craig interview by John O. Anfinson, St. Paul, MN, 20 July 1993, p. 11, Oral History File, St. Paul District, St. Paul, Minnesota.

44 NDSWC, "Assessment of Potential Devils Lake Flood Damages," p. 4; Notes from Thomas Raster, Civil Engineer, St. Paul District, 19 November 2003.

45 U.S. Army Corps of Engineers, St. Paul District, Devils Lake, North Dakota, Contingency Plan (St. Paul, MN: U.S. Army Corps of Engineers, St. Paul District, 1996).

46 U.S. Army Corps of Engineers, St. Paul District, "Devils Lake Levee, North Dakota," <http://www.mvp.usace.army.mil/fl_damage_reduct/default. asp?pageid=31> (6 June 2003); "Three Major Initiatives Underway for Devils Lake," Crosscurrents 19 (September 1996): p. 1.

47 "Testimony of Michael J. Armstrong, Associate Director for Mitigation, Federal Emergency Management Agency, Before the Senate Committee on the Environment and Public Works Regarding the Devils Lake Basin Interagency Task Force," 23 October 1997, <http://80-web.lexisnexis. com.weblib.lib.umt. edu:2048/congcomp/document?_m=7701530145029adf8c74d315 780642db&_docnum=6&wchp=dGLbVtblSlAA&_ md5=5fc5961bbd2a9b8660cc98d187ad88aa> (6 June 2003).

48 "City, State Under Dangerous Siege," The Bismarck *Sunday Tribune*, 15 September 1996.

49 "Farmers, Bedeviled by Rising Lake, Look for a Lifeline," *Los Angeles Times*, 10 November 1996.

50 "Solution Slower Than Rising Waters," *Bismarck Tribune*, 17 September 1996.

51 U.S. Army Corps of Engineers, St. Paul District, *Emergency Outlet Plan: Devils Lake, North Dakota* (St. Paul, MN: U.S. Army Corps of Engineers, St. Paul District, 1996), pp. 1-3; "Three Major Initiatives Underway for Devils Lake," Crosscurrents 19 (September 1996): pp. 1-2; Thomas E. Raster email to John M. Wonsik, Charles E. Crist, William W. Spychalla, David R. Raasch, and Robert F. Post, 16 August 1996, File Devils Lake Stage 2A, Box 6451, SPDAR. The District's Devils Lake Basin Planning Team's work on the Emergency Outlet Plan earned it the Chief of Engineer's Oustanding Planning Team Award in 1996.

52 "Clinton Asks $32.5 Million for Devils Lake," *Grand Forks Herald*, 20 March 1997.

53 Quotations in "Canadian Officials Oppose Devils Lake Outlet," *Grand Forks Herald*, 22 March 1997 and "Canada Takes Tough Stand," *Bismarck Tribune*, 25 March 1997.

54 Marvin Zeldin, "Souris: Mouse That Roars," Audubon 78 (November 1976): pp. 135-138; *U.S. Army Corps of Engineers, Missouri River Division, Water Resources Development in North Dakota 1991* (Omaha, NE: U.S. Army Corps of Engineers, Missouri River Division, 1991), p. 30.

55 "Canadian Dams Play Important Part in Souris Basin Project," *Crosscurrents* 10 (June 1987): p. 6; "Kowalski Reflects on 39 Years of Federal Service," *Crosscurrents* 19 (May 1996): pp. 6, 8; U.S. Army Corps of Engineers, St. Paul District, "Souris River Basin Flood Control Project: N.D.," <http://www.mvp.usace.army.mil/fl_damage_reduct/default.asp?pageid=43> (6 June 2003).

56 Public Law 105-18, 12 June 1997, <http://frwebgate.access.gpo.gov/cgi-bin/getdoc. cgi?dbname=105_cong_public_laws&docid=f:publ18.105> (6 June 2003).

57 "Devils Lake Levee Becomes Critical Priority," Crosscurrents 21 (March 1998): p. 5; Notes from Thomas Raster, Civil Engineer, St. Paul District, 19 November 2003; see also "Panel Approves $5 Million for Devils Lake Outlet," *The Forum* (Fargo, ND), 26 September 1997.

58 "Questions/Answers/Discussion concerning the Emergency Outlet from Devils Lake to the Sheyenne River, ND," 18 February 1998, Attachment A to "Scoping Meeting for the proposed Peterson Coulee Outlet Project for preparation of the Draft Environmental Impact Statement," File Devils Lake Outlet – Correspondence, Box 6453, SPDAR. One of the reasons why the Peterson Coulee route was adopted was because of concerns raised by members of the Spirit Lake Nation about the Twin Lakes proposal. In the summer of 1997, the tribe approved the Peterson Coulee route because it only crossed a few miles of the reservation. The Twin Lakes route, on the other hand, would have run through several hundred acres of reservation land, including tribal trust land. "Route and Plan Selection, Emergency Outlet, Devils Lake to the Sheyenne River, ND: Executive Summary," File Devils Lake Outlet Design and Alternative Reports, Box 6453,

SPDAR; "Spirit Lake Tribe Endorses One of Devils Lake Outlet Proposals," *The Forum*, 26 June 1997.

59 "History and Effects of Devils Lake Flooding," p. 2; "Strategies and Actions: The Three-Legged Stool," Devils Lake Outlet EIS Newsletter 1 (March 1998): p. 3.

60 Colonel J. M. Wonsik interview by John O. Anfinson, St. Paul, MN, 20 January 1998, p. 8, Oral History File, St. Paul District, St. Paul, Minnesota.

61 Col. J. M. Wonsik Memorandum for Commander, U.S. Army Corps of Engineers, 21 November 1997, File Devils Lake Outlet – Correspondence, Box 6454, SPDAR. The Boundary Waters Treaty was not ratified by the U.S. Senate until 1910, meaning that the IJC did not meet for the first time until 1911.

62 See "Capitol Hill Hearing Testimony Before the Senate Committee on Environment and Public Works," 23 October 1997, <http://80-web.lexisnexis.com. weblib.lib.umt.edu:2048/congcomp/doclist?_m=93b5adbc8842f4b5195e90c4089 832a6&wchp=dGLbVtb-lSlAA&_md5=1b43b30249f4dc0c255868433d87b1b6> (6 June 2003).

63 John H. Zirschky, Acting Assistant Secretary of the Army, Memorandum for the Director of Civil Works, 28 January 1998, Miscellaneous Folder on Devils Lake, Box 6447, SPDAR.

64 Raymond Chrétien, Ambassador, to the Honourable John H. Chafee, Chairman, Committee on Environment and Public Works, United States Senate, 22 October 1997, File Devils Lake Outlet – Correspondence, Box 6453, SPDAR.

65 "Draft, Senator Dorgan Questions," 23 March 1998, File Devils Lake Outlet – Correspondence – Congressional, Box 6454, SPDAR.

66 Quotation in Richard Bad Moccasin, Executive Director, Mni Sose Intertribal Water Rights Coalition, Inc., to Robert Whiting, Chief, Environmental Resources Section, 30 September 1998, File Devils Lake Outlet – Correspondence, Box 6453, SPDAR; see also "Devils Lake Emergency Outlet Regulator Meeting Summary, January 13, 1998," pp. 2-3, File Devils Lake Outlet – Environmental Studies and Reports, Box 6453, SPDAR.

67 "Devils Lake, North Dakota, General Information, March 1999," File Devils Lake Outlet – Correspondence – Congressional, Box 6454, SPDAR; "Lake Region Frustrated by Army Engineers' Meanderings," Devils Lake Journal, 25 March 1999.

68 Maj. Gen. Phillip Anderson, "Devils Lake Emergency Tiger Team Memorandum of Instructions," Miscellaneous File on Devils Lake, Box 6447, SPDAR.

69 U.S. Army Corps of Engineers, Mississippi Valley Division, "Mississippi Valley Division Devils Lake Division/District (Tiger) Team Technical Report, June 1999, Executive Summary," <http://www.swc.state.nd.us/projects/pdf/ExecSum.pdf> (6 June 2003).

70 Phillip R. Anderson, Major General, U.S. Army, Division Engineer, to Honorable Edward T. Schafer, Governor of North Dakota, 17 June 1999, File Devils Lake Outlet – Correspondence – State Agencies, Box 6453, SPDAR.

71 "Stalling Outlet for Devils Lake Invites 'Disaster,'" *The Forum*, 11 June 1999.

72 "State, Local Leaders Find Corps Plan Unacceptable," *Devils Lake Journal*, 11 June 1999.

73 Judith M. Ovre to Lt. General Joe Ballard, Chief of Engineers, US Army Corps of Engineers, 29 July 1999, File Devils Lake Outlet – Correspondence, Box 6454, SPDAR.

74 "A Rising Lake Puts Corps in Hot Water," *The Washington Post*, 11 September 2000.

75 David Loss interview by Matthew Godfrey, St. Paul, MN, 21 October 2002, p. 5.

76 Colonel James T. Scott interview by John O. Anfinson, St. Paul, MN, 30 May 1995, p. 11, Oral History File, St. Paul District, St. Paul, Minnesota; see also Notes from Thomas Raster, Civil Engineer, St. Paul District, 19 November 2003.

77 Colonel William J. Breyfogle interview by Matthew Pearcy, St. Paul, MN, 28 November 2001, p. 14, Oral History File, St. Paul District, St. Paul, Minnesota.

78 Quotation in "Senator Wants to Put Corps on Hold," *Devils Lake Journal*, 16 July 1999; see also "A Rising Lake Puts Corps in Hot Water," *The Washington Post*, 11 September 2000; "Devils Lake: Corps Change Earns Praise," *Grand Forks Herald*, 26 July 1999; "Corps Uses Emergency Powers to Speed Devils Lake Solution," North Dakota's Congressional Delegation Press Release, File Devils Lake News Clippings, Box 6100, SPDAR.

79 "A Rising Lake Puts Corps in Hot Water," *The Washington Post*, 11 September 2000.

80 For examples of criticism of environmental groups, see "Devils Lake Situation Getting Some Attention," *Devils Lake Journal*, 14 May 1999. For examples of the environmentalists' explanations of the flooding, see "Statement of Gary L. Pearson on Behalf of the Dakota Prairie Audubon Society Submitted at the Hearing of the Committee on Environment and Public Works, United States Senate, Regarding the Proposal to Construct An Emergency Outlet from Devils Lake to the Sheyenne River in North Dakota," 23 October 1997 (see footnote 39); Kent Conrad, United States Senate, to Joseph Westphal, 16 August 1999, File Devils Lake Outlet – Correspondence, Box 6454, SPDAR.

81 "Merit Award Goes to Devils Lake Levees Project," *Crosscurrents* 25 (August 2002): pp. 3, 8.

82 U.S. Army Corps of Engineers, St. Paul District, "Devils Lake Basin, North Dakota," <http://www.mvp.usace.army.mil/fl_damage_reduct/default. asp?pageid=14> (6 June 2003); U.S. Army Corps of Engineers, St. Paul District, "Outlet Identified as Preferred Alternative at Devils Lake," Press Release, 26 February 2003, <http://www.mvp.usace.army.mil/pressroom/default. asp?pageid=648> (6 June 2003).

83 Loss Interview, p. 11.

84 U.S., Congress, House, Committee on Public Works and Transportation, Oversight and Review Subcommittee, Flooding of the Red River of the North and Its Tributaries: Hearing Before the Subcommittee on Oversight and Review of the Committee on Public Works and Transportation, House of Representatives,96th Cong., 1st sess., 1979, p. 250; U.S. Army Engineer District St. Paul, *Red River of the North Post Flood Report*, 1978 (St. Paul, MN: U.S. Army Corps of Engineers, St. Paul District, 1978), p. 2. At the time, there was no clear reason why flooding became more frequent in the 1960s and 1970s. The District informed the House Committee on Public Works in 1979 that "perhaps all we can conclude [from the increased frequency of floods] is that a number of large floods tend to be grouped into rather short periods interspersed with longer periods without large floods."

85 Quotation in "Corps Outline Farm Dike Control," *Grand Forks Herald*, 26 April 1978; see also "1979 Red River Flood Set Records for Damage," Minneapolis *Tribune*, 10 May 1979; "Flood Danger Eases at Grand Forks," The Forum, 14 April 1978; "Crest Moves North," Minot Daily News, 14 April 1978.

86 "1979 Red River Flood Set Records for Damage," Minneapolis *Tribune*, 10 May 1979.

87 "Staying in Touch! Congressman Arlan Stangeland," *Benson Monitor* (MN), n.d., clipping in File 870 Red River of the North Flood 1979, Box 3858, SPDAR.

88 Quotation in "Levee Plans Not Popular At Meet," Red Wing-*Republican Eagle*, 29 October 1983; see also "EGF to Study Flood Plan Tuesday," Grand Forks *Herald*, 8 October 1983; U.S. Army Corps of Engineers, Water Resources Development in Minnesota 1995, pp. 69-70; "Fact Sheet: General Investigations," File 1110-201150a East Grand Forks Flood Control ('97), Box 8072, SPDAR.

89 Bory Steinberg, "The Federal Perspective," in *Water Resources Administration in the United States: Policy, Practice, and Emerging Issues, edited by Martin Reuss* (East Lansing: Michigan State University Press, 1993), p. 264.

90 Colonel Kenneth Kasprisin interview by Virginia Gnabasik, 13 July 2001, St. Paul, MN, p. 10.

91 "GF Hasn't Dropped Guard in Protecting from Flood," *Grand Forks Herald*, 23 October 1983.

92 Edward McNally interview by Matthew Godfrey, St. Paul, MN, 22 October 2002, p. 3.

93 U.S. Army Corps of Engineers, St. Paul District, *Draft General Reevaluation Report and Environmental Impact Statement, East Grand Forks, Minnesota and Grand Forks, North Dakota* (St. Paul, MN: U.S. Army Corps of Engineers, St. Paul District, 1998), p. 1; "A Day That Began with Sirens Blaring in the Night Ends with Devastation," Grand Forks *Herald*, 18 April 1997; " 'We're Losing': Downtown Grand Forks Hit by Fire as Well as Flood," St. Paul *Pioneer Press*, 20 April 1997; "Flames Beaten in Grand Forks, But Red's Rising," *The Forum*, 21 April 1997; "Flooded Grand Forks, N.D., Will Be Deserted

When Clinton Visits Tuesday," *Grand Forks Herald*, 21 April 1997; "District Puts in Herculean Effort Against the Flood of '97," *Crosscurrents* 20 (Summer 1997): pp. 1-6.

94 McNally Interview, p. 3.

95 "Description of 100-Year City-Wide Plan (Preliminary)," File 10-1-7a Grand Forks Feasibility Study 1995, Box 4575, SPDAR.

96 U.S. Army Corps of Engineers, St. Paul District, *Draft General Reevaluation Report and Environmental Impact Statement*, p. 2.

97 U.S. Army Corps of Engineers, St. Paul District, *Draft General Reevaluation Report and Environmental Impact Statement*, pp. 2, 13-16; " 'Down to One Plan, One Project' at Grand Forks," *Crosscurrents* 21 (March 1998): p. 1; McNally Interview, p. 6. The two cities ultimately received financial help from the states of Minnesota and North Dakota.

98 McNally Interview, pp. 6-7. According to one source, East Grand Forks was the first city to install the invisible floodwall, a structure developed in Germany to minimize scenic changes from flood protection structures. Using the invisible floodwall, the Corps constructed a permanent concrete base along the river. In times of flooding, the Corps would insert vertical columns into the concrete base and connect these columns with inter-locking horizontal planks. Therefore, the floodwall only exists when a flood threatens; at other times, the unobtrusive concrete base is the only visible structure. See "Flood Protection in East Grand Forks," <http://www.draves.com/gf/egf_dike.htm> (12 August 2004).

99 U.S. Army Corps of Engineers, St. Paul District, "Flood Control, Red River of the North: Grand Forks, N.D./East Grand Forks, Minn.," <http://www.mvp.usace.army.mil/fl_damage_reduct/default. asp?pageid=18> (6 June 2003); "District Earns 3rd Planning Award," *Crosscurrents* 22 (September 1999): p. 3.

100 Scott Interview, p. 11.

101 McNally Interview, p. 2.

102 Breyfogle Interview, p. 13.

103 "Flood Control, Red River of the North: Grand Forks, N.D./East Grand Forks, Minn."

104 McNally Interview, p. 9.

105 Scott Interview, p. 8.

106 U.S. Army Corps of Engineers, St. Paul District, *Draft Revised Environmental Impact Statement, Flood Control and Related Purposes, South Fork Zumbro River Watershed, Rochester, Olmsted County, Minnesota* (St. Paul, MN: U.S. Army Corps of Engineers, St. Paul District, 1976), p. 8; "Zumbro Ditch is Cost of Ending Flood Risk," *Post-Bulletin* (Rochester, MN) 17 July 1990.

107 U.S., Congress, House, Committee on Public Works and Transportation, Water Resources Subcommittee, *Water Resources Development Act of 1978: Hearings Before the Subcommittee on Water Resources of the Committee on Public Works and Transportation, House of Representatives*, 95th Cong., 2d sess., 1978, p. 468; "Engineers OK City Flood Control Plans," *Post-Bulletin*, 10 July 1972; "Cooperative Planning . . . Zumbro River at Rochester," *Crosscurrents* 1 (January 1978): p. 3.

108 "Flood Project All Because City Built in Wrong Place," *Post-Bulletin*, 23 February 1993; "Flood Control Provides Recreation Opportunities," *Post-Bulletin*, 4 April 1995.

109 "Statement of Hon. Albert H. Quie, a Representative in Congress from the State of Minnesota," in House Subcommittee on Water Resources, *Water Resources Development Act of 1978*, p. 508.

110 Moore and Moore, *The Army Corps of Engineers and the Evolution of Federal Flood Plain Management Policy*, p. 132. For a discussion of this time period and the events leading up to the passage of the Water Resources Development Act of 1986, see Martin Reuss, *Reshaping National Water Politics: The Emergence of the Water Resources Development Act of 1986* (Fort Belvoir, Va.: U.S. Army Corps of Engineers, Institute for Water Resources, 1991).

111 Moore and Moore, *The Army Corps of Engineers and the Evolution of Federal Flood Plain Management Policy*, pp. 133-134.

112 Quotation in "Rochester Gets Go-Ahead in Water Bill," *Crosscurrents* 10 (January 1987): p. 1; see also U.S., Congress, House, Committee on Public Works and Transportation, Water Resources Subcommittee, *Water Resources Development – Cost-Sharing Aspects of President's Water Policy Initiatives: Hearings Before the Subcommittee on Water Resources of the Committee on Public Works and Transportation, House of Representatives*, 96th Cong., 1st sess., 1979, p. 231.

113 Russel K. Snyder interview by Matthew Godfrey, St. Paul, MN, 23 October 2002.

114 Wonsik Interview, p. 7; "Rochester, Minnesota Flood Control Project," summary provided by Russel K. Snyder, Project Manager, St. Paul District.

115 "Rochester Gets Go-Ahead in Water Bill," p. 1; "Information Paper, Rochester, Minnesota, Flood Control Project, June 1991," Loose Papers, Box 7842, SPDAR.

116 Quotation in "$12.4 Million Requested for Flood Control," *Post-Bulletin*, 4 February 1991; see also "Flood Project May Go Into 1997," *Post-Bulletin*, 30 October 1990; Colonel Roger L. Baldwin interview by John O. Anfinson, St. Paul, MN, 1 July 1991, p. 8, Oral History File, St. Paul District, St. Paul, Minnesota. Neither Baldwin nor Foley explained what caused the significant increase in cost; Baldwin merely said that "the job is a more expensive job than we had anticipated." "$12.4 Million Requested for Flood Control," *Post-Bulletin*, 4 February 1991.

117 Quoted in "Some Not Happy with Flood Control Project," *Post-Bulletin*, 10 July 1990.

118 Quoted in "Zumbro Ditch is Cost of Ending Flood Risk," *Post-Bulletin*, 17 July 1990.

119 David F. Hansen Letter to the Editor, *Post-Bulletin*, n.d., clipping in File 22840 IHF Rochester, MN 1990, Box 4144, SPDAR.

120 "Minnesota Engineers Honor Rochester Project," *Crosscurrents* 19 (February 1996): pp. 1, 3; "Project's End Gets Flood of Praise," *Post-Bulletin*, 29 September 1994.

121 Mark Heywood, Regional Fisheries Manager, Minnesota Department of Natural Resources, to Randy Devendorf, Corps of Engineers, 21 October 1994, File 11-2-240a Zumbro River at Rochester, Box 2964, SPDAR; Louis Kowalski, Deputy District Engineer for Project Management, to Mr. Mark Heywood, 5 December 1994, ibid.; "Rochester Flood Control Project: Summary"; "Flood Control Provides Recreation Opportunities," *Post-Bulletin*, 4 April 1995.

122 "Zumbro Ditch is Cost of Ending Flood Risk," *Post-Bulletin*, 17 July 1990.

123 "City Surprised by Low Bids for Flood Project," *Post-Bulletin*, 2 October 1991.

124 "Minnesota Engineers Honor Rochester Project," p. 3; "Rochester Flood Control Project: Summary," p. 3.

125 Chuck Canfield, Mayor, City of Rochester, to Colonel J. M. Wonsik, Army Corps of Engineers, 19 March 1996, File 672 Awards, Box 7823, SPDAR.

126 Frank Star interview by Matthew Godfrey, St. Paul, MN, 21 October 2002, p. 4.

127 "Rochester Flood Control Project," p. 3.

128 Quotation in "Minnesota Engineers Honor Rochester Project," p. 1.

129 "District Project Earns Top Honors," *Crosscurrents* 19 (April 1996): p. 4; "St. Paul District Achieves Top Recognitions in '96," *Crosscurrents* 19 (December 1996): p. 1; Terry Birkenstock email to Matthew T. Pearcy, March 1, 2004, copy supplied to the authors.

130 "Deb Foley: Corps Project Manager of the Year," *Crosscurrents* 19 (June 1996): p. 5; "Minnesota Engineers Honor Rochester Project," pp. 1, 3.

131 Snyder Interview.

132 "Rochester Flood Control Project: Summary," p. 1.

133 Scott Interview, p. 9.

134 Kasprisin Interview, p. 14.

Wetlands: St. Paul District encompasses a variety of wetland types. (Photo by Steve D. Eggers, courtesy of St. Paul District, Corps of Engineers)

5 The Regulatory Mission

The Corps has a responsibility to protect the nation's wetlands. By authority of the Federal Water Pollution Control Act Amendments of 1972, the Corps regulates activities that involve the discharge of dredge or fill material in waters of the United States – including wetlands. The St. Paul District, encompassing an area that contains more wetlands than any other Corps' district outside of Alaska, has played a significant role in the development of the Corps of Engineers regulatory program.

The protection of wetlands is an exceedingly political process, often pitting developers against environmentalists. In Minnesota and Wisconsin, the main threat to wetlands stemmed from agricultural activities. Farmers encountered new restrictions on what they were able to do with their own property. When environmental regulation impinged on private property rights, tension ran high. During one controversy in 1989, upset farmers posted a handbill on grain elevators and farm supply stores across western Minnesota lambasting the Corps. "Farmers Take Notice Now," this handbill read. "The U.S. Corps of Engineers is trying to tighten its stranglehold on all farm drainage with even stronger wording in Section 404 of the Clean Water Act ... Don't lose your right to improve your property. The Corps of Engineers has too much authority already. Don't give them anymore!"[1] A political cartoon in the Mankato, Minnesota, newspaper at this time showed a farm with a patch of cattails in the foreground. Sticking out of the cattails was a sign: "Property of the U.S. Government."[2] In order to implement an effective wetlands protection program in this political climate, the St. Paul District had to work assiduously to win the trust and cooperation of farmers and rural county governments. Owing in part to the farmers' outcry, Minnesota and Wisconsin both developed strong wetland protection programs at the state level. One way in which the St. Paul District distinguished itself nationally was through its innovative coordination with these two progressive state programs.

Much of the controversy surrounding wetlands protection stems from the complicated nature of this resource. Wetlands provide a variety of public values: for their role as filters in preserving water quality, for their function in absorbing water in time of flood and storing water in time of drought, for their importance to biota and for their recreational value to hunters, fishers and wildlife watchers. Yet wetlands can be difficult to recognize, classify and delineate. Even within a two-state area such as Minnesota and Wisconsin, wetlands are extremely varied. Types of wetlands include prairie potholes, shallow lakes, inland fresh meadows, marshes and swamps.

The prairie pothole region, a legacy of the Ice Ages, includes parts of Minnesota, Iowa, North Dakota and South Dakota in the United States and parts of Manitoba, Saskatchewan and Alberta in Canada. When the continental glaciers retreated more than 12,000 years ago, they left behind millions of depressions in the glacial drift. Today, these potholes trap rainwater and snowmelt to form isolated ponds of varying depths and sizes, each one an oasis of aquatic plants and animals. The region's climate is characterized by mid-continent extremes of temperature and precipitation. The potholes are replenished in spring when snowmelt runs off the frozen soil. Most precipitation falls in summer in the form of short, violent cloudbursts. Variations in spring temperatures and the amount of summer rainfall may result in a pothole drying up one year and remaining wet throughout the next.[3]

Prairie potholes provide breeding habitat for immense numbers of waterfowl. These wetlands are estimated to support more than fifty percent of all waterfowl in North America. In wet years, the percentage is even higher. Agricultural usage has made enormous inroads on this type of wetland in Minnesota, reducing the total area from approximately 12 to 3 million acres.[4] A national wetlands inventory produced by the U.S. Fish and Wildlife Service in 1984 described the prairie pothole region as one of nine "National Problem Areas."[5]

Another group of wetlands in Minnesota and Wisconsin that are of unusual importance are the patterned peatlands. These areas exhibit many distinct landforms, including string bogs, ovoid islands, teardrop islands, bogs and fens.[6] Like the prairie potholes, the peatlands are also a product of the Ice Ages. As the continental glaciers receded in northeastern Minnesota and northern Wisconsin, glacial meltwater periodically inundated the land. Drowned vegetation, instead of decomposing, accumulated in layers of organic sludge that turned to waterlogged peat. Today, these water-saturated, acid-peat soils form bogs. The bogs of northeastern Minnesota constitute the largest peatland complex in North America, while smaller bogs dot northern Wisconsin. Poor in nutrients, these bogs are colonized by sphagnum mosses, which in turn provide a mat for tenuous invasions by evergreen shrubs, tamarack and black spruce.[7]

In 1987, the St. Paul District published a pictorial field guide, *Wetland Plants and Plant Communities of Minnesota & Wisconsin*. Patterned after popular field guides to wildflowers and other plant communities, the book sought to make wetland ecosystems recognizable to general readers. The authors, Steve D. Eggers, ecologist with the St. Paul

Wetlands: St. Paul District encompasses a variety of wetland types. (Photo by Steve D. Eggers, courtesy of St. Paul District, Corps of Engineers)

District, and Donald M. Reed, principal biologist for the Southeastern Wisconsin Regional Planning Commission, divided wetland plant communities in the two states into fifteen vegetation types. While the authors' focus on vegetation highlighted just one of three factors used in defining wetlands (it downplayed soil and hydrology), it emphasized the most visible feature. The book was offered as a companion to the more technical publication, *Wetlands and Water Quality: A Citizen's Handbook on How to Review Section 404 Permits.*[8]

Eggers and Reed followed the wetland classification system developed by John Curtis in *The Vegetation of Wisconsin* (1971). They divided the wetland vegetation types between two major floristic provinces, the first characterized by "prairie-forest" and the second by "northern forest." The transition or "vegetation tension zone" between the two provinces divided both states approximately in half on a meandering northwest-southeast diagonal running from Roseau County, Minnesota, to Milwaukee County, Wisconsin. The prairieforest floristic province, included the eastern edge of the prairie pothole region. The authors classified wetland plant communities into eight types: shallow, open water communities, marshes, inland fresh meadows, bogs, shrub swamps, wooded swamps, floodplain forests and seasonally-flooded basins (prairie potholes). Most of these classifications included at least two subclassifications. One noteworthy subclass comprised calcareous fens – distinguished by wet, seepage sites where calcium and magnesium bicarbonates and sulfates in the soil surface restricted

117

vegetation to a select group of calcium-tolerant plants. Calcareous fens exhibited the rarest plant community in Minnesota and Wisconsin, and probably one of the rarest in North America. The fens usually had a disproportionate number of rare, threatened or endangered plant species.[9]

It has been estimated that Minnesota contained more than 18 million acres of wetlands – an area amounting to one-third of the state – prior to non-Indian settlement.[10] In Minnesota, as in other regions, agricultural interests spearheaded the assault on wetlands. In the mid-nineteenth-century, settlers moved into the region and began at once to drain wetlands in order to bring more land under cultivation. These early settlers, many of whom were immigrants from Germany, Ireland, Scandinavia and other European countries, soon obtained active support of the state government, which saw the large-scale conversion of wetlands as a public good. The state government was abetted by the Federal Swamp Lands Acts of 1849-50, which granted inundated lands to states. In 1861, Governor Alexander Ramsey of Minnesota addressed the state legislature on wetlands: "From their nature and situation they are capable of easy reclamation. In a climate so dry as ours, we may naturally expect that lands of this class will eventually be the most valuable in the state."[11] Minnesota state laws promoted the formation of corporations for the purpose of draining lands. A state drainage commission oversaw all drainage ditch construction. Although the drought and economic depression of the 1930s temporarily halted wide-scale drainage efforts, the destruction of wetlands resumed in the 1940s and 1950s. While the state legislature of Minnesota began to enact laws for the conservation of wetlands – notably in response to the Pittman-Robertson Act of 1937, which offered federal funds to participating states for wildlife restoration projects – these measures were largely confined to public or navigable waters. It was not until 1973 that the Minnesota state legislature enacted a law that expanded the definition of public waters to include "all waters which serve a beneficial public purpose, thereby including wetlands."[12] By this time, the total extent of Minnesota's wetlands had been reduced by about half. In the prairie pothole region the loss of wetlands was much higher.

Conservation of wetlands in Minnesota and Wisconsin, as elsewhere, initially focused on their value as wildlife habitat. While wetlands generally drew public disdain because they inhibited most kinds of development, people appreciated the value of these forbidding landscapes as breeding grounds for ducks and other game birds. Beginning in the early twentieth century, the federal government began to set aside wetlands as bird refuges or wildlife refuges. The Fish and Wildlife Service sought to raise public awareness of the plight of duck populations whose breeding areas were drying up. At that time, both the prairie pothole region and the many sloughs along the Mississippi River gained national attention for their significance to waterfowl. During the 1930s and after, Congress enacted numerous laws aimed at coordinating protection of wetlands and other wildlife habitat with other land uses. Yet as long as wetlands protection remained narrowly focused on the conservation of wildlife, it could not withstand other social forces working toward the destruction of wetlands. In particular, the American belief in the sanctity of private property contributed to the demise of this resource, because wetlands almost invariably became more economically productive when they were drained. With the rise of environmental awareness in the 1960s, public policy toward wetlands began to change. Perhaps no other type of environment in the United States underwent such dramatic change in land use and public policy as wetlands.

Origins of the Section 404 Program

The Corps' authority to regulate use of the navigable waters of the United States dates from the early years of the Republic and derives from the federal government's constitutional power to regulate interstate and foreign commerce. The Corps' regulatory program took more specific form in the River and Harbor Act of 1899, which prohibited obstructions to navigability of waters of the United States. Section 10 of the act required the Department of the Army to issue a permit for any work involving navigable waters, including dredge and fill operations. Section 13 required a federal permit for any discharge of refuse matter except liquid sewage into navigable waters or their tributaries. Although the law extended the Corps' regulatory jurisdiction to areas upstream from navigable waters, in practice the regulatory function was limited to protection of navigation. Consequently, the Secretary of War and the Chief of Engineers used their authority judiciously on activities affecting navigation, rarely addressing matters concerning the environment.[13]

Decades later, in response to growing public concern for the environment, the Corps enlarged the scope of its regulatory function in 1968 to include not just the effect of a proposed action on navigation but also its effects on fish and wildlife, water quality, ecology and the general public interest. The following year, Congress passed the National Environmental Policy Act of 1969, or NEPA, which required all federal agencies with regulatory functions to prepare a detailed Environmental Impact Statement for permit actions that would significantly affect the quality of the human environment. NEPA specifically mandated that the review process involve public input and that it take an interdisciplinary approach by considering ecological, social and economic impacts. In response to NEPA, the Corps expanded its regulatory program to include interdisciplinary teams engaged in a general public interest review process, but its main focus remained on navigable waterways. This changed with the Federal Water Pollution Control Act Amendments of 1972, Federal Water Pollution Control Act, or Clean Water Act.[14]

The Federal Water Pollution Control Act established a national goal of eliminating discharge of pollution into waters by 1985. The law placed the Environmental Protection Agency in charge of a permitting program aimed at stopping pollution at its source.[15] While the Environmental Protection Agency had primary responsibility for the program, Section 404 of the act required the Corps assist the Environmental Protection Agency in its mission, stating in part: "The Secretary of the Army, acting through the Chief of Engineers, may issue permits, after notice and opportunity for public hearings[,] for the discharge of dredged or fill material into the navigable waters at specified disposal sites." The Federal Water Pollution Control Act defined navigable waters as "the waters of the United States, including the territorial seas." Given the law's ambitious goal to eliminate water pollution by 1985, Environmental Protection Agency interpreted the law liberally to include tributaries of navigable waters. The

Corps initially insisted upon a narrow interpretation of "waters of the United States" based on navigation, but environmentalists pressed the Corps through court action to take a more expansive view of its Section 404 authority.

In 1975, environmentalists won a landmark decision in Natural Resources Defense Council v. Callaway. District Judge Aubrey Robinson held that the Corps' definition of "waters of the United States" was too narrow and must be revised in accordance with Congress's intent in the Federal Water Pollution Control Act. In the court's opinion, Congress had intended that the Federal Water Pollution Control Act provide for the exercise of "federal jurisdiction over the nation's waters to the maximum extent permissible under the Commerce Clause of the Constitution." As a result of this decision, the Corps, in cooperation with the Environmental Protection Agency and with input from environmental organizations, prepared four alternative regulations for publication in the *Federal Register*.[16]

While this effort was underway, however, Corps' leadership continued to argue that a broad construal of its Section 404 authority to include wetlands would create a public outcry and a political backlash against the federal program. Although Corps' leaders obtained support for their position from the Department of Agriculture and the Department of Commerce, they failed to convince either the Department of the Interior or the Department of Justice, which refused to appeal the Callaway decision. Nor could Corps' officials get any policy guidance on Section 404 from the White House. As a result, senior officials in the Office of the Chief of Engineers determined to state their case directly to the American people through a press release. In so doing, they hoped to prompt congressional review of the Section 404 program and clarify congressional intent. To elicit a public response, officials directed the Public Affairs Office to craft a press release that would grab media attention and provoke widespread public opposition to the permit program. Released on the same day that the alternative regulations were published in the *Federal Register*, the press release warned that "millions of people may be presently violating the law" and stated that convicted offenders could be "subject to fines up to $25,000 a day and one year imprisonment." The St. Paul District, together with other districts, helped disseminate the information.[17]

The press release succeeded in provoking a public outcry. Thousands of protests poured into congressional offices. *The New York Times* accused the Corps of attempting a power grab. Secretary of Agriculture Earl Butz condemned the proposed regulation as a "dangerous extension of the long hand of the federal government into the affairs of private citizens." One official was quoted as stating that the Corps, lacking other means, would rely on farmers to snitch on one another in order to ensure compliance with its Section 404 permits. Environmental groups, meanwhile, lambasted the Corps for misrepresenting the facts and for attempting to sabotage the court ruling in Callaway.[18]

While the press release earned notoriety, it drew thousands of comments on the proposed regulations in the *Federal Register*. The Washington, D.C., office received more than 4,500 written comments from governors, congressmen, federal, state and local agencies, as well as organizations and individuals in the private sector. Working with the Environmental Protection Agency, the Corps issued an interim draft of revised regulations on July 25, 1975. The Corps then developed a public relations plan to sell its wetlands protection program, which it launched on September 4, 1975. District engineers were to inform the public that the "Corps of Engineers will be reasonable, moderate, objective and practical in administering the program." Brigadier General Kenneth McIntyre, Acting Director of Civil Works, explained the Section 404 program to state administrators. "The farming, ranching, and lumbering industries can rest assured that plowing, cultivating, seeding and harvesting will continue to be permitted without regulation," he said.[19]

During the next two years, Congress held hearings on the controversial Section 404. Various bills were introduced to modify or clarify the Corps' regulatory authority. Early in 1977, Congressman John Breaux (D-Louisiana) introduced a bill that would dramatically curtail the Corps' Section 404 jurisdiction, eliminating federal safeguards for about seventy- five percent of the nation's wetlands. Breaux had strong ties to development interests on the Lower Mississippi. With backing from House Majority Leader Jim Wright of Texas, the measure passed in the House by a wide margin. The Senate voted down the bill, but in joint conference later that year, the measure was used as a bargaining chip to extract concessions in a further set of amendments to the law. Congress passed the amendments on December 15, 1977, and President Carter signed them into law thirteen days later. The amended law was called the Clean Water Act of 1977. Environmentalists claimed victory insofar as the law affirmed the Corps' Section 404 jurisdiction as established by Callaway. But opponents won key exemptions from the permit process for normal farming, ranching, and silviculture activities, including minor ditch and road construction. In another key concession, states were allowed to administer portions of the permit program as soon as they would adopt regulatory standards deemed acceptable by the Environmental Protection Agency and the Corps – a prerogative that Minnesota and Wisconsin would both exercise about a decade later.[20]

The Clean Water Act of 1977 was a turning point in wetlands protection. From 1972 to 1977, the main issue surrounding Section 404 was whether Congress would repeal Section 404 (or amend it so drastically as to make it ineffective). After 1977, congressional support for Section 404 was no longer in doubt and the program acquired legitimacy. In the years ahead, the program would continue to be controversial, but environmentalists and developers would debate how to make it function better rather than argue over whether to implement or scrap the program.[21] During these formative years from 1972 to 1977, the Corps improved its relationship with environmental organizations – at least with regard to its regulatory mission. Historian Jeffrey K. Stine investigated the origins of the Section 404 program and concluded that the Corps' performance after 1975 won the respect of the environmental community. "Throughout the controversy over the extent of the Corps' jurisdiction under Section 404, environmental groups rarely tried to reduce the power of the Corps or to slow it down, as they had done repeatedly in the area of civil works," Stine wrote. "Despite occasional disagreements over individual permit decisions, a new basis for cooperation was clearly established."[22]

The St. Paul District faced an overwhelming task in assuming its Section 404 responsibilities in the 1970s. With some ten million acres of wetlands in Minnesota and five million acres in Wisconsin, no other Corps' district outside of Alaska contained so many wetlands, and few Corps' districts would process as many Section 404 permit applications. Moreover, the political landscape within the St. Paul District was challenging. Farmers in Minnesota and Wisconsin (and North Dakota, which remained within the district's regulatory purview in the 1970s) were highly suspicious of the program. Many county governments reflected the farmers' concerns. On the other hand, the large urban populaces of Minnesota and Wisconsin generally supported strong environmental regulations for protecting water quality. Reflecting these urban-based values, the Minnesota and Wisconsin state governments demanded higher standards for wetlands protection than most other states in the nation, while the North Dakota state government gave priority to protecting the state's farm-based economy.[23]

The St. Paul District phased in the Section 404 program over a two-year period, gradually applying the permitting requirements to wider geographic areas. In the first phase, from July 1975 to September 1976, the Corps required permits for discharges into the tributaries of navigable waters and wetlands adjacent to navigable waters. In the second phase, from September 1976 to July 1977, it required permits for discharges into tributaries of navigable waters and wetlands adjacent to those tributaries. Finally, beginning in July 1977, the program was extended to all water bodies in the district including mud holes, ponds, backwaters, lakes, rivers and streams.[24]

Initially, the Regulatory Branch had two sections. The permit evaluation section did all the preliminary work on each permit application. After establishing a permit file, making the public notice and receiving comments from other agencies and interested parties, the permit evaluation section turned over each permit application to the research and analysis section for an environmental assessment. The latter section was composed of biologists. After the biologists completed their work, the permit evaluation section could issue the permit – usually under certain conditions to protect the environment. By 1977, it had become clear that the Corps needed to track whether the permit holder complied with the terms of the permit, so it formed a third section, the surveillance and enforcement section. In time, the St. Paul District had about eight or nine investigators working in the surveillance and enforcement section.[25]

Ben Wopat, a long-time senior official in the St. Paul District office, joined the Corps in April 1976 when the district's Regulatory Branch was beginning to increase staff. Initially, Wopat was one of just four personnel in the unit. As the program expanded, the surveillance and enforcement section quickly outgrew its office space on the eleventh floor of the old Post Office building and had to relocate two floors below. There was no formal change in the organizational structure, but the staff group was physically set apart and was informally perceived within the organization as "the investigators down on the 9th floor." The staff came from a variety of academic disciplines other than engineering. Wopat, for example, had a law degree, as well as a master's degree in history. While the rest of the organization was providing public

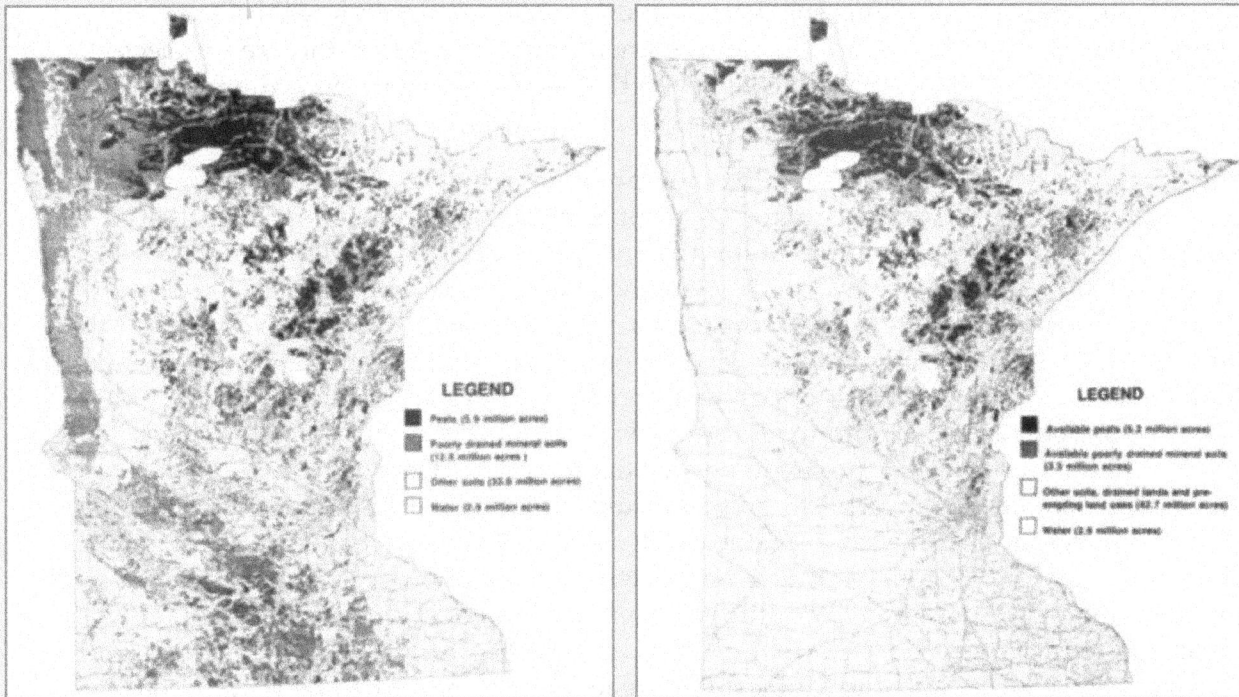

Original Minnesota wetlands (left). Existing Minnesota wetlands (right).
(Map courtesy of U.S. Fish and Wildlife Service)

services and building flood control projects, the Regulatory Branch was busy controlling development. "We were the guys with the black hats," Wopat wryly recalled in a recent interview. "Here we were down here telling people what they could not do with their own property. It was heathen and communistic."[26]

The demands on the Regulatory Branch were enormous. By the time the Section 404 program was fully operational in 1977, the St. Paul District covered an estimated 9 million acres of wetlands in Minnesota, Wisconsin and North Dakota. After two-and-a-half years, the staff processed some six hundred twenty permits involving 10,040 acres of wetlands. Approximately two-thirds of the applications resulted in permits, while the Corps and the applicants resolved most of the remainder by modifying the proposed action so that it did not require a permit. Only a handful of applications were rejected without some kind of alternative resolution for the applicant. During the same period, the Regulatory Branch authorized another 300 projects under general permits and issued nearly three hundred permits under Section 10 of the River and Harbor Act of 1899. The latter, so-called Section 10 permits, allowed placement of structures in navigable waters.

Despite this effort, the St. Paul District's regulatory staff cautioned that a huge amount of activity was occurring without regulation. Using information obtained from state programs, the Corps estimated that unauthorized actions during the same two-and-a-half-year period covered a whopping 1.8 million acres. Most of the noncompliance

123

resulted from public ignorance of the law. To tackle this problem, Corps' personnel joined state officials on various speaking tours. As public awareness of the Clean Water Act requirements spread, the ratio of unauthorized versus authorized projects diminished. St. Paul District officials believed that as of December 1977, the Section 404 program covered most major projects that posed significant threats to wetlands.[27]

Public ignorance of the law was not the only problem, however. Sometimes developers purposely skirted the Corps' regulatory authority or opposed it in court. In 1978, Ron McDaniels applied for a permit to build a Toyota car dealership in Maplewood, a suburb of St. Paul. The Ramsey County Soil and Water Conservation District found the proposed development site, which bordered a county drainage ditch, to be "critical" for filtering pollutants and sediments that would otherwise run into nearby Kohlman Lake. Moreover, if the site were blacktopped to accommodate the car lot, area homes would be prone to flood damage. Both the Ramsey-Washington Metro Watershed District Board and the Corps found the site to be a wetland, and the Corps finally denied McDaniels' federal permit application in the summer of 1979. McDaniels then sued the Corps, arguing that the site was not a wetland. Soon, the Maplewood City Council aligned itself with McDaniels, while a homeowners association opposed the developer. In the spring of 1980, District Court Judge Miles Lord ruled in McDaniels' favor: according to the judge, the site was not a wetland. But this did not end the matter. Four days after the court ruling, the Minnesota state legislature passed a law that placed the proposed development site under the jurisdiction of the Minnesota Department of Natural Resources. This extraordinary action by the state legislature forced McDaniels to work with the Minnesota Department of Natural Resources and the Corps after all.[28]

Ben Wopat, December 1981.
(Photo by Lyle Nicklay, courtesy of St. Paul District, Corps of Engineers)

As the St. Paul District's regulatory staff tried to raise public awareness of the Clean Water Act permitting requirements, they sometimes encountered frustration from members of the public who did not know who to contact for permit applications. In most cases, a developer such as Ron McDaniels had to satisfy three levels of government: federal, state and county. Sometimes, the situation demanded a permit from a municipality as well. The St. Paul District regulatory staff developed a single application form that could be filled out by the applicant and supplied to all four offices – federal, state, county and municipal. As a result, instead of going through a series of permit application processes, the applicant could initiate one process and all four offices would proceed simultaneously. Some state officials resisted the uniform application form but eventually became convinced that a joint federal-state application form best served the public.[29]

Just as Wopat had to work with multiple state offices on this issue, so too did state officials have to work with more than one district of the Corps of Engineers. Because of the need for public outreach and coordination with multiple levels of government, Wopat argued that the Section 404 program would be strengthened if the St. Paul District's jurisdiction followed political rather than watershed boundaries. With the support of his district engineer, and eventually under orders from Corps' headquarters, Wopat negotiated with his counterparts in neighboring districts to achieve a realignment of St. Paul District boundaries for purposes of the Section 404 regulatory program. First, by mutual agreement, the St. Paul District relinquished its small portion of Iowa in exchange for the Rock Island District's little piece of Minnesota and the Rock River watershed in Wisconsin. Next, the St. Paul District gave up its portion of North Dakota to the Omaha District. Then it exchanged the Upper Peninsula of Michigan for the Detroit District's Fox River watershed and its Lake Michigan watershed in Wisconsin. Finally, it obtained from the Chicago District the southeastern corner of Wisconsin. By this series of mutual agreements, the St. Paul District's Section 404 program came to serve all of Minnesota and Wisconsin and no parts of other states. In some other parts of the nation, districts followed this lead so that Section 404 permitting conformed to state lines rather than watershed boundaries.[30]

Nationwide Permit 26 and the Rise of State Programs

In order to process tens of thousands of Section 404 permit applications annually, the Corps developed a two-tiered approach using individual and general permits. Individual permits involved large or unusual actions that required a full public interest review. General permits involved small, routine actions that were believed to have minimal environmental impact. Once the Corps determined an action could be handled under a general permit, the action was essentially pre-approved and did not need to undergo the same level of public notice and review. For example, Corps' headquarters developed a general permit for bank stabilization projects. If a proposed bank stabilization project could be designed to meet the environmental conditions specified by the general permit, the permitting process was considerably expedited. Although the general permits dealt with relatively benign actions, they were significant because of the cumulative environmental impact of so many similar but separate actions going forward under one set of standards. At best, the two tiered approach facilitated an appropriate scaling of effort that discouraged excessive regulation. At worst, it was no more than a form of triage for dealing with loss of wetlands on many fronts. Environmentalists viewed the Corps' approach in this negative light and focused on general permits as the weak link in the Section 404 program. In time, state agencies responsible for wetlands protection began to share environmentalists' concerns.

The two-tiered approach to Section 404 permitting won congressional approval in the Clean Water Act amendments of 1977. Immediately, the Corps began to develop a number of "nationwide" (general) permits to address various activities. One of these permits, Nationwide Permit 26 (NWP 26), covered actions that involved discharges of dredged material above headwaters and in isolated waters (such as prairie potholes).

NWP 26 provided a vehicle for the Corps to handle the vast geographic scope of Section 404. As such, it was the only nationwide permit to deal with a type of wetland environment rather than a type of construction activity.[31] For thousands of farmers in Minnesota and Wisconsin whose property included wetland, NWP 26 offered a fast track through the Section 404 process.

With the advent of the Reagan Administration in 1981, Corps' leadership anticipated a rollback in the Section 404 program. Ronald Reagan had campaigned for president on a platform of smaller government. He fervently believed in reducing government red tape. In particular, he wanted to ease the burden of environmental protection for agriculture and industry. His primary tactic in bringing about regulatory reform, it soon became clear, was to starve selected regulatory programs of funds. As Secretary of the Interior James Watt explained, "We will use the budget system [as] the excuse to make major policy decisions."[32] Reagan's appointee to oversee the Army Corps, Assistant Secretary of the Army for Civil Works William R. Gianelli, immediately began to study alternatives for shrinking the Section 404 program. Broader use of nationwide permits – with the reduction in federal oversight that that shift entailed – was central to his plan.

In July 1982, the Corps published a revision of Section 404 regulations. The new rules included a broadening of NWP 26 authority.[33] A coalition of environmental organizations filed suit in U.S. District Court in Washington, D.C., charging that the new rules would exempt millions of acres of wetlands from the requirement to obtain individual permits to dispose of dredged material, violating the intent of the Clean Water Act. While administration officials defended the new rules as necessary in the face of limited funding, environmentalists accused the administration of "abandoning the nation's wetlands under the guise of regulatory reform."[34]

State agencies in Minnesota and Wisconsin also criticized the new rules. The Minnesota Pollution Control Agency citizens' board voted unanimously to sue the Corps on the basis that the NWP-26 permit would not require state review of the proposed action. According to one Minnesota Pollution Control Agency official, the new rules would lift state authority over vast peat bogs in northern Minnesota, as well as several million acres of waterfowl-rich marshes in the prairie pothole region.[35]

St. Paul District Engineer Colonel William W. Badger supported the rollback of Section 404 regulations in principle. He responded favorably to the Reagan Administration's emphasis on cutting red tape and pushing economic development. He was impatient with those whom he called "termites" in the agency, the low-level technocrats who eschewed action in favor of further study and deliberation. However, he was also mindful that the people of Minnesota and Wisconsin were more supportive of environmental regulations than the nation as a whole. "We in the St. Paul District are in a very environmentally sensitive region," he told an interviewer in July 1981. "We have the potholes, the wetlands, and the 10,000 lakes and the people that we serve are locked in step to preserve these wetlands." Consequently, Colonel Badger wanted to work with the Minnesota and Wisconsin Departments of Natural Resources and adapt Section 404 regulations to meet their requirements. The St. Paul District ought to "fine-tune" and "retain" the Section 404 program, Badger held, rather than "roll it back."[36]

Badger encouraged Ben Wopat and others in the regulatory branch to negotiate with state officials in the Minnesota and Wisconsin DNRs over adjustments to NWP 26 and other nationwide permits. The idea was to modify the rules to reflect regional conditions – both environmental and political. As a result of these discussions, the Wisconsin DNR published state guidelines in November 1982. The Minnesota DNR completed its guidelines in April 1984. These efforts laid the groundwork for a more comprehensive effort to coordinate wetlands protection at the federal and state levels through the development of programmatic general permits with each state. The programmatic general permit defined various actions affecting wetlands that fell within both federal and state jurisdiction. Any action that required an application for a programmatic general permit would be reviewed by federal and state agencies. The arrangement satisfied state officials that they would not be bypassed in the federal permitting process, especially where NWP 26 was employed. Federal officials, for their part, received assurance that the review process would not become bogged down; both the Corps and the DNRs were committed to respond to programmatic general permits applications within ten days. In addition, the district engineer had discretionary authority to require an individual permit for any area outside the purview of the programmatic general permit that he considered to be sensitive. The district engineer invoked this authority to protect those rare and minuscule wetlands known as calcareous fens.[37] By the mid-1980s, the St. Paul District was a leader in developing coordinated federal and state procedures to fulfill the purposes of Section 404 of the Clean Water Act.

In the meantime, the lawsuit brought by environmental groups over NWP 26 was settled out of court. According to the settlement terms, NWP 26 was rewritten so it was limited to projects that would impact up to ten acres of wetlands in headwaters or isolated waters. Any project that would impact more than ten acres would no longer be authorized under the nationwide permit. Moreover, the Corps would take a closer look at projects that would impact one to ten acres. Any project that would impact more than one acre would require public notice. The Corps issued the new regulations, including modification of NWP 26, in October 1984.

Environmentalists still distrusted the intent of NWP 26. In the 1990s, they attacked the ten-acre limit as too lenient; however, for the time being it was allowed to stand.

Wetlands Delineation

One of the most controversial aspects of wetlands protection was how to define a wetland. Even after Congress and the courts resolved the issue of whether the "waters of the United States" extended to wetlands, the problem remained of establishing guidelines so that people could agree on where wetlands ended and uplands began. In general, wetlands were defined as areas inundated or saturated by water at a frequency and duration sufficient to support plants that were adapted to saturated soil conditions. Ecologists recognized wetlands by the vegetation that grew on them. Experts could not agree on specific guidelines, however, and the public remained befuddled about what constituted a wetland. Gradually, it became apparent that the Corps needed a scientifically sound and workable definition – one that could be applied in the field with consistency so that the jurisdictional boundaries of Section 404 were made clear.

The Corps' generous use of NWP 26 in the early 1980s fueled the controversy over wetlands delineation. Environmentalists argued that many thousands of acres of wetlands were being destroyed each year under NWP 26 authorizations. Regulators noted that without uniform standards as to what constituted a wetland, environmentalists' estimates concerning the total extent and rate of loss of wetlands had to be treated circumspectly. Farmers, for their part, were leery of any definition of wetlands that could bring previously converted wetlands – croplands that were lying fallow, for example – under the Clean Water Act's purview. In short, environmentalists, regulators and farmers all had their own agendas for wetlands delineation. The question of what is a wetland, though posed to science, stemmed from politics.

Nowhere, perhaps, was wetland delineation more controversial than in Minnesota, where county drainage ditches crisscrossed the countryside, forming a peculiar network of man-made wetlands. The ditches had been constructed in the early decades of the twentieth century to drain wetlands and render adjoining areas suitable for agriculture. Often, they ran parallel to county roads. The ditches gradually filled with debris, which interrupted the flow of water, so that they had to be periodically cleaned to keep them functional. For decades, county ditch boards oversaw the maintenance of ditches on a public need basis, but many ditches had been abandoned and the county ditch boards had ceased to exist. As counties fell behind on maintenance, the process of land conversion was reversed. The ditches clogged, the water ceased to flow and the surrounding area returned to wetlands. As these clogged ditches became less effective in draining surrounding agricultural fields, the resulting wetlands performed a new function: they acted as filters to absorb farm chemicals and other pollutants that would otherwise flow into natural streams and rivers. Moreover, they provided habitat for wildlife. The Corps was bound by the Clean Water Act to protect these linear wetlands, but rural county governments saw the Corps' responsibility as an intrusion into local affairs. Speaking on behalf of the public need for a particular ditch repair, Meeker

County Commissioner Steve Dille expressed a concern common to many rural residents when he remarked, "The thing that bothers me is the loss of local control and the need to contact Washington for permission."[38]

As public awareness of wetlands increased, ditch improvement proposals often proved divisive among area residents. Farmers might desire ditch maintenance to get waterlogged fields back into production, while nearby townspeople preferred to protect downstream water quality. When controversy arose, the St. Paul District held public hearings to gather information that would assist in its determination of whether a permit served the public interest. In a notable example, the Corps scheduled a public hearing in Stevens County to garner testimony on a proposed ditch project. Proponents wanted to improve County Ditch 6 for drainage and flood control. Opponents claimed the ditch improvement would pollute the waters of Page Lake, harming its recreational and economic value. Twice the meeting was postponed at the request of county officials. An editorial in the Hancock *Record* admonished readers to participate: "The upcoming public hearing concerning the proposed alteration of County Ditch 6 and Page Lake is perhaps the single most important hearing that the citizens of Hancock and surrounding area can ever attend." When the hearing finally occurred in December 1981 in the town of Morris, Minnesota, population five thousand, some two hundred people packed the courthouse hearing room.[39] Evidently the public response served to kill the project.

Rural county governments often bristled at involvement by the Corps, even when the Corps sought to facilitate public review of project proposals. In 1986, the Corps denied a permit application to improve Ditch 5 in McLeod County, which lies in Minnesota's prairie pothole region. Later that year, the Board of Commissioners of McLeod County narrowly approved a resolution that effectively barred future expansion of Ditch 5. The resolution, drafted by attorneys in the St. Paul District office for the county commissioners, sought to clear the way for Corps' approval of a county permit application involving two other ditches. Two of the five commissioners opposed the resolution on the grounds that it smacked of "arm twisting" by the Corps.[40]

The problematic relationship between agricultural drainage ditches and wetlands was not unique to the St. Paul District, but the connection was perhaps more complex there than in any other part of the nation. Beginning about 1984, a wet cycle in the region's climate caused water tables to rise, spurring counties to initiate ditch repair projects for the first time in many years. As with Ditch 5 in McLeod County, most of these projects went beyond maintenance, thereby threatening destruction not only of wetlands that had become reestablished along the ditch corridor itself, but wetlands in adjoining areas as well.[41] Insofar as regulators sought to distinguish between existing versus previously converted wetlands, ditch projects were particularly confounding.

The problem of defining wetlands undoubtedly perplexed rural residents more than it did urban residents, but it could turn up anywhere. In 1986, district ecologist Steve Eggers discovered a calcareous fen in Savage, a Minneapolis suburb. This rare type of wetland, blooming with plants and grasses that the state had classified as threatened species, was found at the end of a gravel road behind a concrete-panel casting factory. To the newspaper reporter who accompanied Eggers to the Savage fen site, the small spring-fed wetland looked like nothing but a "patch of weeds." According to Eggers, the Corps was aware of three other calcareous fens in the Twin Cities metropolitan area.[42]

Eggers, like other Corps' ecologists, recognized a wetland by the composition of wetland plant species. In theory, only certain species of plants could grow in water-saturated soils, and these plant species were then indicators of a wetland. Eggers' field guide presented a classification scheme for wetland types. However, Eggers and other ecologists in the Corps increasingly saw the need for a more precise and legally defensible method for delineating wetlands. In 1987, the Corps accordingly produced a manual. Based on seven years of research and testing, it offered numerical standards for the three basic attributes of wetlands – water, soil and vegetation. For example, the hydrology (water) standard included this requirement: to qualify as wetland, the soil must be inundated or saturated within major portions of the root zone (within twelve inches of the surface) during at least five percent of the growing season.[43]

However, the manual did not satisfy critics. The Reagan Administration directed four agencies, the EPA, the Corps, the Fish and Wildlife Service and the Soil Conservation Service, to develop standards that all four could agree upon; and in 1989, the agencies produced the "Joint Four-Agency Wetland Delineation Manual." It was similar in most respects to the Corps' 1987 manual. On the specific hydrology standard noted above, however, the 1989 manual stated soil must be inundated or saturated to a depth of six to eight inches for at least seven consecutive days during the growing season. This seemingly subtle difference marked the 1989 manual as more inclusive in its definition of a wetland.[44]

Pro-development critics blasted the 1989 manual primarily on the grounds that it would redefine millions of acres of farmland as wetland. Apparently by mistake, the 1989 manual included an estimated 53 million acres of farmland that had been exempted from Section 404 regulations under provisions of the Food Security Act of 1985. Also, critics complained that the hydrological definition was too broad and that the 1989 manual had not undergone a public review process.[45]

With wetland policy in the national limelight, newly elected President George H.W. Bush announced his administration's goal of "no net loss of wetlands." Bush called for a review and revision of the 1989 manual and appointed a panel of experts, the Federal Interagency Committee for Wetland Delineation, to accomplish this task. After a two-year study, the committee announced its findings. Taking a more restrictive view of wetlands than either the Corps' 1987 manual or the four agencies' 1989 manual, the committee's draft revisions, if implemented, would have eliminated 50 million acres of widely recognized wetlands. Indeed, field testing of the proposed criteria revealed that parts of the Everglades in Florida and the Great Dismal Swamp in North Carolina would be excluded from federal jurisdiction. Now it was the environmentalists' turn to cry foul. Coming to the environmentalists' support, both the EPA and the Corps found the committee's revisions were unscientific and unusable in the field.[46]

Congress responded to the uproar by requesting yet another study of wetlands delineation by the National Academy of Sciences. At the same time, Congress directed the Corps to drop its use of the 1989 manual in favor of its earlier 1987 guidelines. Other agencies followed suit in adopting the Corps' original criteria for wetlands delineation. By the time the National Academy of Sciences completed its study in 1995, the controversy had subsided. The National Academy of Sciences concluded that the existing federal wetlands regulatory program was scientifically sound and effective in most respects.[47]

Swampbuster

In the spring of 1985, the House Agriculture Committee introduced a provision in the farm bill that would deny agricultural subsidies to any farmer who planted crops on wetlands. Known as "Swampbuster," the provision was modeled on a similar conservation measure, called "Sodbuster," which aimed at discouraging farmers on the Great Plains from plowing up new sod. Like Sodbuster, the Swampbuster provision would reverse outmoded farm policy that actually gave farmers incentive to convert wetlands to agriculture even when this action undermined wetland policy. The concept of pushing a conservation measure by tying it to eligibility for farm subsidies appealed to a Congress searching for ways to cut federal subsidies. It also appealed to environmental groups, including conservation-oriented farm groups such as the National Association of Conservation Districts.[48]

President Ronald Reagan signed the Food Security Act into law on February 23, 1985. According to the Swampbuster provision, any farmer who planted crops on wetlands after the date of the act would lose eligibility for commodity price supports, disaster payments, Farm and Home Administration loans and crop insurance. The law used a definition of wetlands similar to that developed by the Corps in its Section 404 regulations – based on soil, hydrology and vegetation. Drainage projects that were in progress could be completed if they had been initiated prior to February 23, 1985.[49]

Enforcement of Swampbuster fell primarily to the Soil Conservation Service in the U.S. Department of Agriculture. The Soil Conservation Service and the U.S. Fish and Wildlife Service jointly developed guidelines and disseminated them through state and county offices in March 1986. Like the Corps a decade earlier, the Soil Conservation Service acquired the enormous task of identifying and monitoring wetlands throughout farm country. Although it had some seven thousand personnel in the field, Soil Conservation Service agents were not trained to recognize wetlands nor were they anxious to do surveillance. Soil Conservation Service agents enjoyed the role of helping farmers negotiate the maze of federal programs, and they resisted assuming what amounted to a role reversal. "In small farm communities where everyone knew everyone and there was only one coffee shop to go to in the morning, the pressure not to enforce the provision was tremendous," historian Ann Vileisis wrote.[50] Reported violations were rare, and sanctions against violators were even rarer.

In theory, Swampbuster should have buttressed the Section 404 program because farmers who violated their Section 404 permits could face additional penalties from the Soil Conservation Service. Initially, the Corps received excellent cooperation from Soil Conservation Service officials in sharing information on their respective programs. As

Corps' officials went from their Soil Conservation Service contacts in state offices to Soil Conservation Service agents in the field, however, they found much less willingness on the part of the agents to assist with wetlands protection. Whereas the Soil Conservation Service agents had been "the guys in the white hats that were helping the farmers with programs," Ben Wopat recalled, "all of a sudden here they were viewed as the bad guys who were now telling them what they couldn't do rather than helping them do things that they wanted to do to improve or expand their agricultural production."[51]

Farm groups objected to Swampbuster and vigorously lobbied for changes in the law when it came up for reauthorization in 1990. Congress made minor adjustments to Swampbuster in the Food, Agriculture, Conservation and Trade Act, which was signed into law on November 28, 1990. One key change was the introduction of graduated penalties for unintentional violations. Farmers were allowed one violation in ten years, and they stood to lose benefits of $750 to $10,000, depending on the severity of the violation. The law also redefined the Swampbuster prohibition itself. Rather than prohibiting the planting of crops in wetlands, it prohibited any act of draining, dredging, filling, leveling or otherwise altering wetlands to produce an agricultural commodity.[52]

While these amendments removed some of the teeth from Swampbuster, the program's main shortcoming continued to be weak enforcement by the Soil Conservation Service and other federal agencies. Soil Conservation Service agents were supposed to report violations to the Agricultural Stabilization and Conservation Service, which oversaw local committees of farmers that were tasked to assess penalties. The Agricultural Stabilization and Conservation Service committees proved highly recalcitrant, granting "good faith" exemptions to hundreds of violators. In 1991, the National Wildlife Federation sued the Agricultural Stabilization and Conservation Service for granting exemptions to farmers who drained eighteen prairie potholes in the Yellow Medicine River watershed in Minnesota. The circuit court of appeals ruled that the farmers must restore the potholes or forfeit their farm subsidies. Despite this rebuke from the court, the Agricultural Stabilization and Conservation Service continued to issue exemptions. An audit of Agricultural Stabilization and Conservation Service actions in Nelson County, North Dakota, in 1993 revealed that the Agricultural Stabilization and Conservation Service granted exemptions in eleven of thirty randomly-selected cases. Other audits in 1993 disclosed $1.2 million in subsidies paid to six farmers who had violated Swampbuster. Total forfeiture of subsidies under Swampbuster amounted to just $12 million for the period 1986-1992. After the government subsequently restored a large portion of these subsidies, total penalties amounted to less than $3,000 per farm for some five hundred forty-four violators.[53]

Critics also pointed out that the Soil Conservation Service was lax in mapping wetlands. In 1994, environmentalists compared Soil Conservation Service wetlands maps and Fish and Wildlife Service wetlands maps for twenty-one counties in Minnesota and found that the Soil Conservation Service identified only fifty-seven percent of the area that the Fish and Wildlife Service identified as wetlands. Although officials in the two agencies refused to comment on the disparity, environmentalists charged that some 2,678 acres of wetland were "missing" from Soil Conservation Service maps in the twenty-one counties. Extrapolating from those counties to the rest of the state, environmentalists observed that "approximately 875,000 acres of Minnesota wetlands could have been drained with Soil Conservation Service consent."[54]

Swampbuster revealed how difficult it was to protect wetlands when responsibility for wetlands protection was divided between multiple federal agencies. As Corps' officials continually reminded the public, Section 404 was extremely broad in its reference to "the nation's waters," but it was narrow in its concern only with dredged and fill material. While the Corps had shown some success in defining what a wetland is, it was not responsible for mapping or inventorying wetlands or monitoring losses, and most experts agreed that the total extent of wetlands continued to shrink despite federal policy to promote "no net loss."

Defining the Section 404(f) Farming Exemption

As noted above, the Clean Water Act amendments of 1977 included a handful of exemptions, the most significant one being for normal farming activity. The exemptions were part of a larger compromise to recognize property rights in the national Section 404 program. When farmers faced the dual effects of Swampbuster and more restricted use of NWP 26, they countered by claiming exemption under Section 404(f) of the Clean Water Act. Like the Soil Conservation Service, the Corps did not want to engender widespread resistance to wetlands protection from the farm community, so it worked with farm groups to reach an understanding.

Agricultural drainage ditches once again forced the issue. In 1984 – an unusually wet year in Minnesota – a number of counties began taking steps to repair old drainage ditches. Since many of these ditches had been abandoned for several decades, it was questionable whether the ditch repairs should be defined as maintenance or new construction. The Corps initially chose to take all ditch repairs at their face value as maintenance, but environmental groups protested. After environmental groups sued the Corps in District Court in Washington, D.C., the Corps changed its position. The Corps published regulations on November 22, 1985, requiring permits for all drainage projects that would expand the original size of the ditch.[55]

One of the first counties to respond to this change of policy was Stearns County, in central Minnesota, where several ditch improvement projects were underway. The county duly applied for Section 404 permits for each project, and then placed a moratorium on the work pending the Corps' response. In the meantime, the Stearns County commissioners passed a resolution calling on the Association of Minnesota Counties and the U.S. Congress to prevail on the Corps to revise its policy to accord with the definition of ditch repairs used by the Minnesota DNR. According to the Minnesota DNR, all ditch repairs constituted maintenance. One such project in Becker County in northwest Minnesota called for restoring a ditch to its condition in 1920. The project was classified as "repair" in the hope that the Corps would not require a permit. County commissioners recognized that defining the project as a "repair" was something of a charade, because in practical terms it did not make sense to restore ditches to their original shape. "Nobody wants to do that," conceded Don Ogaard, president of the Wild Rice Watershed District, "because that's the reason they eroded in the first place. They want to change the design and backslope and properly slope the sides."[56]

During the next year, the St. Paul District denied numerous applications for ditch repairs on the grounds that they would drain surrounding wetlands. In particular, the Corps noted that most "repair" projects included construction of new lateral ditches and placement of new tile drain systems, not to mention enlargement of the original ditch.[57] But with hundreds of thousands of dollars already invested in planning, county governments were stung by these permit denials. Moreover, farmers with standing water on their fields could not obtain relief. Resentment toward federal regulators grew.[58] One newspaper headline announced with obvious irony: "Flooded county ditches create 'wetlands' in federal view."[59]

Farming & Wetlands

Section 404 permitting addressed encroachment of wetlands by cropland development such as seen in these photographs. (Photos by Steve D. Eggers, courtesy of St. Paul District, Corps of Engineers)

In January 1987, the St. Paul District hosted a meeting of federal and state regulators to discuss differences of interpretation over ditch repairs. Ben Wopat headed the team of Corps' staff, Doug Ehorn represented the Environmental Protection Agency and others attended from the Soil Conservation Service, the Minnesota DNR and the Minnesota Pollution Control Agency. Wopat explained that the Corps' current interpretation of the exemption was that the project qualified as "maintenance" if it returned the ditch to its original size and configuration. There was a presumption that this would not bring a drained wetland into a new use but would restore earlier agricultural land use. Ehorn stated that the Environmental Protection Agency wondered whether "legitimate farming" had ever been done on lands that had long since returned to wetlands. They were also skeptical of ditches that dated back to the 1910s and 1920s that had never seen any maintenance. The meeting pointed to the need for interagency agreement on what constituted ditch maintenance.[60]

At Wopat's initiative, District Engineer Colonel Joseph Briggs detailed Wopat to work with Doug Ehorn of the Environmental Protection Agency's Region 5 office in Chicago. Their task was to develop an enforceable standard that would measure whether an area had been subjected to regular if not continuous farming use. Only then would their agencies certify that a project would not convert an area of wetland to a new use. The result of their deliberations was a joint policy for the St. Paul District known as the "51-51 policy." Colonel Briggs announced the policy on November 23, 1987.[61]

The policy called for a dual test that measured both the extent and duration of past farming in a given area. To qualify for the Section 404(f) exemption, it was necessary to show that 51 percent of the wetlands physically connected to a drainage ditch had been subject to the plowing, seeding and cultivating agricultural cycle for fifty-one percent of the time for which credible agricultural records existed and were available. In addition to the "51-51 test," the policy affirmed the Corps' requirement that the ditch must be returned to its original condition. It was the applicant's responsibility to document the original size and configuration of the ditch by providing such evidence as engineering plans, soil borings and contractor records. The record of past agricultural usage would be documented through aerial photos, crop histories, agricultural subsidy records and personal statements.[62]

As the 51-51 policy was implemented, the St. Paul District found the historical assessment to be a labor-intensive exercise, yet the results were illuminating. "We'd draw out the drainage basin, and take a look at the aerial maps – usually they went back to about 1936, '37, and we'd bring them up to the present," Wopat recalled. "And we'd look at the span of fifty or sixty years and we would look at how much wetland there was adjacent to that ditch and how much of it actually was reflected as being cropped during those years."[63] In most cases, the project did not meet the 51-51 test. Indeed, during the next eighteen months, the St. Paul District evaluated twenty ditch maintenance permit applications, of which it granted three and denied seventeen.[64]

The 51-51 policy caused further dismay in the farm community and contributed to a sudden flap over another proposed rule change by the St. Paul District in the winter of 1988-1989. The controversial proposal pertained specifically to the prairie pothole region. It designated fifty-one counties in western Minnesota – covering the prairie pothole region – as exempt from NWP 26. This nationwide permit applied to dredge and fill actions that would impact wetlands in headwaters or isolated waters. NWP 26 required a predischarge notification and evaluation process for proposed actions that would impact from one to ten acres. The purpose of the rule change, the Corps belatedly tried to explain to farmers, was simply to bypass the predischarge notification and move applicants straight into the individual permit review process because experience had shown that most proposed actions in the fifty-one western Minnesota counties did not meet the regional conditions attached to NWP 26 anyway. "The intent was to streamline the administrative burden posed by the predischarge notification process," one official in the Corps later insisted. These subtleties were lost on the region's farmers, however, who saw the suspension of NWP 26 as a ploy to tighten restrictions on use of lands bordering prairie potholes.[65]

The reaction from the farm community surprised Corps' officials. "Many of the comments received in response to the public notice for the proposed exercise of discretionary authority over the prairie pothole region reflected widespread confusion and misunderstanding of the Corps' regulatory program, especially as it applied to agricultural drainage projects," one official noted. "In addition, the public was virtually unaware of the regional conditions that apply to the nationwide permit for discharges of dredged or fill material into waters located above the headwaters of a stream or into isolated waters." The regional conditions had been introduced several years earlier to comply with environmental standards developed by state agencies. In an effort to increase public understanding of Section 404 requirements, the Corps held five public meetings in the prairie pothole region of Minnesota in February 1989. District Engineer Colonel Roger Baldwin also withdrew the proposed rulemaking that same month.[66]

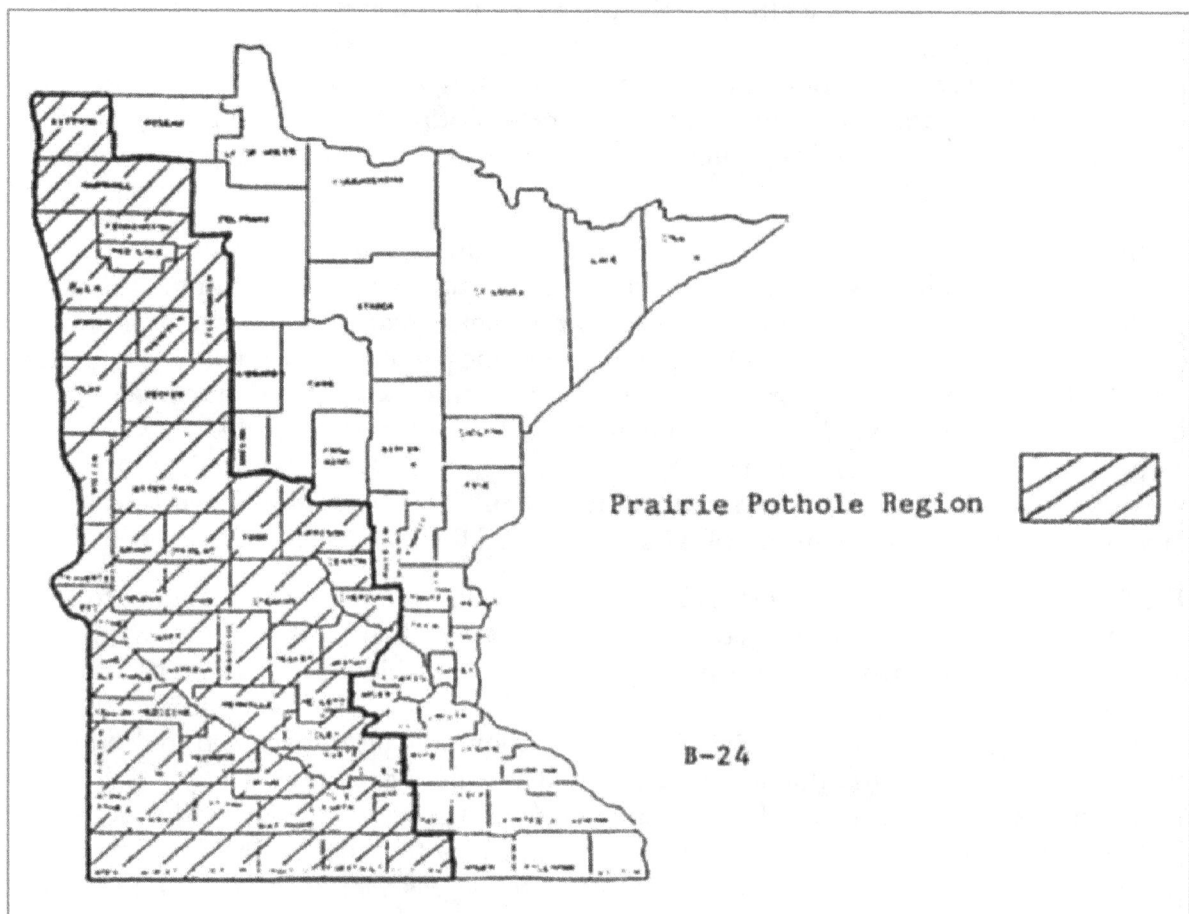

Prairie Pothole Region: Map of 51 counties in western and southern Minnesota that the Corps ruled ineligible for Nationwide Permit 26 because of sensitive prairie pothole wetlands. (Map courtesy of St. Paul District, Corps of Engineers)

The controversies surrounding agricultural drainage ditches and NWP 26 prompted a congressional hearing in St. Cloud, Minnesota, in April 1989. In preparation for the hearing, Wopat prepared testimony for Principal Deputy Assistant Secretary of the Army (Civil Works) John S. Doyle, Jr. The Corps hoped to get clarification from Congress on the Section 404(f) exemption for farming activity. Congressman Arlan Stangeland (R-Minnesota), whose district included St. Cloud in Stearns County, conducted the hearing. At the conclusion of the hearing, the congressional subcommittee went by helicopter to inspect Stearns County Ditch 29, a project the Corps determined could not be permitted. The congressional hearing in St. Cloud raised interest in the murky problems surrounding the Section 404(f) exemption for farming use, but Corps' officials were disappointed that it did not result in amendatory legislation.[67] Later, Stearns County went forward with Ditch 29, challenging the Corps' Section 404 authority. The Corps sued Stearns County, hoping a court ruling would provide judicial guidance on whether ditch maintenance came under the Section 404(f) exemption. However, the Department of Justice settled the case out of court, so this, too, did not provide the desired clarification.[68]

Having failed to obtain clarification of the farming exemption from Congress or the courts, the Corps and the Environmental Protection Agency found they had no choice but to adopt a more accommodating position on the issue. The two agencies issued a joint memorandum on May 4, 1990. Signed by Assistant Secretary of the Army for Civil Works Robert W. Page and Environmental Protection Agency Assistant Administrator Walter LaJuana S. Wilcher, the statement read: "The exemptions ... recognize that American agriculture fulfills the vitally important public need for supplying abundant and affordable food and fiber, and it is our intent to assure that the exemptions are appropriately implemented." The memorandum launched a broad effort on the part of the Corps and the Environmental Protection Agency to rebuild trust with the farm community on issues involving wetlands.[69] In September 1990, Major General Patrick J. Kelly, Director of Civil Works, issued a guidance letter to all Corps' districts aimed at further placating farmers. Kelly's statement held that "prior converted croplands" would not require Section 404 permits. In general, this applied to wetland that had been manipulated for agricultural production before December 23, 1985 – prior to Swampbuster. "This guidance," the statement continued, "will allow the Corps to focus its limited regulatory resources on the nation's truly important and significant aquatic resources."[70]

Cranberry Farms and Mitigation Banks

Cranberry farmers in Wisconsin raised another issue connected with wetland conversion. The Corps supported a conservation approach called "mitigation banking." A mitigation bank was any private land area where wetlands were saved, restored or created and "sold" as credits to balance the loss of equivalent wetlands acreages elsewhere. When the cranberry industry began to expand sharply in Wisconsin in the 1980s, the Corps took a permissive view of wetland conversion to cranberry farms. The reason for the Corps' leniency was that cranberry farms arguably enhanced the value of existing wetlands, much like mitigation banks. The controversy over cranberry farms paralleled a wider debate over mitigation banks.

Cranberry farmers situated their cranberry beds in acidic, sandy soils. During the growing season, cranberry farmers tried to keep the water table between nine and twelve inches below the surface elevation of the beds. Construction of reservoirs was typically integral to the operation, as large quantities of water had to be delivered to the beds to keep them saturated. The reservoirs created a more stable hydrology. "In many cases," Tom Lochner, executive director of the Wisconsin Cranberry Growers Association remarked, "we end up with a higher quality wetlands system that attracts a tremendous diversity of wildlife."[71]

Corps' officials supported the industry position. "The cranberry growers are obviously attuned to a number of environmental concerns," District Engineer Colonel Roger Baldwin stated during a tour of cranberry fields by members of Congress in 1989. Their growing practices, Baldwin said, demonstrated "tremendous environmental awareness." Cranberry growers needed vast amounts of water in the surrounding area in order to maintain a high water table. For every acre that they put into cranberry beds, growers set aside about thirteen acres of woodland, fields and wetlands for the purpose of recharging groundwater and controlling storm water runoff. These surrounding lands also provided habitat for wildlife and plants.[72]

Environmentalists were not so sanguine. They noted cranberry operations involved stripping and leveling the land put into cultivation. Moreover, use of pesticides and fertilizers on cranberry beds impacted water quality in surrounding areas. Environmentalists wanted cranberry growers to expand into uplands, not wetlands – an alternative that growers claimed to be prohibitively expensive.[73]

In the early 1990s, the St. Paul District took steps to counter environmentalists' concerns about the Wisconsin cranberry industry. First, it developed a general permit for expansion of existing cranberry operations where the total acreage of disturbance would not exceed ten acres of wetlands. The permit included construction of new cranberry beds adjacent to existing beds, as well as construction or extension of dikes for reservoir expansion. The ten-acre limit would be measured over a five-year period. The Corps noted that with approximately a hundred and fifty cranberry farms in existence, the loss of wetlands over a five-year period would be no greater than 1,500 acres – far less than what critics of the cranberry industry supposed. Moreover, mitigation measures (such as mitigation banking) would offset the losses. The Corps wanted the general permit so that growers would not have to obtain individual permits and the Corps would be able to divert resources away from these controversial actions to permitting actions that were, in the Corps' view, more important.[74]

At the same time, the St. Paul District conducted a comprehensive study of cranberry operations in Wisconsin authorized under Section 404 of the Clean Water Act. The point of the study was to rebut a Wisconsin DNR study, which found that cranberry operations were responsible for more than half of wetland losses in the state between 1981 and 1989. Whereas the state's study indicated a loss of 9,247 acres, the Corps' study showed a loss of 2,737 acres. Whereas the state's study considered cranberry beds as a loss, the Corps classified cranberry beds as modified wetlands with diminished function and values. In Ben Wopat's view, the state's study was motivated by the DNR's desire to obtain regulatory control of the industry, which it could only accomplish by the repeal of a troublesome state statute of 1867. That statute exempted cranberry growers from permit requirements for damming, ditching and other activities that were normally regulated under Wisconsin laws. The Corps, for its part, sought to justify its approach to Section 404 permitting, with its emphasis on mitigation over prevention. The Corps' study began with a more inclusive definition of wetlands, and it took a much different view of the mitigation process and results.[75]

The Corps was strengthened in its position by the course of debate over mitigation banks. When the concept was first developed in the 1980s, critics argued that natural and man-made wetlands did not necessarily contain equivalent biological richness; therefore, acre-for-acre compensation did not protect environmental quality. Michael Bowen, a doctoral student in ecology and Corps' scientist himself, argued that mitigation banking was no panacea for wetlands protection when it merely reduced wetlands to equivalent acres. Even when the equivalent acres of wetland habitat were located nearby the project site, there was no certainty that animal populations would move from one place to the other, or that the newly created wetland would be occupied by wetland species. "All we will build," Bowen wrote, "are large, wet, 'dead' areas containing fewer species than the original 'protected' wetland."[76]

The Minnesota and Wisconsin DNRs also doubted the efficacy of mitigation banking in the 1980s. Without state support, the St. Paul District could make little use of mitigation banking, as mitigation credits were not at the disposal of developers in these two states. Unfortunately, the alternative – requiring the developer or landowner to mitigate wetland impacts on the site where the development activity was to occur – was generally more costly and less effective. As the Environmental Protection Agency's Robert H. Wayland III testified before a congressional subcommittee, mitigation banks were "an innovative, market-based way for landowners to effectively and efficiently compensate for unavoidable wetland impacts ... Through mitigation banking, the responsibility for providing mitigation is transferred to an entity that has the financial resources, scientific expertise, and incentives necessary to ensure that the mitigation will be ecologically successful."[77]

In the 1990s, improved techniques in wetland development led to greater support for mitigation banking. Minnesota and Wisconsin both sanctioned the approach. The Clinton Administration made efforts to increase scientific and technical knowledge that would enhance mitigation capabilities. The new administration's announced policy on wetlands, "Protecting America's Wetlands," released in August 1993, contained a strong endorsement of the approach: "Mitigation banking provides for the restoration or creation of wetland functions in advance of development impacts reducing thereby the uncertainty of mitigation success. As such, mitigation banking may expedite the permit review process for projects that qualify. By consolidating compensation requirements, there may be ecological advantages accrued, as well as economies of scale relating to planning, monitoring, and management."[78]

In November 1995, the Corps and other federal agencies provided guidance to promote the establishment and use of mitigation banks under Section 404. The new mitigation banking policy provided for proper location and design of mitigation banks. It required that bank sponsors meet certain standards of financial security and long-term commitment to monitoring and management of the wetlands. By 1997, some two hundred mitigation banks had been approved or were under development nationwide.[79]

Statewide General Permits

As noted above, one important and long-standing goal of the Corps' Section 404 program was to assist the states in assuming greater responsibility for wetlands protection. Coordination of Section 404 regulations with state programs was important for two reasons: first, to facilitate state control; and second, to avoid duplication of effort by the government that resulted in overly burdensome requirements for the public. The Corps was under constant pressure by Congress to streamline its Section 404 permitting process, and coordination with state programs was one area in which the Corps could significantly improve efficiency without sacrificing the Section 404 program's effectiveness. Since Minnesota and Wisconsin both had relatively strong environmental laws, the St. Paul District was often a leader among Corps' districts in coordinating the Corps' regulatory program with state programs.

In 1991, the Minnesota Legislature passed the Wetland Conservation Act, one of the most comprehensive wetland laws in the nation. The law expressed a goal of no-net-loss of wetlands and described a "sequencing" process similar to the Corps' Section 404 program for mitigating impacts. According to the law, anyone proposing to drain or fill a wetland was required first to try avoiding the wetland; second, to try to minimize the impact; and, as a final resort, to replace any lost wetland acres, functions, and values. The law was to take effect in stages, becoming fully operational in 1994.[80]

In 1995, the St. Paul District issued a new programmatic general permit, GP-17, on a trial basis. This permit covered certain activities regulated and approved under the Minnesota law. The state law exempted some activities and types of wetland covered by Section 404, so the programmatic general permit was not a "perfect overlay," but it avoided duplication in most cases. This permit was later incorporated into the Corps' existing programmatic general permit for Minnesota, GP-01-MN.[81]

The St. Paul District made refinements to a similar programmatic general permit for Wisconsin. Although Wisconsin had no state law comparable to Minnesota's Wetland Conservation Act, the Wisconsin Department of Natural Resources vigorously exercised its role in the Section 404 process through the state's Section 401 certification authority. Consequently, the public was urged to apply for the programmatic general permit in Wisconsin, GP-01-WI, through a joint application form addressed to both the Corps and the Wisconsin DNR. As in Minnesota, applicants were advised to submit the application to the DNR, which then forwarded the application, along with its recommendation, to the Corps.[82]

In 2000, the St. Paul District issued three packages of general permits for Minnesota, Wisconsin and Indian reservations. Each package covered a variety of actions previously addressed by the Corps' nationwide permits. A significant innovation in these permits was that each permit had to be accompanied by a "letter of permission" from the appropriate local governing authority. Governing authorities varied and might involve city or county governments, watershed management organizations, soil and water conservation districts, townships or Indian tribal governments. As such, the new permits were designated GP/LOP-MN (for Minnesota), GP/LOP-WI (for Wisconsin) and GP/LOP-IR (for Indian reservations).

The St. Paul District developed an extensive training program to implement the GP/LOP process. The district provided training to tribal environmental staff, as well as various other local government bodies. The Minnesota Wetland Conservation Act empowered more than four hundred local government units to implement the permitting system, few of which commanded any expertise in wetland protection. Most of the people assigned to administer the state program at the local level, Ben Wopat remarked, "could see standing water and cattails and not call it a wetland." The Corps' training sessions were normally one week in length and included classroom training as well as field training.[83]

With the implementation of the GP/LOPs, the St. Paul District no longer dealt with nationwide permits, including the controversial NWP 26. By the late 1990s, the nationwide permits engendered so much scrutiny and protest by state natural resource officials and environmental groups in Minnesota and Wisconsin that they had become more hindrance than help. By abandoning use of the nationwide permits, the St. Paul District tailored its program more closely to the strong state wetland protection programs finally in place in Minnesota and Wisconsin. Still, both states stopped short of assuming control of the Section 404 program itself (as provided for under the Clean Water Act amendments of 1977), preferring to have the continued partnership with the Corps.[84]

The Crandon Mine Controversy

No environmental controversy tested the St. Paul District's ability to exercise its regulatory function more publicly than the complicated proposal to develop the Crandon Mine. Located a few miles south of the town of Crandon in Forest County, northern Wisconsin, the proposed mine would have accessed a rich deposit of zinc and copper ore that was claimed to be one of the ten largest ore bodies of its type in North America. Discovered in 1976, the ore body stirred enormous economic interest and political opposition. Because any major mining operation would have involved the discharge of fill material into jurisdictional wetlands, the Corps was involved through the Section 404 process. The controversy over the potential development of the Crandon Mine involved the Corps with the ore body owners, the Wisconsin DNR and three separate Wisconsin Indian tribes. Other parties in the controversy included the governor, the Environmental Protection Agency, the U.S. Fish and Wildlife Service and local and national environmental groups. At the center of the controversy were the evolving plans and environmental impact statements concerning how the mine would be developed. "Crandon Mine is the granddaddy of all EISs," Ben Wopat remarked. "It's a world-class EIS."[85]

Exxon Coal and Minerals Company began mineral exploration in northern Wisconsin in 1969 and announced its discovery of the deposit south of Crandon in 1976. Exxon applied to the Wisconsin DNR and the Corps for the necessary permits to develop a mine in 1982, proposing a $540 million project that would involve daily production of about ten thousand tons of zinc and copper ore. While the DNR and the Corps reviewed the proposal, metal prices fell and Exxon withdrew its applications in 1986. Seven years later, Exxon formed a partnership with a Toronto-based company and created a subsidiary, Crandon Mining Company. The following year, in 1994, the new company again applied for permits to open the Crandon Mine, proposing to extract 55 million tons of ore at a rate of 5,500 tons per day. Although the scale of operations was reduced in the new proposal, environmental regulations had become more restrictive. No fewer than twenty permits were involved, including a Section 404 permit for discharge of fill material in wetlands.[86]

Skunk Lake & Bur Oak Swamp

Skunk Lake (left), a small lake located just east of the formerly proposed Crandon Mine and mill site. The mining company was proposing to pump additional water into the lake to mitigate for the water that would have been lost due to groundwater drawdown. Bur Oak Swamp (right) is located near the formerly proposed Tailings Management Area. This wetland was of special concern to the Tribes because it is the home of hybrid white and bur oak trees, wich are relatively uncommon. (Photos by John Ahlness, courtesy of St. Paul District, Corps of Engineers)

A further modification of the Crandon Mining Company proposal in 1995 involved the Corps in another key issue. The proposed project was located in an area of extensive wetlands – the headwaters, in fact, of four separate watercourses: the Wolf, Brule, Peshtigo and Pine rivers. The waters of Forest County include some five hundred miles of trout streams and a hundred and ninety named lakes. Mining engineers determined the mine operation would require discharge of an average of 42 thousand gallons an hour of treated wastewater, much of it from groundwater seepage into the mine. In the modified proposal, the wastewater would flow through a thirty-eight-mile pipeline, entering the Wisconsin River south of the town of Rhinelander in Oneida County. Previously, the proposal was to discharge the wastewater into the Wolf River. Since the surface waters in Forest County drain into Lake Michigan, while the Wisconsin River flows into the Mississippi River, the question arose whether this plan would have involved a diversion of water out of the Great Lakes Basin.[87]

The proposed decision had legal and political significance because the Water Resources Development Act of 1986 prohibited any new diversion of Great Lakes water for use outside the Great Lakes Basin without approval by the governor of each of the Great Lakes states. The Wisconsin DNR held that the law only applied to surface waters and did not apply in the case of the Crandon Mine. Michigan's Governor John Engler disagreed. In a letter to Wisconsin's Governor Tommy Thompson in February 1998, Governor Engler argued that a draw down of the groundwater in Forest County could effectively tap Great Lakes water; therefore, a transfer of water from Forest County to the Wisconsin River was unacceptable to the state of Michigan.[88]

The issue was resolved when Exxon sold its interest in the mining venture to an Australian-based company, and the new subsidiary, Nicolet Minerals, once again modified the proposal. In its revised proposal, Nicolet Minerals altered the milling process to remove purite from the tailings to be deposited on the surface and thereby reduce acid drainage. It also included a plan for the additional treatment of wastewater on site, discharging it into infiltration fields from which it would seep back into the groundwater. Nicolet Minerals revised the proposal in response both to the Michigan governor's challenge and to a new mining law passed by the state of Wisconsin. The Wisconsin state law, tagged the mining moratorium law, introduced stricter standards to protect the environment from acid mine drainage during the life of the mine and after its closure.[89] The changes adopted by Nicolet Minerals ostensibly eliminated the need for pumping wastewater to the Wisconsin River.[90]

Each modification of the mining proposal forced the Corps and the Wisconsin DNR to begin practically anew on environmental impact studies. Documentation submitted by the succession of mining concerns grew upwards of seventy thousand pages. The Corps was under strong pressure to find efficiencies in this lengthy and expensive process, such as combining efforts with the Wisconsin DNR, but it also faced demands from Indian tribes to give consideration to federal trust responsibilities that were outside the DNR's scope. Legal counsel for the tribes argued that the Corps, representing the federal government, had fiduciary responsibilities to protect Indian trust resources both on and off the Indian reservations near the mine site. Moreover, legal counsel for the tribes contended that the Corps was not fulfilling the Clinton Administration's stated policy of implementing government-to-government relations with tribes. In response to these charges, the St. Paul District developed an issue paper about the Corps' trust responsibilities toward Indian tribes in the regulatory permitting process. In 1999, the tribes responded with their own issue paper, insisting that the Corps' commitment did not go far enough.[91] The St. Paul District determined that the trust relationship between the federal government and the tribes required it prepare an independent EIS – although it would continue to share data with the DNRs and other federal agencies. To assist in developing the EIS, the Corps contracted with an environmental engineering firm, Montgomery Watson Harza.[92]

As the mining proposal crept toward seeming finality, the Mole Lake Band moved to center stage among mine opponents. It established stringent water quality standards on the reservation two miles downstream from the mine site, requiring that the water entering the reservation be as pristine as though there were no mine. The Wisconsin Department of Natural Resources sued, contending the Environmental Protection Agency exceeded its authority in approving the water quality standards of the tribe. The court ruled in favor of the Environmental Protection Agency and the tribe. The DNR appealed the decision, and the Seventh U.S. Circuit Court of Appeals again found in favor of the Environmental Protection Agency and the tribe. The DNR took the case to the U.S. Supreme Court, which upheld the lower court's decision in June 2002. In response to the high court's ruling, Nicolet Minerals president Dale Alberts stated that the company could comply with the tribe's "nondegradation standard."[93] Later that summer, a delegation of the Mole Lake Band traveled to Johannesburg, South Africa, to talk with members of the board of Nicolet Minerals' parent corporation in an effort to get the company to sell the property to the state.[94] With the company claiming it would have all necessary permits in hand by the first quarter of 2004, negotiations got underway to purchase the mine property and finally lay the controversy to rest. A coalition of environmental organizations and local and tribal governments advanced a proposal for state acquisition of the property. The proposal would turn the site into a "conservation area dedicated to sustainable land management practices, tribal cultural values, and tourism suitable to this environmentally sensitive area."[95] When this initiative fizzled, the Forest County Potawatomi and Mole Lake Band negotiated their own buyout of the mining interests. On October 28, 2003, the two Indian tribes purchased the property for $16.5 million. The tribes withdrew all permit requests, ending more than two decades of controversy.[96]

Conclusion

Since 1975, the heart of the St. Paul District's regulatory mission has been the protection of wetlands. This resource is exceptionally significant in the St. Paul District – owing both to its extensiveness and its vulnerability to agriculture. The district pioneered a major innovation in the Section 404 program when it revised regulatory boundaries to conform to state lines and focused on cooperation with state wetlands protection programs in Minnesota and Wisconsin. Through astute political decision-making, the district obtained the respect and cooperation of urban dwellers, as well as farmers, environmentalists and developers. However, as the Crandon Mine controversy demonstrated, it continued to face challenges in preventing the degradation of this vulnerable resource.

1 "Farmers Take Notice Now," paid advertisement in *Tribune* (Granite Falls, Minnesota), 5 January 1989.

2 *The Land* (Mankato, Minnesota), 10 February 1989.

3 Jay A. Leitch, "Politicoeconomic Overview of Prairie Potholes," in *Northern Prairie Wetlands*, edited by Arnold Van Der Valk, (Ames: Iowa State University Press, 1989), p. 3.

4 Ralph W. Tiner, Jr., *Wetlands of the United States: Current Status and Recent Trends*, (Washington: Government Printing Office, 1984), pp. 44-45.

5 Tiner, *Wetlands of the United States*, pp. 35-36.

6 Steve D. Eggers and Donald M. Reed, *Wetland Plants and Plant Communities of Minnesota & Wisconsin*, U.S. Army Corps of Engineers report, (St. Paul, MN: U.S. Army Corps of Engineers, 1987), p. 10.

7 Ann Vileisis, *Discovering the Unknown Landscape: A History of America's Wetlands*, (Washington: Island Press, 1997), p. 19.

8 Eggers and Reed, *Wetland Plants and Plant Communities of Minnesota & Wisconsin*, pp. vii-ix.

9 Eggers and Reed, *Wetland Plants and Plant Communities of Minnesota & Wisconsin*, p. 100.

10 Tiner, *Wetlands of the United States*, pp. 44-45.

11 Governor Ramsey quoted in "Background on Wetland/Public Waters Issues," <http://www.bwsr.state.mn.us/wetlands/wca/history.html, October 2002.>

12 Chapter 315 cited in "Background on Wetland/Public Waters Issues," <http://www.bwsr. state.mn.us/wetlands/wca/history.html, October 2002.>

13 Charles D. Ablard and Brian Boru O'Neill, "Wetland Protection and Section 404 of the Federal Water Pollution Control Act Amendments of 1972: A Corps of Engineers Renaissance," Vermont Law Review, 1 (1976): pp. 54-57; Robert K. Tener, "Federal Regulation of the Nation's Wetlands, An Analysis of Government Policy," unpublished report, Environmental Protection Agency Region VIII Library, Denver.

14 Ablard and O'Neill, "Wetland Protection and Section 404 of the Federal Water Pollution Control Act Amendments of 1972: A Corps of Engineers Renaissance," pp. 57- 58.

15 <http://www.epa.gov/history/topics/fwpca/05.htm> (August 17, 2004).

16 Jeffrey K. Stine, "Regulating Wetlands in the 1970s: U.S. Army Corps of Engineers and the Environmental Organizations," *Journal of Forest History* 27 (April 1983): p. 66.

17 Stine, "Regulating Wetlands in the 1970s: U.S. Army Corps of Engineers and the Environmental Organizations," pp. 66-67. Stine's is the most detailed study of this controversial episode and explains the roles of key individuals in the planning and preparation of the press release.

18 Peter J. Bernstein, "Here Come the Dredgers! Sneak Attack on the Wetlands," *The Nation*, 225 (10 December 1977): p. 615; Stine, "Regulating Wetlands in the 1970s: U.S. Army Corps of Engineers and the Environmental Organizations," p. 68.

19 Stine, *"Regulating Wetlands in the 1970s: U.S. Army Corps of Engineers and the Environmental Organizations,"* p. 70.

20 Bernstein, "Here Come the Dredgers! Sneak Attack on the Wetlands," p. 616.

21 Michael C. Blumm, "The Clean Water Act's Section 404 Permit Program Enters Its Adolescence: An Institutional and Programmatic Perspective," *Ecology Law Quarterly*, 8 (1980): p. 411.

22 Stine, "Regulating Wetlands in the 1970s: U.S. Army Corps of Engineers and the Environmental Organizations," p. 71.

23 U.S. Army Corps of Engineers, Office of the Chief of Engineers, Engineer Profiles: The District Engineer, Interviews with Colonel William W. Badger, by Frank N. Schubert (Washington, U.S. Army Corps of Engineers, 1983), p. 43; Leitch, "Politicoeconomic Overview of Prairie Potholes," in *Northern Prairie Wetlands*, p. 4.

24 Raymond Merritt, "Years of Transition: the St. Paul District Corps of Engineers 1976-1982," unpublished manuscript, p. 53.

25 Wopat Interview, 25 April 2002, pp. 4-6.

26 Ben A. Wopat, interview by Matthew Pearcy, St. Paul, 25 April 2002, pp. 2, 5, 18.

27 "Regulation Protects Wetlands," *Crosscurrents* 1 (December 1977): p. 6. See also, Henrik Strandskov, "General Regulatory Branch Joins MN/DOT on Whirlwind Tour," *Crosscurrents* 2 (April 1979): p. 5.

28 *Maplewood Review*, 29 May 1980, Vadnais Heights – Little Canada Press, 15 April 1980, *Free Press* (White Bear Lake Area), 15 April 1980.

29 Wopat Interview, 25 April 2002, pp. 23-24.

30 Wopat Interview, 25 April 2002, pp. 24-25.

31 U.S. Senate Subcommittee on Clean Air, Wetlands, Private Property and Nuclear Safety of the Committee on Environment and Public Works, Wetlands: Review of Regulatory Changes: Hearing before the Subcommittee, 105th Cong., 1st sess., 26 June 1997, p. 60.

32 Vileisis, *Discovering the Unknown Landscape: A History of America's Wetlands*, pp. 275-276.

33 "Who Benefits in Reform of Wetlands Laws," *Science News*, 122 (24 July 1982): p. 56.

34 Grand Forks *Herald*, 23 December 1982.

35 Grand Forks *Herald*, 29 October 1982.

36 Badger Interview, pp. 42-44.

37 Jacqueline Peterson, "Regulations and the Changing Role of the Corps," *Crosscurrents*, 7 (June 1984): p. 4.

38 Litchfield *Independent Review*, 18 September 1986; Ben Wopat Interview, 24 October 2002.

39 Hancock *Record*, 2 December 1981, 8 December 1981, Morris *Tribune*, 19 November 1981.

40 Glencoe *Enterprise*, 29 May 1986; *Brownton Bulletin*, 5 November 1986.

41 U.S. House Subcommittee on Water Resources of the Committee on Public Works and Transportation, Status of the Nation's Wetlands and Laws Related Thereto, Hearing before the Subcommittee, 101st Cong., 1st and 2d sess., 14 April 1989, p. 214.

42 Unidentified news clipping, File 870 Gen. History Environmental Gen. (1986), Box 3848, St. Paul District administrative records.

43 Carroll Pursell and William Willingham, "Protecting the Nation's Waters: A History of the U.S. Army Corps of Engineers' Regulatory Responsibilities 1899-1999," Draft Report, 25 February 1999, copy available at Office of History, HQUSACE, Fort Belvoir, VA, pp. 108-109.

44 Pursell and Willingham, "Protecting the Nation's Waters," pp. 108-109.

45 "Master Briefing Manual, House of Representatives Hearing, Water Resources Development Act of 1996, H. Martin Lancaster Assistant Secretary of the Army (Civil Works) 28 February 1996," Civil Works/Policy Division/Legislative Initiatives Branch (Room 7112), Headquarters, U.S. Army Corps of Engineers, Washington, D.C.

46 Pursell and Willingham, "Protecting the Nation's Waters," pp. 110-111; "Master Briefing Manual."

47 "Master Briefing Manual."

48 Vileisis, *Discovering the Unknown Landscape*, pp. 299-300.

49 Vileisis, *Discovering the Unknown Landscape*, p. 300.

50 Vileisis, *Discovering the Unknown Landscape*, p. 301.

51 Ben A. Wopat, interview by Matthew Godfrey, 24 October 2002, pp. 9-10.

52 "The 1990 Farm Bill," *Soil and Water Conservation News*, 12, no. 1 (May-June 1991): pp. 4-5.

53 Vileisis, *Discovering the Unknown Landscape*, pp. 304-305.

54 *Star Tribune* (Minneapolis), 3 April 1994.

55 Detroit Lakes *Tribune*, 30 January 1986.

56 Detroit Lakes *Tribune*, 30 January 1986.

57 U.S. Congress, House, Subcommittee on Water Resources of the Committee on Public Works and Transportation, Status of the Nation's Wetlands and Laws Related Thereto, Hearing before the Subcommittee, 101st Cong., 1st and 2d sess., 14 April 1989, p. 214.

58 *Glencoe-McLeod County Chronicle*, 28 May 1986; *Brownton Bulletin*, 5 November 1986.

59 Litchfield *Independent Review*, 18 September 1986.

60 Record of Meeting, 30 January 1987, in Binder – Congressional Hearing Info, St. Cloud, Minnesota, 14 April 1989, Ben Wopat files, St. Paul, Minnesota.

61 U.S. Congress, House, Subcommittee on Water Resources of the Committee on Public Works and Transportation, Status of the Nation's Wetlands and Laws Related Thereto, Hearing before the Subcommittee, 101st Cong., 1st and 2d sess., 14 April 1989, p. 214; Wopat Interview, 24 October 2002, p. 8.

62 Joseph Briggs, District Policy on Section 404(f)(1)(c) Exemption, 23 November 1987, in Binder – Congressional Hearing Info, St. Cloud, Minnesota, 14 April 1989, Ben Wopat files, St. Paul, Minnesota.

63 Wopat Interview, 24 October 2002, p. 9.

64 U.S. Congress, House, Subcommittee on Water Resources of the Committee on Public Works and Transportation, Status of the Nation's Wetlands and Laws Related Thereto, Hearing before the Subcommittee, 101st Cong., 1st and 2d sess., 14 April 1989, p. 214.

65 "Complete Statement of John S. Doyle, Jr., Principal Deputy Assistant Secretary of the Army (Civil Works) before the Subcommittee on Water Resources, Committee on Public Works and Transportation, U.S. House of Representatives," 14 April 1989," in Binder – Congressional Hearing Info, St. Cloud, Minnesota, 14 April 1989, Ben Wopat files, St. Paul, Minnesota, p. 12.

66 "Complete Statement of John S. Doyle, Jr.," p. 12.

67 Wopat Interview, 24 October 2002, p. 8.

68 Information Paper, June 1991, Box 7842, SPDAR, St. Paul.

69 "EPA, Corps clarify wetlands rule for farmers," *Engineer Update*, (June 1990): p. 3.

70 News Release 90-17, File "Wetlands/Regulatory," Box labeled "Hatch," William Baldwin's files, Office of History, HQUSACE, Fort Belvoir, VA.

71 *Christian Science Monitor*, 27 June 1990.

72 *Daily Tribune* (Wisconsin Rapids), 4 October 1989.

73 *Christian Science Monitor*, 27 June 1990.

74 Public Notice, 28 December 1992, File 228-10 Historical Files Wetlands (89), Box 4144, SPDAR, St. Paul.

75 U.S. Army Corps of Engineers, St. Paul District, Impacts of Activities Authorized by Section 404 of the Clean Water Act: State of Wisconsin, September 1993, pp. 1-5.

76 Michael Bowen, "What's Wrong with Mitigation Banks?" *The Military Engineer*, 573 (October/November 1995): p. 20.

77 Senate Subcommittee on Clean Air, Wetlands, Private Property and Nuclear Safety of the Committee on Environment and Public Works, Wetlands: Review of Regulatory Changes, 105th Cong., 1st sess., 1997, p. 55.

78 "Protecting America's Wetlands," The Clinton Administration's 24 August 1993 Announcement, File 1110 – Tribal Coordinator, Box 4154, SPDAR.

79 Senate Subcommittee on Clean Air, Wetlands, Private Property and Nuclear Safety of the Committee on Environment and Public Works, Wetlands: Review of Regulatory Changes, 105th Cong., 1st sess., 1997, p. 55.

80 Minnesota Board of Water and Soil Resources, "1999/2000 Minnesota Wetland Report," October 2001, p. 3, available at <http//www/bwsr.state.mn.us/wetlands> (September 2002).

81 Michael M. Weburg, Policy Analyst, St. Paul District, communication with authors, 25 September 2002.

82 Department of the Army Permit GP-01-WI, <http://www.mvp.usace.army.mil/ regulatory /proposals/gp01wi98.pdf>, October 2002.

83 Wopat Interview, 24 October 2002.

84 Weburg Communication. As of 2000, only Michigan and New Jersey had assumed control of Section 404 permitting.

85 Wopat Interview, 24 October 2002, p.14.

86 Information Paper, January 2001, John Ahlness files, St. Paul District Office, St. Paul.

87 Milwaukee *Journal Sentinel*, 11 February 1997.

88 Rhinelander *Daily News*, 23 October 1997 and 6 February 1998.

89 Rhinelander *Daily News*, 23 October 1997.

90 "Company attempts to reopen Crandon Mine," *Mining Engineering* (February 1999): p. 12; *Wisconsin State Journal*, 10 December 1998.

91 See Chapter 9 for a discussion of these issue papers.

92 Information Paper, January 2001, provided to authors by John Ahlness.

93 Rhinelander *Daily News*, 4 June, 2002.

94 Wopat Interview, 24 October 2002, p. 24.

95 Forest *Republican*, 26 June, 2002.

96 *Pioneer Press* (St. Paul, MN), 29 October 2003; Matt Pearcy, "Crandon Mine producestons of controversy," *Crosscurrents* 26 (December 2003): pp. 8-9.

Grand Portage proposed small boat harbor: The Grand Portage project was cancelled when research indicated that the entire bay might qualify as a Traditional Cultural Property of the Grand Portage Band. (Illustration courtesy of St. Paul District, Corps of Engineers)

6 Cultural Resources and History

For most of its history, the Corps of Engineers has provided flood protection and facilitated navigation. Along with these and other important functions, the organization, in company with the rest of the federal government, initiated cultural resource management programs in the late twentieth century. Although still embryonic in the mid-1970s, this duty had matured by the twenty-first century and had become vital to the Corps' public interaction even though it was not one of the Corps' defined missions. Mandated by the National Historic Preservation Act of 1966, the cultural resource management function included assessing the effects of Corps' undertakings on historic properties and interacting with Native American tribes to preserve their resources. Along with its cultural resource management responsibilities, the St. Paul District also implemented an active program to discover, protect and explain the Corps' own history. Although the historical program is not considered part of the Corps' cultural resource management responsibilities, both functions served a major role in "educat[ing] the public about Corps' history and its mission."[1]

Cultural Resources

The Bureau of Reclamation has defined cultural resources as "the physical remains of a people's way of life that archaeologists and historians study to try to interpret how people lived."[2] The St. Paul District's cultural resource management section, which included the position of district historian, described the term more expansively, stating that cultural resources consisted of "everything from prehistoric archeological sites to historic buildings, from historic engineering structures to historic documents and oral records of past events."[3] Because of the insight these materials provided to the past, they facilitated a comprehension of other cultures, as well as an understanding, of architecture and engineering.[4] By preserving both prehistoric and historic cultural resources and by providing means of interpreting them for the public, the St. Paul District's archeologists and historians made the past come alive.

In the early 1900s, individuals in the United States became aware of the need to protect the unique cultural resources that the nation had. Accordingly, the 1906 Antiquities Act and the 1935 Historic Sites Act provided a measure of protection for historic and prehistoric resources. The St. Paul District initially worked to excavate archeological resources by cooperating with the National Park Service under the Inter-Agency Archaeological Salvage Program. By the 1960s, the recreation section in the Planning Branch coordinated these activities, which were almost always subcontracted to private organizations.[5] In 1966, the passage of the National Historic Preservation Act ushered in a new era of preservation by making the federal government an active participant. The law created three major elements to help government agencies implement preservation practices. First, it established the National Register of Historic Places to list all "districts, sites, buildings, structures and objects significant in American history, architecture, archaeology, engineering and culture." Second, Section 106 of the National Historic Preservation Act required the heads of any federal or federally assisted project to "take into account" the effects of undertakings "on any district, site, building,

Upper and Lower Locks at St. Anthony Falls, Minneapolis: The falls were the highest point of navigation on the Mississippi River when the Corps of Engineers opened an office in St. Paul in 1866. (Photo courtesy of St. Paul District, Corps of Engineers)

structure, or object that is included in or eligible for inclusion in the National Register." Third, it created the Advisory Council on Historic Preservation, and authorized it and State Historic Preservation Offices to oversee the Section 106 process and the National Register in a federal-state partnership.[6] These provisions meant that whenever the Corps began an undertaking, it had to investigate what prehistoric or historic resources would be affected, and then consult with State Historic Preservation Offices, or SHPOs, and the Advisory Council on how to avoid or mitigate the consequences.

Preserving Cultural Resources

In order to comply with the National Historic Preservation Act, Corps' districts began hiring archeologists to conduct the necessary research. In 1970, Tulsa District became one of the first districts with a full-time archeologist; and in the mid-1970s, the St. Paul District followed Tulsa's lead by hiring Dan Bowman as its first full-time, permanent archeologist.[7] Bowman only stayed a couple of years; and in 1978, the district hired David Berwick as archeologist. Berwick, together with John O. Anfinson, a historian first employed by the district in 1980, became the backbone of St. Paul's cultural resource management program, which fell under the jurisdiction of the Environmental Resources Branch. As Robert F. Post, chief of the branch from 1974 to 1982 related, Berwick and

Anfinson "were largely responsible for establishing the outstanding foundation of the CRM [cultural resource management] program the district has today."[8]

From the beginning, the main responsibility of the cultural resource management unit was the coordination of the Section 106 process with civil works projects. To streamline Section 106 implementation, the Advisory Council developed regulations explaining what agencies had to do to comply with the law. Under these regulations (36 CFR Part 800), the council mandated that when a federal undertaking occurred, the responsible agency had to consult with the SHPO to determine what properties listed in or eligible for the National Register would be affected. The agency also had to confer with public and private organizations, local governments, Native Americans and others who might know about potential resources and would have to conduct literature searches and field surveys as well. Once the resources had been identified, the agency and the SHPO determined the undertaking's effects. If the two agreed there were no adverse effects, the project could continue. If adverse effects existed, the two had to develop ways to avoid or mitigate them and then sign a memorandum of agreement or a programmatic agreement, depending on the complexity of the project, outlining these methods. In cases of dispute between the agency and the SHPO, the council mediated.[9] In order to fund these necessary functions, Congress passed the Archeological and Historic Preservation Act in May 1974 (also known as the Moss-Bennett Act), permitting federal agencies to spend up to one percent of project funding to recover historic and archeological resources. Robert M. Vogel, the head of the Smithsonian Institution's Science and Technology Department, believed this law allowed the Corps to expand its cultural resource management efforts, transforming its historic preservation reputation from one "so rotten it had no way to go but up" to one "ever so much better."[10]

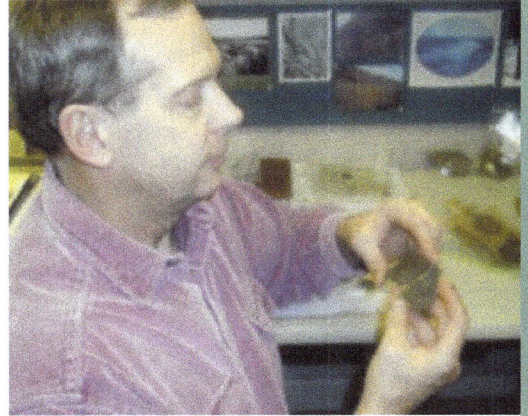

Brad Johnson, archaeologist, displays a prehistoric pottery shard from a site at Sandy Lake Recreation Area. (Photo by Mark Davidson, courtesy of St. Paul District, Corps of Engineers)

With Moss-Bennett funds in place, Corps' cultural resource management units followed the Section 106 regulations. According to Berwick, the St. Paul District used several factors to determine a site's significance, including the potential for scientific information and "engineering features, architectural styles, or an association with an important event, era, or person." If the Corps and the SHPO determined that resources were eligible for the National Register and that the project would adversely affect them, the cultural resource management staff took efforts to diminish the effects. With archeological sites, such mitigation usually took the form of excavation. Fortunately, Berwick explained, "The St. Paul District does not do a lot of excavation work, because we have a good track record in avoiding as many sites as possible."[11] Such avoidance was not easy, however, especially since humans naturally tend to live near water, meaning that some areas under the district's jurisdiction had had human habitation for at least twelve thousand years.[12] At Lake Ashtabula, a reservoir

153

created by the Corps' construction of Baldhill Dam a few miles north of Valley City, North Dakota, surveys recorded thirty-seven prehistoric and historic archeological sites ranging from burial mounds and bison processing areas to homestead dugouts.[13] Likewise, investigations in the 1990s at Grand Forks, North Dakota, and East Grand Forks, Minnesota, located nine historic or prehistoric archeological sites in the Red River Valley.[14]

When large acreage surveys or site excavations were necessary, the cultural resources management staff hired archeological contractors to perform the work. Prior to the passage of a federal regulation in 1990 entitled "Curation of Federally Owned and Administered Archeological Collections" (36 CFR Part 79), these contractors would often curate the artifacts recovered from the fieldwork. In 1994, the Corps designated the St. Louis District as the Mandatory Center of Expertise for the Curation and Management of Archaeological Collections to help districts establish formal curation agreements with state historical societies and universities whose storage facilities met the requirements of regulations. However, the curation center mainly concentrated on complying with the Native American Graves and Repatriation Act (see below) and provided little help or funding for curation. This forced the St. Paul District to continue to rely on contractor storage of artifacts from pre-1990 fieldwork.[15] This method of curation created some problems, including the scattering of collections across North Dakota, Minnesota and Wisconsin. In addition, small cultural resources management contractors sometimes went out of business before artifacts were curated at appropriate facilities, and a backlog of material began to accumulate in boxes outside of the district's cultural resource management cubicles. Because of these problems, Virginia Gnabasik, a senior archeologist for the district, considered effective storage and curation of archeological collections as one of the crucial funding issues that the Corps needed to address.[16]

Lake Ashtabula and Balhill Dam: The Corps excavated thirty-seven prehistoric sites prior to filling the reservoir. (Photo courtesy of St. Paul District, Corps of Engineers)

If the affected resources were historical rather than archeological, such as individual buildings, housing districts or other edifices, the Corps implemented other methods to avoid harm. In 1998, for example, the St. Paul District determined that the area of the flood control project at Grand Forks/East Grand Forks contained more than a hundred properties either listed on or eligible for the National Register of Historic Places. In order to alleviate the effects on these structures, the district entered into a programmatic agreement with the Advisory Council, the North Dakota SHPO and the Minnesota SHPO, stating that the Corps would "to the extent feasible, avoid historic properties either through project design changes, use of temporary fences or barricades during construction, realignments, landscaping, or other measures."[17] In accordance with the agreement, the district employed innovations, such as mechanically stabilized earthwalls and invisible flood was, which, in the words of

154

technical manager Edward McNally, "save[d] a number of areas that probably would have been impacted with our initial alignments."[18]

In other cases, the Corps could not preserve the structures. In 1983, the St. Paul District confronted five dangerous bridges on the Kickapoo River between Rockton, Wisconsin, and La Farge, Wisconsin, on State Highway 131. Two of the bridges were eligible for the National Register because they were the only two pre-1936 Warren Through Truss bridges left in Wisconsin, but safety issues forced the Corps to take drastic measures. Initially, the district tried to close off the bridges through gates and dirt mounds, but people used cutting torches to remove the gates and maneuvered around the dirt, forcing the district to remove the structures. In order to alleviate the effects of removal, the district documented and photographed the structures. In this case, public safety took precedence over historical value.[19]

Because of the numerous historic and archeological resources in the St. Paul District, the cultural resource management unit and the Corps implemented additional preservation policies. Several operational management plans counseled Corps' resource managers, rangers and project personnel to "be aware of the documented archeological and historic/architectural sites around the project" and to report "any suspicious activities near or acts of vandalism at recorded sites." The Archeological Resources Protection Act of 1979 levied fines of up to $10,000 and imprisonment for up to one year for illegally removing artifacts from federal lands, and the cultural resource management staff asked Corps' personnel to enforce this law at all times. In accordance with the National Historic Preservation Act, the Corps also restricted information regarding the location and character of significant cultural resources to prevent vandalism and removal.[20]

Native American Relations

Congress amended the National Historic Preservation Act in 1992 to provide more fully for the preservation of Native American sites and properties. Among the amendments were provisions clarifying that properties containing religious or cultural significance to Indian tribes or Native Hawaiians were eligible for the National Register. The amendments also granted "consulting party" status to tribes in the Section 106 process by authorizing them to assume SHPO responsibilities if they developed their own cultural resource management programs.[21] According to Virginia Gnabasik, these amendments increased district interaction with tribes, especially after five groups – the Leech Lake Band and Mille Lacs Band of Ojibwe in Minnesota, the Turtle Mountain Band of

Archaeological site: (Left to right) Allen Westover, Corps' archaeologist; Jim Zorn, Great Lakes Indian Fish and Wildlife Commission attorney; Christine Harrison, principal investigator, Archaeological Resource Services; Jeff Steere, Sandy Lake operations manager; and Terry Ladd, Sandy Lake park ranger. (Photo courtesy of Brad Johnson, St. Paul District, Corps of Engineers)

155

Chippewa in North Dakota and the Ho-Chunk and Menominee in Wisconsin – assumed the Section 106 functions of the SHPO and appointed tribal historic preservation officers. In most cases, Section 106 coordination with tribes started with sending a formal letter notifying each tribe of possible religious and cultural resources in a project area and then consulting with the tribe if it expressed an interest. Although the Corps had to contact every affected tribe, regardless of whether or not it had a cultural resource management component, tribes with cultural resource management programs, Gnabasik explained, were "easier to work with" because they had "a point of contact" with a knowledge of the Section 106 process. These developments enabled the St. Paul district to develop good working relationships with the tribes.[22]

Native American Graves Protection and Repatriation Act

Another law, passed in 1990, mandated Corps' interaction with tribes. For many years, removing Native American remains and funerary objects from the earth was a common practice in the United States, and many of these objects made their way to museums and other repositories. In the 1980s, numerous tribes and other organizations lobbied Congress to stop this desecration and to return collected remains to their rightful owners. In response, Congress passed the Native American Graves Protection and Repatriation Act on November 16, 1990. The act provided that, when Native American human remains or funerary objects were found on federal or tribal lands, they be returned to the tribe that had the "closest cultural affiliation with such remains or objects." In addition, the law established penalties for violations and required federal agencies and museums to inventory their collections and return any remains or objects to pertinent tribes.[23] This meant the St. Paul District had to examine any human remains or funerary items excavated under the Corps' authority and make the necessary returns.

Sissel Johannessen, a district archeologist, took charge of this effort, which was funded by the center of expertise in St. Louis. According to Johannessen, the district followed certain steps in its Native American Graves Protection and Repatriation Act compliance. First, district staff mapped the boundaries of fee title land for each water resource project. Second, they examined all of the cultural resource investigations that had taken place on that land, scrutinizing the reports for any artifacts that could possibly fit Native American Graves Protection and Repatriation Act criteria. Third, the staff contacted whatever curation facilities housed the relevant items in order to inspect them and also collected additional information about the materials. Fourth, archeologists developed arguments about the probable cultural affiliation of each artifact (or its lack of one) and sent a letter to each tribe with an interest in the area, explaining the findings. From all of these investigations, there were only a few instances where materials had to be returned or reburied. For example, the district gave the remains of three individuals found in eroding banks at Lake Ashtabula, North Dakota, to the North Dakota Intertribal Reinternment Committee in 1992. Likewise, items excavated in 1969 from Gull Lake in the Mississippi Headwaters, including the skeletal remains of eighteen individuals and associated funerary items, such as ceramic vessels, potsherds and stone tools, were returned to Eastern Dakota tribes in

1998. By 1999, Johannessen had finished inventorying all of the district's collections, and the surrounding tribes seemed satisfied with the district's work.[24]

Traditional Cultural Properties

Another area that stimulated involvement with American Indians evolved in the 1990s from the concern of some historians, anthropologists and indigenous groups that properties important to a community's religious beliefs or culture were not receiving adequate protection. In 1990, the National Park Service published *National Register Bulletin* 38, which stated that a cultural resource could be eligible for the National Register if it had "traditional cultural significance." According to the bulletin, such resources, called Traditional Cultural Properties, or TCPs, consisted of any item – whether a building, a structure or a natural location – eligible for the National Register "because of its association with cultural practices or beliefs of a living community that (a) are rooted in that community's history, and (b) are important in maintaining the continuing cultural identity of the community."[25]

Grand Portage proposed small boat harbor: The Grand Portage project was cancelled when research indicated that the entire bay might qualify as a Traditional Cultural Property of the Grand Portage Band. (Illustration courtesy of Brad Johnson, St. Paul District, Corps of Engineers)

Most TCPs the Corps and other federal agencies encountered belonged to Native Americans. Because of the different world views of Indians and Euro-Americans about these objects, tribal TCP claims sometimes led to confusion and outright disbelief on the part of the federal government. As archeologist David W. Cushman explained, "What one group sees as vital to its cultural identity, the other often does not even recognize." When a tribe claimed that portions of Lake Superior were important as places of religious and cultural awakening, for example, many Euro-Americans failed to understand the significance. Other problems resulted from taboos existing in many tribes to discourage the revelation of information about places of traditional cultural value, especially to outsiders. These taboos sometimes made it difficult for cultural resources management personnel to obtain the information necessary to evaluate a site's eligibility.[26]

Such problems confronted district historian John Anfinson in his dealings with TCPs. In 1994, Anfinson became involved with deliberations on whether or not to approve a permit to place a 700-foot-long dock on Grand Portage Bay, located at the northeastern tip of Minnesota. The Grand Portage Band of the Chippewa Indians' reservation surrounded the entire bay, and the tribe complained to the Corps that the dock and the accompanying boat traffic would harm the bay, which was important to the tribe's religion and culture. According to Anfinson, "People within the district found that a hard argument to accept," so he investigated the bay's status as a TCP.[27] Anfinson interviewed seven residents of Grand Portage, both Indian and non-Indian, to explain further Chippewa' beliefs. These discussions convinced Anfinson that the bay was "the focal point or heart of the Grand Portage Reservation." Many of the Grand Portage Chippewa believed the bay had spirits and that a marina would force the spirits to move. "One person noted that a mountain near the bay had been inhabited by a thunderbird spirit," Anfinson related. "So many people had started going to the mountain that the spirit had left. This, they worry, could happen with the spirits of the bay." Others believed the bay was a part of their soul: "to mistreat [it] could make them ill individually and as a people."[28] Anfinson's research led district officials to deny the permit; he had effectively indicated that tribal claims about the bay were not "just some spurious thing."[29]

Another TCP encounter presented different problems. In 1992, a company began pulling logs off the bottom of Lake Superior at Chequamegon Bay for salvage. These logs had sunk in the 1800s on their way to sawmills during the early logging era of the Great Lakes. Because of the lake's low oxygen content and cold temperatures, the submerged logs remained in their original condition, meaning they could be sold for as much as $10,000 apiece. By 1997, the St. Paul District received approximately two hundred applications for permits to obtain these logs, but the Red Cliff and Bad River bands of Chippewa Indians registered their objections, stating that both the lake and the logs themselves were sacred. In this instance, Anfinson was not convinced of the tribes' claims, mainly because many members of both bands were either Catholic or Lutheran and did not attribute any special significance to the logs. But Thomas King, an archeology and historic preservation consultant to the Advisory Council, claimed that the logs were TCPs, a conclusion Anfinsen believed was "extremely weak."[30] Ultimately, the Council decided the bay itself was a TCP, but that the sunken wood was not, although the individual logs could be part of submerged logging complexes eligible for the National Register. The district circulated this determination, stating that individuals or companies interested in logging would thereafter have to comply with special conditions in order to avoid adverse effects to the bay. According to project manager Maria T. Valencia, "This seemed to dissuade potential applicants because no further permit requests" were received after that time.[31] Anfinson saw this incident as "one of the classic examples of the problems of TCPs in trying to figure out what's significant ... in a way that's fair and true."[32]

Appendix C and Section 106 Compliance

TCP designations were not the only issues leading to Corps' clashes with the Advisory Council. In 1990, a conflict developed between the two over the implementation of the Section 106 process as it applies to the Corps' Regulatory Program. Under Section 404 of the Federal Water Pollution Control Act of 1972, as amended by the Clean Water Act of 1977, the Corps had the responsibility of issuing permits for any undertaking on navigable bodies of water in the United States. Because the Corps was the permitting entity, any project that required a permit became subject to the Section 106 process. Since the Corps was only serving a regulatory function and not performing the actual work, complying with Section 106 assumed different features for the regulatory branch than it did for civil works.[33]

These differences led the Corps to develop its own guidelines for Section 106 compliance in the permitting process. When the Advisory Council produced 36 CFR Part 800 regulations implementing Section 106 of the National Historic Preservation Act, it provided that agencies could develop "alternate procedures" in place of portions of Part 800 if the procedures were consistent with the Council's regulations. If the Council approved the "alternate procedures," they defined the Section 106 process for the agency.[34] On June 29, 1990, the Corps issued its alternative as Appendix C to 33 CFR Part 325. According to one summary, Appendix C explained, "The steps the Corps follows to fulfill the requirements set forth in the National Historic Preservation Act, other applicable historic preservation laws, and the Presidential directives as they relate to the regulatory program."[35] The Advisory Council did not approve the substitute; regardless, the Corps used Appendix C after 1990 to govern its compliance with Section 106.

Few disparities existed between the Advisory Council's regulations and Appendix C, but the discrepancies were significant. The main area of contention revolved around the differences between "Permit Area" as defined in Appendix C and the "Area of Potential Effect" as defined in 36 CFR Part 800. The "Permit Area" was the geographic area in which the project's activities were dependent on the work or structures authorized by the Corps' permit, including waters of the United States and upland areas.[36] The Council's "Area of Potential Effect," meanwhile, was the "geographic area or areas within which an undertaking may directly or indirectly cause alterations in the character or use of historic properties."[37]

Central to this problem was the definition of undertaking and the SHPO's perception that Corps' regulatory involvement "federalized" an entire project. The Corps defined "undertaking" as the authorization of work or structures in the waters of the United States and not the larger project. Upland project areas could be included in the Corps' scope of analysis if the project activities in those locations would not occur but for the authorization of the work or structures or if those upland activities were an integral part or directly related to the work or structures. If these criteria were not met, the Corps believed it lacked sufficient control over the project features to avoid their potential effects on historic properties. SHPOs generally saw this interpretation as too narrow. Regardless of the situation, both sides adhered to their different positions.[38]

In some circumstances, conflicts over the "Permit Area" and the Area of Potential Effect could only be resolved by litigation, but in the St. Paul District, the differences merely led to expressions of discontent. Dennis Gimmestad, the compliance officer for the Minnesota SHPO, stated that Appendix C was the biggest frustration he had with the district, especially when he had to declare the Corps out of compliance with Section 106. "It doesn't mean necessarily I don't think they're doing their job," he explained. "It's just that I can't concur in good conscience with what I've been told that I need to follow." District personnel might believe that Gimmestad was taking a hard line, but he was only following the guidelines laid out by the Council "I can't just throw [the Council's regulations] out and go by [Appendix C] because I would not be doing my job," he related.[39] Scott Anfinson, John Anfinson's brother and a National Register archeologist with Minnesota's SHPO, agreed, but believed that district employees were caught in the same bind – if they did not interpret the permit area according to Appendix C, they were deficient in their own positions. "I think a lot of the staff over at the Corps in the cultural resources management wing is sympathetic and they want to preserve sites," Anfinson stated, but "when orders come down you obey those orders."[40]

In an effort to improve coordination with SHPOs, the St. Paul District assigned Brad Johnson, a district archeologist, to work with the Regulatory Branch on a one-year assignment. One important result of this endeavor was an understanding that was reached on the Permit Area/Area of Potential Effect controversy between the council, the Minnesota SHPO and the Corps during consultations pertaining to the effects of a housing development on the Rose McAllister farmstead in Chanhassen, Minnesota. In November 2002, the council essentially agreed that the Area of Potential Effect for a regulatory undertaking should be based on the effects of project activities in the permit area and that the undertaking was the authorization of the work or structures in the waters of the United States and not the larger project. The Council and the SHPO concurred that the effects to the McAllister farmstead were not the result of wetland fill or the townhouse lots dependent on that fill but resulted from the larger project development over which the Corps had little control.[41] Whether the council continued to interpret permit areas in this way remained to be seen, but as the McAllister farmstead incident indicates, Johnson's temporary appointment to the Regulatory Branch helped to further the working relationships between the district, the SHPO and the Advisory Council.

Historical Activities

Along with its cultural resources management program, the St. Paul District also actively implemented historical activities in the last quarter of the twentieth century. Led mostly by John Anfinson, district historian from 1980 to 2000, the district worked to preserve its own past, complete environmental site histories and develop interpretive materials at district visitor centers. Although Anfinson periodically had to justify his own position and responsibilities to district officials, St. Paul established a strong historical program that effectively portrayed its past.

The district saw the value of its history even before it hired Anfinson in 1980. In the 1970s, the Corps contracted with Raymond H. Merritt, a professor at the University of Wisconsin-Milwaukee, to compose a history of the St. Paul District from its beginnings to 1978. District personnel embraced the book after its 1979 publication, with District Engineer Colonel William W. Badger claiming that it "did a very good job of showing what the Corps does."[42] Despite their enthusiasm, district leaders were still uncertain about hiring a full-time historian, questioning whether or not such a position was justified. When the district engaged Anfinson's services in 1980, it actually hired him as an archeologist because he had a double major in history and anthropology. Not until 1985 did the district change his job title to historian and, even then, it did so reluctantly.[43]

Throughout Anfinson's tenure as a district historian, however, he gradually built up the historical program, aided by Corps' headquarters in Washington, D.C., which had a strong contingent of historians. In the 1980s, headquarters issued ER 870-1-1, outlining the responsibilities of district historical programs. According to this directive, historians should "develop in Corps' personnel knowledgeable interest and pride in the history of the Corps of Engineers," publish histories of individual district activities, prepare policy-study reports, compile research materials, preserve records, conduct oral history interviews, collect historic artifacts, support public affairs activities and provide information for visitor centers.[44] As part of these obligations, the St. Paul District implemented an oral history program in the 1980s, consisting of end-of-tour interviews with district engineers to provide perspectives and "lessons learned" for future commanders.[45] Frank "Mickey" Schubert, a member of the Corps' headquarters Office of History staff, carried out annual interviews with Colonel William W. Badger and Colonel Edward Rapp, both district engineers in St. Paul, in the early 1980s, and Anfinson assumed the responsibility thereafter, conducting end-of-tour interviews with North Central Division commanders as well.[46] These histories became valuable sources for information about the St. Paul District and the Corps in general. A 1991 interview with outgoing District Engineer Colonel Roger L. Baldwin, for instance, covered a "typical" day in his life, his leadership philosophies, information about Life-Cycle Project Management and explanations about cost-sharing, the drought of 1988, civil works projects, regulatory issues, the International Joint Commission, congressional relations and the Corps' reorganization.[47]

Along with these end-of-tour interviews, the district began other projects in response to Corps' headquarters request that districts "conduct interviews with as broad a spectrum of the [district's] active and retired personnel as possible."[48] In 1986, the cultural resources management staff interviewed former Mississippi River headwaters employees, including dam tenders. According to Anfinson, these interviews were intended to show "how the headwater's [sic] staff perceived what the district office was saying and how they carried it out."[49] Another project involved interviewing individuals who had helped construct and operate Mississippi River Locks and Dams 3, 4, 5, 5A, 6, 7, 8, 9 and 10. The report on these interviews explained that they "preserve[d] important information not contained or poorly detailed in written documents."[50] According to Berwick, these interviews helped make "present employees proud of what the district has done in the past."[51]

Henry P. Bosse's photo of wingdams on the Mississippi River: The Bosse collection of 136 photographs, found by the district, is a historical treasure. (Courtesy of St. Paul District, Corps of Engineers)

In the 1990s, the cultural resources management unit assumed the function of completing environmental site histories, performed mostly by Jane Carroll, who worked as a second historian for the district during that decade. These studies, which included archival research, as well as site visitation, eliminated delays in civil works projects, especially the construction of urban levees. Frequently industries had operated on sites where the Corps wanted to construct a levee, and sometimes these businesses left behind contaminated soil. If the Corps did not discover the polluted areas until late in the project, it could, in the words of Anfinson, "significantly delay a project or cause an increase of costs." Carroll and Anfinson thus conducted environmental site histories in the planning process to determine where potential contaminated soils were in order to forestall any late discoveries. After Carroll left the district, Anfinson and his successor, Matthew Pearcy, had little time to continue such studies because of the pressing demands of other projects, so they became the responsibility of the district's Geotechnical and Geology Section.[52]

In addition to these responsibilities, Anfinson focused on preserving the Corps' own historic resources. In the early 1990s, the district discovered a book of rare photographs of the Mississippi River taken by Henry P. Bosse, who worked for the Corps in the late 1800s. The album, entitled *Views on the Mississippi River*, contained a hundred and thirty-six photographs showing some of the Corps' initial work on the waterway. One copy of the rare album had retrieved $217,000 at a 1990 auction. Many believed the district's copy was worth as much as $1.5 million.[53] In order to promote these photographs, Anfinson composed a brochure about them and made presentations to interested public audiences. The photographs proved to be tremendously popular, and Anfinson estimated that he lectured at least thirty times about them. In addition, the Corps itself embraced the photographs as an important resource, with officials at Corps' headquarters calling it a great treasure.[54] In 2003, prints of the photographs still lined the second floor corridor of the St. Paul District office, showing the importance the district placed on them.

Other Corps' resources were equally significant, especially the locks and dams under the district's jurisdiction. In the early 1980s, the district undertook an examination of each of its locks and dams to determine their hydropower potential, and, at the same time, began a major rehabilitation of these complexes, including repairing structures, installing new wiring and building new central control stations. As with all federal undertakings, these projects had to go through the Section 106 process, and the State Historic Preservation Offices in the various Upper Mississippi River states asked the Corps to determine whether the locks and dams themselves were eligible for the National Register. The district hired historian Jon Gjerde in 1983 to study the edifices, which had been built between 1932 and 1938, and Gjerde and Anfinson together determined that Locks and Dams 3 through 10 were eligible. According to Anfinson, they represented the orderly "spirit of the Progressive Era" and "the public works associated with the New Deal and Keynesian economics of Franklin D. Roosevelt." Their design also showed "both the influence of the Art Moderne movement and the austerity of the Great Depression."[55] But a study commissioned by the Rock Island District in the mid-1980s to evaluate Locks and Dams 11 through 22 disagreed with Gjerde's and Anfinson's assessments, stating that the structures might have local and regional significance, but they had no national importance. The study recommended that only one of the complexes be determined eligible as a representative example. After reviewing both reports, the various SHPOs agreed with Gjerde's and Anfinson's arguments and declared the locks and dams eligible for the National Register.[56]

When Corps' officers learned about the determination, they were not pleased, believing that eligibility would just make it harder for the agency to maintain and operate the dams. Fearing that Section 106 requirements would adversely impact operation and maintenance, the Corps, especially Rock Island and St. Louis districts, balked at complying with the decision. As Anfinson related, the determination did not "fit well with the construction-operations mentality" of the Corps.[57] The St. Paul District, however, was less reluctant to accept the decision, perhaps because it recognized the importance of preserving the engineering history of the locks and dams. To that end, the district entered into a contract with the National Park Service in 1986 to produce Historic American Engineering Record documentation for Locks and Dams 3 through 10. In 1990, Rock Island and St. Louis followed St. Paul's lead; and in 1992, the National Park Service issued a report on the locks and dams entitled *Gateway to Commerce: The U.S. Army Corps of Engineers 9 Foot Channel Project on the Upper Mississippi River* which specifically explored the structures' engineering aspects. All of the documentation, including photographs, manuscripts and inventories, were stored in the Library of Congress in the Historic American Engineering Record archives, thereby preserving the historical record of the Nine-Foot Channel Project.[58]

Ultimately, the eligibility determination did increase the difficulty of lock and dam operation and maintenance. In order to preserve the structures' integrity, the Corps had to remove any "features inconsistent with the historic character of the locks and dams" when possible, in addition to consulting frequently with SHPOs to mitigate any effects that major rehabilitation efforts might have.[59] To ease the implementation of this increased bureaucracy, Anfinson, as head of the cultural resources management unit, argued for its "early involvement ... in all construction and maintenance projects that may potentially affect eligible properties."[60] Although the determination hindered and delayed some structure rehabilitation, it helped to preserve a vital part of the Corps' history, however reluctantly the organization agreed to this protection.

Another way the St. Paul District tried to maintain the history of the district's locks and dams was through the establishment of visitor centers. In the 1970s, Lieutenant General John W. Morris, Chief of Engineers, initiated a program instituting local, regional and national visitor centers. Corps' headquarters reiterated the importance of these units in the 1990s with a regulation stating that it was Corps' policy to operate centers at water resource development projects in order to "educate and inform the public with regard to the history and mission of the Corps, its role in water resources development, the project, its purpose, benefits and costs."[61] One of the earliest visitor centers in the St. Paul District was at Upper St. Anthony Falls Lock and Dam, completed in 1963 at the site of the only naturally occurring waterfall on the Mississippi. The center initially was only an open overlook structure on the top of the control building. In the late 1970s, the district proposed a renovation but funding for the construction was cut in 1978.[62] It was not until the late 1980s and early 1990s that the Corps made a concerted effort to

(top) A commercial pleasure boat passes the visitors center. (below) A view of the river from inside St. Anthony Falls Visitor Center. (Photos by Frank Star, courtesy of St. Paul District, Corps of Engineers)

restructure St. Anthony Falls Visitor Center the overlook and establish first-rate exhibits telling the story of Upper St. Anthony Falls and the Corps.

This push for an expanded visitor center occurred for a couple of reasons. First, the Corps itself requested that more time be spent on developing interpretive materials at visitor centers.[63] Second, in 1988 the Minnesota State Legislature created the St. Anthony Falls Heritage Interpretive Zone in the area of the lock and dam and established a Heritage Board to administer it. As part of its plans for the region, the Heritage Board proposed the development of a trail system throughout the zone that would help interpret the historic riverfront. The board proposed making the district's Upper St. Anthony Falls Visitor Center one of the primary features of the trail. If the board implemented the trail and other interpretive features, the Corps estimated that the center's current visitation of 30 to 40 thousand visitors annually could triple. This would necessitate an expansion in order to manage the increased visitation.[64]

However, the center was located within the St. Anthony Falls Historic District. Because of this, as an officer at the Minnesota SHPO related, even though the lock and dam was not eligible for the National Register, the Corps still had to treat it as "a contributive element" to the historic district and prevent extensive modifications that "could have considerable impact."[65] Officials and citizens concerned with historic preservation worried about the effects of the Corps' expansion, especially given its track record in the area. When it first constructed the lock and dam in 1963, for example, the Corps altered

Stone Arch Bridge 1962: The Corps altering the 1880s Stone Arch Bridge in Minneapolis prior to building Upper St. Anthony Falls Lock and Dam in 1963. (Photo courtesy of St. Paul District, Corps of Engineers)

the historic Stone Arch Bridge, built by railroad magnate James J. Hill in the 1880s, by replacing two arches and installing a steel truss bridge to accommodate barges.[66] Although the bridge had since been recognized as a National Civil Engineering Landmark, the damage had been done. In order to ensure changes to the visitor center did not likewise disrupt the historic character of the St. Anthony Falls District, Russel Snyder, a landscape architect for the St. Paul District, and Anfinson met frequently with the St. Anthony Falls Heritage Board to receive their input on the renovation designs. Among other things, the board successfully convinced Snyder and Anfinson not to block off the south windows of the observation deck for a display area, believing "the view from the observation deck was critical to interpretation of the area and the Corps' role."[67]

With the approval of the Heritage Board and the SHPO, the district completed the necessary renovations in the mid-1990s. These improvements included installing an elevator to the observation level and a rest room at the ground level to make the center more accessible for people with disabilities. At the same time, new exhibits told the story of Upper St. Anthony Falls and the Corps' involvement there. The new displays, generated by Anfinson and John Fisher of the district's Engineering Division, explained the general history of the Corps and its missions, the general history of the St. Anthony Falls area, how the Corps preserved the falls from destruction in the late 1800s, the construction of Upper St. Anthony Falls Lock and Dam and how the lock and dam operated. In addition, an interactive kiosk allowed users to simulate the locking of a vessel and the dredging of a waterway. The Corps hoped such displays would teach the public more about the district and its activities, as well as about the history of the falls.[68] These improvements generated increased visitation, but some interaction was lost in September 2001, following coordinated terrorist attacks against the United States. Because of the resulting security concerns, the Corps barred any public contact with its locks and dams and shut down the Upper St. Anthony Falls Visitor Center until the middle of 2002. When the center reopened, its hours were changed from 6 a.m. to 10 p.m. to 10 a.m. to 6 p.m. The lock continued to follow these visitor hours in 2003, with no indication of when or if they would return to the longer hours.[69]

Conclusion

The Upper St. Anthony Falls Visitor Center was a good example of some of the ways the St. Paul District sought to provide information about the Corps and its structures to the general public. With such activities, coupled with existing programs in oral history and environmental site histories, Anfinson built a strong district history program. Meanwhile, David Berwick and other archeologists implemented the district's cultural resources management program, including the Section 106 process for Corps' undertakings and the mediation between SHPOs and the Regulatory Branch over Appendix C. Both the history and cultural resources management components educated the public about the Corps' past and the history of the region under the St. Paul District's jurisdiction. As John Anfinson related, those personnel comprising the cultural resources management section, be they archeologists or historians, successfully explained history and prehistory to the public in a way that enabled citizens to "really use [cultural resources] and learn about them."[70]

Chapter Six Endnotes

1 John O. Anfinson Memorandum for Robert F. Post, Chief, Engineering and Planning Division, 31 March 1994, copy provided by John O. Anfinson, Cultural Resources Specialist, Mississippi National River and Recreation Area, National Park Service. Anfinson worked as a historian within the St. Paul District's CRM division from 1980 to 2000.

2 U.S. Bureau of Reclamation, "Bureau of Reclamation Cultural Resources Management," <http://www.usbr.gov/cultural> (6 June 2003).

3 "Cultural Resources Input, Operational Management Plan, Upper Mississippi River, 19 March 1990," File MR-HPP, Cultural Resources Management Administrative Files, St. Paul District of the Army Corps of Engineers, St. Paul, Minnesota [CRM Files].

4 "Bureau of Reclamation Cultural Resources Management," <http://www.usbr. gov/cultural> (6 June 2003).

5 *U.S. Conference of Mayors Special Committee on Historic Preservation, With Heritage So Rich* (New York: Random House, 1966; reprint, Washington, D.C.: The Preservation Press, 1983), p. 191; Lisa S. Mighetto and William F. Willingham, *Service – Tradition – Change: A History of the Fort Worth District, U.S. Army Corps of Engineers, 1975-1999* (Fort Worth, TX.: U.S. Army Corps of Engineers, Fort Worth District, 2000), pp. 33-36; David Berwick, personal communication with the authors, 31 October 2002; Robert F. Post, personal communication with the authors, 6 January 2003. Post was Chief of the Environmental Resources Branch from 1974 through 1982.

6 Quotations from "National Historic Preservation Act of 1966, as amended through 1992," in U.S. Department of the Interior, Federal Historic Preservation Laws (Washington, D.C.: U.S. Department of the Interior, 1993), pp. 7, 9-10, 22; see also Mike Wallace, *Mickey Mouse History and Other Essays on American Memory* (Philadelphia: Temple University Press, 1996), p. 190.

7 Mighetto and Willingham, *Service – Tradition – Change*, pp. 33-36; Bob Post, personal communication with the authors, 6 January 2003.

8 Quotation in Post, personal communication with the authors, 6 January 2003; see also "Cultural Resources Unit," *Crosscurrents* 10 (June 1987): p. 7; Berwick, personal communication with the authors, 31 October 2002; John O. Anfinson interview by Matthew Godfrey, St. Paul, MN, 25 October 2002, p. 1. The program was originally established as a unit under the Environmental Resources Branch, but became a section in 1989. "Cultural Resources Section Input, District Historical Report," File Planning Division AR 89, Box 6412, St. Paul District administrative records, St. Paul, Minnesota [SPDAR].

9 Advisory Council on Historic Preservation, "Section 106 Regulations (Effective 11 January 2001)," 36 CFR Part 800, <http://www.achp.gov/regs.html> (6 June 2003); see also Adina W. Kanefield, *Federal Historic Preservation Case Law, 1966-1996: Thirty Years of the National Historic Preservation Act* (Washington, D.C.: Advisory Council on Historic Preservation, 1996), pp. 11-12.

10 Both quotations in James Kahn, "History Takes a Step Forward," *Water Spectrum 7* (Fall 1975): p. 40.

11 "Cultural Resources Unit," p. 7.

12 U.S. Army Corps of Engineers, St. Paul District, "Native American History in the Mississippi Headwaters Region," <http://www.mvp.usace.army.mil/history/native_am> (6 June 2003).

13 "Lake Ashtabula Operational Management Plan," File Baldhill Dam/Lake Ashtabula OMP, Homme Dam OMP, Lake Ashtabula/Homme Lake EA, CRM Files.

14 U.S. Army Corps of Engineers, St. Paul District, "Final Environmental Impact Statement, Flood Control, East Grand Forks, Minnesota, Grand Forks, North Dakota," p. 30, <http://www.mvp.usace.army.mil/docs/projs/eisfinal.pdf> (6 June 2003).

15 Mighetto and Willingham, *Service – Tradition – Change*, p. 41; Virginia Gnabasik interview by Matthew Godfrey, St. Paul, MN, 22 October 2002, p. 9.

16 Gnabasik Interview, p. 9.

17 Quotation in "Programmatic Agreement Among the U.S. Army Corps of Engineers, St. Paul District, the Advisory Council on Historic Preservation, the North Dakota State Historic Preservation Officer, and the Minnesota State Historic Preservation Officer Regarding Implementation of Flood Protection Measures for the Cities of Grand Forks, North Dakota and East Grand Forks, Minnesota," Revised Draft – July 1998, p. 7, File 1110-2-1150a East Grand Forks Flood Control Programmatic Agreement ('98), Box 8076, SPDAR; see also U.S. Army Corps of Engineers, St. Paul District, "Final Environmental Impact Statement, Flood Control, East Grand Forks, Minnesota, Grand Forks, North Dakota," p. 34.

18 Edward McNally interview by Matthew Godfrey, St. Paul, MN, 22 October 2002, p. 7.

19 "Draft, Environmental Assessment, LaFarge Bridges Removal/Relocation, Kickapoo River, Near La Farge, Wisconsin," pp. 1-9, File 1501-07 Ref. Paper Files – La Farge – Tech. Drawings, Box 7932, SPDAR; Richard Otto interview by Matthew Godfrey, St. Paul, MN, 23 October 2002, pp. 11-12; John Anfinson Interview, p. 8.

20 Quotation in "Homme Dam Operational Management Plan," File Baldhill Dam/Lake Ashtabula OMP, Homme Dam OMP, Lake Ashtabula/Homme Lake EA, CRM Files; see also "Archaeological Resources Protection Act of 1979," in U.S. Department of the Interior, Federal Historic Preservation Laws, p. 55; Charles

P. Spitzack Memorandum for CENCS-DDPM (Crist), 9 April 1997, File La Farge Correspondence, Box 6407, SPDAR.

21 "National Historic Preservation Act of 1966, as amended through 1992," in U.S. Department of the Interior, Federal Historic Preservation Laws, pp. 14-15.

22 Gnabasik Interview, pp. 7-8. For an example of a Corps letter requesting tribal participation, see Kenneth S. Kasprisin, Colonel, Corps of Engineers, to Honorable Phillip "Skip" Longie, Jr., Chairman, Spirit Lake Tribal Council, 19 November 1999, File 1110- 21150a Baldhill Dam Pool Raise ('99), Box 6417, SPDAR.

23 Quotation in "Native American Graves Protection and Repatriation Act," in U.S. Department of the Interior, Federal Historic Preservation Laws, p. 65, 67; see also U.S. Congress, 101st Cong., 2d sess., "Providing for the Protection of Native American Graves, and For Other Purposes," House Report 101-877, 1990, pp. 13-17, <http://www.cast.uark.edu/other/nps/nagpra/DOCS/lgm001.html> (6 June 2003).

24 Sissel Johannessen, "Notes on NAGPRA," 28 May 2003, document provided to the authors; Gnabasik Interview, pp. 6-7.

25 Patricia L. Parker and Thomas F. King, "Guidelines for Evaluating and Documenting Traditional Cultural Properties," *National Register Bulletin* 38, <http://www.cr.nps.gov/nr /publications/bulletins/nrb38> (6 June 2003). For background on TCPs, see Antoinette J. Lee, "Recognizing Cultural Heritage in the National Historic Preservation Program," CRM 16 (1993 Special Issue – *Traditional Cultural Properties*): pp. 7-8.

26 David W. Cushman, "When Worlds Collide: Indians, Archeologists, and the Preservation of Traditional Cultural Properties," CRM 16 (1993 Special Issue – *Traditional Cultural Properties*): pp. 49-51 (quotation on p. 50).

27 John Anfinson Interview, p. 11.

28 "Oral Interviews: The Significance of Grand Portage Bay to the Grand Portage Chippewa Band," memorandum provided to the authors by John Anfinson.

29 John Anfinson Interview, p. 11.

30 Quotation in John Anfinson Interview, p. 12; see also "Watery Logs Expand Wood Products Industry," Federal Reserve Bank of Minneapolis *Fedgazette* (July 1997) <http://minneapolisfed. org/pubs/fedgaz/97-07/wi.cfm> (6 June 2003).

31 Maria T. Valencia to Ben A. Wopat, 17 December 2002, email message supplied to the authors by Ben A. Wopat.

32 John Anfinson Interview, p. 12.

33 Dennis Gimmestad interview by Matthew Godfrey, St. Paul, MN, 23 October 2002, p. 1; Scott Anfinson interview by Matthew Godfrey, St. Paul, MN, 24 October 2002, p. 5. Gimmestad served as the Minnesota State Historic Preservation Office's Compliance Officer, while Anfinson was a National Register Archeologist for Minnesota's SHPO.

34 Advisory Council on Historic Preservation, "Section 106 Regulations (Effective 11 January 2001)," 36 CFR Part 800, Section 800.14, <http://www.achp.gov/regs.html> (6 June 2003).

35 "Department of the Army Regulatory Program – An Overview," June 1997, in U.S. Army Corps of Engineers Regulatory Executive Training Session Binder, 7-9 March 2000, Headquarters, U.S. Army Corps of Engineers [HQUSACE] administrative records, Washington, D.C.

36 U.S. Army Corps of Engineers, "33 CFR Part 325, Appendix C – Procedures for the Protection of Historic Properties," <http://www.usace.army.mil/inet/functions/cw/cecwo/reg/33cfr325.htm#appendixC> (6 June 2003).

37 Advisory Council on Historic Preservation, "Section 106 Regulations (Effective 11 January 2001)," 36 CFR Part 800, Section 800.16 – Definitions, <http://www.achp.gov/regs.html#800.16> (6 June 2003) (emphasis added).

38 Gimmestad Interview, p. 7; Brad Johnson, personal communication with the authors, 15 March 2004.

39 Gimmestad Interview, p. 6.

40 Scott Anfinson Interview, p. 5.

41 SHPO No. 2000-1434, as related in Johnson, personal communication with the authors, 15 March 2004.

42 U.S. Army Corps of Engineers, Office of the Chief of Engineers, Engineer Profiles: The District Engineer, Interviews with Colonel William W. Badger, by Frank N. Schubert (Washington, U.S. Army Corps of Engineers, 1983), pp. 37-38 [hereafter cited as Badger Interviews].

43 John Anfinson Interview, p. 1.

44 Albert J. Genetti, Jr., Colonel, Corps of Engineers, Chief of Staff, "Historical Activities: Field Operating Activities Historical Programs," Regulation No. 870-1-1, 30 April 1990, p. 2, File Hist. Cmte. (1989-90), Box 6412, SPDAR.

45 William A. Stofft, Brigadier General, Chief of Military History, Memorandum, 2 July 1986, File Oral History – General, Box 7842, SPDAR; John Anfinson Interview, p. 2.

46 John O. Anfinson, personal communication with the authors, 30 December 2002; Paul K. Walker Memorandum for Commander, U.S. Army Engineer Division, North Central, 18 August 1989, File Oral History – General, Box 7842, SPDAR. Schubert had a summer cabin in Minnesota, giving him opportunities to implement the oral history program in the St. Paul District.

47 Colonel Roger L. Baldwin interview by John O. Anfinson, St. Paul, MN, 1 July 1991, 3 July 1991, Oral History File, St. Paul District, St. Paul, Minnesota.

48 Genetti, "Historical Activities: Field Operating Activities Historical Programs," p. 5.

49 Quotation in "District Begins Oral History Program," *Crosscurrents* 10 (August 1987): p. 6.

50 Jo Blatti, "Oral History of the Mississippi River Locks and Dams Nos. 3-10: Draft Final Report," p. 3, File MR Oral History 2, Box 7842, SPDAR.

51 Quotation in "District Begins Oral History Program," p. 6.

52 Quotation in John Anfinson Interview, p. 4; see also Charles E. Crist, Chief, Planning Branch, Memorandum for Robert F. Post, Chief, Engineering and Planning Division, 31 March 1994, document provided to the authors by John Anfinson; Berwick, personal communication with the authors, 31 October 2002; Matthew T. Pearcy, personal communication with the authors, 29 December 2002. The Geotechnical Section usually contracts these histories out to a private firm.

53 John Anfinson, "Detailed Overview: Henry P. Bosse Exhibit," File 200 Cultural Resources, General Folder #1, Box 4338, SPDAR.

54 John Anfinson Interview, p. 5.

55 John O. Anfinson to Sverdrup, 6 December 1988, File Lock and Dam 4 – Major Rehab., CRM Files.

56 John O. Anfinson, "The Nine-Foot Channel: Eligibility and Protection," File Lock and Dam 4 – Major Rehab., CRM Files.

57 John Anfinson Interview, p. 4.

58 William Patrick O'Brien, Mary Yeater Rathbun, and Patrick O'Bannon, *Gateways to Commerce: The U.S. Army Corps of Engineers' 9-Foot Channel Project on the Upper Mississippi River, edited by Christine Whitacre* (Denver: National Park Service, Rocky Mountain Region, 1992), p. 7; John Anfinson Interview, p. 5. The Historic American Engineering Record is under the purview of the National Park Service.

59 "Mississippi River – OMP," pp. 7-9, File Locks and Dams – History, CRM Files.

60 Joseph H. Mose, Acting Chief, Environmental & Economic Analysis Branch, Memorandum for MVP-CO/Ken Buck, n.d., File Section 106 and Con-Ops, CRM Files.

61 Robert L. Herndon, Colonel, Corps of Engineers Chief of Staff, "Planning, Development, Management and Operation: Visitor Center Program," ER 1130-2-401, 15 February 1991, p. 2, File SAF Visitor's Center, CRM Files; see also Raymond Merritt, "New Directions: Transitions in the St. Paul District, Corps of Engineers, 1976-1982," unpublished manuscript, St. Paul District, p. 61.

62 "Fact Sheet: Upper St. Anthony Falls Lock and Dam Visitor Center Improvements," 20 August 1990, File SAF Visitor's Center, CRM Files; see also Steven

Lenhart interview by Matthew Godfrey, Minneapolis, MN, 21 October 2002, p. 19. Lenhart is the lockmaster at USAF Lock and Dam.

63 See, for example, Herndon, "Planning, Development, Management and Operation: Visitor Center Program."

64 "Fact Sheet: Upper St. Anthony Falls Lock and Dam Visitor Center Improvements"; "Plan Summary Draft Text (13 November 1989)," pp. 4-5, File SAF History, CRM Files.

65 Ted Lofstrom, Review and Compliance Officer, Minnesota State Historic Preservation Office, to Mr. Robert J. Whiting, St. Paul District, Corps of Engineers, 13 April 1990, File SAF History, CRM Files.

66 Minnesota Historical Society, "Railroad Properties: Stone Arch Bridge (in the St. Anthony Falls Historic District)," <http://nrhp.mnhs.org/property_overview. cfm?propertyID=79> (6 June 2003).

67 Russel Snyder, "Meeting with St. Anthony Falls Heritage Board Technical Advisory Committee, November 28, 1988: Memo for the Record," 6 December 1988, File SAF Historic District, CRM Files.

68 U.S. Army Corps of Engineers, St. Paul District, *Interpretive Prospectus: Morgan J. Tschida Visitor Center, Upper St. Anthony Falls Lock and Dam* (St. Paul, MN: U.S. Army Corps of Engineers, St. Paul District, 1995), pp. 2, 6-8; John Anfinson Interview, p. 3; Lenhart Interview, pp. 2, 15-16.

69 Lenhart Interview, p. 12; U.S. Army Corps of Engineers, St. Paul District, "Corps of Engineers Opens Most Lock and Dam Visitor Centers Along the Mississippi River," Press Release, 10 May 2002, <http://www.mvp.usace.army.mil/pressroom/ default.asp?pageid=329> (6 June 2003).

70 John Anfinson Interview, p. 14.

Ranger Kyle Curtiss, Pokegama Dam and Recreation Area, Grand Rapids, Minn., assists a camper in making a pinecone bird feeder. (Photo by Tammy Wick, courtesy of St. Paul District, Corps of Engineers)

7 Recreation

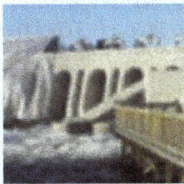

In 1988, Colonel Joseph Briggs, outgoing district engineer of the St. Paul District, related that the Corps' "recreational business is growing in leaps and bounds."[1] The Corps received the responsibility from the federal government to develop recreational opportunities in conjunction with its civil works projects in the mid-twentieth century. As Briggs explained, recreation had become an increasingly important function of the Corps as the century progressed, although it was never considered as important as the navigation and flood control missions. Emphasizing the value of recreation, however, a 1996 Corps' engineering regulation declared that one of the primary goals of the Corps was "providing quality public outdoor recreation experiences to serve the needs of present and future generations." By the twenty-first century, the Corps had become one of the largest operators of recreation units on federal land.[2] Yet the Corps sometimes shied away from fully developing recreational opportunities, in part because of environmental concerns and in part because of conflicts with other missions and federal agencies. An examination of the recreational function in the St. Paul District in the late twentieth century highlights some of these features.

Although Congress has never authorized the Corps to build a dam and reservoir solely for recreational purposes, the Corps obtained authority in the 1944 Flood Control Act to build recreation facilities. The 1965 Federal Water Project Recreation Act allowed the Corps to include recreation as a contributing factor to benefit-cost ratios, while also mandating that non-federal sponsors bear at least fifty percent of the construction costs.[3] With these authorities, the Corps developed campgrounds, day-use areas, boat ramps and swimming beaches around the bodies of water it managed. As more and more Americans participated in outdoor recreation in the 1960s and 1970s, Corps' resources became increasingly popular. The Corps estimated in 2003 that 360 million people annually visited the 2,500 recreation areas at the more than 450 projects that it operated, as well as the 1,800 other sites leased to state, local or private recreation managers. However, the Corps' responsibilities did not merely consist of providing areas of enjoyment. According to one manager, they also extended to "insur[ing] the public safety and health of the visiting public, ... protect[ing] natural resources for future generations, and ... charg[ing] fees where appropriate to offset operation and maintenance costs." Because of these diverse duties, Corps' regulations required that its Natural Resources Management Program staff be drawn from "personnel having expertise in areas such as forestry, wildlife management, recreation management, fisheries management, parks management, landscape architecture, biology, soil science, interpretation, visitor assistance and contract administration."[4]

In the St. Paul District, recreation management was a part of the Natural Resources section of the Construction-Operations Division. Project managers within the Construction-Operations Division administered project sites, and recreation personnel reported to the on-site supervisor. The main recreational attractions in the district included the Mississippi River, its headwaters and several other reservoirs and waterways scattered across North Dakota, Minnesota and Wisconsin. Essentially, the district's recreational operations lay in four major areas: developing new opportunities on civil works projects; maintaining existing projects; conducting public outreach ventures, including safety programs; and assisting in natural resources management. Most of these functions could best be carried out at the projects themselves, meaning the district did not have a large recreation staff in its St. Paul office. Instead, most recreation and natural resource employees were located in the field, and these individuals labored to ensure the public had ample recreational opportunities and satisfactory experiences.[5]

Developing New Opportunities

One of the main functions of the district's recreation staff included the development of recreational features as part of new civil works projects. After 1936, the Corps built numerous large dams for flood control, and the resulting reservoirs were some of the major attractions for the general public. Numerous factors, including the environmental movement and increasing costs, however, reduced the Corps' dam/reservoir construction in the 1970s in favor of more non-structural solutions.[6] Yet recreation opportunities still existed, and the Corps continued to develop these possibilities whenever feasible.

One of the major successes for the St. Paul District stemmed from the construction of the South Fork Zumbro River Flood Control Project in Rochester, Minnesota, completed in the 1990s and the recipient of several awards (see Chapter Four). Recreation was an important component of this project from the beginning.[7] According to Frank Star, an outdoor recreation planner for the district, the involvement of the recreation staff in Rochester was typical of its participation in most civil works projects. First, Star related, the district had to determine whether recreational aspects were feasible. If so, it had to discover whether local entities were willing to share the costs of these developments. The City of Rochester expressed an early willingness to pay the fifty percent cost requirement, meaning the district's recreational staff worked closely with the city to determine just what features were desirable. "Once we had figured out what the project was going to consist of, which was channel work in the city itself," Star stated, "then we looked at what kind of recreational opportunities ... that afford[ed]." The two sides ultimately decided that the best utilization lay in bicycle and pedestrian trails and picnic areas along the Zumbro River where much of the Corps' work was occurring.[8]

Recreation: Swimmers at the Crosslake Recreation Area in Cross Lake, Minnesota. (Photo by Shannon Bauer, courtesy of St. Paul District, Corps of Engineers)

During the project's construction in the late 1980s and early 1990s, many citizens in Rochester grew excited about the opportunities. As one newspaper report related, "Not only will the project protect the city from flooding, but it will provide outdoor enthusiasts with an array of new opportunities through a network of bike trails, a series of reservoirs and new parks and campgrounds." These features, the newspaper concluded, showed that the Corps, as well as other entities involved in the project, was "work[ing] hard to combine flood protection and fun."[9] In essence, the recreation developments consisted of 6.5 miles of walkways and bicycle paths along the Zumbro in downtown Rochester, as well as pedestrian plazas, picnic shelters and better access points to the river. Even before the project was completed, the general public extensively used these features, and frequently commented favorably.[10] One woman was grateful for the bike paths because her daughter could ride without worrying about automobiles and curbs. Another man, on an "after-dinner stroll," expressed his pleasure with the trails, stating that the area was "much improved over what it was."[11] According to project manager Deborah Foley, the well-accepted recreation developments, funded in part by the city, were "key" reasons why the project received "top honors" in 1996.[12]

The South Fork Zumbro River Project was representative of the way the district developed recreational aspects on civil works projects. Although not all local parties were as willing to foot fifty percent of the bill, other undertakings, including the St. Paul and the Grand Forks/East Grand Forks flood control projects, also had significant recreation features. However, as with the Zumbro, once the Corps completed construction of these developments, it turned the recreation units over to the local sponsor for operation and maintenance. Thereafter, the Corps had little to do with the projects, aside from periodic inspections to ensure they were being operated and maintained correctly. Local assumption of responsibility commonly occurred in the last half of the twentieth century. According to Richard Otto, who began working with the St. Paul District's recreation program in 1975, because most of these facilities were "small areas and parks ... used by local people," common sense dictated that local governments operate them.[13]

However, the Corps quickly learned that local governments sometimes caused problems in the management of recreation facilities. In 1980, for example, Vernon County, Wisconsin, which leased Blackhawk Park on the Mississippi River from the Corps, decided to terminate its operating lease and return the park to Corps' control. The county also informed the St. Paul District it would no longer maintain the access road to the park, even though the street provided service to private residences and public utilities. In addition, the county refused to construct safety features on the road, including warnings at a railroad crossing. Because of the county's unwillingness to take responsibility for the road and the safety concerns, the Corps closed Blackhawk Park for

a couple of months in the spring of 1984. The loss of tourist revenue hurt the surrounding communities, leading 2,843 people to sign a petition demanding the county assume responsibility for the road. The county finally accepted that duty in May, allowing the Corps to reopen in time for the Memorial Day weekend. Although the situation eventually resolved itself, it showed some of the difficulties that could result from a local government's lack of participation in recreation projects.[14]

The Mississippi National River and Recreation Area extends from the mouth of the Crow River below Lock and Dam 1 (shown here) through the Twin Cities to the mouth of the St. Croix River. (Photo courtesy of St. Paul District, Corps of Engineers)

Mississippi National River and Recreation Area

The Mississippi River was another site for recreational development in the last quarter of the twentieth century, although the Corps was at times dubious about pursuing recreation on the river. As part of the Great River Environmental Action Team's (GREAT I) study of the Upper Mississippi River in the 1970s (see Chapter Three), a recreation work group, consisting of representatives from the Corps, the U.S. Fish and Wildlife Service, the Heritage

Conservation and Recreation Service and the states of Iowa, Wisconsin and Minnesota, issued recommendations in 1979 for increasing recreation on the Mississippi. The work group suggested that:

- The Corps should consider recreation enhancement when disposing of dredged material on the river;

- Congress should give the Corps authority to maintain recreational areas on federal lands along the river in cooperation with other agencies without local cost-sharing;

- The Corps should maintain backwater accesses;

- Federal agencies should "provide a diversity of recreational opportunities" on the river; and

- Recreation should be included as a "project purpose" of the Nine-Foot Navigation Project.[15]

When the St. Paul District issued its report on the implementation of GREAT I's recommendations, it noted that its nine-foot navigation channel increased recreational boating opportunities on the river and recognized the popularity of islands in the Mississippi created by the disposal of dredged material. However, the district only promised to give "additional consideration" to recreation on the river, recognizing that other programs, such as environmental management, took priority.[16] Accordingly, when the district later received authority for its Upper Mississippi Environmental Management Program in the 1980s, the recreation component received no funding from Congress "due to a low" federal priority.[17] As Frank Star explained, "The big problem is that the recreation community is not [as] well organized as some of the environmental community is ... There's no big group of campers or hikers or somebody to raise the stakes."[18]

Wildlife Refuge: Don Powell served as project manager for the Fish and Wildlife Service's Trempealeau Refuge Project as part of the Upper Mississippi Environmental Management Program. (Photo by Shannon Bauer, courtesy of St. Paul District, Corps of Engineers)

Although GREAT I's recommendations did not significantly alter recreational opportunities on the Mississippi, it enabled Congress and environmental organizations to examine how recreation could be integrated more fully into river management plans. These dialogues eventually culminated in the introduction of legislation in the late 1980s by U.S. Representative Bruce F. Vento (D-Minnesota) for the establishment of a Mississippi National River and Recreation Area. It would encompass an 80-mile stretch of the river beginning near the Crow River in Minnesota and running through the Twin Cities to the confluence of the Mississippi and the St. Croix rivers at the Wisconsin-Minnesota border. Vento foresaw this area as falling under the jurisdiction of the National Park Service, with a coordinating committee aiding its governance. He believed the designation would "maximize the River's potential and assure a fair balance between commercial and recreational interests."[19]

The St. Paul District, however, was not enthusiastic about Vento's plan, believing, in the words of District Engineer Colonel Briggs, that "another layer of coordination would unduly delay the essential time required to accomplish the things that we have to do," such as navigation, flood control and environmental regulation. Vento disagreed with the Corps' complaints, believing the real reason why Briggs opposed the project was because he did not want the National Park Service infringing on the district's "turf," a charge Briggs denied.[20]

Despite the Corps' reservations about the new system, the bill had enough support to become law on November 18, 1988. Along with designating the 80-mile section of the river as a national river and recreation area under the jurisdiction of the National Park Service, the law also established a Mississippi River Coordinating Commission "to assist federal, state, and local authorities in the development and implementation of an integrated resource management plan." Representatives from the National Park Service, the Fish and Wildlife Service, the state of Minnesota and the Corps all had a seat on the commission.[21] This helped the St. Paul District work closely with the National Park Service to develop recreational activities on the Mississippi, including installing interactive kiosks at visitor centers and initiating the Mighty Mississippi Passport program, whereby children could earn a Mighty Mississippi Junior Ranger Badge and certificate by visiting a certain number of sites on the river. Although district officials were initially reluctant to support the designation of the river as a national recreation area, they eventually accepted it as a good way, in the words of Frank Star, to "encourage people to come down and look at the river and [our] stewardship."[22]

Recreation Boating: Canoeists paddle through the Lower St. Anthony Falls Lock and Dam in Minneapolis during an annual Independence Day event. (Photo courtesy of St. Paul District, Corps of Engineers)

Lower St. Anthony Falls Whitewater Park

Other possibilities for Mississippi River recreation also existed. In the late 1990s, the Corps began discussions with the Minnesota DNR about the creation of a whitewater park at Lower St. Anthony Falls in Minneapolis. The Mississippi Whitewater Park Development Corporation provided the impetus for the facility, forming specifically to outline plans for the park. The development corporation envisioned the establishment of a rapids channel adjacent to the Lower St. Anthony Falls Lock and Dam, along with a park and trail system on the east bank of the Mississippi. The channel would be 40 feet wide and 2,000 feet long and would utilize the dam's vertical drop of 25 feet. Proponents believed that canoeists, kayakers and rafters would use the conduit, which would also provide fishing opportunities. In addition, not only would the channel restore the whitewater rapids that existed on the river decades before, but the park itself would enhance the aesthetics of a desolate portion of the river. In 1999, Minnesota's DNR completed a feasibility report on the park, and Congress authorized the project in the Water Resources Development Act of 2000. The Corps and the DNR entered into a cooperative agreement in 2002 to begin planning and design, but the outcome of the project was unclear after President George W. Bush omitted it from his fiscal year 2003 budget. Regardless, most supporters believed it was only a matter of time before the park would be constructed, and, when completed, it would, according to the Mississippi Whitewater Park Development Corporation, "expand the concept of a 'user-friendly' river, increasing environmental awareness, [and] giving Minnesotans the opportunity to make the Mighty Mississippi a part of their lives."[23]

Maintaining Existing Facilities

Along with planning new recreational developments, the St. Paul District also maintained existing facilities under its control. Several of these were located at the headwaters of the Mississippi in northcentral Minnesota, including the Cross Lake, Pokegama Lake, Sandy Lake, Leech Lake, Gull Lake and Lake Winnibigoshish recreation areas. The Corps created these reservoirs between 1884 and 1912 by constructing several dams at the Mississippi Headwaters to store water for release during the summer to support navigation below St. Paul. After the Corps developed the nine-foot navigation channel on the Mississippi River in the 1930s, these reservoirs became less important for navigation but more significant for wildlife habitat and recreation. In 1964, the first official recreation facilities were designated at the lakes with the completion of a recreational development master plan for the Pine River Reservoir, another name for Cross Lake. After that time, the Corps developed master plans for the other lakes as well.[24] In addition to the headwaters, the St. Paul District supervised recreational facilities at several other locations, including Orwell Lake, Lake Traverse and Lac Qui Parle Dam in Minnesota; Homme Lake and Lake Ashtabula in North Dakota; and Eau Galle Lake and Blackhawk Park in Wisconsin. Finally, the Mississippi River itself provided numerous recreational resources, including beaches and islands made from dredged materials.[25]

Pine River Dam in Crosslake, Minnesota, received a facelift from 1999 to 2003. Improvements included an accessible fishing pier. (Photo by Shannon Bauer, courtesy of St. Paul District, Corps of Engineers)

One of the Corps' essential responsibilities in managing these facilities was determining public needs and improving parks accordingly. Most of the sites, whether in Minnesota, North Dakota or Wisconsin, offered essentially the same water-related activities: boating, swimming, camping, fishing and picnicking. Some provided hiking, playground areas and visitor centers as well. With so many facilities scattered throughout the three states, district employees spent much time maintaining resources and ensuring the public's satisfaction with the areas. In 1985, for example, the Corps decided that changes were necessary at Leech Lake Dam. Traditionally an excellent spot for fishing, the lake had experienced only nominal annual increases in visitation in the 1980s. The Corps determined that more appealing activities for families, retired couples and persons with disabilities might increase visitation, so it installed a game area with horseshoe pits, shuffleboard, volleyball, badminton and basketball courts. The district also constructed landscaped stairways, ramps and walkway bridges to increase access. The improvements worked, and visitation increased by seventeen percent in 1986 and nine percent in 1987.[26]

The number of campers, coupled with a decreasing number of Corps' employees at Leech Lake, compelled the district to instigate a volunteer campground host program. Under this plan, volunteers became the principal contact point for visitors to the area, handling questions and distributing information. According to the Corps, "hosts never enforce rules and regulations or become involved in any domestic disputes." Instead, they performed "common daily duties, allowing rangers additional time to perform more professional duties." Although the district never widely implemented the volunteer host program, it helped Leech Lake cope with a lack of personnel in the late 1980s.[27]

Funding and personnel issues were always problems for the St. Paul District and the Corps in general. Not only did recreation recommendations made by study groups such as GREAT I receive little money, but existing recreation areas, dependent on congressional appropriations, sometimes faced paltry funding as well. In 1989, for example, President Ronald Reagan's fiscal year 1990 budget slashed the St. Paul District's recreation operations and maintenance budget by nearly twenty-five percent. This meant most sites had to cut back on activities.[28] The St. Paul District was not alone; in 1989 the Bush Administration called for the closing of 654 Corps' recreation areas nationwide. Fortunately for the Corps' recreational employees and local economies depending on these sites, Congress rejected the plan. Because of these budget constraints, the Corps examined new ways to fund recreation projects in the early 1990s. As Frank Star said, funding was "always an issue" for recreation, in part because of its "non-essentiality." Whereas transportation networks needed highway repairs, the maintenance of campgrounds was less important. This made recreation an "easy target" for budget cuts.[29]

User Fees

One of the ways the Corps attempted to bolster its funding was by charging user fees at its facilities. Congress first authorized the Corps to impose recreation fees in the 1965 Land and Water Conservation Fund Act. This law stated that federal agencies administering outdoor recreation sites could levy recreation use charges, mandating that such costs be "fair and equitable." Other than campground fees, however, the Corps did not implement any charges at that time. With funding cuts for recreation in the 1990s, however, the agency decided user fees could rectify the situation. Accordingly, Congress included in the 1993 Omnibus Budget Reconciliation Act a provision allowing the Corps to implement day-use charges at appropriate areas.[30]

Subsequent Corps' regulations claimed that the fees had five major purposes: to recover some of the operation and maintenance costs of facilities, to reduce overcrowding, to provide quality recreational experiences which would support the national economy, to control vandalism and disruptive behavior and to foster a responsible user ethic among its guests. The resulting revenue went into a special Corps' account in the U.S. Treasury and was ultimately returned as Special Recreation Use Funds to those projects producing the revenue.[31] Although fees meant increased costs for the consumer, the public generally accepted the charges, in part because it knew the Corps used the revenue to offset operation and maintenance costs. As Star related, "If you can show them that the money is coming back and you're actually making use of it to improve facilities, then [the public is] more accepting of it."[32] In addition, the fees were not burdensome. At the beginning of 2003, the public could purchase annual passes allowing yearlong day-use of Corps facilities for $30, while persons 62 years of age and older could buy a Golden Age Passport, which provided a fifty percent discount on all recreation fees, for $10. Individual day-use charges ranged from $1-3 per person, depending on whether or not the individual accessed a boat ramp or a swimming area.[33]

National Recreation Reservation System

Another change the Corps implemented was the creation of the National Recreation Reservation System. In the late 1990s, the Corps joined with the Forest Service and the Bureau of Land Management, and later, the National Park Service, to establish a national reservation system for federal campgrounds. According to the Corps, this would "enhance customer service for users of our public lands by providing, with a single phone call, the ability to make reservations for fee-based, recreation facilities." The organizations contracted with ReserveAmerica to provide this service, thereby facilitating the camping experience for those willing to make and pay for advance reservations. Although the Corps characterized this program as a "win-win-win service for our customers," it did lead to some problems early on, mainly with the service provided by ReserveAmerica. Company representatives at times provided misinformation about the availability of campsites, while others placed non-disabled people on sites set aside for those with disabilities. The Corps also discovered the reservation system made it easier for individuals to skirt around policies such as the number of days a group could stay at a campsite. Frank Star expressed some frustration with the contractor, stating it was "not responsive at times to some of our complaints or problems," but he still recognized the system was valuable at least for "reduc[ing] some of our workload."[34]

Public Outreach and Safety Programs

The Corps faced other problems at its recreation sites. Some trouble arose because of the proximity of these areas to urban regions. The Corps prided itself on providing recreational opportunities to cities, but this same feature created difficulties in the twenty-first century. Alcohol had long been a source of concern at Corps' facilities and forced the agency to conduct periodic assessments of its prevalence at larger sites, but the appearance of methamphetamine labs at some Corps' campgrounds was disturbing as well.[35] So, too, was the danger that some Corps' rangers faced. Because rangers did not have any law enforcement authority, working only to implement rules and regulations, they could not carry or use weapons, meaning they sometimes had little means of protecting themselves against assaults. The need to provide for ranger safety was emphasized in the 1970s when escapees from the Oklahoma State Prison abducted two park rangers in Arkansas, critically injuring one and killing the other. Such incidents caused concern, and, in 1995, the government appointed a task force to investigate ranger safety. This group issued a report and policy letter in 1996 addressing concerns and providing recommendations. One of the results of this study was the implementation in 1999 of a pilot program in the Fort Worth District allowing rangers to carry pepper spray. Based on the success of this experiment, the Corps issued a circular in April 2002 allowing all of its park rangers to carry and use the spray for self-defense. St. Paul District rangers welcomed this authorization, especially after discovering that in the summer of 2002 a highly dangerous sex offender was located not many miles from one of its camping sites in Minnesota. As Star related, "It's getting a little more scary out there for our employees."[36]

Water Safety: Frank Star, wearing his ranger uniform, introduces the Corps' Seamoor the Sea Dragon to children in La Crosse, Wis. Seamoor's job is to teach water safety. (Photo by Shannon Bauer, courtesy of St. Paul District, Corps of Engineers)

As visitation at Corps' facilities expanded, littering problems increased as well. The St. Paul District, for example, had trouble with trash problems on the dredged material islands in the Mississippi River. Richard Otto, one of the district's natural resources managers, explained there was little the district could do to ensure that visitors to these islands cleaned up their trash because "we don't have any staff to patrol on the water."[37] Instead, the district sponsored annual volunteer cleanups at the islands, but littering continued. At other sites manned by the Corps, rangers regularly patrolled campgrounds and water areas both for safety reasons and for trash control, but as one district engineer related, "with limited resources, we cannot assign 24-hour ranger patrols to each recreation area."[38]

In large part because of its staff and its outreach programs, the St. Paul District was able to provide a satisfying experience at its recreation facilities. The district received numerous letters from pleased visitors applauding Corps' personnel and various recreation programs. One couple expressed their approval with the district's Gull Lake campground. "It is nice to know that there is always such a great place to go for camping," they commented, "and it is especially nice to know that we see the same familiar, friendly and helpful staff."[39] Neil R. Hunt, the president of a local Parent-Teacher Association, echoed these sentiments after a grade-school class toured the Cross Lake Recreation Area with two summer interns. "The kind of human level, service-oriented actions" exemplified by the employees, he observed, did "more to improve the attitude of taxpayers than any program or brochure coming out of Washington."[40]

Outreach programs provided an excellent means for the Corps to interact with the public, especially youth. School groups routinely visited recreation areas for tours, environmental workshops and fishing lessons, while youth also attended summer fishing clinics and contests. In 1978, for example, several recreation sites sponsored "Eco-Expoz," where students participated in tours, games and exercises dealing with the environment. According to Richard Otto, the students enjoyed the different programs, convincing the district to continue them in future years.[41] In a similar way, the St. Paul District participated in the Mississippi River Project in 1993, where different federal agencies coordinated a day of water quality awareness education for youth along the Mississippi from its headwaters to the Gulf of Mexico. As part of this program, students in the St. Paul District went to Lake Itasca, Harriet Island in St. Paul and Locks and Dams 3, 7 and 9 to help with water sampling and testing. At Lock and Dam 7, Otto and Corrine Hodapp, a park ranger at Blackhawk Park, discussed commercial navigation and water safety before the students conducted their experiments. As a district account of the event concluded, "By the end of the day, more than 300 future stewards of the Mississippi River had a better understanding of the river and its problems and promises."[42]

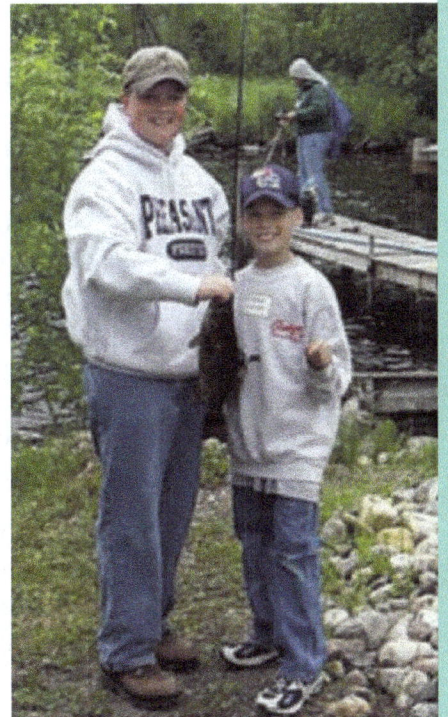

Recreation: Young fishermen at Lake Ashtabula in North Dakota (Photo by Jeff Kapaun, courtesy of St. Paul District, Corps of Engineers)

Fishing activities were also popular. In June 1991, the staff at Sandy Lake Dam sponsored a clinic for campground visitors and a local 4-H club. Forty youth attended the event and learned how to identify different species of fish and how to tie various knots, while also gaining knowledge in artificial lures, casting, the uses of live bait and the proper way to release fish. At the conclusion of the workshop, the 4-H group asked the Corps to hold such clinics every year.[43] Meanwhile, the Lake Ashtabula staff conducted an annual program entitled "Take A Kid Fishing Day," held each June in conjunction with National Fishing Week. Rangers helped the children fish in the morning, and then talked to them about water safety and the "Mr. McGruff" safety program in the afternoon. Upon leaving, each child received a bag with safety literature, coloring books, a National Fishing Week Educational Activity Book and various prizes donated by Valley City, North Dakota, businesses.[44]

Safety Programs

As the Lake Ashtabula clinic showed, safety was an important feature of the Corps' outreach programs. Because so many recreational opportunities revolved around water, the Corps was concerned about the public's safety. The locks and dams on the Mississippi River constituted some of the most dangerous places because of the strong currents and powerful undertows close to the structures. To combat this problem, the Corps established restricted areas both above and below the locks and dams, but accidents still occurred.[45] The safety hazards that water posed led lock operators and park rangers to gain training in rescue, CPR and first aid, and this preparation was sometimes very useful. In May 1989, for example, park rangers at Leech Lake conducted two separate rescue operations within three days of each other. The first involved a fisherman who had become lost on the lake, while the second saved two couples stranded in a boat filled with water. Park Rangers Clint Fishel, Corrine Hodapp and Jeff Steere all participated in the rescues, leading one Corps' publication to express its gratitude for the "training and expertise of the park rangers at our recreation areas."[46]

In addition to ensuring its employees had proper rescue skills, the Corps conducted safety programs at its recreation sites. Lake Ashtabula, for example, presented "Kids in Boats" workshops to teach children about personal flotation devices, hypothermia, rescue techniques and knot tying. Although students could attend the session at the lake, rangers also took the program to various locations in North Dakota in support of the North Dakota Game and Fish Department and the North Dakota Safety Council. According to one ranger, the workshops were so popular the staff could not fill every request. Likewise, personnel at the Cross Lake Recreation Area provided water safety presentations to grade school classes at the end of every school year in preparation for summer water activities.[47] According to park ranger Kevin Berg, these programs helped "the public better understand the importance of thinking 'safety' while on the water."[48]

Other forms of outreach included Corps' participation in outdoor recreation conferences and professional societies. The St. Paul District often had booths at recreation and sports shows, where it explained its recreation operations. Frank Star claimed these shows enabled the Corps to "tell our story" to people unaware of "how big the Corps was and what it did." Several district employees, some in leadership positions, were also active in professional societies, including the National Association of Interpreters, the National Recreation and Parks Association and the National Society for Park Resources. All of these efforts resulted in increased public exposure of the Corps' recreation mission.[49]

Assisting in Natural Resources Management

Recreation employees also helped the Corps manage its natural resources. Part of this mission consisted of ensuring that recreation use on reservoirs and rivers did not harm the surrounding environment. One way the St. Paul District accomplished this was through environmental studies. As part of the Upper Mississippi River-Illinois

Waterway System Navigation Study in the 1990s, for example, the district undertook an examination of the effects of recreational boating traffic on the Upper Mississippi River for the project's EIS. The study related that recreational vessels caused "wake waves, propeller turbulence, noise in air and under water, release of petroleum and combustion products into air and water, and consumption of petroleum fuels." In addition, they contributed to "shoreline erosion, sediment resuspension, and land use changes for marina facilities and boat landings." Finally, although boating was an enjoyable activity, the plan stated, it produced "conflicts for lockage with commercial vessels, boating accidents, use of nonrenewable resources for leisure, and disturbance of other recreational users." The study addressed how an expansion of navigation on the Mississippi River would affect these conditions but offered few solutions to the problems.[50]

This was not the first time the district examined the difficulties of recreational boating on the Mississippi. In 1977, the Corps held public workshops on locking delays faced by recreational boaters on the Mississippi River. Because commercial barges had priority at the locks, recreational vessels sometimes had to wait as long as two-and-a-half hours for the availability of a lock. The Corps commissioned a study on the issue, and this report contained seven alternatives for relieving the congestion, including using signs to inform boaters of the length of the wait, providing special tie-up areas for recreational boaters, implementing designated lock times for recreational vessels and constructing separate recreation locks.[51] In 1978, the Corps examined the feasibility of these alternatives, and the district eventually decided that the best ways to alleviate the congestion were to use signs and to establish better waiting areas. Unfortunately, these methods did not resolve the issue. In 2002, Frank Star still considered lock delays "a problem" for recreational boaters.[52]

Additional studies of the environmental effects of recreation on waterways also occurred. The Long Term Resource Monitoring Program of the Corps' Environmental Management Program, conducted by the U.S. Fish and Wildlife Service, studied the characteristics of waves from recreational watercraft in 1992 in order to determine their effects on the environment. The report recognized that waves from recreational vessels could exacerbate bank erosion and "cause resuspension of fine sediments and increased turbidity, which can then be carried to the side channels and backwater areas and may impair riverine ecosystems."[53] Meanwhile, in 1996 the River Resources Forum Recreation Work Group, an interagency organization chaired by Richard Otto, studied water-based recreational activities in Pools 7 and 8 of the Mississippi River in order to gather information useful "in determining future recreational uses of the river." The group discovered that the most popular activities on the river were boat fishing and recreational boating and that personal watercraft, such as jet skis, were becoming more prevalent. Such conditions led "a large number of boaters" to "avoid certain parts of the river because there are 'too many other boats' or 'too many [boat] wakes.'"[54] However, as with the Upper Mississippi Navigation Study, these reports did not offer many solutions.

But as a Minnesota DNR brochure explained, there were measures that could be taken. It was the boater's responsibility to reduce his or her speed and wake size in order to mitigate shoreline erosion and other problems, the brochure claimed, but the Corps could implement mandatory speed and wake restrictions. "If all boaters become aware of the wakes their boats create and take action to reduce them when necessary," the brochure concluded, "the shoreline erosion can be reduced and conditions should improve."[55] The St. Paul District did not necessarily disagree. Richard Otto, for example, believed if the Corps did a better job of getting information to boaters, environmental effects could be lessened.[56]

In the meantime, district officials continued to serve on natural resource studies. In the first years of the twenty-first century, Frank Star participated in an examination of a system-wide operating plan for the headwaters of the Upper Mississippi. Called the Reservoir Operating Plan Evaluation Study, or ROPE study, it was conducted in partnership with the Forest Service, attempted, in the words of the St. Paul District, "to evaluate alternative plans and to recommend a new operating plan for the Mississippi Headwaters Reservoirs system with consideration given to tribal trust, flood control, environmental concerns, water quality, water supply, recreation, navigation, hydropower and more."[57] In essence, Star explained, the ROPE study would enable the Corps to operate the headwaters "more as a system." Some of the alternatives the study examined were allowing more natural flow releases from the lakes in the spring and changing the levels of some of the lakes. It remained to be seen how extensively the study would change the Corps' recreational practices at the headwaters, but the coordination of different purposes would at least provide better communication between agencies and groups responsible for the headwaters.[58]

Mississippi River Boathouses

One of the major controversies involving recreation and natural resources in the St. Paul District occurred in the 1970s and 1980s, but its beginnings stretched back into the 1920s. In 1924, Congress established the Upper Mississippi River Wildlife and Fish Refuge along a stretch of the river running from Wabasha, Minnesota, to Quincy, Illinois, and placed it under the jurisdiction of the Fish and Wildlife Service. In order to preserve habitat, the Fish and Wildlife Service purchased land along the Upper Mississippi. When Congress authorized the nine-foot channel navigation project in 1930, the Corps began buying land as well. This resulted in a checkerboard pattern of land ownership along the Upper Mississippi, in which the Corps owned some land and the Fish and Wildlife Service held other tracts. As people purchased property along the Mississippi River, the shoreline remained under the control of the two agencies. Against the wishes of the Fish and Wildlife Service, however, the Corps allowed individuals to place boathouses and docks on shorelines and did nothing to regulate this until 1960, even though some people moved amenities into the structures in order to have a place to stay on the weekends.[59]

In 1960, the Corps, concerned that these property owners were using public land for private purposes, developed Special Use Licenses for anyone wishing to place a structure on the shoreline, and these licenses specifically prohibited human habitation in the units. The Corps revised the license in 1973 to state that specific items, such as beds, stoves and heaters, were not allowed. Four years later, the St. Paul District, led by District Engineer Colonel Forrest T. Gay, strictly implemented these provisions and issued both public statements and private letters stating the Corps would remove units out of compliance.

It was unclear why Gay decided to take a stand at this time, but it is likely that he was partly motivated by pressure from the Fish and Wildlife Service, which considered the boathouses to be incompatible with the river's wildlife refuge designation.[60]

Whatever Gay's reasoning, a public outcry arose against enforcement. Minnesota State Representative Tom Stoa from Winona prepared a state resolution opposing the Corps' licenses, arguing that "the vast majority of boathouses are neither a hazard to navigation nor detrimental to the river environment." Stoa suggested the Corps target industrial pollutants, such as the Metro Waste Commission, "rather than harass the little guy who likes to spend the weekend at his boathouse."[61] At the same time, the city of Brownsville, Minnesota, the site of numerous boathouses, supported the property owners; the city council declared that they saw "no harm with an overnight or weekend stay, to be able to relax, do a little fishing or boating, providing [property owners] keep their area respectable and refrain from polluting." Finally, citizens formed CARP (Concerned About River People), an organization which championed an owner's right to stay in his or her boathouse on occasional weekends.[62]

Boathouse: An individual fishing from a boathouse on the Mississippi River. (Photo by Richard Otto, courtesy of St. Paul District, Corps of Engineers)

The conflict continued into the 1980s, when the St. Paul District announced it would begin on-site inspections of structures near Brownsville that it suspected were out of compliance with the regulations. On September 30, 1980, Ted Loukota and Joe Murphy of the district's real estate section conducted the inspections. One newspaper reported that "there was no apparent animosity between the inspection team" and the boathouse owners, but citizens were still displeased. La Crosse County Supervisor William Ipsen wondered whether the crackdown would "push our kids back on the streets" because they would not want to go to the river "and sit in a bare room." Loukota and Murphy expressed sympathy but argued that "if we allow the boathouses to be improved so they can be lived in we are granting exclusive rights to a few."[63]

After these inspections, the issue remained dormant until 1982 when the Corps and the Fish and Wildlife Service began preparing a Land Use Allocation Plan for the Upper Mississippi. In a discussion of how to handle private use of the shoreline, the Fish and Wildlife Service declared that the boathouses, whether livable or not, were incompatible with the river's designation as a wildlife refuge. The Fish and Wildlife Service claimed that lands purchased with tax dollars should be public land – they should not be leased out for private exclusive use. In a spirit of cooperation with the Fish and Wildlife Service, the Corps agreed as part of the Land Use Allocation Plan to refuse to issue any new licenses for boathouses on the river and to phase out all existing boathouses and docks by grandfathering them only for the life of the current owner. Once that owner died, the Corps would demolish the structure.[64]

The Land Use Allocation Plan and the Corps held public meetings in towns along the river throughout 1982 to announce this plan. But, in the words of Richard Otto, who operated as the district's spokesman on the issue, "We got crucified pretty badly." Hundreds of people attended the meetings and were almost universally opposed to the plan. "They made a very strong point that they wanted their ... privileges to continue," Otto related.[65] In order to bolster their case against the Corps, CARP and other concerned citizens turned to the National Inholders Association, an organization whose mission was to fight bureaucracy on behalf of private property interests. The National Inholders Association pledged $35,000 annually to battle the Corps.[66]

Despite the National Inholders Association's efforts, the Land Use Allocation Plan, as published, called for the elimination of the boathouses, stating that the grandfathering would occur in 1989. A Corps' newsletter published that same year unequivocally stated the Corps' reasons for instigating the plan: "Special private use of Federal land is becoming increasingly less appropriate and is not in the best public interest ... All available Federal land along the river will be needed to help meet future public use demands." Although it seemed that boathouse owners had little recourse after this policy was issued, the National Inholders Association assured them there were several avenues still open. Even Otto admitted that "though the plan is in the very final stage, there is a chance that the public could have it changed through legislation." This was the exact approach that the National Inholders Association took.[67]

For the next few years, the National Inholders Association lobbied Congress to allow the boathouses to remain; and in 1986, its dedication paid off. In the Water Resources Development Act of 1986, Congress mandated that no existing structure could be phased out on Corps' land. Because of this legislation, the Corps had to change its plan to say it would grandfather the structure instead of the owner, meaning that transfers of ownership could occur. As Otto explained, the boathouses thus "could be perpetuated way on into the future," although the Corps still refused to grant permits for new units. This meant, essentially, that the number of structures was frozen. "If there's 92 structures," Otto said, "there will never be 93." This new plan went into effect in 1988 and forced the Corps to use one full-time person to inspect the structures every year to ensure they were up to code. According to Otto, "habitation [was] still prohibited; it [was] just very difficult to enforce."[68] The presence of the Mississippi boathouses, then, represents a good example of the conflict that arose between private property and the Corps' mission to manage its waterways for the benefit of the general public. It also showed that at least in some instances, public opinion could change Corps' policy.

Conclusion

Whether the St. Paul District was developing recreation opportunities at new projects, maintaining existing facilities, providing outreach programs or managing natural resources, its recreation staff interacted to a great extent with the public. Although at times the district, and the Corps in general, was reluctant to embrace its recreational mission fully, whether because of interagency conflicts, environmental concerns or the preeminence of other functions over recreation, the St. Paul District offered numerous services to the public. Indeed, recreation provided good exposure for the Corps, established good public relations and offered services many people appreciated. Because of this service function, recreation officials sometimes considered themselves to be public servants rather than just Corps' employees. "I often tell people I don't work for the Corps in the same sense that you work for General Motors," Frank Star related. "I work for the public."[69] With this commitment, the St. Paul District's recreation program effectively brought information about the Corps and its mission to the people, enhancing the Corps' visibility in the process.

Chapter Seven Endnotes

1 Colonel Joseph Briggs interview by Mickey Schubert, St. Paul, MN, 24 May 1988, p. 22, Oral History File, St. Paul District, St. Paul, Minnesota.

2 U.S. Army Corps of Engineers, "Recreation Operations and Maintenance Policies," Engineering Regulation [ER] No. 1130-2-550, p. 2-1 (each section has its own page numbers), <http://www.usace.army.mil/publications/eng-regs/er1130-2-550/entire.pdf> (6 June 2003).

3 U.S. Army Corps of Engineers, "Visitor Assistance: Program Summary," <http://corpslakes. usace.army.mil/employees/visitassist/pback.html> (6 June 2003).

4 Quotation in Jean Harrison, "The Corps' Stake in Recreation," Parks and Recreation 10 (March 1975): pp. 2b-3b, 7b; see also U.S. Army Corps of Engineers, "Recreation," <http://www.usace.army. mil/public.html#Recreation> (6 June 2003); U.S. Army Corps of Engineers, "Recreation Operations and Maintenance Policies," ER No. 1130-2-550, p. 2-2; Frank Star interview by Matthew Godfrey, St. Paul, MN, 21 October 2002, p. 1.

5 Star Interview, pp. 2, 12.

6 See, for example, Marvin Zeldin, "Corps' New Look in Flood Control: No Dams, Levees," Audubon 77 (July 1975): pp. 103-104.

7 "Cooperative Planning: Zumbro River at Rochester," Crosscurrents 1 (January 1978): p. 3.

8 Quotation in Star Interview, pp. 2-3; see also "Rochester Gets Go-Ahead in Water Bill," Crosscurrents 10 (January 1987): p. 1.

9 "On the Waterfront," Post-Bulletin (Rochester, MN), 24 August 1991.

10 Star Interview, p. 3.

11 Quotations in "Some Not Happy with Flood Control Project," *Post-Bulletin*, 10 July 1990.

12 "District Projects Earn Top Honors," *Crosscurrents* 19 (April 1996): p. 4.

13 Richard Otto interview by Matthew Godfrey, St. Paul, MN, 23 October 2002, p. 20.

14 "Delay in Opening Corps Park," *Crosscurrents* 7 (April 1984): p. 7; "Blackhawk Reopened?" *Crosscurrents* 7 (August 1984): p. 3; "Nonagreement Causes Park Closure," *Courier Press* (Prairie du Chien, WI), 28 March 1984; "Support the Park," *Vernon County Broadcaster*, 28 March 1984; "Blackhawk Park to be Closed," *La Crosse Tribune*, 23 March 1984.

15 Great River Environmental Action Team, GREAT I: Recreation, Work Group Appendix – Upper Mississippi River (Head of Navigation to Guttenberg, Iowa) (Des Moines, IA: Great River Environmental Action Team, 1979), pp. 1-23.

16 U.S. Army Corps of Engineers, St. Paul District, Implementation for GREAT I Study (St. Paul, MN.: St. Paul District, U.S. Army Corps of Engineers, 1981), pp. 14-15, 28.

17 U.S. Army Corps of Engineers, North Central Division, Upper Mississippi River System Environmental Management Program, Sixth Annual Addendum (Chicago: U.S. Army Corps of Engineers, North Central Division, 1991), p. 2.

18 Star Interview, pp. 3-4.

19 Quotation in U.S., Congress, House, Committee on Interior and Insular Affairs, National Parks and Public Lands Subcommittee, Miscellaneous National Park Issues: Hearings Before the Subcommittee on National Parks and Public Lands of the Committee on Interior and Insular Affairs, House of Representatives, 100th Cong., 1st and 2d sess., 1987-1988, p. 177; see also U.S., Congress, Senate, Committee on Energy and Natural Resources, Public Lands, National Parks and Forests Subcommittee, Miscellaneous Parks and Public Lands Measures: Hearing Before the Subcommittee on Public Lands, National Parks and Forests of the Committee on Energy and Natural Resources, United States Senate, 100th Cong., 2d sess., 1988, pp. 43-44.

20 House Subcommittee on National Parks and Public Lands, Miscellaneous National Park Issues, pp. 238-243 (quotations on pp. 239-240).

21 Public Law 100-696, 18 November 1988, <http://80-web.lexisnexis. com. weblib.lib.umt.edu:2048 /congcomp/ document?_m=9815b4f857438c030d4436e3483e4 ab2&_docnum=1&wchp=dG LbVtz-lSlAA&_md5=0fb6b5db5ee9e907aec0087c936ceb 6d> (6 June 2003).

22 Star Interview, p. 10.

23 Quotation in Mississippi Whitewater Park Development Corporation, "Who We Are," <http://www.whitewaterpark.canoe-kayak.org/MWPDC_Info.html> (6 June 2003); see also U.S. Army Corps of Engineers, St. Paul District, "Lower St. Anthony Falls

Rapids Restoration, Mississippi River, Minneapolis, Minn.," <http://www.mvp.usace. army.mil/finder/display. asp?pageid=110> (6 June 2003); "In Search of a Bumpy Ride," St. Paul *Pioneer Press*, 14 January 1999; "A Drifting Dream," *Star Tribune*, 28 April 2000; Star Interview, p. 11.

24 U.S. Army Corps of Engineers, St. Paul District, "History of the Headwaters Recreation Areas," <http://www.mvp.usace.army.mil/history/headwaters> (6 June 2003); "Mississippi River Headwaters," *Crosscurrents* 7 (July 1984): pp. 4-5.

25 U.S. Army Corps of Engineers, St. Paul District, "Recreation," <http://www. mvp.usace.army. mil/recreation> (6 June 2003).

26 "Leech Lake Dam: A Family Recreation Area," *Crosscurrents* 11 (April 1988): p. 6.

27 "Leech Lake Campground Host Program First in District," *Crosscurrents* (August 1988): p. 6.

28 "Potential Rec Area Closures in FY 90," *Crosscurrents* 12 (February 1989): p. 3.

29 Quotation in Star Interview, p. 5; see also "Corps Seeking New Ways to Fund Projects," *The Forum* (Fargo, ND), 22 April 1990; "Corps Considers Alternatives," *Valley City Times-Record* (ND), 22 November 1989; "Information Paper: Corps of Engineers Recreation Study," January 1990, File Information Papers – National Recreation Study, Box 6412, SPDAR.

30 "Land and Water Conservation Fund Act of 1965," Public Law 88-578, pp. 9-10, <http://www.house.gov/resources/105cong/reports/105_a/lwcf65_.pdf> (6 June 2003); "Corps Seeking New Ways to Fund Projects," *The Forum*, 22 April 1990; "User Fees Okayed for Corps Recreation Areas," *Crosscurrents* 16 (December 1993): p. 4. 31 U.S. Army Corps of Engineers, "Recreation Operations and Maintenance Policies," pp. 9-1 – 9-8.

32 Star Interview, p. 7.

33 U.S. Army Corps of Engineers, St. Paul District, "Annual Day Passes Available for 2003 Recreation Season at Corps of Engineers Parks," Press Release, 18 November 2002, <http://www.mvp.usace.army.mil/finder/display.asp?pageid=541> (6 June 2003); U.S. Army Corps of Engineers, "Recreation Operations and Maintenance Policies," p. 9-6.

34 Star quotations in Star Interview, p. 9; other quotations in Daniel R. Burns, Chief, Operations, Construction and Readiness Division, Directorate of Civil Works, Memorandum for See Distribution, 19 October 1995, File I-39A-4 Reading File, HQUSACE administrative records, Washington, D.C. See also U.S. Army Corps of Engineers, "Reservations at Federal Recreation Facilities," <http://www.usace.army. mil/inet/recreation> (6 June 2003).

35 U.S. Army Corps of Engineers, "Recreation Operations and Maintenance Policies," p. 2-3; Star Interview, pp. 8-9.

36 Quotation in Star Interview, p. 11 (see also p. 12); U.S. Army Corps of Engineers, "Visitor Assistance: Program Summary"; U.S. Army Corps of Engineers, "Oleoresin Capsicum (Pepper Spray) Program," Engineer Circular [EC] No. 1130-2-214, 22 April 2002, p. 1, <http://www.usace. army.mil/publications/eng-circulars/ec1130-2-214/entire.pdf> (6 June 2003). Corps regulations emphasize that "the authority of resource managers and park rangers is limited to the enforcement of rules and regulations as designated in Title 36 and does not extend to arrest authority or the enforcement of state and local laws, including game laws." Rangers or any other Corps personnel could not be deputized while on duty and could not perform any law enforcement activity on civil works installations even if not on duty. U.S. Army Corps of Engineers, "Recreation Operations and Maintenance Policies," pp. 6-1 – 6-2.

37 Otto Interview, p. 19.

38 Joseph Briggs, Colonel, Corps of Engineers, District Engineer, to Honorable Kent Conrad, U.S. Senate, 10 July 1987, File Congressional Correspondence, Box 6412, SPDAR.

39 Larry and Diane Uhlir to Mr. Gregg Struss, Resource Manager, Gull Lake Recreation Area, 9 June 2001, reprinted in "Campers' Kudos to Staff at Headwaters Sites," *Crosscurrents* 24 (July 2001): p. 7.

40 Neil R. Hunt, President, CCS PTA, to Ray Nelson, Crosslake Recreation Area, 12 June 2001, reprinted in "Campers' Kudos to Staff at Headwaters Sites," p. 7.

41 "Classroom Without Walls," *Crosscurrents* 1 (June-July 1978): p. 7.

42 "St. Paul District Participates in Water Quality Project," *Crosscurrents* 16 (June 1993): pp. 1-3 (quotation on p. 3).

43 "It Won't Be Long Before They're at This Again! Fishing Clinics at Sandy Lake," *Crosscurrents* 14 (April 1991): p. 8.

44 "Feed-a-Kid-a-Line (Fishing Line, That Is)!" *Crosscurrents* 13 (October 1990): p. 5.

45 "Drownings Lead to Change in Restricted Areas," *Crosscurrents* 6 (April-May 1983): p. 1; Otto Interview, p. 19.

46 "A Tale of Two Rescues," *Crosscurrents* 12 (August 1989): p. 5.

47 " 'Kids in Boats' Program at Lake Ashtabula Teaches Safe Boating and Water Safety," *Crosscurrents* 22 (October-December 1999): p. 4; "Special Programs at Crosslake," *Crosscurrents* 14 (October 1991): p. 8.

48 "Water Safety," *Crosscurrents* 12 (August 1989): p. 4.

49 Star Interview, p. 4.

50 U.S. Army Corps of Engineers, St. Paul District, "Study Plan Navigation Study Environmental Work Unit 11: Effects of Recreational Boating," 28 December 1994, pp. 3-

4, File 10-1-7a Mississippi River Illinois Waterways Navigation (1994), Box 5601, SPDAR; see also U.S. Army Corps of Engineers, St. Paul District, "Effects of Recreational Boating on the Upper Mississippi River System," <http://www.mvp.usace.army.mil/finder/display.asp?pageid=187> (6 June 2003).

51 "Small-Boat Locks at Area Dams Studied by Corps of Engineers," *Post-Bulletin*, 2 December 1977; "Corps Looks at River Lock Delays," Red Wing *Republican-Eagle*, 13 August 1977.

52 Quotation in Star Interview, p. 8; see also Howard Needles Tammen and Bergendoff, "Recreational Craft Locks Study Selected Alternatives: Upper Mississippi River, Minneapolis to Guttenberg, for U.S. Army Corps of Engineers, St. Paul District," October 1978, File 1517-08 Mississippi River – Upper Mississippi River Recreation (1980), Box 1065, SPDAR.

53 Nani G. Bhowmik and Ta Wei Soong, Waves Generated by Recreational Traffic: Part I, Controlled Movement (Champaign, IL: Illinois State Water Survey, 1992), p. 3.

54 River Resources Forum Recreation Work Group, Recreation Use Profiles: Upper Mississippi River Pools 7 and 8 (La Crosse, WI: Wisconsin Department of Natural Resources, 1996), pp. 1-5.

55 Quotation in Minnesota Department of Natural Resources, Mississippi River Bank Erosion and Boating: Facts and Solutions (St. Paul, MN: Minnesota Department of Natural Resources, 1993), n.p.

56 Otto Interview, p. 20.

57 U.S. Army Corps of Engineers, St. Paul District, "Reservoir Operating Plan Evaluation (ROPE) Study for Mississippi Headwaters," <http://www.mvp.usace.army.mil/environment/default.asp? pageid=143> (6 June 2003).

58 Star Interview, p. 11. For more information on the ROPE study, see "Corps Leads Public-Private Headwaters Study," *Crosscurrents* 25 (November 2002): pp. 3, 6.

59 Colonel Forrest T. Gay, III, District Engineer, to Mr. Theodore Ranzenberger, 8 April 1977, File 1501-07 Reference Paper Files (Mississippi River) 1977, Box 1660, SPDAR; Otto Interview, pp. 13-14.

60 "Corps Zeroes in On the Area's 'River Rats,' " *Houston Signal* (MN), 11 September 1980; Gay to Ranzenberger, 8 April 1977; Major Walter L. Heme, Acting District Engineer, to Honorable Albert H. Quie, 26 April 1977, File 1501-07 Reference Paper Files (Mississippi River) 1977, Box 1660, SPDAR.

61 "Stoa Hits Corps on Boathouse Ban," Minnesota House of Representatives News Release, 5 July 1977, File 1501-07 Reference Paper Files (Mississippi River) 1977, Box 1660, SPDAR.

62 Giles Quillin, Mayor, and Harold Harer, Clerk, to Mr. Albert, Mr. Reisdorf and all members of "Save the Boathouse Ass'n," 8 July 1977, File 1501-07 Reference

Paper Files (Mississippi River) 1977, Box 1660, SPDAR; "Boathouse Hassles Following Course of River," *Houston County News* (La Crescent, MN), 18 September 1980.

63 Quotations in "Boathouses for Boats or People?" *La Crosse Tribune*, 1 October 1980; see also "Corps to Crack Down on Squatters," *The Forum*, 15 September 1980.

64 Otto Interview, pp. 14-15.

65 Quotations in Otto Interview, p. 15; see also "Proposed Land-Use Allocation May Doom Future of County Boathouses," *Houston Signal*, 18 December 1982.

66 " 'Pro' Joins River Battle," unidentified newspaper clipping, File 228-10 IHF-MR, Box 3854, SPDAR.

67 Quotations in "Mississippi Land Use Plan Finalized," unidentified newspaper clipping, File 228-10 IHF-MR, Box 3854, SPDAR; see also "Shoreline Management Plan," p. P2-29, document provided by Richard Otto.

68 Quotation in Otto Interview, pp. 15-16; see also "Shoreline Management Plan," pp. P2-33, P2-36, P2-38.

69 Star Interview, p. 1.

Lake Winnibigoshish Reservoir at the center of controversy during the drought of 1988. (Photo courtesy of St. Paul District, Corps of Engineers)

8 Emergency Operations and Recovery

In the 1950s, Congress mandated the Corps of Engineers to provide relief to communities stricken by floods. Additional laws expanded the Corps' responsibility, authorizing it to provide emergency operations in water-related disasters such as hurricanes and drought. In the regions served by the St. Paul District, the Corps' emergency response was extremely important. The high water tables and severe winters of North Dakota, Minnesota and Wisconsin caused flooding almost every spring, as melting ice and snow poured into river basins in five separate floodplains. In times of disaster, the district's Readiness Branch provided logistical and technical support to incapacitated communities, building emergency levees and supplying equipment and manpower to fight floods. As it participated in these activities in the late twentieth century, the Corps earned accolades from those it aided, which improved its public image and boosted the morale of its employees. The Corps basked in this praise, frequently commenting on the worthwhile service it provided and the good feelings this engendered. As Robert F. Post, chief of the Engineering and Planning Division from 1987 to 1999, related after a 1997 flood on the Red River, "The professionalism and dedication displayed by the more than 200 men and women of the Corps' Flood Emergency Response Team during this event was truly awesome."[1]

The Corps' emergency operations mission was a relatively new development. In June 1955, Congress passed Public Law (PL) 84-99, which created a $15 million emergency fund to be used by the Corps "in flood emergency preparation; in flood fighting and rescue operations, or in the repair or restoration of any flood-control work threatened or destroyed by flood."[2] Subsequent amendments to the act expanded the Corps' authority to deal with hurricane and shore protection, contaminated water and drought. In such instances, the Corps could engage in any action "which is essential for the preservation of life and property," such as strengthening existing flood control structures, constructing temporary levees, clearing channels and removing debris and wreckage once a flood had receded and providing clean water to regions in need.[3]

Supplementing PL 84-99 was the 1974 Disaster Relief Act, which empowered the president of the United States to provide federal assistance during major natural disasters of any kind upon a governor's request. If the president determined a disaster exceeded the capabilities of a state, he would authorize federal emergency operations to begin.[4] To provide a central coordinating agency for this federal response, President Jimmy Carter issued an executive order in 1979 that created the Federal Emergency Management Agency.[5] In 1988, Congress formalized FEMA's role in the Robert T. Stafford Disaster Relief and Emergency Assistance Act.[6] Under the provisions of this law, FEMA reviewed governors' requests for federal assistance and then made recommendations to the president on whether or not aid was warranted. If the president decided assistance was required, he issued a disaster declaration and chose a federal coordinating officer who supervised FEMA's direction of relief activities.[7]

In order to streamline emergency operations, FEMA developed a Federal Response Plan outlining the responsibilities of different agencies in times of disaster. Under the plan, the Corps became the operating agent for Emergency Support Function #3 (ESF-3), entitled Public Works and Engineering. This made the Corps the lead agency in providing a variety of services, including: technical advice and evaluation, construction management and inspection, emergency repair of water and wastewater treatment facilities, emergency power, inspection of residential and commercial structures to determine damage and the stabilization or demolition of damaged structures or facilities deemed hazardous. In essence, the Federal Response Plan required the Corps to supply both logistical support and materiel in times of disaster.[8]

Whether the Corps acted on its own under the authority of PL 84-99 or under the direction of FEMA depended on the status of the disaster and whether or not it was water-related. If the Corps supplied flood assistance before a presidential disaster proclamation, it used its PL 84-99 authorization and funded the operation in a couple of ways. If the emergency called for strengthening flood control works operated by the Corps, money came from project funds. If local sponsors had responsibility for the flood control works, they paid up to twenty-five percent of the cost. However, in cases where a presidential disaster declaration had been issued and in instances of non-water-related emergencies, the Corps had to wait for FEMA to authorize its ESF-3 function before it could take any action. The Corps then funded these operations with money routed through FEMA.[9] In all cases, Corps' officials emphasized, emergency operations were supplements to local and state actions, not replacements. Local and state officials had to exert "maximum efforts" and officially request aid before the Corps could become involved. In addition, local governments had to "identify specific needs; obtain all necessary easements and rights of ways; provide a local source of borrow material; and coordinate with local landowners."[10]

In the St. Paul District, disaster relief fell under the authority of the Readiness Branch in the Construction-Operations Division. The chief of the Readiness Branch served as the district's point of contact for emergency situations and was responsible for the district's

Emergency Operations Center, an administrative support office within district headquarters that provided central logistical guidance.[11] The chief, together with the district's flood executive officer (who was the chief of the Engineering Division and who provided technical advice to the district engineer), ensured the district had a cadre of well-trained specialists that could be mobilized in times of emergency. Among these were the flood area engineers and operations managers who worked in the field to coordinate flood control activities. In order to keep themselves ready for deployment, these employees participated both in annual flood scenario workshops and training in emergency operations and technology such as ENGLINK, an emergency operations software program. Other exercises included teaching people about contract negotiations for levee construction, practicing deployment of personnel to sites and establishing communication links between individuals in the field and in the office. Such simulations prepared the district for real emergency situations.[12]

Floods

Most of the St. Paul District's disaster operations occurred in response to spring flooding in the five floodplains under its jurisdiction. One of the major trouble spots was the Red River of the North Basin in North Dakota and Minnesota, a predominantly agricultural area. In geologic times, first a continental glacier and then glacial Lake Agassiz covered the region, creating an immature, flat and poorly drained valley through which runs the Red River, a waterway that begins in the vicinity of Breckenridge, Minnesota, and Wahpeton, North Dakota, and runs north into Canada. In the winter, frequent blizzards and below-zero temperatures cause large accumulations of snow. When spring arrives, snowmelt runoff, beginning first in the southern headwaters, generates high flows in the river. As the water moves north, it collides with ice in the river's still-frozen downstream reaches. These jams elevate flood stages and frequently push the waterway out of its banks. When that happens, water runs for miles in every direction because of the flatness of the valley. Surrounding communities and farmland sustain heavy damage.[13]

In the spring of 1950, for example, the river ran 54,000 cubic feet per second, or cfs, at Grand Forks, North Dakota, instead of the usual 32,000 cfs, causing millions of dollars of damage. Despite several projects constructed to restrain the waterway, the river overflowed again in the spring of 1969, this time inundating Fargo, North Dakota, with nearly three times its normal flow.[14] The problems continued in 1978 when a greater than normal snowpack led the district to prepare for flooding. Thirty employees constructed temporary levees along the Red and its tributaries and gathered pumps, sandbags and polyethylene sheeting for the fight. The district also set up an office to coordinate with local officials.[15]

When flooding began in late March and early April 1978, the river reached record water levels at Oslo, Minnesota, and approached records at Twin Valley and Hendrum, both Minnesota, and at Grand Forks. By the middle of April the water had formed a lake 22 miles long and 5 miles wide over rural farmlands just north of Grand Forks. "The water has been coming up so fast, I don't have any idea how many roads we've got flooded," Norman County Sheriff Herman Lovas related. "It's just running wild."[16] Fortunately, the river soon crested, easing the danger, but the damage had been done. U.S. Senator

Grand Forks, North Dakota, during the Red River of the North flood of 1997.
(Photos courtesy of St. Paul District, Corps of Engineers)

Quentin Burdick (D-North Dakota) believed the devastation "thoroughly justifie[d]" a presidential disaster declaration, and twenty-three counties subsequently received disaster assistance.[17] Although many farms and ranches suffered from flooding, the district, using a complicated formula that compared peak flood stage/discharge data with existing stage/discharge damage curves, claimed that its emergency preparations and permanent levees prevented an estimated $40 million in additional damages, especially in urban areas. However, the flood highlighted the need for increased protection in several communities, including Grand Forks and West Fargo in North Dakota, and East Grand Forks, Crookston, Halstad, Hendrum and Roseau in Minnesota.[18]

Before the Corps could take any measures, the basin experienced its worst flood of the century. Initial forecasts in the spring of 1979 indicated that, although flooding was possible along the Red River and its tributaries, water levels would not approach those of 1978. In fact, the National Weather Service downgraded its forecast in April, indicating that, with normal precipitation patterns, only minor flooding would occur. The situation changed in mid-April when heavy rains fell and snow began melting rapidly. In preparation, the St. Paul District established emergency field offices at Fargo and Grand Forks, constructed new emergency levees, and strengthened old ones. In some areas, the water rose too rapidly, and the communities of Warren and Stephen, Minnesota, and Grand Forks, Argusville, Bowesmont and Grafton, North Dakota, were inundated by the end of April. Water spread for 12 miles just north of Grand Forks, topping farmer-constructed dikes and submerging thousands of acres of farmland. By the time the water receded, it had reached heights unseen since 1897 – the worst flood on record – and had caused more than $90 million in damages.[19]

Ninety district employees labored to ease the disaster's effects. The Corps estimated that workers spent 10,186 man hours fighting the flood, serving in one of four units: materials distribution, construction, reconnaissance and communication. The materials distribution group gathered the items necessary for the operation, such as sandbags and pumps, and coordinated the rental of other equipment. The construction unit planned and designed the required levees and negotiated the requisite construction contracts. The reconnaissance team collected field stream gauging data and set high-water marks so that it could better record the peak discharges and stages along the river. The communications unit installed equipment, such as commercial telephone lines and radios, to ensure interaction between the field offices and the emergency centers. These groups also coordinated efforts with other agencies, including the Minnesota and North Dakota National Guards, the Second Coast Guard District, the Air Force, the National Weather Service and the U.S. Geological Survey, among others.[20]

By the end of the fight, the district, in partnership with these entities, had assisted more than fifty communities and constructed 33,470 feet of new emergency levee, while upgrading an additional 42,640 feet of existing levee. It additionally supplied affected areas with 462 rolls of polyethylene sheeting, 104 pumps and nearly 4 million sandbags. According to Corps' calculations, these efforts prevented approximately $40 million in damages, leading the district to claim that its role "was a key one carried out skillfully and tenaciously." The Corps' estimate of damage prevention failed to impress many residents in the Red River Valley who demanded more permanent flood control projects. "More than $300 million of damage has been done by floods in the last 10 years," U.S. Representative Arlan Stangeland (R-Minnesota) declared. "I am tired of facing this devastation every year."[21] The Corps acknowledged that some communities, such as East Grand Forks, required additional flood protection and promised to pursue these projects further, especially after Congress held hearings in the summer of 1979 on Red River flooding problems and solutions.[22]

Throughout the 1980s, however, the Corps had difficulty finding projects in the area with favorable benefit-cost ratios. When it did, local communities, such as East Grand

Forks, sometimes balked at paying their share of the cost (see Chapter Four). Because there were no major floods for most of the decade, the public clamor for projects on the Red River subsided, highlighting the obvious connection between disasters and flood control projects. If flooding occurred several years in a row, the public and its congressional delegation pleaded for projects. If weather patterns produced no flooding for an extended period of time, it was difficult for the Corps to convince communities of potential danger, even if its figures showed a significant flood potential.[23]

In the spring of 1989, the relative lull in the Red River Valley ended when ice jams once again caused the Red to flow out of its banks. The Corps began preparing in March after National Weather Service forecasts indicated that minor to moderate flooding would occur in the Red River Basin. In April, large slabs of ice clogged the river at Breckenridge, Minnesota, and Wahpeton, North Dakota, quickly elevating water levels to dangerous heights. Before the Corps or the cities could act, water flowed into the streets, pouring into Breckenridge's sewer system and flooding more than three hundred houses. "I've been here over 20 years and people just can't believe it," Butch Stollenwerk, a city worker for Breckenridge, related. "They haven't seen anything like this before." Craig Hinton, a St. Paul District engineer, agreed. "You look at the little old Red River during the summer and it's just a little stream," he explained. "Now it's something else."[24] The water forced many citizens to evacuate their homes, leaving behind empty neighborhoods and mobile home parks. "It gives you a spooky feeling," Gary Ferguson, a resident of Breckenridge, commented. "From what I can see, it's pretty deserted."[25]

Although little could be done for Breckenridge and Wahpeton, the St. Paul District quickly set up operations in communities downstream. From these bases, the Corps constructed emergency levees for Fargo and Grand Forks, as well as for East Grand Forks and Moorhead, Minnesota. At the same time, hydrologic teams inspected the Red and its tributaries to develop forecasts for the river's maximum stages. According to the district's After Action Report, sixty-five members of the St. Paul District worked in the Red River Basin "during the peak of operations" in the first two weeks of April. Fortunately, normal temperatures and little precipitation together diminished the flood threat, and many of these workers were able to return home after only a few days in the field. The staff expended a total of 10,117 man hours, and, as with earlier floods, cooperated with several different agencies, including the Minnesota and North Dakota National Guards, the Second Coast Guard District and the Air Force. Breckenridge and Wahpeton experienced serious damage, but few other cities saw drastic flooding, and rural areas, overwhelmed in previous floods, escaped relatively unscathed. In its After Action Report, the district estimated its work prevented $25 million in damages to twenty communities.[26]

One reason for the district's effectiveness was the availability of new technology that facilitated communications between emergency operation centers and field workers. In the 1970s and 1980s, America experienced a technological boom, especially in computing and communications systems.[27] By 1989, the Corps was reaping the benefits of these innovations. During the flood fight, the Corps used technology not available in the 1970s, such as laptop computers, which expedited contract negotiations and reconnaissance reports; facsimile (FAX) machines, which quickly transported contracts, situation reports, correspondence and newspaper articles between offices; and portable radios and beepers.[28] "The development of high technology in the last decade," an article in the district's newsletter explained, "made a significant difference in communications and record keeping operations from the floods of '78 and '79."[29] According to one report, this technology would only "expand in the future," enabling the Corps to further "increase the speed and efficiency of administrative control of emergency operations."[30]

Floodfighting

Flood fighting: (Above, top) Flood responders fight the onslaught of the Minnesota River with sandbags and pumps in Granite Falls, Minnesota, in April 1997. (Above, from left) Bonnie Greenleaf, Dave Haumersen and Josh Cress prepare for a flood fight in Montevideo, Minnesota, in April 1997. (Photos courtesy of St. Paul District, Corps of Engineers)

For the next few years, the Corps enjoyed a reprieve from serious flooding; but in the late spring and early summer of 1993, major rainstorms inundated the Midwest, overflowing numerous rivers. Although states such as Iowa bore the brunt of the storms, North Dakota and Minnesota also experienced problems. In May, the town of Marshall, Minnesota, flooded after receiving nearly 10 inches of rain in one day, and this was repeated in June. Meanwhile, Valley City, North Dakota, experienced a seven-inch rainfall in three hours on July 15. In order to mitigate the resulting floods, St. Paul District officials made a risky but innovative decision: they closed the gates of the Lake Ashtabula reservoir a few miles upstream from Valley City, thereby shutting off its discharge. The closure meant that water overtopped the reservoir's gates by six inches, exerting a significant amount of pressure on the structure. Despite the risk of collapse, the overtopping was necessary because it reduced the amount of water flowing into Valley City, preventing significant damages. Had another large rainstorm passed through the region, the district would have had to release the water, causing even more flooding, but the gamble paid off and the city survived.[31] "If we had . . . stayed within the absolute technical bands in which we were supposed to work," District Engineer Colonel Richard W. Craig explained, "Valley City would be [completely] flooded right now."[32]

As rainstorm after rainstorm pummeled the Midwest in the summer of 1993, the soil in the area became saturated, causing heavy runoff into the streams and rivers feeding the Mississippi River. This started a chain reaction of massive flooding on the Mississippi, especially from the Quad Cities of Illinois to St. Louis, Missouri.[33] Throughout the summer of 1993, Corps' personnel fought to keep the river in its banks. Working in concert with FEMA, the Coast Guard, National Guard units and the American Red Cross, the Corps constructed emergency levees and strengthened existing structures. It also used gage readings to develop numerical models of river stage forecasts – a difficult task because of the wide fluctuations in water levels caused by levee breaks and overtoppings – and supplied sandbags and pumps to local governments. By August 9, more than five hundred Corps' employees were involved in the fight, including a hundred and seventy-one from the St. Paul District. In the district itself, most of the damage occurred when the Minnesota River spilled into towns and farmland before reaching the Mississippi River. Although the Mississippi reached an all-time summer record of 19.2 feet at St. Paul, flood control structures in the Twin Cities prevented major destruction. Unfortunately, flood control structures in other regions, especially privately constructed agricultural levees, were not as strong and water broke through in numerous places outside of the St. Paul District's jurisdiction. By the time the water receded throughout the whole Mississippi Valley, the Great Flood of 1993 had killed fifty-two people, injured 2,300, left 56,000 homeless and caused more than $10 billion in property damage.[34]

Although the flooding sparked a national debate about the effects of the Corps' levees on the Mississippi River (see Chapter Three), the major lessons learned by the St. Paul District focused more on its flood response efforts. An After Action Report explained that accessible basin maps and project locality maps would facilitate staff discussions of future operations. It also called for blackboards, flip charts or other ways to display current hydrological data, location of district personnel, summaries of pertinent events and important telephone numbers. Fighting the flood had demonstrated that cellular telephones were an effective way of communicating during some emergency operations and district officials advocated their future use. Finally, the flood had convinced the district that if local governments would prepare emergency situation guidelines, including emergency notification contacts, inventories of supplies and maps of the region, damage could be reduced.[35]

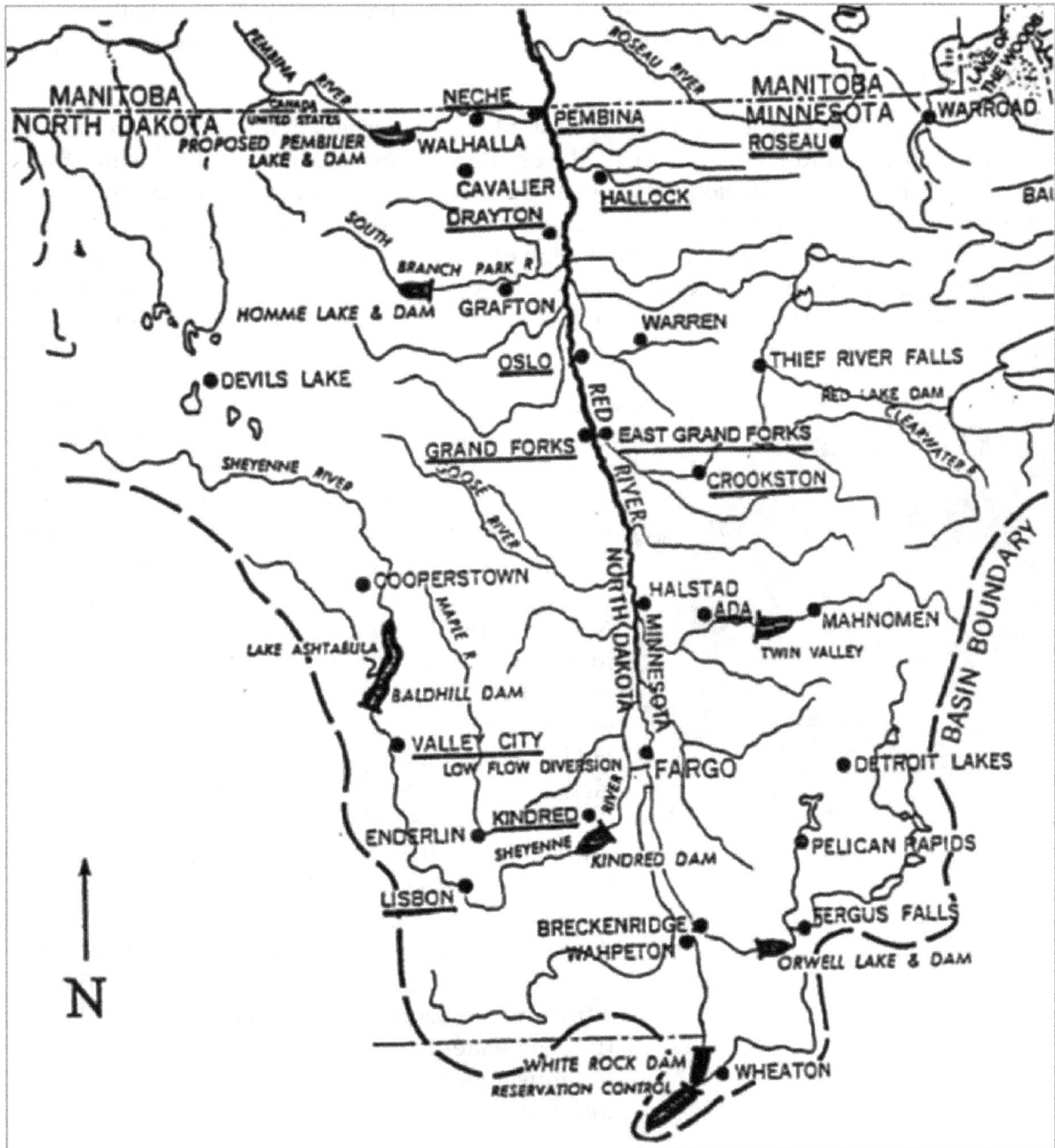

Map: Red River of the North Basin in North Dakota and Minnesota. (Map courtesy of St. Paul District, Corps of Engineers)

The lessons of the 1993 flood served the St. Paul District well four years later when the Red River of the North inundated Grand Forks, East Grand Forks and several other communities. During the winter of 1996 and 1997, six to eight feet of snow accumulated in the Red River basin, breaking records in several places. In February 1997, the huge snowpack caused the National Weather Service to issue a forecast of major flooding, and the Corps began to prepare for the fight. In March, the district initiated approximately twenty-two advance measures in several communities, spending $5 million. When warm temperatures at the end of March hastened melting, swelling the river and its tributaries, District Engineer Colonel J. M. Wonsik authorized the beginning of emergency operations.[36]

During the first week of April, the Corps established emergency operation centers in Fargo and East Grand Forks and worked from these locations throughout the month. Based on a flood stage forecast of 49 feet at Grand Forks, the district constructed emergency levees around the city to a stage of 52 feet and transported sandbags to the area. Then, on April 6, Blizzard Hannah, one of the worst snowstorms in fifty years, hit the region, causing whiteout conditions, heavy wind gusts and wind chill temperatures of forty below zero. The storm dropped an additional 3.5 inches of precipitation on the already-saturated ground.[37]

Cleanup: Corps' contractors cleanup the aftermath left in Grand Forks, North Dakota, by the devastating Red River of the North flooding in 1997. (Photo courtesy of St. Paul District, Corps of Engineers)

After the blizzard ended, temperatures escalated again, producing vast quantities of meltwater. During the third week of April, the Red rose to 54 feet, nearly 40 feet above its normal level. Water spilled over the emergency levees, pouring water into the downtown areas of both Grand Forks and East Grand Forks and forcing massive evacuations. Not long after, broken gas pipes ignited a fire in downtown Grand Forks. Because the water prevented fire fighters from reaching the blaze, eleven buildings burned. In the words of Lisa Hedin, project manager of the Grand Forks/East Grand Forks Flood Control Project, the situation "was like a bad Sunday night movie." By the time the river crested at 54.2 feet, significant damage had occurred. On April 22, President Bill Clinton visited the two communities, declaring them disaster areas and commented that the people of America "could never imagine facing a flood and a fire and a blizzard all at the same time."[38] By the time the water receded, eight people died, tens of thousands had fled their homes and property destruction approached $2 billion.[39]

But Grand Forks and East Grand Forks were not the only communities waging battles in 1997. Breckenridge, Minnesota; Fargo, North Dakota;

and Ada, Minnesota, also experienced flooding, as did areas along the Minnesota River and the Mississippi River. More than a hundred district employees provided emergency services to more than forty communities in the spring of 1997, winning the fight in all but four of them – Grand Forks, East Grand Forks, Breckenridge and Ada. In total, the district estimated it spent $14.8 million and prevented an additional $100 million in damages by supplying state and local governments with 4.5 million sandbags and 235 pumps. "Every flood executive officer hopes that during their career they won't have to deal with any flood, much less a flood of this magnitude," Robert Post, chief of engineering, commented. "Thank God we were prepared and trained for this emergency."[40]

Flood fights continued in the twenty-first century, when the Red River and the Minnesota River overflowed again in 2001. Likewise, after heavy rainstorms in the summer of 2002, the district faced flooding from the Wild Rice River at Ada, Minnesota; the Roseau River at Roseau, Minnesota; and Lake of the Woods at Warroad, Minnesota. As with other floods, the district aided local communities with levee construction, water stage predictions and cleanup efforts. At Lake of the Woods, the district employed a new flood fighting device: geo-cells, which were plastic grid systems filled with dirt and stacked four feet-by-four-feet. The Corps worried about their cost, but because they were recyclable for up to six floods, officials hoped they would prove to be cost-effective. Using such technology, the Corps protected streets, residences and businesses in the three communities. "The entire district supported the flood fight," David Christenson, chief of the Readiness Branch, stated, "and they did it very effectively." A note from a family in Roseau concurred with this assessment, expressing "a sincere thank you" to Corps Employees for "a job well done."[41]

Drought

Although flooding was the major natural disaster the St. Paul District routinely faced, other emergencies occurred as well. In 1977, Congress amended Public Law 84-99 to mandate the Corps provide services in times of drought, such as offering emergency supplies of water and constructing wells in affected areas.[42] To fulfill this mandate, the Corps developed several plans of action. If the National Weather Service issued a drought alert forecast in the vicinity of the Upper Mississippi River, for example, the Corps could use its locks and dams to conserve water in its reservoirs, and then release the stored flow at later dates. If the drought became severe, the Corps could restrict the number of lockages on the Mississippi in order to preserve pool elevations. It could also conduct emergency dredging operations if water levels became too low. When local, county and state resources became exhausted, the Corps could supply emergency drinking water assistance by providing water tank trucks, bottled water, temporary filtration, mobile purification units, temporary pipelines and well-drilling equipment. In such instances, the Corps would cover the transportation costs while the community would pay for the water charges.[43]

The St. Paul District used these plans in 1976 when severe drought conditions affected the Midwest. When the Mississippi River's water flow dipped to 532 cfs between Minneapolis and St. Paul, District Engineer Colonel Forrest Gay and Minnesota Governor

Wendell Anderson called an emergency news conference to ask Minnesotans to conserve as much water as possible. Within two weeks, residents of the Twin Cities had curtailed their water consumption by fifty percent. The district also restricted the number of recreational lockages at St. Anthony Falls and Lock and Dam 1, thereby helping navigation interests on the river. Because of these actions, Minnesotans successfully outlasted the drought until rain finally fell.[44]

Another drought occurred in 1988 when water flows on the Mississippi again declined dramatically. During an unusually dry June, water levels at Anoka, Minnesota (upstream of the Twin Cities), dropped to 1,280 cfs, dramatically lower than the normal 10,000 cfs average for June. Throughout the month, Ed Eaton, chief of the district's water control unit, met with representatives from the Minnesota DNR in a series of technical drought meetings. At the same time, the district's emergency management team prepared a situation report on the conditions in North Dakota, Minnesota and Wisconsin. When water levels continued to fall, the district advised recreational boaters that they could face either locking delays or restrictions on the Mississippi, and the state of Minnesota asked its residents to conserve water.[45]

Conditions worsened in July when no rain was forthcoming. The Minnesota DNR informed the Corps on July 6 that if water levels dipped below 1,000 cfs for three consecutive days, it would request the district release water from its headwaters reservoirs. During the last week of July, three consecutive days of sub-1,000 cfs flows occurred. In response, Governor Rudy Perpich asked the Corps to release 300 cfs of water from the Lake Winnibigoshish Reservoir. The Leech Lake Band of the Chippewa Indians protested the plan, concerned that a release of water at that time would have adverse impacts on its wild rice and fishing operations later. At the same time, St. Paul District officials, including Colonel Roger Baldwin, who had only recently assumed the position of district engineer, did not believe the release would materially affect the low water levels. But because there was no conclusive data to support these claims, the district was reluctant to reject the request. While district officials considered the best course to follow, the river's flow dropped to 842 cfs at Anoka on July 30. Fortunately, only three days later, rain began falling. Using the rainfall as justification, Baldwin informed Perpich, the Leech Lake Band and Minnesota's congressional delegation that he would not release water from Winnibigoshish. For the next two weeks, intermittent heavy rains soaked the area, and, by August 16, the Mississippi's flow was at 2,690 cfs, convincing state officials to rescind water conservation requirements.[46]

Although the August rains meant that no emergency water supplies were necessary in Minnesota, other communities were not as fortunate. In North Dakota, two small towns, Pembina and Edmore, had inadequate supplies after the Pembina River's flow dropped to nearly zero. In need of aid, the cities turned to the St. Paul District. In September, the district installed a 1,100-foot temporary pipeline connecting Pembina's water treatment plant with the Red River of the North. In October, Assistant Secretary of the Army for Civil Works Robert Page declared Edmore drought distressed after the city's main reservoir dried up. When Edmore officials found an old reservoir containing an estimated 4.5 million gallons of water, they called on the St. Paul District for help. The district installed a temporary pipeline and pump that drained the reservoir in

Lake Winnibigoshish Reservoir at the center of controversy during the drought of 1998. (Photo courtesy of St. Paul District, Corps of Engineers)

November. At the same time, district employees, in cooperation with the Omaha District, investigated more than ninety individual water supply requests from farmers in North Dakota and recommended that the North Central Division approve ten of them. The authorization was never given, but when autumn rains began falling, the worst of the drought was over.[47]

These episodes in 1988 taught the Corps several important lessons about drought in general. For one thing, conditions on the Mississippi River demonstrated the necessity of revising the district's thirty-year-old low flow headwaters plan and drought contingency strategy. In the words of Gary Nelson, a Corps' sociologist, "The drought told the staff we had severe information deficits."[48] The St. Paul District immediately began working with state and federal agencies to correct these plans; and by 1991, according to Colonel Roger Baldwin, employees had a better understanding of "the physical nature of the basin" and "the physical nature of the water flows." This enabled the Corps to produce a low flow headwaters plan that was "far superior" to the previous one.[49] The drought also allowed the Corps to conduct water quality studies on the Mississippi River, thereby gaining information on how drought affected the river's basic characteristics and how dam operations could improve water quality. The Corps' Waterways Experiment Station, located in Vicksburg, Mississippi, assisted the St. Paul District with this study, taking samples from Pools 1 and 2 on the river and testing them for dissolved oxygen, pH, conductivity and temperature.[50] Finally, the Corps developed a drought management team, similar to its flood management team, and studied Indian water rights. As Baldwin concluded, "a lot of education took place among all agencies and all players."[51]

For the most part, the St. Paul District's emergency operations focused on disasters within its own boundaries. However, in accordance with the Stafford Act of 1988, the district responded to emergencies in other regions as well. On October 17, 1989, for example, a magnitude 7.1 earthquake known as Loma Prieta rocked the San Francisco Bay area in California. The quake, which was the worst one in the United States since 1906, killed sixty-two people, injured 3,775, left 12 thousand homeless, knocked out San Francisco's power and caused $7.1 billion in damages. President George Bush declared San Francisco and other communities a major disaster area, and on October 20, FEMA requested Corps' assistance in conducting residential inspections to determine whether people were eligible for FEMA's individual assistance program. Normally, FEMA contracted out such inspection work, but because Hurricane Hugo, which had occurred the year before, had depleted the supply of available contractors, FEMA turned to the Corps for help, asking for three hundred people.[52]

Rebuilding: The St. Paul District provides emergency operations support around the world. Here, Mark Koenig, and General Robert B. Flowers, Chief of Engineers, survey the area at Pol-E-Charkhi Army Base in Afghanistan, 2003. (Photo by Captain Taylor Hwong, courtesy of St. Paul District, Corps of Engineers)

On October 21, Corps' headquarters in Washington, D.C., transmitted FEMA's request, asking that divisions send only their best employees since they would be dealing directly with the public. Two days later, ten volunteers from the St. Paul District arrived in Sacramento, California, along with approximately three hundred other Corps' personnel. Two of the district's representatives were Clyde Giaquinto and Arne Thompson, who spent their time inspecting houses in Redwood City and Oakland, California. One of the problems they faced included people fraudulently claiming the earthquake had damaged structures actually destroyed by other means. At one address, for example, Giaquinto found "nothing more than a chain link fence in front of a vacant lot." The applicant claimed the earthquake had destroyed his house, but after interviewing a neighbor and a postal worker, Giaquinto discovered the house had been torn down months before. Although damage claims investigations were not as glamorous as other engineering jobs, employees such as Thompson and Giaquinto understood that such work ensured that assistance only went to those truly in need. Thompson insisted he was glad to help in the situation, especially because the Corps' efforts refuted general criticism levied against federal disaster relief in the aftermath of Hurricane Hugo. Unlike those efforts, the Loma Prieta earthquake response was, according to Thompson, "excellent."[53]

Other relief assignments allowed the Corps to focus more on engineering. At the end of the Persian Gulf War in 1991, several members of the St. Paul District traveled to Kuwait to help the nation rebuild Kuwait City after its invasion and short-lived occupation by Iraq. The Corps had the responsibility of performing damage surveys, participating in emergency and long-term recovery efforts in public works, utilities, transportation and coordinating the reconstruction of key government and defense facilities. More than 2,000 Corps' members volunteered for the response, including nineteen from the St. Paul District. James Ruyak, who served as chief of construction for the district from 1973 to 1979, worked as the resident engineer at the Ali Al-Salem Air Base. He surveyed damage, planned construction projects and mediated between the construction contractor and Kuwait's Air Force. "The city's entire infrastructure [was] pretty well destroyed," Ruyak observed, but the Corps' emergency response experience and its resources helped to restore much of Kuwait's water, power and defense networks.[54]

In 1992, four representatives from the St. Paul District aided the city of Chicago in its recovery from the "Great Chicago Flood." On April 13, 1992, a piling driven into the bottom of the Chicago River caused a small leak in a network of tunnels 50 feet underneath downtown Chicago. Water spread throughout the system, flooding basements in a number of businesses, causing power outages, closing subway routes and forcing thousands to evacuate. Initially, the Corps supplied only technical assistance to the city; but when the city could not stop the leak, FEMA authorized the Corps to assume command. Led by the Chicago District, the Corps set up three emergency operation centers around the city to coordinate repair and water removal. Lieutenant Colonel Mike Mahoney, deputy district engineer for the St. Paul District, supervised the effort to pump water from the tunnels, while Captain Mark Miller of the district's Construction Branch served as chief of the Corps' night shift team at the interagency command center. Dan Reinartz, from St. Paul's hydraulics section, examined water conditions during the pumping operations, while Ken Gardner, chief of the district's Public Affairs Office, aided in media response.[55]

In August 1992, district employees were sent to southern Florida after Hurricane Andrew, a Category Four hurricane, caused $20 billion in property damage and left 160,000 people homeless. To facilitate the cleanup effort, FEMA assigned two major tasks to the Corps: providing temporary roofing to residences and collecting storm debris. In response, more than 1,150 Corps' personnel went to South Florida, including ten from the St. Paul District. Upon completion of its duties, the Corps had covered 43 thousand damaged roofs and extracted 13 million cubic feet of storm debris. "It is amazing how the Corps of Engineers can organize," Greg Porycky, an engineering technician from the district, remarked.[56]

The Corps also played a significant role in disaster response after terrorists destroyed New York's World Trade Center towers and part of the Pentagon on September 11, 2001. At the time of the attacks, District Engineer Colonel Robert L. Ball and Deputy of Programs and Project Management Judith L. DesHarnais were conducting their annual congressional visit with U.S. Representative Ron Kind (D-Wisconsin). Although neither Ball nor DesHarnais were injured in the attack, the St. Paul District became involved in another way. Michelle M. Shafer of the St. Paul District's Operations Branch, who was working at Corps' headquarters in preparation for the upcoming hurricane season, was immediately mobilized along with two other employees as an Emergency Support Team for FEMA, and they spent the next nine days coordinating missions between FEMA and the Corps. The Emergency Support Team sent structural safety assessment teams, debris subject-matter experts and Emergency Support Function leaders to New York City and Washington, D.C., and also responded to telephone calls offering help. "I will never forget the numerous strangers, recognizing the Corps' castle and emergency operations shirt I was wearing, that approached me just wanting to say thanks," Shafer recounted. "It was probably one of my proudest experiences as a Corps' employee."[57]

Conclusion

Whether in the district or outside, St. Paul personnel assisted in emergency operations. Through the leadership and coordination of the Readiness Branch, the district responded to a variety of disasters, including floods, earthquakes and drought. This effort comprised several tasks. In some cases, the Corps provided technical assistance, equipment and coordination of operations; in other instances, the Corps helped in cleanup efforts and structure inspection. Each disaster gave the Corps an opportunity to refine its operations, making it more efficient the next year. Ironically, the suffering of others gave the Corps some of its most positive publicity as it assisted those in need. As Colonel William Badger, district engineer from 1979 to 1982, stated, emergency operations gave the Corps "the highest marks, the highest visibility. That's where we help people the most."[58] Colonel J. M. Wonsik, district engineer from 1995 to 1998, expressed it in a different way: natural disasters provided circumstances where the Corps "had no choice but to excel." Because "each and every member of the district accepted that challenge personally," the St. Paul District displayed its ability to combat emergencies effectively throughout the last quarter of the twentieth century.[59]

Chapter Eight Endnotes

1 "District Puts in Herculean Effort Against the Flood of '97," *Crosscurrents* 20 (Summer 1997): p. 7.

2 Act of 28 June 1955 (69 Stat. 186).

3 Quotation in Public Law 84-99, Emergency Flood Control Work, copy at <http://www.orn. usace.army.mil/pmgt/customer/Water%20Supply/pl84-99. htm> (10 May 2003); see also Act of 7 March 1974 (88 Stat. 12); Act of 20 June 1977 (91 Stat. 233); U.S. Army Corps of Engineers, St. Paul District, "Fact Sheet: Emergency Operations Overview," 23 March 1999, document provided by David S. Christenson. Christenson succeeded Ben A. Wopat as Chief of the Readiness Branch in 1986.

4 The Disaster Relief Act of 1974 (88 Stat. 143).

5 Federal Emergency Management Agency, "FEMA History," <http://www.fema.gov/about/history.shtm> (6 June 2003). FEMA was not the first emergency office; the Office of Emergency Preparedness predated the creation of FEMA.

6 Act of 23 November 1988 (102 Stat. 4689).

7 Saundra K. Schneider, "FEMA, Federalism, Hugo, and 'Frisco," *Publius: The Journal of Federalism* 20 (Summer 1990): p. 99; Senate, Disaster Relief Act Amendments of 1988, 100th Cong., 2d sess., 1988, S. Rept. 100-524, p. 4. Schneider estimated that it usually took a governor fourteen days to request federal aid and the president ten days to approve or reject it, although the response time could be accelerated if urgency and need required it.

8 U.S. Army Corps of Engineers, "Emergency Employment of Army and Other Resources: Civil Emergency Management Program," Engineer Regulation [ER] No. 500- 1-1, 30 September 2001, p. 2-1 (each section has its own page numbers), <http://www.usace.army.mil/publications/eng-regs/er500-1-1/entire.pdf> (6 June 2003); Federal Emergency Management Agency, "FEMA History," <http://www.fema.gov/about/history.shtm> (6 June 2003); Federal Emergency Management Agency, Federal Response Plan, 9230.1-PL (Washington, D.C.: Federal Emergency Management Agency, 1999), pp. ESF #3-1 – ESF #3-8.

9 See U.S. Army Corps of Engineers, "Emergency Employment of Army and Other Resources: Civil Emergency Management Program," pp. 4-6 – 4-7, Glossary-10; Public Law 84-99, Emergency Flood Control Work; Act of 23 November 1988 (102 Stat. 4689); St. Paul District, "Fact Sheet: Emergency Operations Overview"; Federal Emergency Management Agency, Federal Response Plan, pp. 1-2; David S. Christenson, personal communication with the authors, 25 June 2003.

10 St. Paul District, "Fact Sheet: Emergency Operations Overview."

11 David S. Christenson, personal communication with the authors, 7 March 2003. Before the 1990s, the Readiness Branch was its own division under the District Engineer. Christenson described the Emergency Operations Center (EOC) as "an office area with work stations for EOC staff that provide support to field operations. It includes a briefing room, operations center, storage area and project team area. . . It provides computers [and] communications separate from the personnel normal work area. It is the central location for district command staff to manage the emergency response." In times of flooding the Corps also set up field EOCs to perform similar functions. Christenson, personal communication with the authors, 25 June 2003.

12 David S. Christenson interview by John O. Anfinson, St. Paul, MN, 23 November 1993, p. 9, Oral History File, St. Paul District, St. Paul, Minnesota; "Flood Preparations Start Early at the District," *Crosscurrents* 25 (March 2002): p. 1; "District Readies for Spring with Flood Control Exercise," *Crosscurrents* 15 (May 1992): p. 6.

13 U.S. Army Engineer District St. Paul, *Red River of the North and Souris River Post Flood Report: 1979* (Washington, D.C.: Government Printing Office, 1979), pp. 2-6 – 2-12.

14 Raymond H. Merritt, *Creativity, Conflict and Controversy: A History of the St. Paul District U.S. Army Corps of Engineers* (Washington, D.C.: Government Printing Office, 1979), pp. 348-349; United States Army Engineer District St. Paul, Red River of the North Post Flood Report: 1978 (Washington, D.C.: Government Printing Office, 1978), p. 5.

15 United States Army Engineer District St. Paul, *Red River of the North Post Flood Report: 1978*, pp. 38-39.

16 "Some Homes Abandoned as Rural Flooding Spreads," Minneapolis *Tribune*, 8 April 1978.

17 "Crest Moves North," Minot *Daily News*, 14 April 1978. Burdick's remark highlighted a growing belief in America that people were entitled to federal assistance in times of natural disasters even if they lived in areas at high risk. For more information on this subject, see Richard Reeves, "Hurricane$, Earthquake$, and Flood$: If People Want to Build Their Houses in Dangerous Places, Why Should the Rest of Us Pay When Disaster Strikes?" *The Washington Monthly* 26 (April 1994): 10-13.

18 United States Army Engineer District St. Paul, *Red River of the North Post Flood Report: 1978*, pp. 13, 51, 59-64; "Flood Danger Eases at Grand Forks," *The Forum* (Fargo, ND) 14 April 1978; "20-Mile Long Valley Sea," *Grand Forks Herald*, 14 April 1978.

19 United States Army Engineer District St. Paul, *Red River of the North and Souris River Post Flood Report: 1979*, pp. 3-1 – 3-6, 5-1; "1979 Red River Flood Set Records for Damage," Minneapolis *Tribune*, 10 May 1979; "Red River Flood Threat is Decreased," Grand Forks *Herald*, 27 March 1979.

20 United States Army Engineer District St. Paul, *Red River of the North and Souris River Post Flood Report: 1979*, pp. 3-4 – 3-6, 3-22, 4-1 – 4-2.

21 "Staying in Touch! Congressman Arlan Stangeland," Benson *Monitor*, n.d., clipping in File 870 Red River of the North Flood 1979, Box 3858, SPDAR.

22 Quotation in *Crosscurrents* 2 (May 1979): p. 3; see also United States Army Engineer District St. Paul, *Red River of the North and Souris River Post Flood Report: 1979*, pp. 3-9 – 3-10, 5-7 – 5-8, 7-5; U.S., Congress, House, Committee on Public Works and Transportation, Oversight and Review Subcommittee, Flooding of the Red River of the North and Its Tributaries: Hearing Before the Subcommittee on Oversight and Review of the Committee on Public Works and Transportation, 96th Cong., 1st sess., 1979, pp. 1-2.

23 For an example of this, see Edward McNally interview by Matthew Godfrey, St. Paul, MN, 22 October 2002, p. 5.

24 Quotations in "Three Rivers Flood Breckenridge: Red River Hits Record Level, Hasn't Peaked," St. Paul *Pioneer Press*, 5 April 1989; see also "Worst Flood Ever: Wahpeton-Breckenridge May Top Record by 2 Feet," *The Forum*, 5 April 1989.

25 "Perpich Calls Up Guard in Breckenridge Flood," *Star Tribune*, 6 April 1989.

26 Quotation in U.S. Army Corps of Engineers, St. Paul District, *Spring Flood 89: Red River of the North After Action Report* (St. Paul, MN: U.S. Army Corps of Engineers, St. Paul District, 1989), pp. 3-1 – 3-4, 4-1, 5-1; see also "Red River of the North Flood of '89," *Crosscurrents* 12 (May 1989): p. 1; "Drayton is Ready for Red's Crest," *Grand Forks Herald*, 19 April 1989.

27 John M. Murrin, Paul E. Johnson, James M. McPherson, et al., *Liberty Equality Power: A History of the American People. Volume II: Since 1863*, concise 2d ed. (Fort Worth, TX.: Harcourt College Publishers, 2001), p. 821.

28 U.S. Army Corps of Engineers, St. Paul District, *Spring Flood 89: Red River of the North After Action Report*, p. 5-3.

29 "Floodfight Snapshots," *Crosscurrents* 12 (May 1989): p. 4.

30 U.S. Army Corps of Engineers, St. Paul District, *Spring Flood 89: Red River of the North After Action Report*, p. 5-3.

31 Tim Bertschi interview by John O. Anfinson, St. Paul, MN, 1993, pp. 1, 3-4; Christenson Interview, pp. 1-2.

32 Colonel Richard W. Craig interview by John O. Anfinson, St. Paul, MN, 20 July 1993, p. 15.

33 Lt. Col. Gary M. Koenig, "The Great Flood of 1993," File 1993 Flood, Cultural Resource Management Files, St. Paul District, St. Paul, Minnesota; David McConnell, "Mississippi River Flood: 1993," <http://enterprise.cc.uakron.edu/geology/natscigeo/Lectures/streams/Miss_Flood.pdf> (6 June 2003).

34 Michael C. Robinson, "Nightmare in the Heartland: The Great Midwest Flood of 1993," APWA (American Public Works Association) *Reporter* 60 (September 1993): pp. 6-7; "1993 Reviewed," *Crosscurrents* 17 (January 1994): p. 4; Koenig, "The Great Flood of 1993"; David Tenenbaum, "Rethinking the River," *Nature Conservancy* 44 (July/August 1994): p. 11.

35 U.S. Army Corps of Engineers, St. Paul District, *After Action Report: Summer 1993 Flooding in the Upper Mississippi Basin and Red River of the North Basin* (St. Paul, MN: U.S. Army Corps of Engineers, St. Paul District, 1993), pp. 22-23.

36 "District Puts in Herculean Effort Against the Flood of '97," p. 2; U.S. Army Corps of Engineers, St. Paul District, *After Action Report: Spring 1997 Flood in the Red River of the North Basin, Minnesota River Basin and Mississippi River Basin* (St. Paul, MN: U.S. Army Corps of Engineers, St. Paul District, 1997), pp. 4-5; Congressional Record, 105th Cong., 1st sess., 24 April 1997, p. H1866, <http://80-web.lexisnexis. com.weblib. lib.umt.edu:2048/congcomp/document?_m =cfec99d7fffd8c93d0d4c2edf6534444&_docnum=12&wchp=dGLbVzz-lSlAA&_md5= b90242eb6e5e744703d50b29ff1e2954> (6 June 2003). According to Major General Russell L. Fuhrman, Deputy Chief of Engineers and Deputy Commanding General of the Corps the district's preparations were some of the best advance measure work that the Corps had ever performed.

37 "District Puts in Herculean Effort Against the Flood of '97," p. 6; U.S. Army Corps of Engineers, St. Paul District, *After Action Report: Spring 1997 Flood in the Red River of the North Basin*, pp. 5-13.

38 "Transcript of Clinton Remarks April 22 in Briefing on Flood Damage by Local Officials," *U.S. Newswire* (23 April 1997), <http://80-infoweb.newsbank.com. weblib.lib.umt.edu:2048/iw-search/we> (6 June 2003).

39 Quotation in "District Puts in Herculean Effort Against the Flood of '97," p. 6; "After Action Report: Spring 1997 Flood in the Red River of the North Basin," pp. 5-13.

40 Quotation in "District Puts in Herculean Effort Against the Flood of '97," p. 7; see also *After Action Report: Spring 1997 Flood in the Red River of the North Basin*, pp. 14-17; U.S. Army Corps of Engineers, St. Paul District, "Flood of 1997," <http://www.mvp. usace.army.mil/disaster_response/default.asp?pageid=61> (6 June 2003).

41 Quotations in "District Supports Flood Fight in Northwestern Minnesota," *Crosscurrents* 25 (September 2002): pp. 3-10; see also U.S. Army Corps of Engineers, St. Paul District, *Spring 2001 Flood in the Red River of the North, Minnesota River and Mississippi River Basins: After Action Report* (St. Paul, MN: U.S. Army Corps of Engineers, St. Paul District, 2001).

42 Act of 20 June 1977 (91 Stat. 233).

43 "The Corps and Drought: What Can Be Done," *Crosscurrents* 4 (April 1981): pp. 1-2.

44 "The Corps and Drought," p. 2; Raymond Merritt, "New Directions: Transitions in the St. Paul District, Corps of Engineers, 1976-1982," unpublished manuscript, St. Paul District, pp. 3-4.

45 "The Drought of 1988: A Chronology," *Crosscurrents* 11 (September/October 1988): p. 4.

46 "The Drought of 1988," p. 5; Colonel Roger L. Baldwin interview by John O. Anfinson, St. Paul, MN, 1 July 1991, p. 9; "Annual Historical Report for 1988: St. Paul District," n.p., File 870 Annual Historical Report (90), Box 1560, SPDAR.

47 "Two Emergency Water Projects Completed," *Crosscurrents* 12 (January 1989): p. 3; "Annual Historical Report for 1988: St. Paul District," n.p.

48 Quoted in "Drought of '88 Offers Lessons for Minnesota of '89 and Beyond," *Star Tribune*, 26 April 1989.

49 Quotation in Baldwin Interview, p. 9; see also "Annual Historical Report for 1988: St. Paul District," n.p.

50 "Drought Provided Opportunity for Water Quality Study," *Crosscurrents* 12 (April 1989): p. 3.

51 Baldwin Interview, p. 9; see also "Drought of '88 Offers Lessons for Minnesota of '89 and Beyond."

52 Schneider, "FEMA, Federalism, Hugo, and 'Frisco," p. 109; Janet A. McDonnell, *Response to the Loma Prieta Earthquake* (Fort Belvoir, Virginia: U.S. Army Corps of Engineers, 1993), pp. 27-28.

53 Quotations in "Earthquake Team Returns to District," *Crosscurrents* 12 (December 1989): pp. 4-5; see also "Earthquake Update: Corps Responds with Pride and Professionalism," *Crosscurrents* 12 (November 1989): p. 12.

54 Quotation in "Minnesota Engineer Among Those Who Volunteered to Rebuild Kuwait," St. Paul *Pioneer Press*, 3 March 1991; see also Janet A. McDonnell, *After Desert Storm: The U.S. Army and the Reconstruction of Kuwait* (Washington, D.C.: Department of the Army, 1999), pp. 37-39, 210-211.

55 "Great Chicago Flood: St. Paul District Helps Plug Subterranean Flood," *Crosscurrents* 15 (June 1992): pp. 1-2.

56 "Ten from St. Paul District Work Hurricane Andrew Relief Duty," *Crosscurrents* 16 (January 1993): pp. 1, 3.

57 "Shafer Assists FEMA on Pentagon, NYC Recovery," *Crosscurrents* 24 (October 2001): pp. 3, 8; "St. Paul District, Congressional Visits by Colonel Ball and Judy DesHarnais, 10-11 September 2001," File Record of Congressional Visits, St. Paul District, St. Paul, Minnesota.

58 U.S. Army Corps of Engineers, Office of the Chief of Engineers, Engineer Profiles: The District Engineer, Interviews with Colonel William W. Badger, by Frank N. Schubert (Washington, U.S. Army Corps of Engineers, 1983), p. 71.

59 Colonel J.M. Wonsik interview by John O. Anfinson, St. Paul, MN, 20 January 1998, p. 8, Oral History File, St. Paul District, St. Paul, Minnesota.

Native American relations: Swamp Creek flows just north of the formerly proposed Crandon Mine site into the Mole Lake Indian Reservation where the tribe harvests wild rice from Rice Lake. (Photo by Jon Ahlness, courtesy of St. Paul District, Corps of Engineers)

9 External Relationships

During the past quarter century, the U.S. Army Corps of Engineers maintained its traditional close relationship to Congress. At the same time, it developed stronger relationships to state, local and Indian tribal governments. The Corps also cultivated stronger partnerships with other federal agencies, such as when it responded to the U.S. Fish and Wildlife Service on endangered species issues, or cooperated with the Environmental Protection Agency on regulatory matters or provided disaster relief under the auspices of the Federal Emergency Management Agency. In step with the rest of the Corps' organization, the St. Paul District devoted increasing effort to developing and sustaining myriad relationships with other federal agencies, state and local governments and nongovernment organizations. This development reflected the growing complexity of the Corps' mission in the environmental era as well as new realities associated with government reform.

Relationship with Congress

Congress traditionally took a close interest in the Corps of Engineers, particularly in the civil works program, which provided a prize opportunity for federal spending in each congressional member's home state. In a practice known as "logrolling," congressmen refrained from criticizing civil works projects in another member's state in the expectation that the member would return the favor. In this way, the civil works program became a favorite arena for so-called "pork barrel politics" and the Corps became beholden to Congress. Beginning with President Carter and continuing through the Reagan, Bush and Clinton Administrations, the chief executives sought to cut useless "pork" or undesirable projects out of the civil works program and to wean the Corps from its close relationship to Congress. This power struggle affected the Corps primarily at the headquarters level and above – especially in the Office of the

Assistant Secretary of the Army (Civil Works). At the district level, the Corps continued to communicate frequently with members of Congress who represented the respective states. In the St. Paul District, the district engineer communicated primarily with senators and congressmen from Minnesota, Wisconsin and North Dakota. Although Congress's relationship to the Corps in the last quarter century was highly contested at the national level, the relationship of local congressmen to the St. Paul District in this era might be better characterized as business as usual.

Local congressmen communicated directly with the district engineer. The local point of contact was crucial in times of disaster relief, such as during the Midwest floods of 1993. Congressmen also took the concerns of their constituents directly to the St. Paul District office, as when a Section 404 permit application became controversial or a feasibility study hung in the balance. At no time was the relationship of Congress to the district office more apparent than in the 1990s when the Corps' reorganization plan called for elimination of the St. Paul District. Senators Paul Wellstone (D-Minnesota) and Dave Durenberger (R-Minnesota) joined eighteen other senators in protesting the plan. Wellstone and Representative Bruce Vento (D-Minnesota) visited the St. Paul District office and reassured Corps' employees, saying that they were doing all they could to block the Administration's reorganization plan or to develop an alternative plan. This meeting occurred in the cafeteria of the St. Paul Post Office and was attended by most of the district office's 440 employees.[1]

Once each year, the district engineer visited members of Congress on Capitol Hill to inform them of the Corps' various activities in their states and congressional districts. Typically the deputy for planning, program and project management or chief of planning accompanied the district engineer, and prior to making the rounds in the Capitol these two officials would meet with their superiors at Corps' headquarters and the Office of the Assistant Secretary of the Army (Civil Works). Then, they proceeded to Capitol Hill, where they might get appointments with five or six senators and a dozen or more representatives. Sometimes they met with a congressional staff assistant but more often they spoke directly with a senator or congressman. They highlighted what was of most interest to each member – civil works projects, feasibility studies, the environmental management program, the Section 404 program – and they left briefing papers. The St. Paul District accomplished these congressional visits on a yearly basis in order to keep senators and congressmen informed of new developments and to establish or renew personal relationships. Since the district engineers were on a three-year rotation (or two-year rotation from 1991 to 2001) it was important for them to introduce themselves regularly.[2]

Interagency Cooperation

One of the most influential demands of the environmental movement was to force greater cooperation among government agencies. It was not enough to introduce interdisciplinary perspectives within a land-management agency such as the Army Corps. The holistic approach to environmental protection required interagency cooperation as well. Congress responded to this imperative by embedding innumerable requirements for interagency cooperation in environmental laws. The enthusiasm for establishing river basin commissions in the 1970s furthered the trend toward greater interagency cooperation.

In the St. Paul District, the focal point of interagency cooperation was the Mississippi River. Interagency cooperation began at the state level, as Minnesota, Wisconsin and Iowa shared concerns along the river where it formed state boundaries. It was institutionalized in the Upper Mississippi River Basin Commission established in 1972. The commission included the three states together with five federal agencies: the Army Corps of Engineers, the Fish and Wildlife Service, the Soil Conservation Service (now Natural Resources Conservation Service), the Environmental Protection Agency and the Department of Transportation. The Corps worked particularly closely with the Fish and Wildlife Service, for the Corps was responsible for dredging the navigation channel, while the Fish and Wildlife Service was responsible for managing fish and wildlife habitat. Indeed, much of the area was designated as wildlife refuges and came under the jurisdiction of the Fish and Wildlife Service. The placement of dredged material on manmade and natural islands and in back channels, sloughs and wetlands posed both a threat and an opportunity for habitat management.[3] This was a classic example of the need for interagency cooperation.

Interagency cooperation: District personnel consult with U.S. Fish and Wildlife Service staff, 1982. (Photo by Lyle Nicklay, courtesy of St. Paul District, Corps of Engineers)

Environmental groups were vigilant in demanding interagency cooperation in order to make one federal agency serve as a watchdog over another federal agency. The Corps had a long-standing arrangement of transferring funds to the Fish and Wildlife Service to help the latter agency study and recommend ways to modify civil works projects so as to enhance fish and wildlife habitat. The Fish and Wildlife Coordination Act authorized the transfer of funds. When the Army threatened to eliminate the transfers in the early 1980s, a prominent Washington-based environmental group, the Wildlife Management Institute, protested. The departments of natural resources of Wisconsin and Minnesota also stood to lose both funding and input regarding Corps' actions if the Army decision held.[4]

Congress responded to these concerns by mandating more intensive cooperation between the Corps and the Fish and Wildlife Service on the Upper Mississippi.

Congress designated the Upper Mississippi River System a nationally significant ecosystem. It funded a series of "habitat projects" along the river under the Corps' new Environmental Management Program.[5] The habitat projects were a combination of dredge-and-fill operations and bank stabilization efforts, each designed with a view to enhancing fish and wildlife habitat while preserving the navigable waterway. These projects involved the Fish and Wildlife Service in project design and environmental monitoring. The states participated under cost-sharing agreements.[6]

After Congress authorized the Mississippi National River and Recreation Area in 1988, the Corps coordinated with the National Park Service on navigation and recreation issues. The protected area extended for 80 miles along the river from Dayton, Minnesota, to Hastings, Minnesota, and the St. Paul District commander served as commissioner on an advisory board. The Corps already consulted with the National Park Service on matters involving historic properties and other cultural resources under the Corps' jurisdiction, as required by the National Historic Preservation Act of 1966 and NEPA. The historic properties included the system of locks and dams on the Mississippi River. The Corps additionally coordinated with the National Park Service on issues involving the Rainy River drainage in Voyageurs National Park, located on Minnesota's international border with Ontario. Interagency cooperation became yet more structured in the Upper Mississippi River System Environmental Management Program established by Congress. Although the Environmental Management Program was fundamentally a partnership, Congress invested the Corps with overall responsibility for federal management of the program. The Corps actively coordinated with the U.S. Department of the Interior, the Upper Mississippi River Basin Association and the five states of Minnesota – Wisconsin, Illinois, Iowa and Missouri. The Corps' North Central Division managed the program, while three districts – St. Paul, Rock Island and St. Louis – managed the habitat projects within their boundaries. The Environmental Management Program recognized the river's importance both as a system of major national wildlife refuges and a commercial waterway for navigation.[7]

International Cooperation

The International Joint Commission, or IJC, is a permanent body established by the Boundary Waters Treaty of 1909. Its purpose is to deal impartially with problems of mutual concern wherever waters extend along or flow across the international boundary. Historically, the IJC was concerned primarily with obstruction or diversion of water, particularly where it affected navigability. In the latter part of the twentieth century, it became increasingly involved with water quality, especially in the Great Lakes. As the St. Paul District is bounded on the north by the international border with Canada, the district is one of a handful of Corps' districts involved with the IJC. After the St. Paul District boundaries were realigned in 1979, the district was no longer concerned with Great Lakes matters. In its present configuration the St. Paul District encompasses three rivers that flow along or across the international border: the Rainy, Red and Souris rivers.

The IJC consists of six commissioners: three Canadians and three Americans. One member from each nation serves full-time as a cochairman, while the other two commissioners from each nation serve part-time. The commissioners act as a unitary body and are supposed to make decisions which will best serve both nations. While the IJC itself maintains only a small technical staff, it is empowered to establish boards, composed of engineers and other technical experts from both nations, to oversee particular issues. The boards may meet regularly or conduct studies, and they make recommendations to the IJC.[8]

The Souris River at Minot, North Dakota, with levee and channel work performed by the Corps of Engineers. (Photo courtesy of St. Paul District, Corps of Engineers)

In 1980, the St. Paul District district engineer served on seven different boards under the IJC. These were the International Lake of the Woods Control Board (established 1925), International Rainy Lake Board of Control (1940), International Prairie Portage River Board of Control (1939), International Souris-Red Rivers Engineering Board (1948), International Pembina River Engineering Board (1962), International Roseau River Engineering Board (1971) and International Garrison Diversion Study Board (1975). The number of boards proliferated as the IJC became more involved with pollution issues. In 2001, the district engineer served on four international boards: the International Lake of the Woods Control Board, International Rainy Lake Board of Control, International Souris-Red Rivers Engineering Board, and International Red River Board of Control.[9] Each board comprised a small number of public officials from each nation. The International Souris-Red Rivers Engineering Board, for example, included three U.S. officials from the Bureau of Reclamation, Corps of Engineers and the Geological Survey together with two Canadian officials from the departments of Agriculture and Environment.[10]

As has been discussed in Chapter Four, the Souris and Red rivers present difficult problems for flood control. Both rivers flow north. Spring thaw generally occurs upstream (in the United States) before it occurs downstream (in Canada), causing floodwaters to back up and overflow the riverbanks. Moreover, the two river valleys are exceptionally flat and the floodplains cover large expanses containing both urban and agricultural development. The Corps of Engineers operates a number of flood control dams and reservoirs on these rivers and their tributaries in North Dakota and on the Minnesota-North Dakota state line.

Relations with Indian Tribes

At the end of the twentieth century the Corps was no newcomer to political controversies involving Indian tribes and resources. Numerous dam projects had involved the Corps with the Bureau of Indian Affairs and tribal representatives since the 1930s.[11] For most of this period, however, the federal government treated tribes as dependent wards, with the government in the role of trustee and guardian. This began to change in the 1970s, when the Nixon Administration adopted a national policy of Indian self-determination aimed at promoting tribal self-government. Congress enacted the Indian Self-Determination and Education Assistance Act of 1975, which initiated a broad program of federal support for greater tribal autonomy in the management of tribal resources. With federal assistance, tribes took control of programs formerly under the Bureau of Indian Affairs and tribal governments increased their power through the formation of intertribal political organizations. As one example of this trend, tribes in Michigan, Wisconsin and Minnesota formed The Great Lakes Indian Fish and Wildlife Commission, which pressed for the protection of treaty rights through legal action.

Environmental legislation in the 1970s required federal agencies to consult with tribal governments on actions that could affect tribal resources or treaty rights. The National Environmental Policy Act of 1969, the River and Harbor and Flood Control Act of 1970 and the Water Resources Development Act of 1974 provided new requirements for the Corps to deal with Indian tribes. In 1978, these requirements were strengthened by the Council on Environmental Quality, which published "Regulations for Implementing the Procedural Provisions of the National Environmental Policy Act of 1969." Under these regulations, the Corps needed to consult with tribes concerning project development and project de-authorization, real estate acquisition and disposal, water resources planning, wildlife mitigation and other environmental management programs, cultural resources management and regulatory functions. Importantly, these consultation requirements were not limited to actions involving Indian lands but extended to other Indian resources such as cultural sites and off-reservation hunting and fishing grounds associated with treaty rights.[12]

President Jimmy Carter sought to increase coordination between the Corps and tribes on water development projects. In a memorandum concerning federal and Indian reserved water rights dated July 12, 1978, Carter outlined procedures for federal agencies to evaluate Indian water development projects and to increase Indian water development in conjunction with quantification of water rights. Secretary of the Interior Cecil D. Andrus established a federal task force, which held a series of meetings with Indian representatives and made recommendations in a report. It specifically recommended the Corps establish procedures for coordinating with tribes on water development projects and for consulting with tribes on permit applications that might affect tribal resources. While the Corps initially responded favorably to the

226

recommendations, the initiative died with the advent of the Reagan Administration in 1981.[13]

Federal environmental legislation and Indian policy were not the only factors that encouraged tribes to assert tribal sovereignty during the last quarter of the twentieth century. As the courts and the Indian Claims Commission entered judgments awarding money to tribes for past actions by the United States (mainly involving inadequate compensation for land takings), tribes often employed these funds so as to assert themselves in economic planning and development. Moreover, various court rulings in this era reaffirmed tribal sovereignty in matters ranging from the power to tax and create corporations and administer justice for tribal members, to environmental matters such as the authority to regulate water quality on the reservation. In the mid-1980s, the Environmental Protection Agency initiated government-to-government agreements with tribes concerning the setting of water quality standards. Courts subsequently upheld the Environmental Protection Agency's authority to treat Indian tribes as states under the Clean Water Act.

The move toward government-to-government relations significantly advanced when President Bill Clinton signed a memorandum dated April 29, 1994, directing the head of each executive department and agency to improve federal cooperation with tribal governments. Clinton specifically called for a government-to-government framework for dealing with federally-recognized tribes. In response to Clinton's initiative, the Acting Assistant Secretary of the Army for Civil Works, John H. Zirschky, directed the Corps to hold interest-group workshops and gather data aimed at improving the Corps' working relationships with tribal governments. The Corps assigned this responsibility to a Native American Intergovernmental Relations Task Force under the auspices of the Institute for Water Resources.[14]

Between February and June 1995, field personnel met with tribal representatives of 186 tribes. Each district office prepared an after action report on the workshops and supplied the data to the task force. The task force found a nationwide pattern of "conflict ... between the Corps multistage execution of its water resource missions and its obligation, as a federal agency, to honor the commitments made to Federally Recognized Tribes in treaties, statutes, administrative orders, and court cases." It stated the Corps had an obligation "to reconcile these conflicts as they arise."[15]

The St. Paul District participated in two workshops, the first drawing representatives of ten tribes in Minnesota and North Dakota, and the second, held jointly with the Detroit District, drawing representatives of all nine federally-recognized tribes in Wisconsin.[16] The general format of the workshops was a series of presentations on Corps' programs followed by round-table discussions of tribal concerns. Many of the tribes' comments were directed at the regulatory program. For example, the tribes wanted assurance that the Corps would enforce clean water standards where the tribes adopted more stringent standards than the states, and they wanted the Corps to "lobby" against weakening of the Clean Water Act. (On the latter point, Corps' officials stated the Corps does not lobby for or against its programs, and that tribes must take this initiative.) Another theme in the discussions concerned the definition of tribal trust resources. The Corps wanted the tribes to identify their trust resources, and it offered to assist the tribes with wetland mapping, aerial and ground surveys and other means. The tribes stated they lacked money and manpower to do this, and they believed the Corps defined trust resources too narrowly. In particular, they disagreed with the St. Paul District counsel's view that a tribal trust resource must be specifically mentioned in a federal legal document such as a treaty or executive order. The tribes noted that many tribal trust resources related to cultural heritage or spiritual values and could not be described in "Euro-Asian terms" for the Corps.[17]

Part of the workshops' emphasis on the Corps' regulatory responsibilities stemmed from the controversy surrounding the Crandon Mine proposal, which threatened to impact no fewer than eight federally-recognized tribes. Three tribes occupied reservations in the vicinity of the mine: the Forest County Potawatomi Tribe, the Menominee Indian Tribe and the Sokaogon Chippewa Community (Mole Lake Band). Five other tribes reaffirmed in court their rights to hunt, fish and gather in the area around the mine. These tribes were the Red Cliff Band of Lake Superior Chippewa, the Bad River Band of Lake Superior Chippewa, the Lac Courte Oreilles Band of Lake Superior Chippewa, the Lac du Flambeau Band of Lake Superior Chippewa and the St. Croix Band of Lake Superior Chippewa. Additional tribes potentially had trust resources at stake, having ceded lands in the area.[18]

Native American relations: Swamp Creek flows just north of the formerly proposed Crandon Mine site into the Mole Lake Indian Reservation where the tribe harvest wild rice from Rice Lake. (Photo by Jon Ahness, courtesy of St. Paul District, Corps of Engineers)

When the workshops convened, the three tribes whose reservations were near the Crandon Mine had recently produced a study, "The Potential Cultural Impact of the Development of the Crandon Mine on the Indian Communities of Northeastern Wisconsin." This contracted report by two anthropologists and a biologist described the history of resource use by the affected tribes and the potential environmental impacts of mining operations. The report warned of sulfuric acid pollution in Rice Lake and the Wolf River – vital resources to the Mole Lake Band and the Menominee Tribe respectively – not only as a consequence of mining, but also in anticipation of mine abandonment many years in the future.[19] Tribal representatives raised these concerns in the workshop three months later when they admonished the Corps to evaluate projects on a longer time frame. Although the Corps normally considered project lives of fifty to a hundred years, one tribal representative stated, tribal policy was to consider effects on the next seven generations. Therefore, the Corps was urged to weigh the benefits of a mine that might create an economic boom for twenty to forty years against the costs of "decades of restoration work."[20]

Each of the three tribes in the vicinity of the Crandon Mine had unique concerns. The Mole Lake Band occupied a reservation only two miles from the mine site, and the reservation encompassed Rice Lake, from which they harvested wild rice. According to early versions of the mining proposal, wastewater from the mine would enter Swamp Creek and flow into Rice Lake, threatening the wild rice crop. The Potawatomi were located on lands northeast of the mine site and their primary concern pertained to air quality. They did not want airborne pollutants descending on the area and contaminating the plants and animals that formed a substantial part of their diet. The Menominee Reservation, meanwhile, was located south of the mine site and was traversed by the Wolf River. The portion of the river flowing through the reservation is a national wild and scenic river. The tribe was concerned about the water quality of the river, particularly as several tribal chiefs were buried along its banks.[21]

Tribal demands that the Corps define its trust responsibilities toward Indian tribes intensified in 1997, when the Corps handed the Crandon Mining Company a seeming victory in its long effort to develop the mine. Faced with formidable problems in protecting the water quality in the vicinity of the mine, the Crandon Mining Company altered its proposal and requested state approval to pump 600 gallons per minute of treated wastewater some 38 miles to the Wisconsin River. The Corps determined the transfer of water from the Great Lakes basin to the Mississippi River watershed would not be illegal because the federal diversion law applied only to surface waters.[22] Although the Corps' ruling was soon superseded by other developments, it served as a catalyst for an exchange of issue papers between the Corps and the tribes about the Corps' trust responsibilities.

Tribal attorneys accused the Corps of failing to consider its trust responsibilities adequately. In answer to these charges, the St. Paul District developed an issue paper about the Corps' trust responsibilities toward Indian tribes in the regulatory permitting process. Prepared by District Counsel Edwin C. Bankston, the issue paper was reviewed by attorneys in Corps' headquarters, who concurred in its analysis.[23] On September 29, 1997, District Engineer Colonel J. M. Wonsik transmitted the issue paper to the tribes, proposing the Corps meet with tribal representatives sixty days later for consultation.[24] This meeting never took place.[25]

Bankston's eleven-page paper addressed a number of issues, citing federal case law. Fundamentally, the Corps had a responsibility, explicitly recognized in Northwest Sea Farms, Inc. v. U.S. Army Corps of Engineers (1996) to protect Indian treaty rights. In other words, the Corps could not issue a Section 404 or Section 10 permit that would cause a treaty right to be impinged or abrogated.[26] This much was unambiguous.

Most Indian treaties in Minnesota and Wisconsin conditionally secured "usufructuary rights" to hunt, fish and gather wild foods on lands off the reservation. These rights were limited to "ceded lands," or demarcated areas that each tribe had once occupied and ceded to the United States during the nineteenth century. Bankston held that the

Indians' usufructuary rights to resources such as game and fish invested the federal government with a trust responsibility toward those same resources; thus, the Corps had to consider Indian treaty rights both on and off reservations. However, Bankston noted, the usufructuary rights were extinguished when the land passed into private ownership. In contrast, Indian treaties in the Pacific Northwest made usufructuary rights perpetual. Bankston argued the difference was significant, that it affected the federal government's obligation to determine some form of mitigation when treaty rights were involved. The Corps, he wrote, should apply the same criteria to permit applications for activities on or off reservations; however, it was "very likely" that an activity located off reservation would have a lesser impact on tribal resources.[27]

Since the Corps' regulatory program required that it conduct a public interest review for all individual permit applications, Bankston asked: did the Corps' tribal trust responsibilities take precedence over public interests? Bankston argued that tribal resources should be "considered in the public interest review just as any other similarly sized community would be." But, he added, adverse impacts to natural resources could have a greater effect on Indians than on non-Indians, since the "individual Indian may be more closely tied to the defined land area than his non-Indian counterpart."[28]

Native American relations: A consultation between District Engineer Colonel Robert L. Ball (right) and the Menominee Tribe was conducted at the Menominee Indian Reservation. Ken Fish, Menominee Treaty Rights Office, a representative from the Bureau of Indian Affairs, is on the left. (Photo by Jon Ahness, courtesy of St. Paul District, Corps of Engineers)

One-and-a-half years later, the Great Lakes Indian Fish and Wildlife Commission, representing several tribes in Minnesota, Wisconsin and Michigan; the Sokaogon Chippewa Community; and the Menominee Indian Nation jointly prepared a detailed response to the Bankston's issue paper entitled "Tribal Rights and Trust Responsibility."[29] The nineteen page paper explained the legal basis for tribal rights in natural resources for each of the affected tribes, and then it opined on federal trust responsibilities. M. Catherine Condon, an attorney representing the Indian groups, transmitted the paper to the St. Paul District on April 15, 1999.[30]

Tribal representatives and Corps' officials met in St. Paul on April 23, 1999, to discuss the two papers. Although the papers were close on many points, two critical differences emerged. First, the tribes held that the federal government's trust responsibility required the Corps choose the regulatory alternative that

230

would be in the best interests of the tribes; the Corps, on the other hand, insisted that it need only consider tribal interests alongside others. The second difference was a procedural issue that followed from the first point: the tribes believed that the Corps' consideration of trust resources must be decoupled from the public interest review process; the Corps maintained that the two could be handled at once.[31]

Tribal representatives and the Corps had two follow-up meetings in an attempt to resolve differences raised by the issue papers – the first on May 26 in St. Paul, and the second on June 23 in Keshena, Wisconsin. The tribes continued to argue that trust responsibilities required separate consideration. Indeed, representatives of the Mole Lake Band refused to participate in meetings with representatives of the Crandon Mining Company. When the Corps allowed company representatives to attend one of these meetings – because the company was concerned as well about whether tribal interests would be separated out of the public interest review – the Mole Lake Band walked out of the meeting. Henceforth, the Corps initiated dual monthly telephone conference calls: one with the company and one with the tribes.[32] Government-to-government meetings continued between the district engineer and tribal chairpersons in 2001 and 2002.[33]

There was no clear resolution of the question: do trust responsibilities take precedence over public interest review? In terms of process, the tribes appeared to have won their point: the Corps initiated its own EIS rather than team with the state Department of Natural Resources on this mammoth study owing to the federal government's trust responsibilities to the tribes, and its consultation with the tribes took the form of government-to-government talks. But in terms of product, the Corps would not allow its hands to be tied. As the massive environmental impact study neared completion, it remained unclear how trust resources would be defined and what level of protection they would be afforded.

Ultimately, the Forest County Potawatomi and Mole Lake Band concluded the federal government's trust responsibility would not necessarily preclude development of the mine. To assure the mine would not be developed, the two tribes decided to purchase the property with tribal funds. On October 28, 2003, the tribes acquired 5,770 acres in Forest County and 169 acres in Shawano and Oconto counties for $1.6 million. A few days later, the tribes withdrew the application to open the mine, ending twenty-five years of controversy over impending environmental impacts. The Mole Lake Band's chairwoman, Sandra Rachal, stated, "We made this decision to protect our people and our resources." Whether the Corps would have denied a Section 404 permit for the Crandon Mine in the final analysis anyway would never be known, but certainly the controversy forced the St. Paul District to explore facets of the Corps' federal trust responsibility to Indian tribes as no other district had. The district's government-to-government relations with these Indian tribes established a positive foundation for further engagement with tribal governments in the future.

Conclusion

Regional planning and interagency cooperation have become increasingly vital concerns to the Corps in the last quarter century. As land managers seek to balance competing interests and to accomplish tasks with finite resources, they must ensure that one agency's actions do not conflict with another's, and that resources are shared whenever possible. For the St. Paul District, managing the Upper Mississippi River is the most complicated interagency effort it has ever undertaken. Yet, other demands on the district highlighted the trend toward greater government-to-government consultation as well as interagency cooperation. Situated on the boundary with Canada, the Corps consulted with land managers across the border. And, it dealt with the unique relationship between the federal government and Indian tribes, consulting with tribal governments on issues affecting Indian trust resources.

Chapter Nine Endnotes

1 *Star Tribune* (Minneapolis), 8 June 1991 and 3 July 1991.

2 Congressional visits are described in Memoranda for Record. Memoranda for 1989-1997 were provided courtesy of J. A. Stadelman, Chief, Programs Management Branch.

3 George W. Griebenow, "A Team Called GREAT," *Water Spectrum* 9, No. 1 (Winter 1976-77): pp. 20-21.

4 *Courier Press* (Prairie du Chien), 25 April 1984.

5 Richard C. Nelson, field supervisor, to John R. Brown, District Engineer, 10 June 1991, File 1110 Fish and Wildlife Transfer Fund, Box 4466, SPDAR

6 EMP Status Report, 11 August 1994, File 1105 Environmental Management Program Status Report, Box 4467, SPDAR.

7 U.S. Army Corps of Engineers, *Upper Mississippi River System Environmental Management Program: Sixth Annual Addendum*, (Chicago: U.S. Army Corps of Engineers, 1991), p. 4.

8 International Joint Commission, "1980 Annual Report," Box 3539, SPDAR, pp. 4-6.

9 Kenneth Kasprisin, Memorandum 10-1-1, 26 January 2001, <http://mvpiis/ RMOffice/ docs/Mission Statement> (September 2002).

10 Annual Report to the International Joint Commission by the International Souris-Red Rivers Engineering Board for the period October 23, 1990 to October 23, 1991, File 15-1e International Joint Commission, Box 4338, SPDAR.

11 Katherine Weist, "For the Public Good: Native Americans, Hydroelectric Dams, and the Iron Triangle," in *Trusteeship in Change: Toward Tribal Autonomy in Resource Management*, edited by Richmond L. Clow and Imre Sutton (Boulder: University Press of Colorado, 2001), pp. 55-72. Some Corps dealings with Indian tribes

date to the 19th century. Dams in the headwaters of the Mississippi River adversely affected lands belonging to Minnesota Chippewa bands in the late 19th and early 20th centuries. See Jane Lamm-Carroll, "Dams and Damages," *Minnesota History* (Spring 1990): pp. 4-15.

12 Janet McDonnell, "The U.S. Army Corps of Engineers and Native American Tribes," in Native American Intergovernmental Relations Task Force, Assessment of Corps/Tribal Intergovernmental Relations, Vol. 2, IWR Report 96-R-6a (Washington: U.S. Army Corps of Engineers, 1996), p. 4.

13 McDonnell, "The U.S. Army Corps of Engineers and Native American Tribes," pp. 17-18.

14 Native American Intergovernmental Relations Task Force, Assessment of Corps/Tribal Intergovernmental Relations, Vol. 1, IWR Report 96-R-6 (Washington: U.S. Army Corps of Engineers, 1996), p. 1.

15 Native American Intergovernmental Relations Task Force, Assessment of Corps/Tribal Intergovernmental Relations, p. vii.

16 After Action Report Tribal Assessment Workshop, 2 May 1995, and 9 May 1995, in Native American Intergovernmental Relations Task Force, Assessment of Corps/Tribal Intergovernmental Relations, pp. 260, 292.

17 After Action Report Tribal Assessment Workshop, 2 May 1995, in Native American Intergovernmental Relations Task Force, Assessment of Corps/Tribal Intergovernmental Relations, pp. 266-279.

18 M. Catherine Condon to Ben A. Wopat, Assistant Chief, 21 June 1999, John Ahlness Tribal Trust (Crandon Project) file, SPDAR.

19 Charles Cleland, Larry Nesper, and Joshua Cleland, "The Potential Cultural Impact of the Development of the Crandon Mine on the Indian Communities of Northeastern Wisconsin," report prepared under contract with the Sokaogon Band of Chippewa, The Menominee Tribe of Wisconsin, and the Forest County Potawatomi in cooperation with The Great Lakes Indian Fish and Wildlife Commission in behalf of the Lake Superior Chippewa, 15 February 1995, Matt Pearcy Crandon Mine file, SPDAR.

20 After Action Report Tribal Assessment Workshop, 2 May 1995, in Native American Intergovernmental Relations Task Force, Assessment of Corps/Tribal Intergovernmental Relations, Vol. 2, IWR Report 96-R-6a (Washington: U.S. Army Corps of Engineers, 1996), p. 268.

21 Ben Wopat, interview by Matthew Godfrey, St. Paul, 24 October 2002, p. 18.

22 Antigo *Journal*, 13 August 1997.

23 Lester Edelman, Chief Counsel, to District Counsel, 9 July 1997, John Ahlness Tribal Trust (Crandon Project) file, SPDAR.

24 J. M. Wonsik, District Engineer, to James Schlender, Executive Administrator, Great Lakes Indian Fish & Wildlife Commission, 29 September 1997, John Ahlness Tribal Trust (Crandon Project) file, SPDAR.

25 James E. Zorn to Ben Wopat, Assistant Chief, 16 July 1999, John Alhness Tribal Trust (Crandon Project) file, SPDAR.

26 Edwin C. Bankston, "Issue Paper and District Recommendation: The Agency's Trust Responsibilities toward Indian Tribes in the Regulatory Permitting Process," no date, John Ahlness Tribal Trust (Crandon Project) file, SPDAR.

27 Edwin C. Bankston, "Issue Paper and District Recommendation: The Agency's Trust Responsibilities toward Indian Tribes in the Regulatory Permitting Process," no date, John Ahlness Tribal Trust (Crandon Project) file, SPDAR.

28 Edwin C. Bankston, "Issue Paper and District Recommendation: The Agency's Trust Responsibilities toward Indian Tribes in the Regulatory Permitting Process," no date, John Ahlness Tribal Trust (Crandon Project) file, SPDAR.

29 "Tribal Rights and Trust Responsibility," no date, John Alhness Tribal Trust (Crandon Project) file, SPDAR.

30 M. Catherine Condon to Char Hauger, Regulatory Branch, 15 April 1999, John Ahlness Tribal Trust (Crandon Project) file, SPDAR.

31 "Tribal Rights and Trust Responsibility," no date, John Alhness Tribal Trust (Crandon Project) file, SPDAR.

32 Kenneth S. Kasprisin, District Engineer, to Chairman Apesanakwat, undated, John Ahlness Tribal Trust (Crandon Project) file, SPDAR; Wopat Interview, p. 22.

33 Information Paper, September 2002, provided to authors by John Ahlness.

Flooding on Sheppard Road in St. Paul, Minn., at the end of the twentieth century.

10 Conclusion

In the last quarter century, few public agencies could match the record of the U.S. Army Corps of Engineers for reinvention as it transformed itself from the nation's leading dam builder to the nation's leading water resources steward. Some observers admired the agency's commitment and finesse, while others maintained that despite the Corps' best effort to adapt to the environmental era, it still had outlived its usefulness. Regardless, the St. Paul District proved to be one of the Corps' most forward looking districts in its approach to civil works design, protection of wetlands and other Corps' missions. In addition, mirroring the experience of other administrative units of the Corps, the St. Paul District underwent significant organizational change and adopted new ways of doing business in the last quarter of the twentieth century.

In its civil works program, the district worked energetically with commissions such as the Great River Environmental Action Team and the Upper Mississippi River Basin Commission to improve management of the Upper Mississippi River. The Corps demonstrated sensitivity to the environment, albeit with prodding from environmental groups, in its implementation of the Upper Mississippi River System Environmental Management Program, as well as its efforts to preserve the Higgins' eye mussel. Even as the district pointed to these accomplishments, however, the Corps as a whole faced new questions about its commitment to environmental values following the Inspector General's investigation of the Corps' Upper Mississippi River-Illinois Waterway Navigation Study.

Outside of the Upper Mississippi River Environmental Management Program, the St. Paul District faced a decline in workload for civil works as large dam projects were curtailed – indeed, interrupted in mid-construction in the case of the La Farge Dam – due to environmental concerns. The district adjusted to the environmental era by developing a workload that involved smaller, more numerous, and less environmentally destructive projects. Communities continued to look to the Corps for assistance in flood control, but the district responded with measures that were more modest in scale. It also touted nonstructural solutions such as moving buildings out of the flood plain and modifying land uses so that communities were less exposed to flood damages. In the case of the La Farge Dam, the St. Paul District mothballed a project that had already cost $18 million and was forty percent complete. After several years of litigation, the Corps finally officially abandoned the project and mitigated its effects by assisting the State of Wisconsin and the Ho-Chunk Indian Nation in the development of a nature reserve on that section of the Kickapoo River.

Although the St. Paul District no longer proposed large dam and reservoir projects for flood control, it continued to respond to communities' requests for flood protection. Adapting to new cost-sharing approaches mandated by WRDA-86, the district worked successfully with cities such as Rochester, Minnesota, and Grand Forks/East Grand Forks on the North Dakota-Minnesota state line to construct flood control projects under elaborate cooperative agreements. Indeed, new federal guidelines required local communities to take greater initiative, and the district's protracted negotiations with the neighboring communities of Grand Forks/East Grand Forks demonstrated the increased level of public review and political coalition building that the Corps had to undertake in order to secure large civil works projects in this new era.

The environmental era posed new opportunities for the Corps, as well as challenges to its traditional mission of waterway improvements for navigation and flood control. The St. Paul District implemented new Corps' responsibilities with zeal, in part to take the place of civil works projects. After the Corps received the duty of regulating the nation's wetlands, for example, the St. Paul District pioneered a major innovation in the Section 404 program by revising regulatory boundaries to conform to state lines. This enabled the Corps to work in close cooperation with the Wisconsin and Minnesota DNRs on wetlands protection. With the aid of the states, the district improved public compliance with the regulatory program.

But the public did not readily associate the Corps with the protection of wetlands. Section 404 permitting was somewhat of a thankless task, for it incurred the irritation of many landowners and developers who saw excessive government red tape in the Corps' handling of tens of thousands of permits annually. Given the large number of wetlands under its jurisdiction and the strong inclination of farming communities to accept agricultural practices that harmed wetlands, the St. Paul District had an exceptional responsibility for environmental protection. Increasingly, the St. Paul District had to mediate differences between urban dwellers who valued biodiversity in the surrounding countryside and rural residents who wanted farmers to prosper even at the cost of destroying wetlands. The St. Paul District sought to balance these competing interests, or in Colonel Badger's telling phrase, to "swim in the middle of the river." In that way, the St. Paul District gained the public's respect, which ultimately helped the Corps win the public's support of a more regulatory environment.

Under the mandate of the National Historic Preservation Act of 1966, the St. Paul District vigorously implemented a cultural resources program and worked assiduously to maintain the district's own history. Using visitor centers, oral history programs and public outreach, the St. Paul District preserved its past and shared it with others. Even as the Corps struggled with the Advisory Council on Historic Preservation over Section 106 compliance on regulatory projects, the St. Paul District maintained a positive relationship with the Minnesota State Historic Preservation Office. At the same time, district archeologists effectively implemented the Section 106 program on civil works projects and worked with Native American groups to preserve their history and cultural resources.

Recreational use of reservoirs and other waterways under the Corps' management increased significantly in the last quarter of the twentieth century. Water sports gained popularity, boosting demand for public access to these areas even beyond the increases in recreational use that stemmed from population growth and rising affluence. Managing civil works projects for recreational use was not new to the St. Paul District, but it acquired more emphasis in the period since 1975. The recreation program was distinctive because it involved so much interaction with the general public. It entailed issues of public access and visitor safety, as well as outreach programs aimed at encouraging public enjoyment of Corps-built facilities. Public recreation was not as central to the Corps' mission as it was to an agency such as the National Park Service; yet with the amount of water resources under its control, the Corps had to respond to growing public demand for recreational opportunities. The St. Paul District maintained a number of parks connected with dams and reservoirs, and it cooperated with the National Park Service in the management of public recreational use in the Mississippi National River and Recreation Area.

Navigation: Kevin Reesie and James Marquardt test the ice thickness on the Mississippi River at Lake Pepin. (Photo by Mark Edlund, courtesy of St. Paul District, Corps of Engineers)

The region covered by the St. Paul District is susceptible to drought and flood, and the Corps participated in numerous disaster response actions. Notable flood fights included efforts to protect communities along the Red River in 1978, 1979, 1989 and 1997, and the response to the epic Midwest flood of 1993. St. Paul District personnel participated in disaster relief operations outside the district as well, notably in connection with war-stricken areas in the Middle East and in New York City, following the terrorist attack of September 11, 2001. During the past three decades, federal disaster relief efforts as a whole grew more costly and complex, raising issues about the role of the federal government in prevention and response. The Midwest floods in particular led to reevaluation of floodplain management.

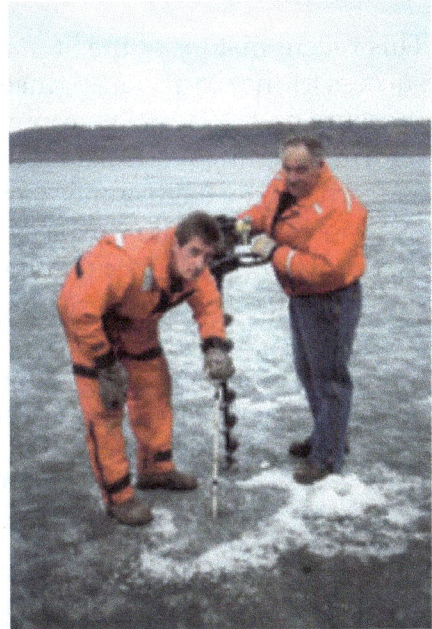

239

Like other districts, the St. Paul District reorganized itself and adopted new methods of operations, both internally and in its relations with other entities, in order to improve efficiency. Cost-sharing and project management were two salient programs. The uncertainty and confusion surrounding the reorganization of the Corps took a human toll, but it also produced bursts of creativity – as evidenced by several award-winning designs produced by the St. Paul District staff – and a stronger organization. In the area of human resources, a noteworthy accomplishment of the district was the number of women who had attained senior staff positions at the end of the twentieth century.

This recent history of the St. Paul District has emphasized two themes: the relative success of the Corps of Engineers in responding to environmentalism and the pressure on the Corps to adopt new business practices as part of a wider effort to reform federal government. Looking ahead, it appears likely that both the public concern for the environment and the search for efficiencies in government will continue to dominate Corps' administration in the next few decades of the twenty-first century. The Corps will be involved with two key environmental concerns in the future: climate change resulting from global warming and pressures on land use from continuing population growth. Long-range projections of the national debt suggest there will be a continuing struggle over the federal budget. The St. Paul District will no doubt face challenges, but these are challenges that it has capably handled during the past twenty-five years.

Acronyms

BRAC	Base Realignment and Closure
CARP	Concerned About River People
DNR	Department of Natural Resources
EIS	Environmental Impact Statement
EMP	Upper Mississippi River System Environmental Management Program
FEMA	Federal Emergency Management Administration
FTE	Full-time Equivalent
GREAT	Great River Environmental Action Team
HQUSACE	Headquarters Division, U. S. Army Corps of Engineers
IJC	International Joint Commission
NEPA	National Environmental Policy Act
ROPE	Reservoir Operating Plan Evaluation
SHPO	Minnesota State Historic Preservation Office
TCPs	Traditional Cultural Properties

District Commanders
1976 - 2007

NAME	YEARS OF COMMAND
Colonel Michael J. Price	2010 -
Colonel Jon L. Christensen	2007 - 2010
Colonel Michael F. Pfenning	2004 - 2007
Lt. Colonel Thomas E. O'Hara	2004
Colonel Robert L. Ball	2001 - 2004
Colonel Kenneth S. Kasprisin	1998 - 2001
Lt. Colonel William J. Breyfogle	1998
Colonel J. M. Wonsik	1995 - 1998
Colonel James T. Scott	1993 - 1995
Colonel Richard W. Craig	1991 - 1993
Colonel Roger L. Baldwin	1988 - 1991
Colonel Joseph Briggs	1985 - 1988
Colonel Edward G. Rapp	1982 - 1985
Colonel William W. Badger	1979 - 1982
Colonel Forrest T. Gay III	1976 - 1979

Bibliography

Caldwell, Lynton Keith. *The National Environmental Policy Act: An Agenda for the Future.* Bloomington, IN: Indiana University Press, 1998.

Carter, Jimmy. *Keeping Faith: Memoirs of a President.* New York: Bantam Books, 1982.

Clarke, Jeanne Nienaber, and Daniel McCool. *Staking out the Terrain: Power Differentials among Natural Resource Management Agencies.* Albany, NY: State University of New York Press, 1985.

Clement, Thomas M., Jr., and Glenn Lopez. *Engineering a Victory for our Environment: A Citizen's Guide to the U.S. Army Corps of Engineers.* Prepared by The Institute for the Study of Health and Society for the Environmental Protection Agency. Washington, D.C.: Government Printing Office, 1972.

Current, Richard N. *Wisconsin: A Bicentennial History.* New York: W. Norton & Company, Inc. 1977.

Garland, John H., ed. *The North American Midwest: A Regional Geography.* New York: John Wiley & Sons, Inc. 1955.

Hays, Samuel P. *Beauty, Health and Permanence: Environmental Politics in the United States, 1955-85.* New York: Cambridge University Press, 1987.

Lass, William E. *Minnesota: A Bicentennial History.* New York: W.W. Norton & Company, 1977.

Mazmanian, Daniel A., and Jeanne Nienaber. *Can Organizations Change? Environmental Protection, Citizen Participation, and the Corps of Engineers.* Washington, D.C.: The Brookings Institute, 1979.

Moore, Jamie W. and Dorothy P. Moore. *The Army Corps of Engineers and the Evolution of Federal Flood Plain Management Policy.* Boulder: Insitute of Behavioral Science, University of Colorado, 1989.

Murrin, John M., Paul E. Johnson, James M. McPherson, et al. *Liberty Equality Power: A History of the American People. Volume II: Since 1863*. Concise 2d ed. Fort Worth, TX.: Harcourt College Publishers, 2001.

Taylor, Serge. Making Bureaucracies *Think: The Environmental Impact Statement Strategy of Administrative Reform*. Stanford: Stanford University Press, 1984.

Thompson, Stephen A. *Water Use, Management, and Planning in the United States*. San Diego, CA: Academic Press, 1999.

Twain, Mark. *Life on the Mississippi*. Boston: James R. Osgood and Company, 1883.

Vileisis, Ann. *Discovering the Unknown Landscape: A History of America's Wetlands*. Washington, D.C.: Island Press, 1997.

Wallace, Mike. *Mickey Mouse History and Other Essays on American Memory*. Philadelphia: Temple University Press, 1996.

Articles and Chapters in Books, Journals and Magazines

"The 1990 Farm Bill." *Soil and Water Conservation News* 12, no. 1 (May-June 1991): 4-6.

Ablard, Charles D. and Brian Boru O'Neill. "Wetland Protection and Section 404 of the Federal Water Pollution Control Act Amendments of 1972: A Corps of Engineers Renaissance." *Vermont Law Review* 1 (1976): pp. 51-115.

Baram, Michael S. "Cost-Benefit Analysis: An Inadequate Basis for Health, Safety, and Environmental Regulatory Rulemaking." *Ecology Law Quarterly* 8 (No. 3, 1980): pp. 473-531.

Bernstein, Peter J. "Here Come the Dredgers! Sneak Attack on the Wetlands." *The Nation* 225 (10 December 1977): pp. 614-618.

Blumm, Michael C. "The Clean Water Act's Section 404 Permit Program Enters Its Adolescence: An Institutional and Programmatic Perspective." *Ecology Law Quarterly* 8 (1980): pp. 409-471.

Bowen, Michael. "What's Wrong with Mitigation Banks?" *The Military Engineer* 573 (October/November 1995): pp. 19-21.

"The Civilian Side of the U.S. Army: The Corps of Engineers." *Ms.* 11 (September 1982): p. 77.

"Company attempts to reopen Crandon Mine." *Mining Engineering* (February 1999): p. 12.

"Corps Finds Itself in Middle of a Heated Policy Debate." *ENR* 225 (26 July 1993): p. 14.

"Cost-Benefit Trips Up the Corps." *Business Week* (19 February 1979): pp. 96-97.

Cushman, David W. "When Worlds Collide: Indians, Archeologists, and the Preservation of Traditional Cultural Properties." *CRM* 16 (1993 Special Issue—Traditional Cultural Properties): pp. 49-51.

Griebenow, George W. "A Team Called Great." *Water Spectrum* 9, No. 1 (Winter 1976-77): pp. 18-25.

Harrison, Jean. "The Corps' Stake in Recreation." *Parks and Recreation* 10 (March 1975): pp. 1b-8b.

Kahn, James. "History Takes a Step Forward." *Water Spectrum* 7 (Fall 1975): pp. 39-45.

Lamm-Carroll, Jane. "Dams and Damages." *Minnesota History* (Spring 1990): pp. 4-15.

Lee, Antoinette J. "Recognizing Cultural Heritage in the National Historic Preservation Program." *CRM* 16 (1993 Special Issue—Traditional Cultural Properties): pp. 7-8.

Leitch, Jay A. "Politicoeconomic Overview of Prairie Potholes." In *Northern Prairie Wetlands*, edited by Arnold Van Der Valk. Pp. 4-12. Ames: Iowa State University Press, 1989.

"The Mississippi River: The 20th Century's Grand Canal?" *Outdoor America* 37 (September 1972): pp. 1, 3.

Reeves, Richard. "Hurricane$, Earthquake$, and Flood$: If People Want to Build Their Houses in Dangerous Places, Why Should the Rest of Us Pay When Disaster Strikes?" *The Washington Monthly* 26 (April 1994): pp. 10-13.

Reuss, Martin. "Coping with Uncertainty: Social Scientists, Engineers, and Federal Water Resources Planning." *Natural Resources Journal* 32 (Winter 1992): 101-135.

Robinson, Michael C. "Nightmare in the Heartland: The Great Midwest Flood of 1993." APWA (American Public Works Association) *Reporter* 60 (September 1993): pp. 6-7.

Schneider, Saundra K. "FEMA, Federalism, Hugo, and 'Frisco." *Publius: The Journal of Federalism* 20 (Summer 1990): pp. 97-115.

Silberman, Edward. "Public Participation in Water Resource Development." *Journal of the Water Resources Planning and Management Division* 103 (May 1977): pp. 111-123.

Slade, Steve. "Army Corps of Engineers: Caught in Midstream." *The Nation* 221 (September 6, 1975): 179-181.

Steinberg, Bory. "The Federal Perspective." In *Water Resources Administration in the United States: Policy, Practice, and Emerging Issues.* Ed. Martin Reuss. Pp. 264-273. East Lansing: Michigan State University Press, 1993.

Stine, Jeffrey K. "Regulating Wetlands in the 1970s: The U.S. Army Corps of Engineers and the Environmental Organizations." *Journal of Forest History* 27 (April 1983): pp. 60-75.

Tenenbaum, David. "Rethinking the River." *Nature Conservancy* 44 (July/August 1994): pp. 11-15.

Upbin, Bruce. "A River of Subsidies." *Forbes* 161 (23 March 1998): p. 86.

"Walton League Opposes Dredge and Fill Projects on Upper Mississippi River." *Outdoor America* 37 (January 1972): p. 9.

Weist, Katherine. "For the Public Good: Native Americans, Hydroelectric Dams, and the Iron Triangle." In *Trusteeship in Change: Toward Tribal Autonomy in Resource Management.* Edited by Richmond L. Clow and Imre Sutton. Pp. 55-72. Boulder: University Press of Colorado, 2001.

"Who Benefits in Reform of Wetlands Laws," *Science News* 122 (24 July 1982): 56.

Williams, Arthur E. "The Role of Technology in Sustainable Development." In *Water Resources Administration in the United States: Policy, Practice, and Emerging Issues.* Ed. Martin Reuss. Pp. 120-129. East Lansing: Michigan State University Press, 1993.

Williams, Ted. "Trouble on the Mississippi." *Audubon* 102 (July/August 2000): pp. 36-45.

Zeldin, Marvin. "Corps' New Look in Flood Control: No Dams, Levees." *Audubon* 77 (July 1975): pp. 103-104.

Zeldin, Marvin. "Souris: Mouse That Roars." *Audubon* 78 (November 1976): pp. 135-138.

GovernmentPublications

Act of 28 June 1955 (69 Stat. 186).

Act of 7 March 1974 (88 Stat. 12).

Act of 20 June 1977 (91 Stat. 233).

Act of 23 November 1988 (102 Stat. 4689).

Bhowmik, Nani G. and Ta Wei Soong. *Waves Generated by Recreational Traffic: Part I, Controlled Movement.* Champaign, IL: Illinois State Water Survey, 1992.

Disaster Relief Act of 1974 (88 Stat. 143).

Eggers, Steve D. and Donald M. Reed. *Wetland Plants and Plant Communities.* St. Paul, MN: U.S. Army Corps of Engineers, 1987.

Federal Emergency Management Agency. *Federal Response Plan.* 9230.1-PL. Washington, D.C.: Federal Emergency Management Agency, 1999.

GREAT I Plan of Study, Upper Mississippi River (Head of Navigation to Guttenburg, Iowa). N.p., n.d.

Great River Environmental Action Team. *GREAT I: Recreation, Work Group Appendix – Upper Mississippi River* (Head of Navigation to Guttenberg, Iowa). Des Moines, IA: Great River Environmental Action Team, 1979.

Interagency Floodplain Management Review Committee. Sharing the Challenge: *Floodplain Management into the 21st Century.* Washington, D.C.: Government Printing Office, 1994.

Kanefield, Adina W. Federal Historic Preservation Case Law, 1966-1996: *Thirty Years of the National Historic Preservation Act.* Washington, D.C.: Advisory Council on Historic Preservation, 1996.

McDonnell, Janet A. *After Desert Storm: The U.S. Army and the Reconstruction of Kuwait.* Washington, D.C.: Department of the Army, 1999.

_____. *Response to the Loma Prieta Earthquake.* Fort Belvoir, Virginia: U.S. Army Corps of Engineers, 1993.

Merritt, Raymond H. *The Corps, the Environment, and the Upper Mississippi River Basin.* Washington, D.C.: Historical Division, Office of Administrative Services, Office of the Chief of Engineers, 1984.

_____. *Creativity, Conflict & Controversy: A History of the St. Paul District, U.S. Army Corps of Engineers.* Washington, D.C.: Government Printing Office, 1979.

Mighetto, Lisa, and William F. Willingham. *Service – Tradition – Change: A History of the Fort Worth District, U.S. Army Corps of Engineers, 1975-1999.* Fort Worth, TX: U.S. Army Corps of Engineers, 2000.

Minnesota Department of Natural Resources. *Mississippi River Bank Erosion and Boating: Facts and Solutions.* St. Paul, MN: Minnesota Department of Natural Resources, 1993.

Native American Intergovernmental Relations Task Force. *Assessment of Corps/Tribal Intergovernmental Relations.* IWR Report 96-R-6a. Washington: U.S. Army Corps of Engineers, 1996.

O'Brien, William Patrick, Mary Yeater Rathbun, and Patrick O'Bannon. *Gateways to Commerce: The U.S. Army Corps of Engineers' 9-Foot Channel Project on the Upper Mississippi River.* Ed. Christine Whitacre. Denver: National Park Service, Rocky Mountain Region, 1992.

Reuss, Martin. Reshaping *National Water Politics: The Emergence of the Water Resources Development Act of 1986.* Fort Belvoir, Va.: U.S. Army Corps of Engineers, Institute for Water Resources, 1991.

_____. Shaping Environmental Awareness: *The United States Army Corps of Engineers Environmental Advisory Board, 1970-1980.* Washington, D.C.: Historical Division, Office of Administrative Services, Office of the Chief of Engineers, 1983.

River Resources Forum Recreation Work Group. *Recreation Use Profiles: Upper Mississippi River Pools 7 and 8.* La Crosse, WI: Wisconsin Department of Natural Resources, 1996.

Tiner, Ralph W., Jr. *Wetlands of the United States: Current Status and Recent Trends.* Washington, D.C.: Government Printing Office, 1984.

U.S. Army Corps of Engineers. *Upper Mississippi River System Environmental Management Program: Sixth Annual Addendum.* Chicago: U.S. Army Corps of Engineers, 1991.

U.S. Army Corps of Engineers, Missouri River Division. *Water Resources Development in North Dakota 1991.* Omaha, NE: U.S. Army Corps of Engineers, Missouri River Division, 1991.

U.S. Army Corps of Engineers, Office of the Chief of Engineers. *Engineer Profiles: The District Engineer, Interviews with Colonel William W. Badger.* Interviews by Frank N. Schubert. Washington, D.C.: U.S. Army Corps of Engineers, 1983.

U.S. Army Corps of Engineers, North Central Division. *Upper Mississippi River System Environmental Management Program, Sixth Annual Addendum.* Chicago: U.S. Army Corps of Engineers, North Central Division, 1991.

_____. *Water Resources Development in Minnesota 1995.* Chicago: North Central Division, 1995.

_____. *Water Resources Development by the U.S. Army Corps of Engineers in Wisconsin.* Chicago: North Central Division, 1979.

U.S. Army Corps of Engineers, Rock Island District, St. Louis District, St. Paul District. *Upper Mississippi River-Illinois Waterway System Navigation Study: Responses to Issues Raised at the Public and NEPA Scoping Meetings of November 1994, Interim Product.* Washington, D.C.[?]: U.S. Army Corps of Engineers, 1995.

U.S. Army Corps of Engineers, St. Paul District. *After Action Report: Spring 1997 Flood in the Red River of the North Basin, Minnesota River Basin and Mississippi River Basin*. St. Paul, MN: U.S. Army Corps of Engineers, St. Paul District, 1997.

_____. *After Action Report: Summer 1993 Flooding in the Upper Mississippi Basin and Red River of the North Basin*. St. Paul, MN: U.S. Army Corps of Engineers, St. Paul District, 1993.

_____. *Devils Lake Feasibility Study: Concept-Level Plan of Study*. St. Paul, MN: U.S. Army Corps of Engineers, St. Paul District, 1995.

_____. *Devils Lake, North Dakota, Contingency Plan*. St. Paul, MN: U.S. Army Corps of Engineers, St. Paul District, 1996.

_____. *Draft General Reevaluation Report and Environmental Impact Statement, East Grand Forks, Minnesota and Grand Forks, North Dakota*. St. Paul, MN: U.S. Army Corps of Engineers, St. Paul District, 1998.

_____. *Draft Revised Environmental Impact Statement, Flood Control and Related Purposes, South Fork Zumbro River Watershed, Rochester, Olmsted County, Minnesota*. St. Paul, MN: U.S. Army Corps of Engineers, St. Paul District, 1976.

_____. *Emergency Outlet Plan: Devils Lake, North Dakota*. St. Paul, MN: U.S. Army Corps of Engineers, St. Paul District, 1996.

_____. *GREAT I Implementation Status Report and Future Program*. St. Paul, MN: U.S. Army Corps of Engineers, St. Paul District, 1992.

_____. *Implementation for GREAT I Study*. St. Paul, MN: St. Paul District, U.S. Army Corps of Engineers, 1981.

_____. *Interpretive Prospectus: Morgan J. Tschida Visitor Center, Upper St. Anthony Falls Lock and Dam*. St. Paul, MN: U.S. Army Corps of Engineers, St. Paul District, 1995.

_____. *Operation and Maintenance Manual: Section 205 Flood Control Project, Devils Lake, North Dakota*. St. Paul, MN: U.S. Army Corps of Engineers, St. Paul District, 1992.

_____. *A Public Trust: An Executive Summary of GREAT I*. St. Paul, MN: U.S. Army Corps of Engineers, St. Paul District, n.d.

_____. *Red River of the North Post Flood Report, 1978*. St. Paul, MN: U.S. Army Corps of Engineers, St. Paul District, 1978.

_____. *Red River of the North and Souris River Post Flood Report: 1979*. St. Paul, MN: U.S. Army Corps of Engineers, St. Paul District, 1979.

_____. *Special Report: Reevaluation of La Farge Dam, Kickapoo River Valley, Wisconsin, Dry Dam and Wet Dam Alternatives*. St. Paul, MN: U.S. Army Corps of Engineers, St. Paul District, 1984.

_____. *Spring Flood 89: Red River of the North After Action Report*. St. Paul, MN: U.S. Army Corps of Engineers, St. Paul District, 1989.

_____. *Spring 2001 Flood in the Red River of the North, Minnesota River and Mississippi River Basins: After Action Report*. St. Paul, MN: U.S. Army Corps of Engineers, St. Paul District, 2001.

U.S. Army Corps of Engineers, Water Resources Support Center. "The Ports of Duluth, MN and Superior, WI; Taconite Harbor, Silver Bay, and Two Harbors, MN; and Ashland, WI." Port Series No. 49. Washington, D.C.: Government Printing Office, 2000.

U.S. Conference of Mayors Special Committee on Historic Preservation. *With Heritage So Rich*. New York: Random House, 1966; reprint, Washington, D.C.: The Preservation Press, 1983.

U.S. Congress. House. Committee on Public Works and Transportation, Investigation and Oversight Subcommittee. U.S. Army Corps of Engineers Proposed Reorganization Plan. 103d Cong., 1st sess., 1993. Serial 103-23.

_____. Proposed Legislation: "Government Reform and Savings Act of 1993," Message from the President of the United States. 103rd Cong., 1st sess., H. Doc. 103-155, 1993.

_____. Committee on Appropriations, Energy and Water Development Subcommittee. Energy and Water Development Appropriations for 2000, Part 1, 106th Cong., 1st sess., 1999.

_____. Committee on Interior and Insular Affairs, National Parks and Public Lands Subcommittee. Miscellaneous National Park Issues: Hearings Before the Subcommittee on National Parks and Public Lands of the Committee on Interior and Insular Affairs, House of Representatives. 100th Cong., 1st and 2d sess., 1987-1988.

_____. Committee on Public Works and Transportation, Oversight and Review Subcommittee. Flooding of the Red River of the North and Its Tributaries: Hearing Before the Subcommittee on Oversight and Review of the Committee on Public Works and Transportation,House of Representatives, Ninety-Sixth Congress, First Session. 96th Cong., 1st sess., 1979.

_____. Committee on Public Works and Transportation, Water Resources and Environment Subcommittee. The Water Resources Development Act of 1994 and Issues Related to Reauthorization of the Civil Works Program of the U.S. Army Corps of Engineers: Hearings Before the Subcommittee on Water Resources and Environment of the Committee on Public Works and Transportation, House of Representatives. 103d Cong., 2d sess., 1994.

_____. Committee on Public Works and Transportation, Water Resources Subcommittee. Status of the Nation's Wetlands and Laws Related Thereto, Hearing before the Subcommittee. 101st Cong., 1st and 2d sess., 14 April 1989.

_____. Committee on Transportation and Infrastructure, Water Resources and Environment Subcommittee. Proposals for a Water Resources Development Act of 1998: Hearings Before the Subcommittee on Water Resources and Environment of the Committee on Transportation and Infrastructure, House of Representatives. 105th Cong., 2d sess., 1998.

_____. Committee on Public Works and Transportation, Water Resources Subcommittee. Water Resources Development—1976: Hearings Before the Subcommittee on Water Resources of the Committee on Public Works and Transportation, House of Representatives. 94th Cong., 2d sess., 1976.

_____. Committee on Public Works and Transportation, Water Resources Subcommittee. Water Resources Development Act of 1978: Hearings Before the Subcommittee on Water Resources of the Committee on Public Works and Transportation, House of Representatives. 95th Cong., 2d sess., 1978.

_____. Committee on Public Works and Transportation, Water Resources Subcommittee. Water Resources Development Act of 1992 and the Reorganization of the U.S. Army Corps of Engineers. 102d Cong., 2d sess., 1992.

_____. Committee on Public Works and Transportation, Water Resources Subcommittee. Water Resources Development—Cost-Sharing Aspects of President's Water Policy Initiatives: Hearings Before the Subcommittee on Water Resources of the Committee on Public Works and Transportation, House of Representatives. 96th Cong., 1st sess., 1979.

U.S. Congress. Senate. Committee on Appropriations. Energy and Water Development Appropriations Fiscal Year 1994. 103d Cong., 1st sess., S. Hrg. 103-299, Part 1, May 1993.

_____. Committee on Environment and Public Works. Reorganization of the Corps of Engineers, Hearing before the Committee on Environment and Public Works. 102d Cong., 2d sess., 30 December 1992.

_____. Committee on Environment and Public Works, Clean Air, Wetlands, Private Property and Nuclear Safety Subcommittee. Wetlands: Review of Regulatory Changes: Hearing before the Subcommittee. 105th Cong., 1st sess., 26 June 1997.

_____. Committee on Energy and Natural Resources, Public Lands, National Parks and Forests Subcommittee. Miscellaneous Parks and Public Lands Measures: Hearing Before the Subcommittee on Public Lands, National Parks and Forests of the Committee on Energy and Natural Resources, United States Senate. 100th Cong., 2d sess., 1988.

U.S. Department of the Interior. Federal Historic Preservation Laws. Washington, D.C.: U.S. Department of the Interior, 1993.

U.S. Senate. Disaster Relief Act Amendments of 1988. 100th Cong., 2d sess., 1988. S. Rept. 100-524. Serial 13866.

Upper Mississippi River Basin Commission. Upper Mississippi River Basin Commission Annual Report/Fiscal Year 1979. N.p., n.d.

Upper Mississippi River Basin Coordinating Committee. Upper Mississippi River Comprehensive Basin Study Main Report. Chicago: Upper Mississippi River Basin Coordinating Committee, 1972.

PeriodicalsandNewspapers

Antigo _Journal._

Benson _Monitor._

Bismarck _Tribune._

Brownton _Bulletin._

Capital Times (Madison, WI).

Christian Science Monitor.

Courier Press (Prairie du Chien, WI).

Crosscurrents.

Daily Tribune (Wisconsin Rapids, WI).

Detroit Lakes *Tribune.*

Devils Lake Journal.

Devils Lake *Outlet EIS Newsletter.*

Duluth *Herald.*

Duluth *News-Tribune.*

Forest *Republican.*

The Forum (Fargo, ND).

Glencoe *Enterprise.*

Grand Forks Herald.

Hancock *Record.*

News (La Crescent, MN).

Houston *Signal* (MN).

Kansas City *Star.*

La Crosse Tribune.

The Land (Mankato, MN).

Litchfield *Independent Review.*

Los Angeles *Times.*

Maplewood *Review.*

Minneapolis *Tribune.*

Minot Daily News.

Milwaukee *Journal Sentinel.*

Morris *Tribune.*

News-Tribune (Minneapolis, MN).

Post-Bulletin (Rochester, MN).

Quad-City Times (IA).

Red Wing *Republican Eagle.*

The Reorganization Wrap-Up.

Rhinelander *Daily News.*

St. Paul *Pioneer Press.*

Star Tribune (Minneapolis, MN).

Tribune (Granite Falls, MN).

USA Today.

Valley City *Times-Record.*

Vernon County Broadcaster.

Washington Post.

Winona Daily News.

Wisconsin State Journal.

UnpublishedManuscripts

Anfinson, John O. Memorandum for Robert F. Post, Chief, Engineering and Planning Division, 31 March 1994. Document provided by John O. Anfinson, Mississippi National River and Recreation Area, National Park Service.

_____. "Oral Interviews: The Significance of Grand Portage Bay to the Grand Portage Chippewa Band." Memorandum provided by John O. Anfinson, Mississippi National River Recreation Area, National Park Service.

Cleland, Charles, Larry Nesper, and Joshua Cleland. "The Potential Cultural Impact of the Development of the Crandon Mine on the Indian Communities of Northeastern Wisconsin." Report prepared under contract with the Sokaogon Band of Chippewa, The Menominee Tribe of Wisconsin, and the Forest County Potawatomi in cooperation with The Great Lakes Indian Fish and Wildlife Commission in behalf of the Lake Superior Chippewa, 15 February 1995.

Crist, Charles E. Memorandum for Robert F. Post, Chief, Engineering and Planning Division. 31 March 1994. Document provided by John Anfinson, Mississippi National River and Recreation Area, National Park Service.

Johannessen, Sissel. "Notes on NAGPRA, 28 May 2003." Document provided by Sissel Johannessen, St. Paul District.

Merritt, Raymond H. "New Directions: Transitions in the St. Paul District, Corps of Engineers, 1976-1982." Unpublished manuscript, St. Paul District.

Moorhus, Donita M., and Gregory Graves. "The Limits of Vision: A History of the U.S. Army Corps of Engineers 1988-1992." Unpublished manuscript, January 1999, Office of the Chief of Engineers, Office of History, Washington, D.C.

Pursell, Carroll, and William Willingham. "Protecting the Nation's Waters: A History of the U.S. Army Corps of Engineers' Regulatory Responsibilities 1899-1999." Draft report, February 1999, Office of the Chief of Engineers, Office of History, Washington, D.C.

"Rochester, Minnesota, Flood Control Project." Document provided by Russel K. Snyder, St. Paul District.

"Shoreline Management Plan." Document provided by Richard Otto, St. Paul District. U.S. Army Corps of Engineers, St. Paul District. "Draft April 2002, Definite Project Report and

Environmental Assessment for Relocation Plan for the Endangered Higgins' Eye Pearlymussel (*Lampsilis higginsii*)." Manuscript provided by Dennis Anderson, St. Paul District.

_____. "Fact Sheet: Emergency Operations Overview." 23 March 1999. Document provided by David S. Christenson, St. Paul District.

_____. "Information Paper, Subject: Proposed De-authorization of the La Farge Dam Project." 24 July 1995. Document provided by Richard J. Otto, St. Paul District.

Web Sources

Advisory Council on Historic Preservation. "Section 106 Regulations (Effective 11 January 2001)." 36 CFR Part 800. <http://www.achp.gov/regs.html> (6 June 2003).

"Background on Wetland/Public Waters Issues." <http.//www.bwsr.state.mn.us / wetlands/wca/history.html> (October 2002).

"Capitol Hill Hearing Testimony Before the Senate Committee on Environment and Public Works." 23 October 1997. <http://80-web.lexis-nexis.com.weblib.lib.umt.edu:2048 / congcomp/doclist?_m=93b5adbc8842f4b5195e90c4089832a6&wchp=dGLbVtblSlAA&_ md5=1b 43b30249f4dc0c255868433d87b1b6> (6 June 2003).

Congressional Record. 105th Cong., 1st sess., 24 April 1997. <http://80-web.lexis-nexis. com. weblib.lib.umt.edu:2048/congcomp/document?_m=cfec99d7fffd8c93d0d4c2edf6534444&_ docnum=12&wchp=dGLbVzz-lSlAA&_md5=b90242eb6e5e744703d50b29ff1e2954> (6 June 2003).

Department of the Army Permit GP-01-WI. <http//www.mvp.usace.army.mil / regulatory/proposals/gp01wi98.pdf> (September 2002).

"Draft Summary Document for the Report to Congress on the Emergency Outlet from Devils Lake, ND to the Sheyenne River." Congressional Record Online via GPO Access 145 (June 28, 1999): pp. S7689-S7690. <http://frwebgate3.access.gpo.gov/cgibin/waisgate.cgi?WAI SdocID=22390328907+0+0+0&WAISaction=retrieve> (1 November 2002).

Dyhouse, Gary R. "Myths and Misconceptions of the 1993 Flood." <http://www.mvs. usace. army.mil/dinfo/pa/fl93info.htm> (6 June 2003).

Federal Emergency Management Agency. "FEMA History." <http://www.fema.gov/ about/history.shtm> (6 June 2003).

Garrison Diversion Conservancy District. "Abbreviated History, 1944-2001." <http:// www.garrisondiv.org/info/history.shtml> (6 June 2003).

"Garrison Diversion and the Devils Lake Outlet: The Canadian Position." <http:// www.canadianembassy.org/environment/garrison-e.asp> (6 June 2003).

Kaplan, Elaine. U.S. Office of Special Counsel. Letter to The President, 6 December 2000. <http://www.osc.gov/reading.htm> (1 November 2002).

Kasprisin, Kenneth. Memorandum 10-1-1, 26 January 2001. <http://mvpiis/RMOffice / docs/Mission Statement.

"Land and Water Conservation Fund Act of 1965." Public Law 88-578. <http://www. house.gov/resources/105cong/reports/105_a/lwcf65_.pdf> (6 June 2003).

McConnell, David. "Mississippi River Flood: 1993." <http://enterprise.cc.uakron.edu/ geology/natscigeo/Lectures/streams/Miss_Flood.pdf> (6 June 2003).

Middleton, Pat. "The Clam Lady of America's Rivers: Marian Havlik." <http://www. greatriver.com/clam.htm> (6 June 2003).

Minnesota Board of Water and Soil Resources. "1999/2000 Minnesota Wetland Report." October 2001. <http//www/bwsr.state.mn.us/wetlands> (September 2002).

Minnesota Historical Society. "Railroad Properties: Stone Arch Bridge (in the St. Anthony Falls Historic District)." <http://nrhp.mnhs.org/property_overview.cfm? propertyID=79> (6 June 2003).

Mississippi Whitewater Park Development Corporation. "Who We Are." <http://www. whitewaterpark.canoe-kayak.org/MWPDC_Info.html> (6 June 2003).

Parker, Patricia L. and Thomas F. King, "Guidelines for Evaluating and Documenting Traditional Cultural Properties." *National Register Bulletin* 38. <http://www.cr.nps.gov/nr/ publications/bulletins/nrb38> (6 June 2003).

Prepared statement of Lt. General Joe N. Ballard, Chief of Engineers, U.S. Army Corps of Engineers, before the Senate Appropriations Committee Subcommittee on Energy and Water Development, April 24, 1997. <http://web.lexis-nexis.com> (September 2002).

Public Law 84-99. Emergency Flood Control Work. <http://www.orn.usace.army.mil/ pmgt/customer/Water%20Supply/pl84-99.htm> (10 May 2003).

Public Law 100-696. 18 November 1988. <http://80-web.lexis-nexis.com.weblib.lib.umt. edu:2048/congcomp/document?_m=9815b4f857438c030d4436e3483e4ab2&_docnum=1&wch p=dGLbVtz-lSlAA&_md5=0fb6b5db5ee9e907aec0087c936ceb6d> (6 June 2003).

Public Law 105-18. 12 June 1997. <http://frwebgate.access.gpo.gov/cgi-bin/getdoc. cgi?dbname=105_cong_public_laws&docid=f:publ18.105> (6 June 2003).

Pye v. United States of America. No. 98-2229, U.S. 4th Circuit Court of Appeals, 22 October 2001. <http://caselaw.lp.findlaw.com/scripts/getcase.pl?navby=search&case =/ data2/circs/4th/982229p.html> (6 June 2003).

Restructured Upper Mississippi River-Illinois Waterway Navigation Study. "Interim Report— Executive Summary." <http://www2.mvr.usace.army.mil/umriwwsns/documents/ IR072502ES.pdf> (6 June 2003).

"Statement of Gary L. Pearson on Behalf of the Dakota Prairie Audubon Society Submitted at the Hearing of the Committee on Environment and Public Works, United States Senate, Regarding the Proposal to Construct An Emergency Outlet from Devils Lake to the Sheyenne River in North Dakota." 23 October 1997. <http://80-web.lexisnexis.com. weblib.lib.umt.edu:2048/congcomp/document?_m=7701530145029adf8c74d315780642db&_ docnum=7&wchp=dGLbVtb-lSlAA&_md5= 259852c2189ade895507a0b950f5775d> (6 June 2003).

"Testimony of Michael J. Armstrong, Associate Director for Mitigation, Federal Emergency Management Agency, Before the Senate Committee on the Environment and Public Works Regarding the Devils Lake Basin Interagency Task Force." 23 October 1997.

<http://80- web.lexis-nexis.com.weblib.lib.umt.edu:2048/congcomp/document?_m= 7701530145029adf8c74d315780642db&_docnum=6&wchp=dGLbVtb-lSlAA&_md5= 5fc5961bbd2a9b8660cc98d187ad88aa> (6 June 2003).

"Transcript of Clinton Remarks April 22 in Briefing on Flood Damage by Local Officials." U.S. Newswire (23 April 1997). <http://80-infoweb.newsbank.com.weblib.lib.umt. edu:2048/ iwsearch/we/InfoWeb?p_action doc&p_docid=0F4B14C2F3529A73&p_ docnum=4&p_nbid=J54 S54QNMTA1NDkyOTA3OC40NjYxNDk6MTo3OjE1MC4xMzE> (6 June 2003).

U.S. Army Corps of Engineers. "33 CFR Part 325, Appendix C—Procedures for the Protection of Historic Properties." <http://www.usace.army.mil/inet/functions /cw/cecwo/ reg/33cfr325.htm#appendixC> (6 June 2003).

U.S. Army Corps of Engineers. "Emergency Employment of Army and Other Resources: Civil Emergency Management Program." Engineer Regulation No. 500-1-1. 30 September 2001. <http://www.usace.army.mil/publications/eng-regs/er500-1-1/entire.pdf> (6 June 2003).

U.S. Army Corps of Engineers. "Oleoresin Capsicum (Pepper Spray) Program." Engineer Circular No. 1130-2-214. 22 April 2002. <http://www.usace.army.mil/publications/ eng-circulars/ec1130-2-214/entire.pdf> (6 June 2003).

U.S. Army Corps of Engineers. "Recreation." http://www.usace.army.mil/public.html# Recreation (6 June 2003).

U.S. Army Corps of Engineers. "Recreation Operations and Maintenance Policies." Engineering Regulation No. 1130-2-550. <http://www.usace.army.mil/publications/engregs/ er1130-2-550/entire.pdf> (6 June 2003).

U.S. Army Corps of Engineers. "Reservations at Federal Recreation Facilities." <http:// www.usace.army.mil/inet/recreation> (6 June 2003).

U.S. Army Corps of Engineers. "Visitor Assistance: Program Summary." <http:// corpslakes.usace.army.mil/employees/visitassist/pback.html> (6 June 2003).

U.S. Army Corps of Engineers, Mississippi Valley Division. "Mississippi Valley Division Devils Lake Division/District (Tiger) Team Technical Report, June 1999, Executive Summary." <http://www.swc.state.nd.us/projects/pdf/ExecSum.pdf> (6 June 2003).

U.S. Army Corps of Engineers, Rock Island District. "Frequently Asked Questions." Restructured Upper Mississippi River-Illinois Waterway Navigation Study. <http://www2. mvr.usace.army.mil/umr-iwwsns/index.cfm?fuseaction=home.faq> (6 June 2003).

U.S. Army Corps of Engineers, Rock Island District. "The Great Flood of 1993 Post-Flood Report," <http://www.mvr.usace.army.mil/PublicAffairsOffice/HistoricArchives / Floodof1993/pafr.htm> (6 June 2003).

U.S. Army Corps of Engineers, St. Paul District. "Annual Day Passes Available for 2003 Recreation Season at Corps of Engineers Parks." Press Release, 18 November 2002. <http:// www.mvp.usace.army.mil/finder/display.asp?pageid=541> (6 June 2003).

_____. "Corps of Engineers Opens Most Lock and Dam Visitor Centers Along the Mississippi River." Press Release, 10 May 2002. <http://www.mvp.usace.army.mil/ pressroom/default.asp?pageid=329> (6 June 2003).

_____. "Corps Reveals Draft Plan to Revive Endangered Mussel Species." Press Release, 18 April 2002. <http://www.mvp.usace.army.mil/news_media/news/PA-2002-0046.htm> (1 November 2002).

_____. "Devils Lake Basin, North Dakota." <http://www.mvp.usace.army.mil/fl_damage_ reduct/default.asp?pageid=14> (6 June 2003).

_____. "Devils Lake Levee, North Dakota," <http://www.mvp.usace.army.mil/fl_damage_ reduct/default.asp?pageid=31> (6 June 2003).

_____. "Effects of Recreational Boating on the Upper Mississippi River System." <http://www.mvp.usace.army.mil/finder/display.asp?pageid=187> (6 June 2003).

_____. "Final Environmental Impact Statement, Flood Control, East Grand Forks, Minnesota, Grand Forks, North Dakota." <http://www.mvp.usace.army.mil/docs/projs/eisfinal.pdf> (6 June 2003).

_____. "Flood Control, Red River of the North: Grand Forks, N.D./East Grand Forks, Minn." <http://www.mvp.usace.army.mil/fl_damage_reduct/default.asp?pageid=18> (6 June 2003).

_____. "Flood of 1997." <http://www.mvp.usace.army.mil/disaster_response /default.asp?pageid=61> (6 June 2003).

_____. "History of the Headwaters Recreation Areas." <http://www.mvp.usace.army.mil/history/headwaters> (6 June 2003).

_____. "Lower St. Anthony Falls Rapids Restoration, Mississippi River, Minneapolis, Minn." <http://www.mvp.usace.army.mil/finder/display.asp?pageid=110> (6 June 2003).

_____. "Mississippi Locks and Dams." <http://www.mvp.usace.army.mil/navigation/default.asp?pageid=145> (6 June 2003).

_____. "Mississippi River Environmental Management Program, Minn/Wis/Iowa." <http://www.mvp.usace.army.mil/environment/default.asp?pageid=74> (6 June 2003).

_____. "Native American History in the Mississippi Headwaters Region." <http://www.mvp.usace.army.mil/history/native_am> (6 June 2003).

_____. "Outlet Identified as Preferred Alternative at Devils Lake." Press Release, 26 February 2003. <http://www.mvp.usace.army.mil/pressroom/default.asp?pageid=648> (6 June 2003).

_____. "Pool 8 Islands Phase II Habitat Project, Stoddard, Wisc." <http://www.mvp.usace. army.mil/environment/default.asp?pageid=136> (6 June 2003).

_____. "Recreation." <http://www.mvp.usace.army.mil/recreation> (6 June 2003).

_____. "Reservoir Operating Plan Evaluation (ROPE) Study for Mississippi Headwaters." <http://www.mvp.usace.army.mil/environment/default.asp?pageid=143> (6 June 2003).

_____. "Souris River Basin Flood Control Project: N.D." <http://www.mvp.usace. army. mil/fl_damage_reduct/default.asp?pageid=43> (6 June 2003).

U.S. Army Inspector General. Agency Report of Investigation (Case 00-019). <http://www.osc.gov/reading.htm> (1 November 2002).

U.S. Bureau of Reclamation. "Bureau of Reclamation Cultural Resources Management." <http://www.usbr.gov/cultural> (6 June 2003).

U.S. Congress. 101st Cong., 2d sess. "Providing for the Protection of Native American Graves, and For Other Purposes." House Report 101-877, 1990. <http://www.cast.uark.edu/other/nps/nagpra/DOCS/lgm001.html> (6 June 2003).

"Watery Logs Expand Wood Products Industry." Federal Reserve Bank of Minneapolis Fedgazette (July 1997). <http://minneapolisfed.org/pubs/fedgaz/97-07/wi.cfm> (6 June 2003).

ArchivalSources

Alexandria, Virginia. U.S. Army Corps of Engineers. Office of Chief of Engineers. Office of History.

St. Paul, Minnesota. St. Paul District. Administrative Records.

St. Paul, Minnesota. St. Paul District. Cultural Resource Management Administrative Files.

Washington, D.C. U.S. Army Corps of Engineers. Administrative Records.

InterviewsandPersonalCommunications

Ahlness, Jon. Personal communication. 20 January 2004.

Anderson, Dennis. Personal communication. 11 July 2002.

Anfinson, John O. Interview by Matthew Godfrey. St. Paul, MN. 25 October 2002

Anfinson, John O. Personal communication. 30 December 2002.

Anfinson, Scott. Interview by Matthew Godfrey. St. Paul, MN. 24 October 2002.

Baldwin, Colonel Roger L. Interview by John O. Anfinson. St. Paul, MN. 1 July 1991.

Bertschi, Tim. Interview by John O. Anfinson. St. Paul, MN. 1993.

Berwick, David. Personal communication. 31 October 2002.

Breyfogle, Colonel William J. Interview by Matthew Pearcy. St. Paul, MN. 28 November 2001.

Briggs, Colonel Joseph. Interview by Mickey Schubert. St. Paul, MN. 24 May 1988.

Christenson, David S. Interview by John O. Anfinson. St. Paul, MN. 23 November 1993.

Christenson, David S. Personal communications. 7 March 2003, 25 June 2003.

Craig, Colonel Richard W. Interview by John O. Anfinson. St. Paul, MN. 20 July 1993.

Gianelli, William R. Interview by Martin A. Reuss. Washington, DC. 1 August 1985.

Gimmestad, Dennis. Interview by Matthew Godfrey. St. Paul, MN. 23 October 2002

258

Gnabasik, Virginia. Interview by Matthew Godfrey. St. Paul, MN. 22 October 2002.

Johnson, Brad. Personal communication. 15 March 2004.

Kasprisin, Colonel Kenneth. Interview by Virginia Gnabasik. St. Paul, MN. 13 July 2001.

Lenhart, Steven. Interview by Matthew Godfrey. Minneapolis, MN. 21 October 2002.

Loss, David. Interview by Matthew Godfrey. St. Paul, MN. 21 October 2002.

McNally, Edward. Interview by Matthew Godfrey. St. Paul, MN. 22 October 2002.

Otto, Richard J. Interview by Matthew Godfrey. St. Paul, MN. 23 October 2002.

Pearcy, Matthew. Personal communication. 29 December 2002.

Post, Robert F. Personal communication. 6 January 2003

Rapp, Colonel Ed. Interview by Mickey Schubert. St. Paul, MN. 7 July 1983.

Raster, Thomas. Personal communication. 19 November 2003.

Scott, Colonel James T. Interview by John O. Anfinson. St. Paul, MN. 30 May 1995.

Snyder, Russel K. Interview by Matthew Godfrey. St. Paul, MN. 23 October 2002.

Spitzak, Charles P. Interview by Theodore Catton. St. Paul, MN. 9 May 2002.

Star, Frank. Interview by Matthew Godfrey. St. Paul, MN. 21 October 2002.

Valencia, Maria T. Personal communication. 17 December 2002.

Weburg, Michael M. Personal communication. 25 September 2002.

Wonsik, Colonel J. M. Interview by John O. Anfinson. St. Paul, MN. 20 January 1998.

Wopat, Ben A. Interview by Matthew Pearcy. St. Paul, MN. 25 April 2002.

Wopat, Ben A. Interview by Matthew Godfrey. St. Paul, MN. 24 October 2002.

Index

Index

O

Two Harbors, Minnesota, 30

Index

X-Y-Z